De

M

w

Jean & Tracey

THE FREEMASONS

Engrav'd by Iohn Pine in Aldersgate Street London.

FRONTISPIECE TO THE 'CONSTITUTIONS OF THE FREE-MASONS',
LONDON, 1723
From the Engraving by John Pine

THE FREEMASONS

*THE HISTORY, NATURE, DEVELOPMENT
AND SECRET OF THE ROYAL ART*

EUGEN LENNHOFF

© 1994

First published in England in 1934
Re-impression 1978
Revised edition 1994
Published by LEWIS MASONIC

LEWIS MASONIC is the publishing imprint of IAN ALLAN REGALIA, Coombelands House, Coombelands, Lane, Addlestone, KT15 1HY, England, who are members of the Ian Allan Group of companies.

Originally published in the German language
under the title *Die Freimaurer*

Translated by Einar Frame

ISBN 085318 206 X

British Library Cataloguing in Publication Data

A Catalogue record for this book is available from the British Library

Printed and bound in Great Britain by Latimer Trend & Company Ltd, Plymouth.

PUBLISHER'S NOTE
TO NEW EDITION

The Freemasons by Eugen Lennhoff was originally published in German under the title *Die Friemaurer* and, in 1930, was awarded the 'Peters-Baertsoen Prize' by the Grand Orient of Belgium. This award was made every ten years for the best masonic publication and had been previously awarded to such eminent writers and historians as R. F. Gould, J. G. Findel, and W. Begemann. The English translation was published by Methuen, London, in 1934 and of this book the reviewer in the June issue of *The Freemason* wrote: 'interestingly and instructively written by Bro Eugen Lennhoff and translated in a scholarly manner by Bro Einar Frame'. Here it was stated that 'the author has treated his subject in the frankest possible way in order to make it a book for Masons and non-Masons alike. He (Lennhoff) lucidly explains facts in connection with the objects and practice of Freemasonry and attacks wholeheartedly the distorted views held by many antagonists, and published in anti-Masonic literature.' At that time, in at least three countries, Russia, Germany and Italy, Freemasonry was under attack. However, the book was intended as a justification for Freemasonry, not an answer to critics of the Order of that period, or earlier, and it became accepted as the work of a competent researcher and historian. Lennhoff displayed his skill in the marshalling of facts and with great ability had presented them in a most readable style. The book went out of print many years ago and copies became scarce being found only in masonic libraries or in private collections. The present publishers felt that an important work of this calibre should be made available to the modern reader and although some parts of the work are inappropriate in a changed climate of opinion and attitude forty years later, rejected the idea of any up-dating of a work of great importance by a competent writer, having in mind that history, whether masonic or otherwise, is an ever-changing scene. Here it is dealt with by one whose style is clear and unmistakable, who comments briefly on the current affairs of his time, but whose work will hold a deep interest for any reader whether expert or inexpert in the subject that continues to attract the support, or the opposition, of people of all nations, class or creed. But may the facts ever be published for those who have the interest and they, of all people, seem to be ever-present.

A. LEWIS Ltd
1978

INTRODUCTION TO
THE SUPPLEMENT

No attempt has been made to rewrite *The Freemasons* which is reproduced in its original form. At that time, Freemasonry was already proscribed by the Communists, Fascists and the newly-elected Nazis, and it was evident that dictators of all kinds shared a common hatred. These dictators were on different sides in World War 2, to the embarrassment of Finland when their friends, the Allies, joined their enemy, the Soviet Union.

The end of the war brought no relief to those countries 'liberated' from the Axis powers by the Soviets, and in much of Europe Freemasonry was to remain in darkness for many years. In contrast, lodges were revived in countries which were liberated by the western Allies and there were many examples of assistance and brotherly love offered in the restoration of Freemasonry among people who had been on different sides as enemies during the war.

Much later, the collapse of the Soviet Union and the disintegration of Communism elsewhere led to the restoration of democracy in Eastern Europe where in some places Freemasonry has already been restored. However, so many years had passed in Russia since the Revolution that there is nobody now alive with any recollection of Freemasonry and it is not yet known when or if it can ever reappear.

The Supplement will briefly outline some of the principal changes which have taken place in more than 60 years since the first edition. The original work has been faithfully copied by the photolitho process and it is just as useful and informative now as when it first appeared.

B. P. HUTTON
1994

TRANSLATOR'S PREFACE

THIS book does not purport to be a comprehensive history of the Craft, but is rather a survey of the legends, history and present activities of Freemasonry throughout the world, and a reply to post-war attacks on the Fraternity with a view to showing that Freemasonry may yet be a world influence for Peace and Goodwill.

The author has asked me to explain in my Preface the reason for the seeming disproportion between the amount of space he has devoted to the Freemasonry of England and that of other countries. He feels that English Freemasonry has been dealt with so thoroughly and efficiently by so many able writers in the English language, that he has not considered himself called upon to give more than the briefest explanatory survey. He has preferred to go more deeply into the various aspects from which Masons in other countries have viewed the Masonic Ideal.

At the same time the author is also fully cognizant of the growing belief that there is much to gain and little to lose by giving greater publicity to the underlying principles and ideals controlling the activities of Freemasons. He has therefore treated the subject in the frankest possible way in order to make it a book for Masons and non-Masons alike, since Freemasonry is not a secret society but a society with secrets.

The fact that the National Socialist Government of Germany under Herr Hitler has prohibited Freemasonry in Germany since this book was written makes it all the more desirable that English-speaking Masons should gain a clearer insight into the aspirations, activities and attitudes of their Continental brethren.

In conclusion I wish to express my gratitude to that staunch advocate of Freemasonry Universal, W. Bro. Max Seiflow, P.A.G.D.C., for the great assistance and encouragement he has given me so whole-heartedly.

LONDON   EINAR FRAME
  15th March, 1934

AUTHOR'S PREFACE

WHEN the first edition of this book was published towards the end of 1928, I said in the Preface :

'Books on Freemasonry, when written by people antagonistic to the Craft, are mostly very one-sided and aggressive, whilst those written by people in sympathy with Masonry are very often works which treat the subject from a highly philosophical standpoint. This book has been written by a Freemason, but it aims, nevertheless, at avoiding philosophical considerations as far as possible. Its principal object is to explain facts about which questions have often arisen, and it will describe the objects and the practice of Freemasonry, as this would seem to be necessary in these days when such distorted views are held regarding the Fraternity. I therefore do not wish to dogmatize, but only to describe ; and above all I shall endeavour to answer the questions which are continually being raised, not only by enemies of Freemasonry, but also by many others who wish to form an honest opinion of the Brotherhood and whose view is constantly obscured by the enormous quantity of anti-masonic literature.

'I believe that my object will be more readily achieved by quoting herein the views of many men who—whether as enthusiastic youths or as firm antagonists—have taken an interest in Freemasonry, and by endeavouring to show, as they have occurred, the many incidents of an international character with which Freemasonry has been brought into contact. Polemics, which I in no way evade, are therefore given a very subordinate position as compared with the facts, which, in view of the breadth of the subject, cannot, of course, be exhausted. In this way I hope, although I am a firm supporter of the great idea of Freemasonry, to be as fair as possible.'

The recognition which the book has met with since then entitles me, I think, to say that it has fulfilled its object, that is, to explain. As early as 1929 it was found necessary to publish a new edition, and in 1932 the book was made available to the general public in the form of a popular edition. This latter edition was published in response to the wish expressed by a large number of people, because to-day, more than ever, people wish to know the actual facts about Freemasonry, seeing that the controversy about the Royal Art has become considerably intensified in the last few years. Many new opponents have joined forces with the old opponents. Almost every month brings additions to the anti-masonic literature. It would therefore seem all the more important to place a book which endeavours to show Freemasonry in its true colours within the reach of all those who desire to form their own opinion about a great movement, irrespective of the slogans of the day.

Eugen Lennhoff

Vienna, *February 1932*

CONTENTS

PART I

FREEMASONRY—ITS NATURE AND DEVELOPMENT

PART II

PRESENT DAY—FREEMASONRY IN VARIOUS COUNTRIES

PART III

OLD AND NEW OPPONENTS

PART IV

MASONIC INTERNATIONALISM

SUPPLEMENT

ILLUSTRATIONS

ILLUSTRATIONS IN SUPPLEMENT
between pages 361–362

THE FREEMASONS

PART I

FREEMASONRY—ITS NATURE AND DEVELOPMENT

CHAPTER I

THE UNDERLYING IDEA

SINCE the end of the World War, Freemasonry has once more become the object of exceedingly violent opposition. It would seem that the truce in regard to subjects of internal controversy, which obtained in most countries during the years of the great catastrophe, must, as a matter of course, be offset by an attack of intensified violence.

This renewed campaign against a society whose motto is 'Humanity', extends over a much wider front than ever before. Whereas before the War it was principally the Roman Catholic Church that put a ban on Freemasonry, since 1918 a number of other powers and groups have entered the lists against it. In Hungary masonic work was prohibited by the State after the overthrow of the Communist Councils. Mussolini destroyed the very foundations of the Italian Lodges by means of the Fascist law against Freemasonry; in Germany a campaign for the suppression of Freemasonry was launched by Nationalist circles of the Right, especially by the supporters of Ludendorff; in France it is the Chauvinistic, anti-German groups that are carrying on a feud against the Craft, whilst the Moscow Soviets have repeatedly pointed out that they are ready to attack Masonry with the utmost energy, should it advance so far as Russia.

The number of catchwords or slogans levelled against Freemasonry is as varied as the horde of its opponents. Some of these opponents—especially the pugnacious Jesuits—have always combated Freemasonry as a dangerous atheist 'anti-Church', a 'Synagogue of Satan', while others maintain that the Mason is the sworn enemy of every patriotic feeling, and that the Lodge is the hotbed of world revolution and Bolshevism ! Yet others describe the Society as an organization in alliance with the Jesuits, the object of which is to establish control of the world by Jewish capitalists, to say nothing of those who denounce the masonic temples as places of wild immorality, as the home of phallism and of the orgies of the Black Mass!

Actually there would seem to be no crime with which Freemasonry has not been charged, and if the assertions of many of its opponents are worthy of belief, then there would seem to be no point in refraining from opening the doors of the jails throughout the world and liberating the inmates. For what are murder and robbery of the individual compared with the heinous crimes which, it is alleged, are daily committed by Freemasonry—by this same Freemasonry which more than one publication has openly accused of having perpetrated every assassination of royalty in the last two centuries or, at least, of having been the instigator of those crimes?

Innumerable are the pamphlets in which the so-called 'people in the know' announce that mysterious hands are constantly at work moulding world events to their sordid plans, and that every evil that has afflicted mankind within the memory of man has been the work of Freemasonry. Their method of proving their assertion is very simple: when a person in any particular circle has an evil reputation he is immediately stamped as a Freemason! And the cry goes up: 'Freemason! Criminal!' till the fools believe it.

Also amongst other classes which are otherwise quite indifferent to Freemasonry there is a belief that it is a powerful force controlled from an invisible centre, and that a movement of tremendous compass can be brought into action when the 'wire-pullers', wrapped in their cloak of secrecy and mystery, so desire it. And even if not everybody believes that the Masons are only working to abolish all international frontiers with the object of setting up a world Republic under their leadership, or to suppress all religion, there is, nevertheless, a firm belief that the Masonic Fraternity is a mutual protection and insurance society which, by secret means, procures situations and lucrative business for its members.

All the fairy-tales in circulation about Freemasons are but irrational gossip. Who stops to consider that the absurd contradictions contained in the accusations themselves demonstrate their entire lack of foundation? Who troubles to point out that Freemasonry cannot serve monarchs and powerful capitalists and at the same time control regicides and social revolutionaries, or be at once the bulwark of both orthodox Protestantism and the most extreme body of Freethinkers? Few indeed! All these accusations are blindly accepted, and it happens only too frequently that institutions promoted by Freemasons, although previously generally recognized as good, suddenly fall into disrepute as soon as one of the antagonists hoists the blue flag of the Lodge above them.

The Arms of ye most Ancient & Honorable Fraternity, of Free and Accepted Masons.

Holiness to the Lord.

The Arms of the Operative, or Stone Masons.

FRONTISPIECE TO 'AHIMAN REZON' BY LAURENCE DERMOTT
LONDON, 1764
From the Engraving by Larken

FRONTISPIECE TO 'AHIMAN REZON'. 'THE CONSTITUTIONS OF THE
ANCIENTS' (RAREST EDITION)
BY LAU. DERMOTT, DEPUTY GRAND MASTER, 1787
Drawn and Engraved by M. A. Rooker

These attacks are not refuted by Freemasons with sufficient frequency. True, the number of masonic publications is legion, and many of the intellectually great have professed themselves enthusiastic followers of the 'Royal Art', as they call Masonry, but, nevertheless, such works as would tend towards enlightenment are all too few. And though in the last few years the flood of antagonistic literature has cried out for an increase in the number of defending publications, the latter treat the subject mainly from a biased point of view. They are biased not so much in the handling of the opposing arguments as in their attitude to the masonic problems themselves. There is, however, nothing new in that. Whosoever cares seriously to take the trouble to examine thoroughly masonic literature will find that this biased consideration has existed for almost the last two centuries. He would also be surprised to make the discovery that all that has been said about a world conspiracy and a world organization, and the like, is fable, for the simple reason that Freemasonry itself is by no means united, but, on the contrary, presents a picture of the greatest disunion. The only thing that is common to all the hundreds of Grand Lodges and to the nearly 28,000 private Lodges, and their members, is the Idea; or, better, the symbolism surrounding it, which is cultivated in a peculiar form reminiscent of the Ancient Mysteries, but the interpretation and the practice of which has, from the very beginning of Freemasonry, been quite different in the various countries. Nor is there any question of a central 'government', or of acting in unity and harmony. Furthermore, many central organizations, obediences of Freemasonry, are almost as divided and varied as the churches, and whereas many orders modelled on the lines of Freemasonry bear the uniform of a real International, Masonry itself appears as a kaleidoscope of a myriad shades. There are Grand Lodges whose rulers are kings or, at least, members of royal families, and there are others that take particular pride in their democratic views. In many countries, especially in the New World, Masonry is practised in the widest spheres of society, whilst in Europe it frequently represents the somewhat exclusive activity of a small intellectual class. When one seeks a definition of Freemasonry one finds thousands, but it is not easy to select one which will apply generally.

Is that credible in the face of such very definite accusations? And if that be so, how can Freemasonry, in spite of the non-existence of the international organization which its opponents allege with such obstinate persistence, withstand these vigorous attacks without being crushed; and why is it that, despite all persecution, there is a continuous increase in the number of its faithful followers in most countries? The answer is simple. The reason is entirely to be found in the infinite strength of the masonic thought that is constantly derived by the majority of Masons from the spirit of their symbols—a thought which has absolutely nothing to do with political aspirations, but is of a purely spiritual nature.

This contention may seem strange to many people, but the truth is that the secret of Freemasonry, which is so passionately abused, lies not in mysterious actions, nor in a definite, secret aim, nor in a mighty world-encircling organization with an object in view, but consists merely in the fact that the Freemason serves a highly abstract idea, which, expressed in symbols, becomes an experience of the deepest inner significance for thousands upon thousands of those who are able to comprehend it—an experience of the mystery of Brotherhood.

It cannot be disputed that Freemasonry has no practical programme that would be common to all its members ; it has never had one, for the men who established its present form of organization never formulated one. This is perhaps most clearly shown by the fact that one of the most important masonic associations of the moment, from an intellectual point of view, the 'Verein deutscher Freimaurer' (Association of German Freemasons), which spurred on its best brains to the formulation of a new aim in the 'seventies of the last century, that is to say, 160 years after the foundation of the first Grand Lodge, in 1908 promoted a prize-competition which had in effect, the same object in view.

What the founders of the Society bequeathed to their followers was, in the main, a book of moral charges. A book of charges which, perhaps, did not impress its exhortations with complete clarity, but which, nevertheless, embodied the whole wonderful idea which encourages and inspires such an infinite number—an idea which has occupied the greatest minds and which, as must freely be admitted, has enabled Freemasonry to become a cultural power in the midst of the tremendous spiritual chaos of the moment ; a decisive factor for the relief of our tormented world.

This idea—laid down in the 'Antient Charges' of 1723, i.e., the fundamental masonic code—is the ancient idea of Humanity, the thought which, in the masonic ritual, is embodied in the beautiful sentence which emphasizes that Masons are working on the erection of the Temple of Human Love, the foundations of which are Wisdom, Strength, and Beauty.

As the building is spiritual, so also is the edifice.

It has already been said that definitions in which this idea finds expression are very numerous. The aim of Freemasonry is very clearly expressed, for instance, in the *Allgemeines Handbuch der Freimaurerei* ('General Handbook of Free-masonry'), the standard work of German Masonry :

'Freemasonry is the activity of closely associated men, who, employing symbolical forms mainly borrowed from the Masonic Craft and Architecture, work for the welfare of mankind, seeking to ennoble themselves, and others, in order thereby to bring into being a universal Brotherhood of Humanity, which they aim to represent in miniature amongst themselves.'

This idea is explained in the Constitutions of Dutch Free-masonry in the following terms :

'The object of Freemasonry is, first of all, to perfect the individual and to guide mankind towards better and more harmonic development. It teaches that the first duty of mankind is to dedicate itself to the welfare of human society and to sacrifice itself if necessary. It searches for the senti-ments common to all men, in order to unite the nations, and pursues the object of destroying the prejudices which are the source of enmity between the nations. It strives to bring these principles into effect in social life and gives support and help wherever efforts are being made to further the welfare of mankind on the same fundamental basis.'

Frederick the Great spoke of Freemasonry, of which he was a ruler, as being 'a means of educating the people to be better members of society, to be more virtuous and more charitable.'

And Lessing, in his dialogue on Freemasonry entitled *Ernst und Falk*, defines a Mason as 'one who so regulates his own life that he can contribute to the perfection of the work of art of the whole life of mankind. Nobody can contribute to the betterment of humanity who does not make of himself what can and should be made of him.'

Most of the authoritative masonic authors conclude therefrom that Freemasonry is an art, the 'Royal Art' as it was already called 200 years ago, in the Book of Constitutions of 1723, but then, of course, still in reference to the real masonic art or science—an art which, for the Lodge, the place of instruction, consists in educating its apprentices in Humanity with the help of masonic symbols, and which, for individual Freemasons, is the art of life, the art of self-knowledge, of strict self-education and harmonic mode of living; the art which declares Love its highest commandment; 'the art of educating the individual soul, as well as mankind, to be the dwelling of the Eternal'.

All these formulæ, regarded superficially, may at first seem to say little that is positive, but their tenor is infinitely rich in truth; it is the valuation of man according to his inner merit and his education to the highest conception of Humanity.[1] It is the profession of the ideal of the Brotherhood of Humanity; the declaration of the will to do ethical work for the good of Humanity. In this valuation of mankind there is contained still another thing, a postulate, which has gathered to the fold of Freemasonry many enthusiastic followers from all quarters, but which has also been the origin of much of the enmity which is seething around it : the idea of tolerance. True Freemasonry does not know the many barriers that have been set up in ordinary everyday life. All 'free men', provided they be actuated by the good intention of dedicating their work in the Fraternity to purely humanitarian ideals, shall have place in its ranks to carry on the common activity, no matter what their national, religious, political, or other opinions may be.

'A mason,' say the Antient Charges, 'is obliged by his tenure, to obey the moral law; and if he rightly understand the art he will never be a stupid atheist nor an irreligious libertine. He, of all men, should best understand that God seeth not as man seeth; for man looketh at the outward appearance, but God looketh to the heart. A Mason is, therefore, particularly bound never to act against the dictates of his conscience. Let a man's religion or mode of worship be what it may, he is not excluded from the order provided he believe in the glorious architect of heaven and earth, and practise the sacred duties of morality. Masons unite with the virtuous of every persuasion in the firm and pleasing bond of fraternal love; they are taught to view

[1] Posner: *The Rough Ashlar*

the errors of mankind with compassion, and to strive, by the purity of their own conduct, to demonstrate the superior excellence of the faith they may profess. Thus masonry is the centre of union between good men and true, and the happy means of conciliating friendship amongst those who must otherwise have remained at a perpetual distance.'

And in another passage:

'All preferment among Masons is grounded upon real worth and personal merit only.'

This idea of tolerance is of such paramount significance in the Freemason's idea of Humanity that, by many, Humanity and Tolerance are regarded as synonymous.

'If we wish to name an idea, which, throughout history, has been visible in more and more extensive form,' said Wilhelm von Humboldt, 'it is the idea of Humanity; the endeavour to break down the barriers which prejudices and arbitrary opinions of all kinds have raised to the detriment of mankind, and to regard the whole of mankind as a large, close-knit family, without consideration of nationality, creed or colour, and as a single unit, the object of which is to attain free development of moral strength.'

Naturally, the Freemason's idea of tolerance signifies not only toleration of other opinions and other ways, but also involves unconditional recognition of freedom of spirit and conscience, and the abandonment of every dogmatic idea. However, freedom of conscience and absence of dogma, by reason of their very nature, allow of few suppositions that cannot be proved. The masonic doctrine must therefore, as Otto Heinichen—one of the German masonic philosophers—so appropriately said, be poor in positive rulings. But all the richer in itself is the doctrine that offers tolerance in place of rigid orthodoxy, and professes the religion of active human love in place of dogmatic faith.

Need further emphasis be laid on the fact that the root of the struggle against Freemasonry lies in this conviction, or that the accusation that Freemasonry is the enemy of religion, that it is godless, that it rejects all faith, and that it is anti-Christian, arose from this idea of tolerance? Is it not clear from the text of the 'Antient Charges', as quoted above, that all these accusations are entirely false?

This text has, it is true, been the subject of much speculation and has had to suffer many interpretations. But there is certainly no question whatsoever of enmity to religion. The charge to believe in God has been given the utmost emphasis by those who raised the 'Antient Charges' to be the Constitutions of Freemasonry, following the example set forth in the gild records of the ancient stonemasons' brotherhoods, on which they are based. But they did not regard the general principles of the monotheistic religions as an empty formula, but as a 'religion in which all men agree'. All that has been brought against this point of view in the last two centuries is inconclusive. And when attempts were made by means of philological subtlety to strain the meaning of 'stupid atheist' and 'irreligious libertine', they were, of course, doomed to failure from the start. Every one, except those who wish deliberately to misunderstand this plain characterization of a religious view, must admit its true interpretation.

Let it be remembered that Freemasonry itself has no desire to be regarded as a religion or church. Within its portals both believers in dogma and the dogmaless meet in true fellowship. The idea of tolerance in Freemasonry does not in any way involve its members in an obligation to be untrue to their creeds; it refers solely to the condition upon which they can take active part in the Fraternity itself. Just as in the eighteenth and nineteenth centuries many dignitaries of the Roman Catholic Church belonged to Freemasonry, there are to-day still many eminent leaders of the various churches amongst its enthusiastic followers. Belief in God (in an undogmatic sense), or, at all events, a belief in the divine creation of the world, is also to-day demanded by the large majority of Grand Lodges. Masonic documents almost without exception bear the symbolic heading:

'In the name of the Great Architect of the Universe.'

Only one grand masonic authority, the much-discussed Grand Orient or Grand Lodge of France, has removed this formula from its Constitution. Not, of course, in order thereby to announce that dogmatic faith is forbidden to its members or that atheism has been made an obligation, but merely in order still more to emphasize the thought of complete freedom of conscience. And yet this very step has caused an absolute revolution amongst those same Freemasons who are alleged to be so antagonistic to religion, and has led to an open breach between Anglo-Saxon Freemasonry and the Grand Orient. If, in spite of numerous attempts, a world organization of

Freemasons, embracing the majority of the Grand Lodges, has not yet been brought into existence, the blame rests, not least, with this conflict, which for fifty years has made constructive international masonic work almost an impossibility. And it has been demonstrated time and again, especially in recent years, that this breach cannot be bridged, even though the Grand Orient of France repeatedly emphasize that they have set at the head of their Constitutions a solemn command to respect all creeds, ideas, and opinions.

All these facts, however, will not be accepted by the opponents of Freemasonry. And to-day, just as 190 years ago, when the first Encyclical of the Pope was issued, the cry still goes up against the 'fundamental antitheistical naturalism of the sect'.

Freemasonry is certainly not a sect, and could not be a sect by reason of its fundamental principles, because, to be a sect, it must have dogma and demand from the brethren that they subject themselves to doctrines of a canonical stamp. That, however, is not the case. Freemasonry is a community of identical conviction—a community, of course, which, as already stated, veils its activity in its own peculiar system of symbolic usage and action, but which, however, has never allowed its symbols to become dogma.

CHAPTER II

SYMBOLS AND RITUAL

VOLUMES have been written about masonic symbolism, but, as in everything concerning Freemasonry, the views and opinions expressed are exceedingly varied and very exaggerated and distorted on both sides. On the one hand, there are those to whom the symbols of the Order are empty and incomprehensible formulæ, to whom the practice of the ritual counts for puffed-up pomposity with empty exercises, and, on the other hand, those misled masses who have been impressed by the false belief that the symbols are the secret signs of a brotherhood of conspirators, in other words, secret orders in symbolic form behind which political and religious secrets are hidden and about which innumerable fables are circulated with never-ending enthusiasm. And then there are the would-be clever ones who would like to twist the meanings of the symbols to their own—often only too confused —ends, and also the out-and-out mystics to whom the rich language of the masonic parables seems too paltry and who ponder and cogitate in the hope of getting on the track, by means of these symbols, of that secret knowledge which is said to have existed in the Dark Ages of antiquity, but which has since been lost.

Amongst those to whom the symbols convey nothing of all that inner wealth which they impart to Masons, there are some who believe that they are solely cultivated with the object of hoodwinking the members of the Fraternity or at least 'the stupid world of the profane' (non-Masons). Dr. Johann Michael Raich, Capitular of Mayence Cathedral, who, thirty years ago, was a leading antagonist of Freemasonry, defended this contention in a lecture in Vienna, quite contrary to most of his fellow-protagonists, to whom every symbol of the 'false gods of Humanity' were torches of war, when he said:

'In the pure religion of reason, in the indifference to Christianity lies the secret, the great secret. . . . All other mysterious words, signs, symbols, legends, and promises, in so far as they do not refer to THE secret, are idle flights

FRONTISPIECE TO JACHIN AND BOAZ, 1776

A Free Mason,
Found out of the Materials of his Lodge.

Behold a Master-Mason rare,
Whose myſtic Portrait does declare
The Secrets of Free Maſonry. —
Fair for all to read and see. —
But few there are to whom they're known,
Tho' they so plainly here are Shown.

SYMBOLICAL PRINT OF THE YEAR, 1754
Engraved by A. Slade

of fancy or the empty inventions of obvious swindlers and frauds, who have designs upon the purses of gullible brethren.'

This is a not infrequently occurring belief, which, in the case of the reverend gentleman, arose from his fundamental attitude towards Freemasonry, but which, in his imitators, is explained by ignorance. However, the majority of those who deny a deeper meaning to the symbols do so for other reasons; for example, they are either lacking in the intellectual capacity to think in symbols, unable to dissociate themselves from everyday life in order to collaborate in symbolic work, or cannot understand the forms which constitute the most highly-prized treasures of the Brotherhood, and which, springing from the heart rather than from the mind, are the necessary expression of the idea of Fraternity and of the whole world of masonic sentiment. They would probably find pleasure in the life of the Lodges were they debating societies, political or religious circles, or active sects. But they are unresponsive to the true nature of Freemasonry, in the same way as Beethoven's most beautiful symphony will neither stir nor move one who has no ear for music, but will bore him beyond all measure. Those are the beings of whom Wieland said:

'A so-called seeker will find nothing worth the seeking here, even if he seek for a thousand years, unless he has within him, when he makes his entry into the Temple, that natural tendency to what constitutes the essential character, and the virtues of, a genuine Freemason. Without this he will be in the same position as the illiterate man who bought a pair of spectacles in order to read and was quite surprised when he discovered that one must first be able to read before the spectacles can assist.'

Those who are unable to comprehend the masonic symbolism will never be able to fathom the meaning of the principle that there is only one secret in Freemasonry—the initiation—and there is only one initiation, namely, to feel oneself spiritually a member of the Fraternity. Whosoever has unveiled this mystery possesses the secret of Freemasonry; he understands the language of Freemasonry—the language which links together innumerable people irrespective of time or place; the language which unfolds in its symbolism its innermost nature as the Church does in its dogmatic theology. He understands that the symbolism is just what is peculiar to the Fraternity, and he will find in these symbols, which are the same in their essentials in the masonic bodies all over the world, the inspiration for that spiritual cultivation which is the aim of all Freemasons. Symbols are capable of making the masonic ideas clearer to him, of bringing them much nearer to him, than any theory expressed in words; for symbols make use of emblems appealing to the senses instead of abstract words, and are more illustrative and impressive in their simplicity. From their very nature they are quite independent of words, and are therefore truly international. The gavel, compasses, and square are much easier to understand than learned dissertations upon the ideas of work, duty, and rectitude which they symbolize, and remain clearer in the memory as strong mental pictures, and are comprehensible, in the same way, to all Freemasons, irrespective of race or nation and quite independent of all idiom. Freemasonry has succeeded, through its symbolism, in making it possible to speak in one language to the seekers after truth in all countries and to convey to them an inner experience, a 'secret', which could never be expressed in words.

Their immutability also constitutes an appreciable advantage over the verbal expression of commandments. Thus, on the one hand, the common fundamental idea is established for all time, and a digression from the original intention is guarded against, whilst, on the other hand, freedom to give expression to the various shades of spiritual or sentimental conviction, though adhering to the common idea, prevents the masonic teaching from becoming stark dogma—a danger which is ever present when clothed in words. And so to-day men receive, with the same intensity, the same moral exhortations in the symbolic acts of the masonic ritual as did their predecessors in the Order 100 and 150 years ago. And finally, even in men of an otherwise most matter-of-fact nature, there lies deep down the inclination towards a cult. The symbolic system in Freemasonry caters for this requirement to the utmost extent.

The symbols have been taken in a large measure from the masonic science of the builders of the cathedrals of the Middle Ages. To what extent the spiritual played a part at that time, and to what extent the individual creativeness of the stonemason was the inspiration of the work, can be judged to-day only with difficulty. Be that as it may, Freemasonry obtained at least its framework from the ancient gild of craftsmen. The application of the theory of the craft to the erection of the spiritual temple is also a science—a task which demands two kinds of work, viz., the erection in the individual heart of an undefiled temple and the striving after a brighter and more beautiful world—a task that demands

Self-knowledge and world-knowledge,
Self-control, and
Self-ennoblement and the striving for the welfare of the community.

This ethical transmutation of the operative work found expression also in the fact that the builders' hut, nestling close to the side of the cathedral, became the Lodge or Temple, a place of devotion of unique kind in which the work was glorified. The Freemason who breaks away from the turmoil of daily life and hastens to the Lodge, there enjoys an atmosphere of peace and tranquillity. The language of the symbols appeals to the intellect, the will, and the soul. When he has put on his apron, the symbol of labour, he passes through a forecourt into the Lodge-room, the predominant colour of which is generally a rich blue. (In the so-called 'Scottish' Lodges the colour of the Temple is red.) The Lodge-room is rectangular in shape. Every Lodge in the world has this appearance, whether it be the gorgeous Temple of a palatial metropolitan Lodge or a primitive hut erected with infinite care and enthusiasm by the brethren themselves in some African or Asiatic wilderness ; everywhere there is the same rectangle forming the boundary of the Temple, and also the idea, based on the mathematical symbolism of Pythagoras, that the world enclosed is a likeness of the cosmos with the starlit vault of heaven above. (According to opponents, however, this is a 'symbol of the exclusiveness of the Fraternity as a secret society'.)

One enters the Temple to the festive strains of the organ. In some temples there are pillars on either side, and, looking towards the east, one sees the altar and, behind it, the master's chair. On the altar the Volume of the Sacred Law,[1] the square, and the compasses, above which shines the flaming star, of which Goethe said:

Zum Beginnen, zum Vollenden,
Zirkel, Blei und Wasserwaage.
Alles starrt und stockt in Händen,
Leuchtet nicht der Stern am Tage.

[1] The Bible

The Volume of the Sacred Law, the square, and the compasses are the 'three great lights' of Freemasonry. The Volume of the Sacred Law is emblematical of the light above us, not as a dogmatic authority but as an expression of belief in the moral order of the world; the square, the light within us, symbolizes the idea of right and duty—moral conduct; the compasses, the light around us, are the symbol of fraternity—service to mankind.

Every tool, every object in this Temple has its symbolical meaning, and even the rhythm of the knocks of the gavel of the master and the two wardens assisting him in directing the building operation speak their own special language. The Mason is constantly reminded that he is a 'rough ashlar', which must be polished if he is to be rendered a fit member of civilized society. And therefore the masonic neophyte is constantly exhorted by the 'Gnothi seauton' of the Greek philosopher, that is to say:

Know thyself

and also

Control thyself
Make thyself noble,

Else wilt thou be unable to help build the Temple of Humanity, and forget not that the fundaments of the same are three pillars:

Wisdom: the intellectual power which directs the work,
Strength: the moral force, which executes it, and
Beauty: which constitutes the harmony of the intellectual power, the consonance between design and deed.

The Freemason, ever 'new born', progresses very gradually in the Royal Art. He is enlightened step by step. He must first have been an Entered Apprentice and then a Fellow Craft before he attains the Master's deep knowledge of Life and Death.

But the masonic work cannot be performed by the individual alone; it must be the work of a community, the work of men of the same conviction, who must join in forging that fraternal chain, which must one day become an unbreakable universal chain, in order that the ancient words of the ritual may come to pass:

'All brethren in all parts of the earth constitute one Lodge only.'

FORM OF TRACING CLOTH

FRONTISPIECE TO 'HIRAM, OR THE GRAND MASTER-KEY TO THE
DOOR OF BOTH ANTIENT AND MODERN FREEMASONRY'

CHAPTER III

THE SECRET

THE 'universal chain', which, to Freemasons, is a distant, ultimate aim, a beautiful dream, is an actual fact to those who will not understand the Royal Art and who constantly vilify it. To them Freemasonry is a secret society the power of which extends over the whole of the earth; the Temple of Humanity is a State dominating all other States, a Church over all churches persecuting all religious beliefs.

Is Freemasonry really a secret society? No! An exclusive society perhaps, but not a secret organization; for all those characteristics which constitute such an organization are absent. Its aim, its organization, its structure, and its history are all known, and its statutes have been approved by the authorities in all those States where the law so demands. There are no 'unknown rulers' and there is no 'unconditional obedience' of the brethren to the commands of the elected leaders. The Lodges do not assemble in secret places. The addresses of Lodges can be found in any directory. All that which secret societies are so anxious not to reveal is readily disclosed by the masonic Fraternity as being of no importance to its fundamental character. Everything that is said about God, the world, mankind, social problems, religion and morals, and everything that might have the slightest savour of politics, is not concealed.

The secret enjoined upon its apprentices consists solely in the obligation to observe silence regarding the various signs of recognition and certain customs. This is demanded by ancient tradition, although since 1723 the year of the appearance of the Anderson Constitution, publications in all languages have been put on the market by business-like opponents, which are obtainable by any one and which describe minutely the signs, words, and grip by which the Mason proves to a brother his membership of the Fraternity. It is also possible to secure copies of the Ritual and complete explanations of the symbols. But what do they betray? Ceremonials, symbols, but nothing of an esoteric secret. The usage without the inspiration of its ethical significance, without creative collaboration, must seem as futile to the uninitiated as—once more making use of a musical metaphor—the reading of a score would be to those in whose minds the musical symbols do not convey a picture of accords and harmonies. However, this secret, this entry into the Holy of Holies of the Royal Art, this spiritual union with brethren throughout the world, cannot be communicated, is inexpressible, even though the printed Ritual seems to say so much:

'The true secret is just that which eternally surrounds you, but is seen by none, although it is there for all eyes to see.'

The fear of profanation plays an important part in the exclusion of the outer world from the work in the Temple, as exemplified by Horace's verse:

Odi profanum vulgus et arceo!

Not to arouse curiosity, nor to attract through mysteriousness, but in order to preserve in the spiritual building of the Lodge that wonderful solemnity without which its vital nerve would be severed.

'Respect by concealment and silence must be paid to certain secrets, even if they should be obvious', said Goethe, who, on another occasion, expressed the same idea in the following. beautiful lines:

Niemand soll und wird es schauen,
Was einander wir vertraut.
Denn auf Schweigen und Vertrauen
Ist der Tempel aufgebaut.

That is not the poetical expression of 'secret intriguing',[1] but is the holy fear of the duly initiated of making public property of the most intimate matters. Freemasonry does not want to go the way of the political parties, but the way of the Ancient Mysteries, whose standard it has, in our time, again planted, although it is not directly descended from them. Like all the cults which aim at bringing about the moral exaltation of mankind, from the Hindus, the Egyptians, and the Greek philosophers down to more recent seekers after truth, it is ruled by the knowledge that ideas revealed to the general public without reservation have always become degraded, because the mob fastened on the heels of the proclaimers and

---

[1] Goethe hated such things, as can be seen from his lines to Lavater: 'I have traces, not to say reports, of a great mass of lies, which slink around in the dark. . . . Believe me, our moral and political world is undermined with passages, cellars, and sewers.'

only too often trod under foot what had been their highest ideal.

Freemasonry also is a mystery society, and, according to August Horneffer,[1] it is the only genuine one at present in existence. It is a mystery society by virtue of its initiation, the Seeker after Light wandering symbolically from step to step,[2] the idea of Brotherhood, the yearning after Light, the belief in Death as another and higher form of Life, and the comforting creed of the spiritual resurrection in the sense of Goethe's words:

> Und solange du das nicht hast,
> Dieses Stirb und Werde,
> Bist du nur ein trüber Gast
> Auf der dunklen Erde.

But what distinguishes Freemasonry from the cults of ancient times is the ideal which it embodies, viz., the ideal of Humanity. It is not, as many would like to make it, a sanctuary for Knights of the Grail. Freemasons do not guard the Holy Vessel into which, on Good Friday, Heaven poured in mysterious manner its eucharistic contents. The Royal Art is not mystical in itself; it possesses no secret wisdom, no key to the secrets of the world; it only builds with worldly material; with the living man. It need not seek secrets outside its own particular world, for it suffices that for generations millions of men have striven, in spite of all internal and external upheavals and supported solely by the power of love, to erect, by self-ennoblement, that edifice which, when it actually does materialize one day, must be a rock-like structure. It is sufficient that the purely abstract idea can rule men with a power that defies all persecution and attack, in a time when life only too often resembles a battle-field and the minds of men are apt to become estranged from all ideals. To serve the masonic cause wholly demands, to-day, an extraordinarily strong inner impulse, for it is harder than ever to ignite the holy flame with the idea of fraternal love. Subjects of controversy, which constantly incite fresh hatred, are becoming more and more numerous. The walls which must be demolished if mankind is to have a better future are getting higher and higher, and many who intended enthusiastically to assist are now becoming daily more wearied and hopeless because of their own suffering.

[1] Ernst Reinhardt: *Symbolik der Mysterienbünde*, Munich.
[2] These wanderings are wonderfully rendered in Mozart's opera *The Magic Flute*.

But those who, in spite of all, continue hopefully to strengthen the building, filled with the conviction that the spiritual resurrection of mankind is necessary, possess the masonic secret. Here are Fichte's words:

'Desert us not, O Holy Palladium of Humanity, O Consoling Thought, that out of each of our works and out of each of our sufferings a new perfection arises for our fellows; that in the place where we now slave and are trampled upon, a race will one day arise which may always do what it wishes, as it will only want to do what is good.'

CHAPTER IV

THE EARLY HISTORY OF FREEMASONRY

FREEMASONRY made its first appearance as a society, i.e. as a distinct organization, in the year 1717. Four Lodges then existing in London, the meetings of which used to be held in various taverns—the Goose and Gridiron Alehouse, St. Paul's Churchyard; the Crown Alehouse, Parker's Lane; the Apple Tree Tavern, Charles Street; and the Rummer and Grapes, Channel Row—combined on St. John's Day of that year to form a Grand Lodge, 'as a centre of concord and harmony', and within a very few years there had developed from this modest foundation an intellectual and spiritual movement of an extent that seems almost fantastic.

England had at that time just emerged from a period of the bitterest political struggles, of the wildest religious quarrels, of awful war and severe economic crisis, and was once more in calm waters. Throughout the whole of the seventeenth century the country, which became Protestant in the year 1553, had been the scene of violent and vicious emotion. Rebellion and revolution had torn it time and again. Under the Stuarts there had been continuous internal strife. King and Parliament, Tories and Whigs, Catholics and the various groups of Protestants, Anglicans, Presbyterians, Puritans, Dissenters, and Independents had all been involved in incessant fratricidal warfare and the blood of the executed flowed in streams. The Republic of the ingenious Cromwell, with its Puritan spirit, the mighty growth of the imperialistic idea, and the marked advance of trade and industry, formed an interlude. Then came the Restoration with its blatant favouritism, the degeneration of the Court, and the most nerve-racking uncertainty in all walks of life. Parliament had to pass the Habeas Corpus Act in 1679 in order to assure the citizen of at least a minimum of personal freedom. In 1688 William of Orange came into power and introduced the Toleration Act. His sister-in-law, Anne, followed him in 1702, and in 1714 George, Elector of Hanover, was called to the throne. An atmosphere of greater freedom then began to make itself felt.

But all the storms and troubles of the times had not been

able to prevent a marked intellectual progress, accompanied by the development of the philosophy of enlightenment which, particularly on English soil, had taken firm root. Newton, by his theory of gravity, had guided thought into different channels, and John Locke, the philosopher, had exploited this to an extraordinary degree. In all branches of learning there was evidence of a marked aversion to the scholasticism

JOHANN AMOS COMENIUS

of the Middle Ages. This system had not been able to withstand the progress of the natural sciences and of mathematical knowledge. The idea of tolerance came into being as a reaction against the infinite hatred which had poisoned the whole of public life. Comenius, the last bishop of the Bohemian Brethren, who, summoned by his friend Hartlib, arrived in London in 1641 and attempted to bring to fruition his ambition of a pansophical society of scholars, was full of enthusiasm for the 'erection of the Temple of Universal Knowledge, which shall be erected according to the rules, laws, and ideas of the Supreme Architect, and shall serve not only Christians but all mankind'.

Toleration was advocated both by Locke, whose *Letters of Toleration* published in 1667 caused a lasting sensation, and by those men who, in the year 1645, formed a coterie of natural philosophers, 'an invisible college' which, in 1662, became the 'Royal Society', and which later gave Freemasonry a large number of its early leaders.

Out of these times there also arose a deistical current, an intellectual tendency which aimed at seeking a standard religious wisdom recognizable to all and sundry (Troeltsch), and also the pantheistic ideas of John Toland, an Irishman, who dreamed of a strange and curious brotherhood, the 'Socratic Brethren'.

When one hears that the year 1717 was the real starting-point of masonic history one would imagine that it would be quite easy to trace the course of the previous history of Free-masonry. This, however, is fallacious. To delve into masonic history is like trying to find one's way through a labyrinth, or, rather, through an innumerable succession of labyrinths; for although works on masonic history are numerous, the views of some of the authors are frequently in direct contradiction to those of others. The reason for this is easily explained: the origin of Freemasonry is shrouded in mystery.

We know approximately what happened in 1717. We know what was then fundamentally decided, but we know nothing whatever of the men who assembled on that 24th day of June which has become so significant. Solely from the fact that the founders of the first Grand Lodge were corporations or Lodges, and not individuals, it is clear that something was there beforehand. But in the course of 200 years of research this 'something' has never been properly determined

The beginnings of Freemasonry are lost in obscurity, an obscurity that is all the greater because the men of 1717 evidently made no attempt to throw even the faintest ray of light on it. Quite the contrary is the case. The author of the first and fundamental Constitutions of 1723,[1] the Rev. James Anderson, who was also the first masonic historian, has bequeathed us an extensive history; but what he wrote can only be regarded as legend, dictated by the desire to make

---

[1] *The Constitutions of the Free-Masons, containing the history, charges, regulations, etc. of that most ancient and right worshipful fraternity.*

the newly created society appear as venerable as possible. No other motive can be attributed to him for the fantastic history with which he endowed the Constitutions of the newly born Grand Lodge, and which, based upon the ancient legends of the gilds, goes back to Adam. However, it has turned out to be a fatal gift for Masonry. There were 'experts' in the eighteenth century who thought that Anderson had not gone back far enough; William Preston, for instance, who, in his *Illustrations of Masonry*, attempted to trace Freemasonry back to the commencement of the world; and Dr. George Oliver (*Antiquities of Freemasonry*), to whom it seemed clear that the masonic science existed on older planetary systems before the formation of the earth. These histories were either based on ancient legends, as in the case of Anderson's work, or were the outcome of the author's own imaginings.

In these legends a great part is played by Jabal, the son of Lamech (or of Enoch),[1] as the 'Inventor of Geometry', the greatest of the seven liberal arts, and as the 'builder of the first house in stone' before the Flood; and also by his brothers Jubal, the discoverer of music, and Tubal Cain, the first artificer in metals, and by his sister Naamah, the first weaver. They knew that the Wrath of God would descend upon the earth, so they hid their knowledge in two pillars, one of which was found after the Flood by Hermes Trismegistus, the great-grandson of Noah, and the other, much later, by Pythagoras, who, according to Anderson, brought the wisdom of the Orient to the Occident and became the head of an academy or lodge of students of geometry to whom he communicated a secret, 'namely, that astonishing principle which is the fundament of all Masonry'.

Hermes (who, by the way, also plays an important part in occultist philosophy, being no other than the Egyptian God Thoth, who wrote the forty-two holy books) became the first teacher of mankind, and thus the 'Father of all Wisdom'.

In this way Masonry came to Babel, where 'much ado' was made about it during the building of the celebrated tower. Nemroth, King of Babylon, himself a Mason, then sent forth sixty masons to build the City of Nineveh, giving them a 'charge'—'the first in the world', as the legend says. Abraham (the 'Father of the Cabala') brought the sciences from the Euphrates to Egypt. There he became teacher to Euclid, who reduced geometry to a system, promoted the building of

[1] Genesis, Chapter iv.

temples and palaces, and gave to Masonry another 'charge', which ran as follows:

'VIII. The First was that they should bee true to the Kinge and Lords they served.

'IX. And that they should love well together And be true each one to other.

'X. And to call each other his fellowe or else his brother And not servant nor knave nor any other foule name.

'XII. And that they should ordaine the wisest of them to bee the Master of their Lords worke And that neither Lord nor man of Great Linage or Riches or for favour should make and ordaine such a one to beare Rule and be governour of theire worke that hath but small knowledge or understanding in the science whereby the owner of the worke should bee evill served and you ashamed of your worke-manship.

'XVI. And alsoe that they should come and assemble themselves together once every yeare That they might take advice and councell together how they might worke best to serve theire Lord and Master for his proffitt and theire owne creditt and honestie And to Correct amongst themselves him or them that erred and trespassed And thus was the Craft or science of Geometrie grounded there.

'XVII. And this worthy Master gave it the name of Geometrie And now it is called Masonrie.'

A golden age for 'Masonry' then came also in Palestine. King David began the building of the great Temple at Jerusalem, which was completed by his son Solomon, the timber for it being supplied by another king, Hiram, whose son Aymon, supported him as the 'chiefest master of all his masons'.

We will not pursue here the strange paths by which these Masons wandered through the times until finally, according to the legends, Athelstan, the Anglo-Saxon, became the first royal protector of the English Lodges.

But even though all this may have sprung from an imagination run riot, and even if Lessing's famous phrase: 'Freemasonry always has been, and is, by its very nature, just as old as society itself', may not be regarded as an attempt to establish historical evidence, it has even now never been established whence the earliest roots of Masonry sprang. It is not even authentically known how it came to pass that the four London Lodges, of which we have just spoken, were the foundations of the present masonic structure. It may safely be asserted, however, that they were not the beginning, but rather the remains of an older structure, though complete documentary evidence is lacking to prove this.

There are, of course, writers of masonic history who doggedly maintain the standpoint *quod est in actis*, and who hold that Freemasonry first saw the light of day in 1717, and had no previous existence in any form. They will not grant that in the founding of the first Grand Lodge a spiritual driving force manifested itself, and to them 'the Honourable Society and Fraternity of Freemasons' of 1717 was a harmless association, a cheerful club, if not a superior brotherhood of gorgers and swillers: that is to say, not the expression of a spirit building for itself a body, but of a body which only in later times found the spirit.

But the vast majority of historical writers have adopted the thesis that the four Lodges which formed the foundation of so proud a structure were the remains of a community going back to previous centuries. Their quarrel, however, concerns the nature of this older institution. And the fact that most of these writers of masonic history approach their task not with open minds, but with private and preconceived views of their own, hardly tends to bring this intellectual dispute to a speedy end. Naturally, their work is not made any easier by the fact that no writings exist concerning the first years of the newly-formed Grand Lodge. There are no minutes, no letters, no records. It is quite certain that such writings did exist, but, for some reason or another they were burned before 1722. Thus the flames devoured much knowledge which would have saved a large amount of mental effort in later years, and which would have spared Freemasonry innumerable theories.

The vast majority of modern Freemasons believe that the craft is a continuation, a descendant, as it were, of the stone-masons who played so important a part, culturally, in many parts of Europe during the Middle Ages. The remarkable thing about this theory is that it did not gain currency in the initial years of the Society, but was first propounded by a non-Mason, the Abbé Grandidier, an Alsatian student of history, in his book on Strasbourg Cathedral, two generations later. Subsequently, when this theory was investigated with the utmost enthusiasm, all kinds of documents and writings came to light which might be quoted in its favour. Up to the present day it has not been possible to forge a complete chain of evidence, and the question is constantly being discussed as to when, and in what manner, the transition took place from a Fraternity of Free Gild Masons to a 'speculative' intellectual Masonry, which, preserving the old symbols, took up the work on an invisible symbolic structure.

It is quite obvious that those of a non-rationalistic turn of mind find no satisfaction in this theory: that is to say, those people who insist on the view that, when discussing the 'Mysteries of Freemasonry', the word 'Mystery', with its two meanings, should not be interpreted as 'handicraft' but as 'secret'. This group defends the opinion that the roots of Freemasonry must have been of an intellectual and mystical nature from the very beginning. But also in this sphere there is a confusing multiplicity of opinions and an abundance of theories, evolved more especially by all those people to whom Freemasonry is not an art but a knowledge, or, rather, an unquenchable thirst for knowledge, the restless quest for the lost 'secret' of the Ancients which the mystery societies have been pursuing throughout the ages from the very earliest times of antiquity. To find a connecting link between these mystery societies—or, at least, between one or the other of them—and Freemasonry has always been the ardent endeavour of many masonic students. And there is probably not a single one of these mystery societies which might not have been connected with Freemasonry; the Priests of the Isis and Osiris cult in ancient Egypt; the Eleusinian Mysteries, with their holy drama of the Rise, Fall, and Resurrection; the Persian Mithras cult with its seven degrees, its deep symbolism, its demand for secrecy, for tolerance, for equality and brotherly love and its dramatic representation of the resurrection of the body; the Pythagoreans; the Essenes; the Culdees of the sixth century—all these have been described as the true forerunners of Freemasonry. Abundant resemblance to the Royal Art has been discovered in their initiation ritual, in their symbols, and in their solemn oaths; but frequently this resemblance was deduced.

In this realm, which confuses unwordly mysticism with the beginnings of Freemasonry, are also to be found those philosophers who seek the origin of Freemasonry in ancient Rosicrucianism, and in a certain sense, therefore, also those who consider that the way for Freemasonry was prepared by Comenius, the great Czech sage, who, imbued with Rosicrucian

FRANCIS, EARL OF MOIRA

ACTING GRAND MASTER OF THE 'MODERNS'

From the Engraving by Henry Landseer, after the Painting by J. Hoppner, R.A.

THE CHEVALIER RUSPINI
FOUNDER OF THE ROYAL MASONIC INSTITUTION FOR GIRLS
Painted and Engraved by I. Jenner

ideas, professed the religion 'in which all men agree' at the beginning of the seventeenth century, and who regarded as his life-work the kindling of the 'Universal Light' for Humanity.

But other connecting links with Freemasonry have also been found; for instance, contemporary English Deism—although it has not been possible to establish the membership of any of the important representatives of this school of thought; the Academies ; the Sodalities; the Neoplatonism of the Renaissance, with its peculiar usage [1] and its system of the three degrees, which—according to Herr G. F. Hartlaub, the Mannheim Art Historian—finds its artistic glorification in Giorgione's celebrated painting, 'The Three Philosophers' (Art-History Museum, Vienna) and the other pictures of the Venetian Master.

We will state our view at once. There is a certain amount of truth in all these theories, but not enough to bridge the vast gulfs which open up on closer examination, and which cannot be spanned by the most audacious hypotheses propounded by clever historical craftsmen, although they may be boldly cloaked as something confirmed by history. This tendency to prove continuity where it does not exist, and, on the other hand, the endeavour to argue away what really does exist, merely because it cannot be proved with mathematical certainty, have thrown masonic history into still greater confusion.

Apart from those who complacently pursue the path of their own theory, and to whom everything else is mere 'bunkum', only he who abandons every attempt to cast light upon the earliest times of Freemasonry and gives up all hope of finding a complete series of facts, confirmed by dates, will find a way out of this chaos. In our opinion it would still prove impossible to forge such an unbroken chain, even if all manner of unknown documents were suddenly brought to light from archives the existence of which we had hitherto not suspected; for the seed of which Freemasonry is the flower germinated in many kinds of soil, and the spirit of the Royal Art was nourished, without a doubt, on the wisdom of centuries. Freemasonry is primarily rooted in the same yearning which, in the earliest times, caused men to gather together in a secret cult community. It enabled ancient ideals to bloom anew.

Even the ancient Egyptians regarded their task at an

---

[1] Especially by Ludwig Keller in *Die geistigen Grundlagen der Freimaurerei*. Jena, Diederichs, 1911, and other publications.

initiation as the unveiling and strengthening of the 'Hidden Light', which, according to their creed, is dormant even in the lowest of men. In letters visible from afar the words 'KNOW THYSELF' sent their message to the faithful, even from above the Apollo Temple in Delphi, and symbol societies whose work was based on Seneca's words: *'Homo res sacra homini'* ('Man shall be sacred to his fellow-men!') were active even in Ancient Rome.

No matter where that seed commenced to grow, it cannot be doubted that in the first stage of Freemasonry, when it was still the 'Freemasonry before Freemasonry' (Horneffer), and, as it were, still lived a subterranean existence, there took place in England a gradual transition from a gild corporation with the character of a fraternity to an intellectual fraternity. That this process of transition took place in obscurity may be explained by the fact that the fraternities of stonemasons and builders, which made so significant an appearance in the fifteenth and sixteenth centuries, and whose work is embodied in those most beautiful and sublime monuments of the archi-tectural science, the Gothic cathedrals which rear their towers aloft into the heavens, began to disintegrate from the beginning of the sixteenth century onwards.

Much difference of opinion also prevails regarding the origin of these fraternities. On one important point they suffer in the same way as Freemasonry itself (like so many other institutions said to have been connected with the earlier history of Freemasonry), in that their origin is also shrouded in obscurity, into which the legends of the gilds throw no useful light. This circumstance has added to Freemasonry's legendary genealogical trees a large number of new ones. The masonic symbols (in reality professional marks), which the excavations of Pompeii laid bare in the mosaic floor of one of its houses, excited the imagination to an extraordinary extent. It is not so very long ago that the true forerunners of the Lodges and of Freemasonry were believed to have been traced back to the Comacines, the Lombardian stonemasons, who went from the neighbourhood of Lake Como to the Rhine, to Spain, and other countries at the beginning of the ninth century. It was just as impossible to prove this as it was to prove the alleged direct derivation from the Roman Colleges of Building, the *collegia fabrorum*, many of whose constructional secrets may have been passed on to subsequent Lodge fraternities.

And there is a further divergence of opinion, for the view

held by some people that the stonemasons' fraternity was of German origin, and only later spread to England, is opposed, probably with good foundation, by the assertion that the reverse was actually the case. It is said that it was the English masons who went to Germany first, and that it was not until much later that the German Steinmetzen began to migrate to England. In any case, the masonic fraternities were brought into being in both countries by the monks, especially by the Cistercians, the Benedictines, and the Oblates, in whose hands originally reposed the knowledge of architecture and the cultivation of the science of building. In the beginning, when churches were being built, a bishop or abbot was the employer, with a cleric or layman possessing a thorough knowledge of the masonic craft as the 'master builder' (*caput magister*), who prepared the plans and models and directed the operations. Abbot Wilhelm of Hirschau, especially, was famous as a *magister operis* in the eleventh century, and with the aid of English masons sent him by the Archbishop of Canterbury, he performed work of such excellence in that sphere that he is often described as the Father of Ecclesiastical Architecture.

As the clerical masons enlisted the services of lay assistants and transferred to them their knowledge and art, these laymen became, to an increasing extent, the actual builders of the cathedrals. Thus developed the lay fraternities, whose 'Charges' were naturally much less strict than the monastic regulations to which the clerical masons were subject. There arose in England the 'Gild of Masons', the 'Lodge'; in France, the 'Compagnonage', and in Germany the 'Bauhütte'.

The great difference between these fraternities and the other craft gilds was the fact that the stonemason's profession did not tie him to any particular place, and the master-builders were forced to wander from place to place in the company of their skilled workmen according to the demand for their services. They were never more than a few years in any place, and, as 'strangers', did not belong to the ordinary local gilds, and therefore they had to have their own widespread organization, so that the building trade of the whole world was more or less organized in a connected fraternity, which was divided into numerous completely independent associations.

The members of this tremendous fraternal community, the builders of the Gothic architectural monuments, were widely renowned and esteemed as the possessors of very special knowledge and traditions—a knowledge which, possessed by them alone, 'enabled them to erect their slender columns to span their broad vaults and far-projecting arches and to calculate how to support the weight resting upon them and properly distribute their mighty burden'.

First of all, let us consider the German 'Bauhütten', or Lodges, which sprang up everywhere. They had their own laws and their own regulations. The head of the 'Hütte' was the master, and the 'Parlierer' acted as his deputy. Three things were peculiar to these Bauhütten, viz., the stonemason's book containing the constructional theory, the regulations applying to the moral behaviour of the brethren amongst themselves and towards strangers, and, finally, the secret of the Ritual of the so-called inner 'Hütte', or Lodge. Goethe, in one of his earlier works (*Über Künst und Altertum in den Rhein- und Maingegenden*') wrote some beautiful words about these peculiarities of the Steinmetzen, whose harmony and concord produced such magnificent artistic and creative energy:

> 'Its great advantages are to be able to make themselves recognizable to their fellows by means of secret signs and sayings. . . . Imagine an organization of an immense multitude of people, of all degrees of skill, giving a helping hand to the Master, inspired by religion, elevated by art, restrained by propriety; then one begins to comprehend how such enormous works are conceived, undertaken and, if not completed, at least made possible. . . .'

At a meeting of Steinmetzen in Regensburg in the year 1459, the German 'Bauhütten', the most important of which were those of Strasbourg, Vienna (St. Stefan), Cologne, Bern, and later, Zürich, were drawn into closer union. Nineteen masters from Swabia, Franconia, Bavaria, Upper Rhine, Switzerland, and Austria participated. The Steinmetzen's association, thus created, set up Constitutions or 'Ordinances', elected chief judges and appointed as the highest authority the master of the chief lodge at Strasbourg Cathedral, at that time Jost Dotzinger of Worms.

There are students of masonic history who regard the Regensburg Assembly, or rather the 'Hütten' Assembly, in Speyer five years later, as, to a certain extent, the foundation of Freemasonry, a hypothesis which does not become any the more tenable by reason of the 'mysteries' of the Bauhütten having been exaggerated and much that never existed having been attributed to them.

The endeavour to trace the complete Ritual of the 'Bauhütten' or to reconstruct them has unfortunately failed. The secret was handed down mainly by word of mouth, and, as time went on, much was lost. What has been handed down to us are merely fragments. It is therefore very difficult to say to what extent the masonic Ritual coincides with that of the ancient 'Bauhütten'. But from what is available—Eugen Weiss has recently written an excellent book on this subject [1]— one is able to see that there is a great similarity between the Steinmetzens' greeting and a part of the masonic usage. Nevertheless, it seems to us that Weiss goes too far when he infers, taking as his chief foundation the fragments of Ritual brought to light by himself, that the German masonic lodges developed directly out of the 'Bauhütten' of the upright, pious, free and liberal Steinmetzen, whose chief principle was brotherly love and whose highest aim in thought and deed was to strive towards the House of God, Virtue and Truth.

The 'secrets' consisted mainly of signs of recognition and the dialogues connected therewith, as, for example, the following colloquy from the Mason's 'proof of his identity':[2]

Altgesell (Elder): 'What dost thou carry under thy hat?'

Stranger: 'A laudable wisdom.'

Elder: 'What dost thou carry under thy tongue?'

Stranger: 'A praiseworthy truth.'

Elder: 'Wherefore dost thou wear an apron?'

Stranger: 'For the honour of the craft and for my own advantage.'

Elder: 'What is the strength of the craft?'

Stranger: 'That which fire and water cannot destroy.'

Elder: 'What is the best in a wall?'

Stranger: 'The bond.'

But such test questions constituted only a part of the secret whereby the members of the Steinmetz fraternity strove to preserve their privileges against intruders. In addition to the greeting, they could recognize each other by the step, by the handshake (with a special grip), and by a password. The stonemason's mark was also of importance. This mark which was entered in the Register of Fellow-Crafts, was received by

---

[1] Eugen Weiss: *Steinmetzart and Steinmetzgeist*, Jena, 1927, Diederichs.

[2] Fallou: *Die Mysterien der Freimaurerei*, Leipzig, 1848. The Steinmetz Ritual is now generally admitted to be a fraud.

the apprentice on being declared free and had to be carved, without fail, into every finished stone.

No person was allowed to cross the threshold of the 'Bauhütten' without 'proof of his identity'. He also had to place his feet at the correct angle and perform the prescribed right-angled genuflexion. The Steinmetz was obliged also to have a knowledge of the rich symbolism of the Fraternity. The secrets of numbers, especially, played an important part there. That was naturally bound up in the fact that the proportions of the growing number of cathedrals were based upon the figures 3, 5, 7, and 9, which have been regarded as sacred since the remotest times. The compasses were a Steinmetz symbol. It was the token of the Fraternity, which symbolized Truth and Wisdom, Love and Harmony. The plumb-rule, the gauge, the common gavel, the trowel, and the tessellated border were their symbols, all of which are still emblems in Freemasonry. Last, but not least, the rose, the symbol of secrecy—a circumstance which later led to even the Steinmetzen being associated with the mysticism of the Rosicrucians. Even the princes who granted their protection to the Hütten, or Lodges, were obliged to be initiated into the Fraternity before they were granted admission to the 'Interior'. Thus the Emperor Maximilian, who confirmed the 'Brother-Book', the result of the deliberations of Regensburg and Speyer, belonged to this Fraternity. And tradition has it that the Emperor Rudolf IV was a member of the Cathedral Hütte of St. Stefan in Vienna.

The existence of the great Fraternity, of whose members Anton Pilgram, the builder of Vienna Cathedral, is counted one of the most important, was, nevertheless, of only short duration. The differences of opinion arising out of the Reformation had a devastating effect upon the organization of the cathedral builders. Violent controversies arose and a legend came into circulation which, much later, was to become current also in Freemasonry, although with the very opposite object in view. The corporations of builders were accused of having originated from the Knights Templars, and this was used as a reason for attacking them violently. The Bauhütten lost more and more of their privileges, and were, for the most part, dissolved in the seventeenth century, by which time the English gilds had also lost their original character.

In England the gilds reach far back. The records of the early times are, however, not very numerous. So far as their subsequent connexion with Freemasonry is concerned, considerable knowledge is to be gained from a number of 'Charges', the oldest of which proves that the original Masonry possessed a literature as early as the end of the fourteenth century. The

FIRST PAGE FROM THE REGIUS MS., WRITTEN ABOUT THE YEAR 1400

oldest manuscript at present known, the Regius Manuscript, was written about the year 1400, and was discovered in the British Museum in 1830, and published in 1840 by James O. Halliwell. It consists of a poem of 794 rhymed lines in the old English language. Following an introduction, there are eight sections, the first of which bears the descriptive Latin title:

'Hic incipiunt constituciones artis gemetrie secundum Euclide',
and, in spite of its significance to Freemasons, it is
quite possible that its late appearance is due to its having

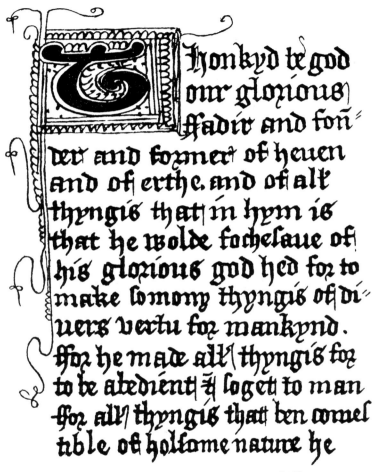

FIRST PAGE OF THE COOKE MS., *c.* 1450

previously been mistaken for some kind of mathematical
treatise. The second important manuscript, the Cooke
Manuscript,[1] probably originated some thirty or forty years

---

[1] A 'Book of charges' annexed thereto may be even older than the Regius
poem and may go back to the year 1388.

after the Regius Manuscript, which, by the way, already contained the expression 'Lodge'. This second manuscript was first published in the year 1861. The most important parts of both these manuscripts, as also in the case of similar ones, are represented by old Gild regulations, fragments of Gild legends, directions for the conscientious fulfilment of the Gild 'charges' and for religio-moral conduct. In addition, the Regius Manuscript contains a reference to the patron saints of the stonemasons, the Quatuor Coronati.

One thing becomes very clear from these manuscripts. Those adventurous legends of which we have just learnt were in vogue even in early times, when they were inscribed on parchment, but with the difference that what was somewhat cautiously described by Anderson as the history of Masonry, here appears clearly as Gild legend, from which it may be concluded that even 300 years before the birth of the first Grand Lodge of Freemasons, English Masons took pride in attributing the origin of their corporation to time immemorial.

The time at which the legends choose firmly to establish the Gild on English soil is the year 926. Legend has it that at that time an assembly of Masons was held at York under the patronage of Prince Edwin, the brother of King Athelstan, who came to the throne in 924, in order independently to regulate the affairs of the Gild on the basis of a Charter granted by the King. This legend has caused undiscriminating people of a very literal turn of mind to propound the obviously wrong theory, 'that the first Grand Lodge of England met, therefore, at York in the year 926'. Consequently, for a certain length of time, the 'York Saga' played an important part in the study of masonic history, and documents were even produced which were afterwards proved to be clever forgeries.

It is only from the fourteenth century that anything positive is known about the Gilds, or Crafts, Mysteries and Companies, as the various kinds of Gilds were called. At that time—it was during the reign of that excellent King, Edward III— these were not only important as commercial and craft organizations, but also as the propagators of religious and moral principles. Miracle plays, which they regularly produced, were extremely popular. It is to these performances that we owe the first positive records of the masonic Gilds, for these latter appear as the organizers of such plays in York in 1350, and in Chester in 1357. However, these plays contained nothing of the present masonic Ritual, but were solely representations of Biblical scenes.

The word 'Freemason' is first encountered in the year 1375.

THE 'WILLIAM WATSON MS.', A.D. 1687

In a record of the assembly of representatives of municipal Gilds in London, mention is made of 'ffremasons'. The word is also found in a list of workmen dated 1396, employed upon the building of Exeter Cathedral. The word 'mason', without the prefix 'free', was in circulation quite a century before. It appeared, for instance, in 1292, in a document concerning the building of a chapel in Westminster Palace. The word (*maszun, massoune mestre*) is of French origin and was brought to England by the Normans. The original meaning of the word 'freemason' has not yet been clearly ascertained. There are many different versions. The addition of the word 'free' is, on the one hand, regarded as merely emphasizing the membership of a privileged Gild, and, on the other hand, as referring to certain liberties, or the freedom to move about from place to place, enjoyed by the freemasons engaged in the building of churches. The most widespread opinion, however, is that the 'freemasons' were specially qualified builders who worked artistically on the 'freestone', i.e., the ornamental stone which projects from a wall, and who also possessed other architectural knowledge, in contradistinction to the 'roughmasons', who only performed the simple work, and did not prepare the stones but only placed them in the walls.

After a period of suppression under Henry VI, the masonic Gild very soon gained fresh impetus, first of all as a purely professional organization. A coat of arms of the 'Hole craft and felawship of masons' dates from the year 1472, whilst in 1481 reference is made to a distinctive livery. The laws of the Gild coincided in material points with the regulations of the German Steinmetzen. In many respects its usage, as in Germany, differed very considerably from the customs of the other craft Gilds. Here also was the secret, here also the precise rules for Apprentices, Fellow-crafts, and Masters, which were read out before the taking of the oath at the initiation. G. Kloss has called special attention to three points in the 'charges', which he had studied very closely: the brotherly equality of the members of the Gild; the care for their technical education; and the precise injunctions for their moral conduct.

But what particularly distinguished the British Lodges from the German 'Bauhütten' was the admission of non-operative masons, which took place to an ever-increasing extent as time went on. · The 'Mary's Chapel' Lodge in Edinburgh preserves as its most valued treasure the oldest existing masonic minute book, the entries in which go back to the year 1598. As early as the 'aucht day of Janij the zeir of God 1600 yeirs', the registration of the first 'Non-Operative'—John

Boswell of Auchinleck—took place. It is recorded on the 20th May, 1640, that the members of this Lodge

'doeth admit amongh them the right honerabell Alexander Hamiltone, generall of the artillerie of thes Kindom to be felow and Mr. of the forsed craft'.

This admission to be 'felow and Master' is all the more interesting because it has been maintained until quite recent times that the division into the three degrees of entered apprentice, fellow-craft, and master was not known in the Lodges of the operative masons before 1717, and that in each one of them there had only been one master mason, the 'master of the craft', the others being merely 'fellows of the Society'. ('Fellow' not in the sense of 'Fellow Craft' but as 'member'.)

In the year 1641 Robert Moray, Quartermaster-General of the Scottish Army, was initiated in Newcastle, i.e. on English soil, by the Edinburgh Lodge. Five years later one of the greatest scholars of the seventeenth century, the Rosicrucian Elias Ashmole,[1] was made a Freemason in Warrington. He entered the date of his initiation—which took place at the same time as that of Col. Henry Mainwaring—in his diary as the 16th day of October, 1646. He regarded the membership, as it says in the *Biographia Britannica*, as of 'an excellent character'. That it was not just a passing interest is proved by a subsequent entry in his diary. Thirty-six years later, in 1682, Ashmole took part in an initiation at 'Masons Hall', London, and, once again, the newly initiated included many non-operative brethren.

In 1665 Randle Holm of Chester, the antiquary, described himself as a Freemason. He was a clever man, to whom we are indebted for a copy of the 'Antient Charges', the so-called Harleian Manuscript, and, consequently, for the knowledge of an oath which mentions the 'Words and Signs of a Freemason'.

Another prominent scholar, Dr. Robert Plot, who wrote a celebrated Natural History of Staffordshire (1686), speaks in this book of 'people of the most eminent quality who consider it worth-while to belong to the Society of Freemasons'. He also quotes customs which to-day still obtain in Freemasonry; for instance, the custom of giving the neophyte

[1] Elias Ashmole (1617–1692) was officer, physicist, astrologer, alchemist, botanist, and historian at Oxford. His chief works are *Theatrum Chemicum Britannicum* and *The Way to Bliss*. A museum founded by him is even to-day one of the sights of Oxford. It bears his name.

1646

Oct. 16. 4^H 30'. P.M. J was made a Free Mason
at Warrington in Lancashire, with Coll: Henry
Mainwaring of Karincham in Cheshire.
The names of those that were then of the Lodge
Mr. Rich: Penket Warden, Mr. James Collier, Mr. Rich.
Sankey, Henry Littler, John Ellam, Rich. Ellam
& Hugh Brewer.

March 1682.

10: About 5 H. P.M. J rec^d: a Summons to app^r at a
Lodge to be held the next day, at Masons Hall London.

11. Accordingly J went, & about Noone were admitted
into the Fellowship of Free Masons,
Sr William Wilson Knight, Capt. Rich: Borthwick,
Mr Will: Woodman, Mr Wm Grey, Mr Samuell
Taylour & Mr William Wise.
J was the Senior Fellow among them (it being 35
years since J was admitted) There were present
beside my selfe the Fellowes after named.
Mr Tho: Wise M^r of the Masons Company this
p^rsent yeare. Mr Thomas Shorthose, Mr Thomas
Shadbolt, ... Waindsford Esqr
Mr Nich: Young, Mr John Shorthose, Mr William
Hamon, Mr John Thompson, & Mr Will: Stanton
Wee all dyned at the halfe Moone Taverne in
Cheapeside, at a Noble Dinner prepaired at the charge
of the New = accepted Masons.

EXTRACTS FROM THE DIARY OF ELIAS ASHMOLE

gloves for the woman 'nearest to his heart', a custom which Goethe, as is well known, mentioned in two letters to Frau von Stein on the occasion of his sending her these gloves after his initiation.

The *Natural History of Wiltshire*, by John Aubrey, also contains important references to the membership of 'Speculatives'. Aubrey speaks not only of an assembly which he himself attended, but also of many things which Sir William Dugdale, who was a Freemason, reported to him about the Fraternity to which he belonged. From Aubrey also comes the story that in the 'eighties of the seventeenth century Sir Christopher Wren, the gifted builder of St. Paul's Cathedral, London, was a member of the London 'Lodge of Antiquity No. 2', which worked in the 'Goose and Gridiron' Tavern and was one of the four original Lodges of 1717. The correctness of this statement is disputed in other quarters, but has recently been confirmed in a history of the Lodge. The three beautiful old candlesticks in the Temple of this Lodge are traditionally described as being the gift of Wren.

We will not adduce here any further evidence to prove that the number of 'accepted Masons', as they were called, was by no means small in the Lodges of the seventeenth century, nor to show that they attained office in many places, as, for instance, in the venerable Scottish Lodge 'Mother Kilwinning' in 1697, nor to demonstrate that in other places they constituted the majority of the members, as, for example, in Aberdeen in 1670, where out of fifty-nine Lodge members only seven were working masons, seven others being tilers and carpenters, and the remainder noblemen, clerics, merchants, doctors, and professors. The same may be said of another Scottish Lodge, in Haughfoot, in 1702. It was in this way that the process of transition from the 'Company' to the 'Society' took place, the deepest foundations of which have not yet been uncovered. The work in the craft, of which the Lodges had originally been the home, slipped into the background and the symbolic work on the invisible temple came to the fore.

How can one explain this infiltration into a Gild of people having really very little to do with it? How came it that the Gild charges of the Stonemasons changed into spiritual charges? Or that the Lodge suddenly had temples and altars? The 'exact' or precise school of masonic research has an explanation for it. This is to the effect that extensive associations connected with the Gild had been formed, the members of which were

The might of the father of heaven
the wisdome of the glorious son through
ye grace and goodnes of ye holy Ghost
ye bene three psons and one God be
with us att our begininge and geve
us grace soe to governe us here in
our liveing, that wee maie come to
his blisse that never shall have
endinge, Amen

Good brethren and followes
my purpose is to tell you, how and in what
manner wyse this worthey craft
of Masonrie was begone. And
afterwaxdes how it was kepte by worthey
kinges and princes, and by maine
other worshipfull men And allsoe to those
that here we will tharge by the charyes
that belongeth to every freemason to
keepe for in good faith and they take good
heede to it it is worthey to be well kepte for it is
a worthey crafte and a curious Siconce ffor
there be seaven Liberall Sciences of which

A PAGE OF THE BAIN MS., ONE OF THE OLDEST MASONIC WRITINGS
In the possession of the West Yorkshire Provincial Grand Lodge

SITHENCE Long time after when the Children of ISRAEL were come into the Lād of the IEBUSITES which is now call'd IERU :SALEM King DAVID began the *Temple* that is call'd (TEMPLUM DOMINI) with us the TEMPLE of IERUSALEM, alias the TEMPLE of the LORD.

THE same King DAVID Loved MASONS and Cherished them, and gave y^m Good Pay. And he gave them the Charges in man -ner as they were given in EGYPT, by EUCLYDE, and other Charges more, as you shalt Hear afterwards.

AFTER

A PAGE FROM THE INIGO JONES MS.

noblemen, priests, citizens, and peasants whose task was to procure and transport building materials coming from afar. The highly placed protectors, the employers and other dilettanti of the art, the local cleric, the sons of Freemasons having attained their twenty-second year, and all kinds of building workpeople, e.g. carpenters, plumbers, glass-painters, etc., were allowed, in the fifteenth century, to enter Lodges on certain conditions, whereby a kind of 'outer ring' of 'speculative masons' was formed: a Fraternity surrounding the real organization. It was a Lodge alongside the Craft, which, later on, when the Gilds fell into decline, became the 'inner ring', and, without any special spiritual background, carried on the ancient traditions and customs and enabled them, in a new shape, to continue their existence after the year 1717. Many representatives of this point of view lay great stress on the fact that round about the year 1717, these Lodges no longer held their meetings in 'Masons' Hall', but in taverns, and that every initiation was followed by a sumptuous repast ('noble dinner', says Ashmole), in order to draw the conclusion that, in the transitional stages, it was chiefly a 'special form of noble companionship surrounded by ancient usages'.

However, this absolutely unspiritual descent does not agree with the spiritual picture which the young Grand Lodge of England presented immediately after its foundation, nor with a passage from an autobiography of the learned physician, Dr. William Stukeley, the first man to become a Freemason in the early days of the Grand Lodge, who wrote the following, under the date '1720':

'His curiosity led him to be initiated into the mysteries of Masonry, suspecting it to be the remains of the mysteries of the antients. . . .'

If Stukeley, who was a member of the 'Royal Society', suspected that, he must have had some reason for it. And the question may also be asked, Whether previously other 'accepted masons' had not sought magic secrets in the Lodges? Or perhaps philosopho-metaphysical mystagogy? Or an esoteric exclusive society in an exoteric garb? Were they not seeking the 'Word'? Were they seeking that primeval knowledge of the ancients—the Alpha and Omega that is said to be hidden in the masonic symbols?

'For we be brethren of the Rosie Crosse;
We have the Mason's Word and second sight,'

as it ran in a poem, 'Muses Threnodie', by Henry Adamson, published in Edinburgh in 1638.

That need not be, as Vibert[1] believes, the earliest reference to a special masonic word, that is to say, a password; it may very easily refer to the 'lost word', which the Rosicrucians and members of other mystery societies have sought to recover from the earliest of times—the lost word, the 'great secret of the Master', which the ancient mystics are supposed to have known, and which is called by the alchemists 'the Philosopher's Stone' and by others 'the great Alcahest'.

This coincides with the ideas of those who wish to trace the Freemasonry of 1717 back to ancient Rosicrucianism. It is, however, not particularly easy to follow the defenders of the Rosicrucian theory in this sphere, for even in regard to that Rosicrucianism which is mentioned for the first time at the beginning of the seventeenth century as an 'old Order', there are, in the main, only hypotheses and legends. How strongly these are impressed upon people's minds is demonstrated by the fact that only a short time ago the distinguished Belgian author Wittemans, who professes to have been for many years on the track of Rosicrucianism in Holland, maintained in all earnestness that the latter goes back to King Amenhotep, and that Paracelsus, from whose teachings the Rosicrucian ideas have evolved, was a member of this ancient secret society. On the other hand, one may accept with all seriousness the statements of the German writer Will-Erich Peuckert, who, with real fervour, saturated himself in the chiliastic dreams of the Middle Ages and lost himself in the works of Rosicrucian writers, and who could 'espy with the greatest respectful awe the birth of a new religion'—which one can believe of him when one reads his book. He proves that the Rosicrucians did not exist at all as a secret brotherhood before the seventeenth century; that a religio-intellectual emotion had at that time developed in the minds of individual persons who wanted positive Protestantism, the proper continuation of the Lutheran Reformation; but that almost all the 'secret societies' of the seventeenth century were on a Rosicrucian basis, and that possibly in this manner the ideas of Rosicrucianism were carried into the masonic Lodges.

Thus it may be said of the Rosicrucians, as of the Freemasons, that their true antecedents will probably never be

[1] Lionel Vibert: *Freemasonry before the Existence of Grand Lodges.*
[2] Will-Erich Peuckert: *Die Rosenkreutzer*, Jena, Diederichs, 1927.

discovered. In 1614, on the eve of the Thirty Years' War, they were mentioned in literature for the first time, in a booklet entitled: *Allgemein und General Reformation der Gantzen weiten Welt. Beneben der Fama Fraternitas Dess Löblichen Ordens des Rosencreutzes an alle Gelehrte und Häupter Europae geschrieben usw.*, published in Cassel in two parts. This booklet written by the Swabian theologian Johann Valentin Andreae (1586–1654), deals, in the second part entitled *Fama Fraternitas oder Brüderschaft des Hochlöblichen Ordens des R.C.*, with a highly mysterious person named Christian Rosenkreutz, supposed to have been born in 1378, who, towards the end of the fourteenth century, made a pilgrimage to Jerusalem, and, on the way, first in Damascus and later in Fez, is said to have been initiated into the ancient secret wisdom and knowledge of the Arabians. With three friars and four other companions he had then founded the Rosicrucian Brotherhood in Germany, with the object of leading the Church back to the original Christianity and establishing human welfare in Church and State. An obscure house, styled Sancti Spiritus, served as a place of refuge for the brethren, who, according to Andreae, went forth into various lands in order to find new adepts and followers. Rosenkreutz died in 1484, at the age of 106 years, and though no one had known the resting-place of his mortal remains, the brotherhood continued to live. It was only after 120 years that the tomb of the founder of the order was discovered in the house Sancti Spiritus, and in it the secrets of the Rosicrucians, which were now to be made public.

Andreae, who followed his *Fama* with a *Confessio*, maintained, therefore, that a secret brotherhood with reformative tendencies, whose 'seal, mark and character' was R.C., that is to say, 'Rose and Cross', actually existed. Soon after the publication of his first work it was declared that Andreae had been guilty of fabrication, that his brotherhood had never existed, and that he had really only attempted to write a satire on the alchemistic and theosophic enthusiasm of those strangely excited times that teemed with miracle-workers, spiritualists, astrologers, faith-healers, and sectarians. On the other hand, there were many people who believed in Andreae. His works brought forth numerous pamphlets from many other pens. There were books, chiefly on alchemy, whose authors described themselves, almost without exception, as 'members of the Antient Brotherhood of Rosicrucians', although those Rosicrucian societies with alchemistic tendencies which were referred to in a work entitled *Occulta Philosophia,* published in 1737, did not make their appearance until some considerable time after the publication of the *Fama.*

Andreae might well have imagined the development otherwise. He was a disciple of Paracelsus, and his works were intended to propagate pansophic ideas. Christian Rosenkreutz was not real, he was only a personification of the true pansophist, who would be able unerringly to lead the way out of the intellectual and spiritual chaos of the times. Andreae would have liked, as he wrote to Comenius, 'to have founded such an order as he had described; an order or an international society in which Christian freedom would embrace noble men in the tie of Love; free from all partisan spirit and quarrelsomeness'.[1] It is certainly that same idea which is to be found, in a still more comprehensive form, in the sphere of masonic ideas, although it is not possible to say whether it had already found its way into the Lodges of the seventeenth century.

That a change may have been in progress may be assumed from the statements of an Austrian enthusiast of Rosicrucian ideals named Permeier, who was also connected with England in the 'thirties of the seventeenth century, contained in a letter addressed to a friend in Danzig (first reported by Peuckert), in which the work for peace, which Permeier desired to initiate, was clothed in words that are strongly reminiscent of the masonic vocabulary.

The Catholics and Lutherans, he wrote, 'wish to bring the new Solomonic Books of Peace into the open, and I have enquired in England whether or not the third, the Calvinist Party, is not also thinking of it; since people have, for a long time, according to the century-old Augsburg custom, wanted to bring out and apply, towards the summer solstice, or St. John's Day, the set-square and measuring tape to the preliminary plan or sketch of the first foundation stones and timbers of the great existing Edifice of Peace. . . . It is necessary, therefore, for all workmen, whether declared as such by themselves or whether qualified, to be registered and entered beforehand in the new Jerusalemic Architectural Book with name and office. . . .'

In this letter one can, as already stated, see a valuable indication; but it would be well in this case, as also in everything else concerning the early history of Freemasonry, to set to work very cautiously. One day, perhaps, we shall learn

[1] Heinrich Boos: *Geschichte der Freimaurerei.*

ANTON PILGRAM, ARCHITECT OF VIENNA CATHEDRAL
From the Sculpture in the Stephanskirche, Vienna

A ROSICRUCIAN PHILOSOPHER

more of the masonic workings of the Rosicrucian, Ashmole, and also find confirmation of the conclusion arrived at by the Hamburg scholar, Sonnenkalb, who believed that a Freemason named Flood—who presented the London 'Masons' Hall' with an improved Book of Constitutions at the beginning of the seventeenth century—was no other than the most celebrated of all English Rosicrucians, the London physician and alchemist Robert Fludd (1574–1637), who, in his turn, was a friend of the German Rosicrucian, Michael Maier of Nuremberg, Physician-in-Ordinary to Rudolf II.

It is quite certain that Ashmole and his friends sought a centre for their common work. They were all intellectuals, physicists, mathematicians, doctors. But a mixture of scientific and fanciful conceptions common to all of them urged their actions strongly towards spiritualistic spheres in which they encountered all kinds of alchemists, astrologers, magicians, and occultists, in whose ideas they then became completely absorbed. 'The general reformation of the whole world' was to be brought about by the changing and ennobling of the human character. The dream of these Rosicrucians was an ideal community which guaranteed the maximum human happiness, as indicated by the ancient poets and again brought to life by the Humanists of the Renaissance. Homer's 'Elysian Fields', Hesiod and Pindar's 'Isles of the Blessed', Plato's 'Critias' beckoned like magic distant lights through the suffocating cloud that weighed down upon Life. They visualized with enthusiasm a Kingdom of Virtue, Justice, and Atonement even on this earth, and a union of Antiquity with Christianity, under the beautiful symbol which Goethe also set up in the fragment *Die Geheimnisse*, from his *Religiösen Humanitätsepos*:

Es steht das Kreuz mit Rosen dicht umschlungen
Wer hat dem Kreuze Rosen zugestellt?
Es schwillt der Kranz, um recht von allen Seiten
Das schroffe Holz mit Weichheit zu begleiten.

Und leichte Silberhimmelswolken schweben,
Mit Kreuz und Rosen sich emporzuschwingen,
Und aus der Mitte quillt ein heilig Leben
Dreifacher Strahlen, die aus einem Punkte dringen,
Von keinen Worten ist das Bild umgeben,
Die dem Geheimnis Sinn und Klarheit bringen.

In 1646, Ashmole, together with William Lilly, the astrologer, Thomas Warton, the physician, William Ougthred, the mathematician, and Doctors John Harwitt and John Pearson, and others, founded Solomon's House, which was to be the sanctuary of their ardent search for the deepest mysteries of Nature and the secret of human happiness. The utopian *New Atlantis* of Francis Bacon, Lord Verulam, supplied the outward characterization for their secret society, which, however, did not follow his theory that science promotes happiness, but pursued the mystical chime of bells which Robert Fludd, under the pseudonym 'Robertus de Fluctibus', caused to ring in a Rosicrucian Tractatus Apologeticus as early as the year 1616.

'Solomon's House' was set up in Masons' Hall, Masons' Alley, Basinghall Street, that is to say, the Rosicrucians became the tenants of the Lodge. That occurred, therefore, in the same year as that in which Ashmole was 'accepted' as a Mason. The learned society took up quarters with the Handicraft Society under whose sure protection it could work undisturbed. Unfortunately, there are no positive indications as to whether this was the point at which the gradual fusion took place. August Horneffer [1] assumes that the professional secrets (Astrology, Alchemy, Magic, and Medicine), which for the learned societies became the bearers of deeper secrets, were attracted to the Handicraft societies because similar truths were there found in other ways, which were then cultivated and propagated by mystical means. 'Their common enemies were the pure dogmatists and analysts, on the one side, and the egoistic materialists (utilitarians) on the other. The Rosicrucian work symbolized the unconscious development in Nature, the vegetative striving of everything existing towards greater perfection, whilst the masonic activities have for their object the systematic working of mankind, a conscious, moral, and social creative activity, also with perfection as its aim. The one therefore supplemented the other.' Consequently there was so much symbolically in common. Hence the change from the 'House' to the 'Temple' of Solomon.

There is one thing, however, which is undoubtedly correct. Many of the masonic symbols point indisputably to a Rosicrucian pansophic origin. On the other hand, the recently published Ritual of the subsequent 'Gold and Rosy Cross' by Dr. Bernhard Beyer-Bayreuth [2] seems to suggest that in many respects the Masons were the donors.

[1] *Symbolik der Mysterienbünde*, 2nd ed., 1924.
[2] In the first volume of the series: *Das Freimaurermuseum*.

CHAPTER V

THE FOUNDERS

THE Grand Lodge of 1717 was certainly not the beginning; it was a re-beginning on a new foundation. Of those people who were prominent in the early days only a few names, such as those of the Rev. Dr. James Anderson, Anthony Sayer, the Rev. Dr. John Theophilus Desaguliers, George Payne, and John, Duke of Montagu, are familiar in Freemasonry to-day.

Of these, James Anderson is the best known. The Book of Constitutions of 1723, which he elaborated on the instructions of the Grand Lodge, is generally known as the Anderson Constitution, although it may not have been the result of his work alone, and even the 'Antient Charges', as now in use almost everywhere, are coupled with his name. He was born in Aberdeen in Scotland in 1680 and became a minister in London after studying at Marischal College. He was the zealous pastor of a French Presbyterian congregation in Swallow Street. As a Dissenter he was a member of the Whig Party, where he was held in high respect. Like all others of his political views he was very loyal to the House of Hanover.

His leisure hours were devoted to genealogy, and he showed great talent, not merely as a dilettante, for his studies are recorded in numerous works.

Whether he had already participated at the inauguration of Grand Lodge in 1717 or was only chosen in after years to play such an important part in its construction is not certain. It is presumed that he was initiated in the year 1710, and, according to a newspaper notice, he was appointed Chaplain to the Masons. It is possible, however, that he had become a member of a Scottish Lodge before he came to London. In any case, he was commissioned in the autumn of 1721—during the fifth Grand Mastership—to adapt the old constitutions to the times and to the new aims, and to impregnate them clearly with the spirit of Tolerance, which should be authoritative for the future work. He carried out his task with extraordinary quickness. As early as the occasion of the Winter Festival of St. John he was able to lay his work before a

Committee, which, on the 25th March, 1722, after making a few alterations, recommended it to be printed and published. The hurry of the work, in conjunction with the desire to show that a new society was not being founded, but that it was the continuation of a time-honoured evolution, may have contributed to the fact that the 'History', the first part of the Constitutions, turned out to be unscientific and confined itself solely to repeating ancient legends. But the form which Anderson gave to the 'Antient Charges' and his liberal conception of the idea of Humanity, which even now constitutes the basis of the Fraternity, stamped the 'Antient Charges' as 'new charges' of imperishable value. In 1711, Sir Richard Steele, who later became a Freemason, had suggested in the 'Moral Weeklies' that a society of decent men drawn from all parties should be formed in order to further internal peace. Here was the fundamental statute for such a society.

Anthony Sayer was the first Grand Master. He was elected by majority at the historic meeting in the Goose and Gridiron Tavern. Of this man very little is known to-day. In Anderson's records he is merely described as:

'Mr. Anthony Sayer, Gentleman.'

Not one word more does he say, for Anderson was ever sparing of details concerning himself and his friends. Nothing further as to Sayer's origin has ever been gleaned from other quarters. Just 'Gentleman'—that is all. Rather in the same way as the 'accepted masons' were known in Scotland as 'Gentlemen Masons'. There was, therefore, no kind of halo about the brow of the first Grand Master, who conducted the affairs of the Lodge in the early years, together with Jacob Lamball, a carpenter, and Captain Joseph Elliot. His name still lives on, but no book records what kind of man he was. It may possibly have been that Sayer was merely called to the chair of the Grand Lodge as a makeshift, for they had in mind, right from the beginning, more illustrious figures for this office.[1]

A clearer description is given of Sayer's successor, George Payne, elected Grand Master in 1718, who played a definite part in London society and belonged by birth to the nobility. He was a Government official—a Secretary to the Tax Office— and was also well known as an antiquary. He was an energetic and active man, exceedingly well-connected in all circles.

---

[1] Sayer died a poor man in 1742. Many Masons attended his funeral. He was interred in the cemetery of Covent Garden Church.

ANTHONY SAYER, FIRST GRAND MASTER, 1717
Engraving by John Faber, after the Painting by Joseph Highmore

DR. JOHN THEOPHILUS DESAGULIERS, F.R.S., GRAND MASTER, 1719
Engraved by P. Pelham, after Painting by H. Hysing

Next to Desaguliers he was, in many respects, the *spiritus rector* of the new Freemasonry. He showed his great interest also as Master of the Rummer and Grapes Lodge. He demonstrated this enthusiasm on the formation of Grand Lodge, chiefly by framing the constitutions. With the aid of an old gild manuscript, he formulated thirty-nine General Regulations governing the activities of Grand Lodge, and he supplied Anderson with much valuable material.

The Rev. Dr. John Theophilus Desaguliers, the Grand Master of 1719, regarded the spiritualization of Freemasonry as his task in life. He was the strongest personality in the 'Revival', and the one who gave Grand Lodge its spiritual countenance, and who, probably as a result of animated discussions with his intimate friends Martin Folkes, Vice-President of the Royal Society, Dr. William Stukeley, the first neophyte of the Lodge in 'Salutation Tavern', and Anderson, gradually introduced much of the programme of the 'Royal Society', which aimed at instructing its learned members to pursue a philosophy of humanity.

This man was of French origin and came to England as a small child in 1685. His father, a Protestant minister, emigrated after the revocation of the Edict of Nantes when nearly half a million French Protestants left their native land. He preached in the same chapel in London as that in which Anderson later held his services. The young Desaguliers studied philosophy and natural science. In 1713, when hardly thirty years of age, he was lecturing in London on physics. The great Newton was his friend, and his admission into the Royal Society without payment of the prescribed fee speaks for his standing in scientific circles. Desaguliers graduated also in theology, and became a Doctor of Laws as well. His learned works are abundant, especially in connexion with physics. He was one of those who prepared the way for the theory of electricity, and the sciences of the Gilds are indebted to him for his research work.

Desaguliers was initiated in the Apple Tree Lodge, but the date is unknown. He did not take part in the inaugural assembly in 1717, otherwise he would have gone to the top at once. The composition of the Book of Constitutions has more than once been attributed to him, although quite wrongly, as only the preamble came from his pen. There is no doubt that he assisted Anderson in his work, and, according to the account of the latter, Desaguliers revived the 'old, regular and peculiar toasts or healths of Free Masons', which even to-day play an important part in Masonry and are still current as an integral part of the work in all English Lodges. The idea of Brotherhood and the Mason's obligation to toil permeated his whole soul. He remained in a prominent position in the Grand Lodge for twenty years, and he acted as Deputy Grand Master for the three Grand Masters who followed him. In 1731, when Francis Stephen, Duke of Lorraine, afterwards Emperor Francis I, applied for initiation, Desaguliers headed a deputation to The Hague in order to carry out the initiation in an impressive manner. And in 1737, when the first member of the English Royal Family—Frederick, Prince of Wales— joined the Fraternity, it was Desaguliers who initiated him.

The first exalted aristocrat to undertake the leadership of Grand Lodge, the Duke of Montagu, was also introduced to Freemasonry by Desaguliers. Under the Duke's Grand Mastership the Grand Lodge began the great advance. The Duke was one of the wealthiest peers in England, and had come into contact with Desaguliers in the Royal Society. It was he who commissioned Anderson to arrange the 'old Gothic Constitutions' in a 'new and better' version. At the wish of the Lodge he appointed those fourteen brethren who examined Anderson's work and ordered it to be printed after it had been approved. The title-page of the first edition of the Constitutions, showing the Duke handing over the Book of Constitutions to his successor, is a picture which has become celebrated.

His successor, like all Grand Masters in the time to come, was an exalted member of the nobility, Philip, Duke of Wharton.

THE SIGN OF THE GOOSE AND GRIDIRON TAVERN, LONDON

CHAPTER VI

THE DEVELOPMENT IN ENGLAND

IN the Book of Constitutions of 1723 Anderson made very few references to the events which took place in 1717 and the succeeding years. The only allusion occurs at the end of the historical portion, and is as follows:

'And now the Freeborn British Nations, disintangled from foreign and civil Wars, and enjoying the good Fruits of Peace and Liberty, having of late much indulg'd their happy Genius for Masonry of every sort, and reviv'd the drooping Lodges of London, this fair Metropolis flourisheth, as well as other Parts, with several worthy particular Lodges, that have a quarterly Communication and an annual grand Assembly, wherein the Forms and Usages of the most ancient and worshipful Fraternity are wisely propagated, and the Royal Art duly cultivated, and the Cement of the Brotherhood preserv'd; so that the whole Body resembles a well built Arch.'

In the year 1738, when Anderson wrote his second Book of Constitutions, which differed from the first in many respects, he attempted to make good what he had omitted. But also on this occasion he reports very sparingly on the decisive events which occurred at the time of the Constitution and thence until 1722.

According to his narrative the Constitution came about in the following manner!

The members of the Lodge had assembled on two occasions, first of all under the chairmanship of the oldest Master Mason in the Apple Tree Tavern. On this occasion the Grand Lodge was constituted *pro tempore*, and it was decided to elect a Grand Master at the annual festival, that is to say, on St. John the Baptist's Day.[1] At this second assembly—held in the Goose and Gridiron Alehouse—Sayer was elected by a show of hands.

When George Payne became Grand Master a year later,

[1] Hence the Lodges working according to the English system are called 'St. John's Lodges'.

he drew attention to the necessity of instituting a search for the missing historical records from the time of the Gilds and requested the brethren 'to bring to the Grand Lodge any old Writings and Records concerning Masons and Masonry in order to shew the Usages of antient Times: And this Year several old Copies of the Gothic Constitutions were produced and collated'—preparatory work for Anderson, who, in 1721, was commissioned to digest a 'new and better method' from these Constitutions.

On the 17th January 1723 the Grand Warden, J. Timson, was able to present the new Book of Constitutions duly printed.

The Constitutions consisted, as we have already indicated, of 'the History, Charges, and General Regulations' of Payne, in addition to which there were several songs.

The 'Charges' were entitled:

'The Charges of a Freemason, extracted from the ancient records of Lodges beyond the Sea and of those of England, Scotland, and Ireland, for the use of the Lodges in London to be read at the making of New Brethren or when the Master shall order it.'

They dealt with:
 I. God and Religion.
 II. Civil Magistrate, Supreme and Subordinate.
 III. Lodges.
 IV. Masters, Wardens, Fellows and Apprentices.
 V. Management of the Craft in Working.
 VI. Behaviour:
   1. In the Lodge while constituted.
   2. Behaviour after the Lodge is over, and the Brethren not gone.
   3. Behaviour when Brethren meet without strangers, but not in a Lodge formed.
   4. Behaviour in presence of strangers, not Masons.
   5. Behaviour at Home and in your neighbourhood.
   6. Behaviour towards a strange Brother.

Speculative Masonry is, therefore, still interspersed with regulations for operative Masonry, for the latter had not yet completely severed itself. But those who read the 'Antient Charges' in their new form looked beneath the surface; they smiled at, or argued about, the 'History', but they recognized the spirit of the masonic Magna Charta; the will to avoid

THE 'GOOSE AND GRIDIRON' TAVERN IN ST. PAUL'S CHURCHYARD
MASONRY WAS REVIVED HERE IN 1717, AND THE FIRST GRAND LODGE OF
ENGLAND—AND OF THE WORLD—WAS FOUNDED

ANDREW MONTGOMERY, GARDER OF THE GRAND LODGE, 1738

Engraving by A. V. Haecken, after the Painting by Æ. V. Meuten

anything tending towards disunion; the yearning for 'the friendly alliance with the antagonists'; the rejection of dogma, the possibility of a synthesis of work and contemplation. This may not have been so immediately upon the publication of the Book of Constitutions, but it was not long before the seed germinated and the masonic idea demonstrated its power of attraction. All those who were 'men of ardent longing', as Comenius once called them, were attracted by the new masonic art, whose materials were 'neither wood nor stone, nor metal nor mortar, but Life and Soul'. It almost seemed, as August Horneffer [1] expresses it, that an invisible power drove the best men of the various nations, and of the various schools of thought, into the fold of this mysterious Gild and that a much stronger power held them in it and forged them into a true community of identical convictions in spite of the diversity of their points of view. Within the next ten years Lodges were formed everywhere—in Spain, India, France, and Bohemia.

In England the increase of the Lodges and the flood of applications for membership from the intellectual classes began very early. 'Masons are made here' was to be read in many a tavern. In 1725 there were already fifty-two Lodges, including some, of course, which had existed previously and had once again commenced working. By 1732 no less than 109 Lodges belonged to Grand Lodge. In the majority of them many good names were to be found. In 1725 the membership of the Rummer and Grapes Lodge, in addition to Payne, Desaguliers, and Anderson, included Lord Paisley, the Dissenter, Sir Richard Manningham, physicist and member of the Royal Society, Lord Waldegrave, the diplomat, and Count Albrecht Wolfgang von Lippe-Bückeburg, who later drew the attention of King Frederick the Great to Masonry. The younger Lord Stanhope, the celebrated statesman and author, Dr. Beal, the physician, and Martin Folkes, the numismatist, belonged to other Lodges.

Under the Grand Mastership of the Duke of Wharton, Freemasonry began to come before the eye of the public. The Masons walked in procession clothed in 'masonic apparel', with leathern apron and symbolic badges, to Stationers' Hall, where it was customary to hold assemblies. Ceremonious processions were organized for the welcome of the Grand Master, in which the Sword of State of the Grand Lodge and the Book of

[1] August Horneffer: *Der Bund der Freimaurer*, Jena, 1913, Diederichs.

Constitutions were later carried, and it became the custom for the laying of the foundation stones of churches and other public buildings to be carried out by Freemasons in a very solemn manner.

There was, of course, no dearth of attacks. To the Tories and the Jacobites, the followers of the Stuarts, who, banished to France, were thinking of nothing but their return, following a revolution, the 'secret societies', most of whose members belonged to the Whigs, were objects of suspicion. Attempts were made as early as 1723 to introduce politics into the Lodges during the Grand Mastership of the vacillating Duke of Wharton, whose election had not proved a happy one, and endeavours were made to draw individual Lodges into the Jacobite camp, but such attempts met with little success. There was hostility also from other quarters. Sensational 'exposures' informing the curious of all kinds of things about the Ritual found their way to the bookshops. The first was a kind of catechism, 'The Mason's Examination' (published in 1723 in the *Flying Post*). Samuel Prichard's pamphlet *Masonry Dissected* attained special notoriety and had a ready sale. Humorous antagonists of Freemasonry took pleasure in jeering at masonic processions and in organising mock processions of their own. These 'Mock Masons' or *Scald Miserables* rode on donkeys through the town escorting a hearse, in which a tattered ragamuffin paraded bearing a Grand Master's badge, followed by a bawling troop carrying columns and waving masonic symbols.

In 1738 a revolutionary movement arose in Catholic countries against the 'deistical and indifferent Freemasons', as the result of which an anti-masonic Bull [1] was issued by Pope Clement XII. But all that was unable to check the progress of Freemasonry.[2] No more success fell to the lot of a vociferous Jacobite counter-organization, the 'Most Ancient Order of Gormogons', which, appearing in Chinese robes, aimed at lowering the masonic Ritual in the eyes of the public, at making masonic brethren disloyal to the Grand Lodge, and at furthering the cause of the Stuarts, whose supporters at that time sang in the alleys the defiant song:

> We'll have no Prince Hanover
> Let James, our King, come over.

[1] See the chapter entitled: 'Papal Bulls'.
[2] In 1722, even the leader of the English Catholics, Lord Petrie, became a Mason and was a very zealous Grand Master.

GEORGE, PRINCE OF WALES
GRAND PATRON
Drawn and Engraved by Edmund Scott

Under the immediate recommendation of HIS MOST GRACIOUS MAJESTY WILLIAM IV, the POWERFUL GRAND PATRON.

This Print of H.R.H. Prince Augustus Frederick Duke of Sussex K.G.R.T.K.G.H. &c. &c. &c. M.W. Grand Master, of the United Free & Accepted MASONS of ENGLAND.

Is most respectfully Inscribed to (The Grand Lodge of England.) By their most Oled. Humble & Devoted Serv.t

Brother JOHN HARRIS, P.M.

PRINCE AUGUSTUS FREDERICK, DUKE OF SUSSEX
AS M.W. GRAND MASTER
Painted and Engraved by John Harris

A masonic rejoinder to all this malice maintained that the Fraternity remained true to its principles:

'Although a Lodge is no theological school, the brethren are, nevertheless, instructed in the great principles of its ancient Religion, its Morality, its Humanity and its Friendship, namely, to avoid all persecution, and to be peaceful citizens of the realm wheresoever they may be resident.'

Many others felt in the same way as the unknown author of the foregoing lines, and they were not to be diverted from their purpose because the work in the Lodge did not always come up to their expectations. Even the Lodges were not impregnable places of worship. The not altogether ideal life of the day was not always left behind at the entrance to the Temple. The people who constituted the Fraternity did not by any means imagine that they were in the higher walks of Humanity; they came as the raw material, not as the finished article, and discords were therefore unavoidable. There were some who quickly disappeared, and there were others who retained their enthusiasm.

Not all the Lodges existing in 1717 joined the new Grand Lodge. Many old operative masons could not reconcile themselves to the Constitutions which so expressly stipulated the 'Religion in which all men agree'; that seemed to them a much too revolutionary innovation, an invasion of the traditional edifice, which they had suddenly recalled to mind. Others stood aside because the leading men in the Grand Lodge seemed to be too closely associated with the régime in power. There were also many who had no liking for the fact that Freemasonry was now entirely on a symbolical basis, and who clung to operative masonry and caused the ancient manuscripts to be reprinted. Others finally went their own way for purely technical reasons: 'The Regulations,' they said, 'contained prescriptions which infringed warranted rights.'

The Lodge of York, which had served as the 'centre of union' for the highly placed personages of the county since 1705, likewise held aloof. This Lodge, supported by Anderson's legends, boasted of its tradition as the oldest Lodge, attributing its origin to before the year 1000. It proclaimed itself an independent 'Grand Lodge of all England' in 1725, without, however, founding any daughter Lodges during the first forty years of its existence. It drew up its own Statute Book, known as the 'Old Rules of the Grand Lodge of York'. This

Grand Lodge of York, which existed until about 1790, also maintained the fundamental principle of the Freemasons of London, namely, 'Brotherly Love, Relief and Truth'. This was expressed in a speech—the earliest masonic address recorded—which was made in 1726 by the Grand Junior Warden, Francis Drake, in which he declared that they had no wish to dispute the rank of the London Grand Master, but that the title 'Totius Angliae' belonged to the Grand Master of York. He also said that Masons should 'so behave themselves that the distinctive trait in the character of the whole Fraternity shall be that they are known as good Christians, loyal Citizens, true Friends and Freemasons'.

Although no difficulties arose for the London Grand Lodge because of the existence of its sister Lodge in York, great difficulties resulted from another foundation. In 1751, a second exceedingly ambitious Grand Lodge appeared in London. Very many false accounts have been circulated as to the reasons which led to this. However, it came about in this way. Certain Irish Freemasons, chiefly humble people, such as painters, tailors and artisans of all kinds, who had worked in London with strict observance of certain peculiarities of their native Lodges, combined with some of the opposition Lodges. In Laurence Dermott, born in Ireland in 1720, they found an enthusiastic and inspiring leader. He was initiated in a Dublin Lodge in 1740, and in 1746 became Worshipful Master ; two years later he joined a Lodge in London, but met with many things of which he did not approve, such as certain alterations in the Ritual, which had been found necessary on account of the 'exposures' then in circulation, and the much too prominent aristocratic element. Dermott was no 'revolutionary' who furthered discord in order to attain his own ignoble ends; he was a man possessed of the urge to masonic activity; a man who believed himself to have a mission. Many regarded him as the most remarkable English Freemason of the eighteenth century. With the greatest enthusiasm he set about the erection of the second House of Freemasonry. Together with brethren from seven Lodges he laid the foundation of the 'Grand Lodge of England according to the Old Institutions' on the 17th July 1751 in the Turk's Head Tavern.

'Universal Masonry !' and 'No innovation' were his slogans, although the new Grand Lodge itself fostered not inconsiderable innovations, for, in addition to the degrees of Entered Apprentice, Fellow-Craft, and Master, it included a fourth—the 'Royal

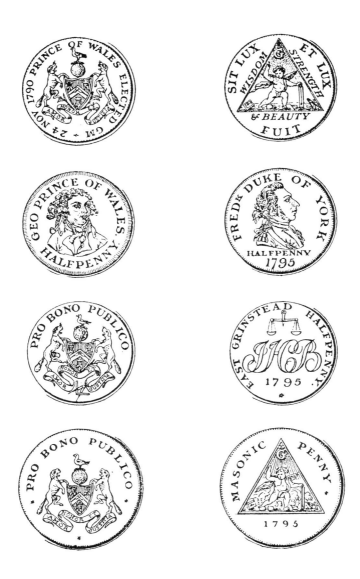

ENGLISH FREEMASONS' PENNIES AND HALFPENNIES OF THE
EIGHTEENTH CENTURY

Arch', which was intended as the completion of the Third Degree and ostensibly gave answers to the questions which the legends of the Master's degree left open.

Dermott, who became Grand Secretary of the Grand Lodge, possessed an impetuous temperament which urged him constantly forward. His honest purpose, and above all, his great literary talent, which found expression in the new Constitution *Ahiman Rezon, or A Help to a Brother*, written by him and published in 1756, had a very fruitful effect upon the development of his foundation, the *leimtotiv* of which he thus expressed in the dedication of the book to the Earl of Blessington:

> 'At the request of several Worthy Free-Masons, I undertook to publish the following Sheets, wherein I have endeavoured to let the young Brethren know how they ought to conduct their Actions, with Uprightness, Integrity, Morality, and Brotherly Love, still keeping the ancient Land-Marks in View.
>
> 'On the Perusal, Your Lordship will find that the Whole is designed not only for the Good of the Fraternity, but also to shew the mistaken Part of the World, that the true Principles of Free-Masonry are to love Mercy, do Justice, and walk humbly before God.'

In 1752 the Grand Lodge had twelve, in 1756 forty-five, and in 1766 eighty-eight affiliated Lodges; at the beginning of the nineteenth century—at the conclusion of peace—there were recorded on its registers 359 Lodges, of which, however, many were no longer active. Not a few Regimental Lodges were to be found in the list. In 1755 both London Grand Lodges had followed the example set them by Ireland in 1732: they founded military Lodges. In the course of time no less than 116 Charters were granted under Dermott's auspices for such Lodges 'travelling' with regiments.[1]

Dermott very cleverly traced his new creation back to the alleged principles of the alleged first Constitution of the Anglo-Saxon Prince Edwin of 926, and derived therefrom the right to describe himself and his friends as the 'Antients' and the others as the 'Moderns'. Many peers and members of the Royal Family soon joined him. The special interest which

---

[1] On the other hand, the elder Grand Lodge approved temporarily three 'Sea Lodges': in 1760 on board the warship *Vanguard*, and later, on board H.M.S. *Prince* and H.M.S. *Canceaux* (Gilbert W. Daynes: *The Birth and Growth of the Grand Lodge of England, 1717–1926*. London, 1926).

the Duke of Atholl, as Grand Master, showed for the cause of the 'Antients', caused many of these to describe it as the 'Atholl Grand Lodge'.

For sixty years the two Grand Lodges developed side by side, not, however, without the desire for union growing stronger, especially when they encountered one another in matters of

A LIST,
of the present
GRAND OFFICERS.

The Right Hon.ble
Lord Petre, G.M.

The Most Noble,
and Right Honourable,
Robert Edward Petre,
Lord Petre,
Baron of Writtle,
in the County of Essex,
Grand Master.

Rowland Holt Esq.r .... D.G.M.
Thomas Parker Esq.r .... S.G.W.
John Hull Esq.r .... J.G.W.
Rowland Berkeley Esq.r .... G.T.
James Heseltine Esq.r .... G.S.
The Rev.d D.r William Dodd .... G.C.
Francis Johnston .... G.S.B.

A.D.1775   A.L.5775.

FIRST PAGE OF FREEMASONS' CALENDAR, 1775

charity, where they both rendered beneficial service. Finally, even Dermott described it as his aim in life to bring about the alliance of the 'Antients' with the 'Moderns', but he did not live to see it. The union, for which Lord Moira of the Moderns had so emphatically declared himself, took place in 1813. The Peace was sealed in the 'Articles of Union Between the two Grand Lodges of Freemasons in England' in an extra-ordinarily solemn manner, and the 'United Grand Lodge', with nearly 640 Lodges, was formed at a magnificent assembly on the 27th December. This 'Grand Assembly' is described, with every reason, as one of the greatest events in English Freemasonry. In solemn procession both Grand Lodges made their entry into the Grand Temple of Freemason's Hall—one dignitary of the 'Moderns' always being accompanied by the

FIRST PAGE OF ENGRAVED LIST OF MASONIC LODGES, 1768

corresponding dignitary of the 'Antients', and at the rear, arm in arm, came the two Grand Masters of the Royal House, the Duke of Sussex for the Antients [1] and his younger brother, the Duke of Kent, for the Moderns. With the strains of the mighty organ resounding through the Temple the 'eternal

[1] August Frederick, Duke of Sussex, son of George III, became a Freemason in Berlin in 1798, and, in April 1813, Grand Master of the 'Antients', as successor to his brother, the Prince Regent, later King George IV.

union' was proclaimed by the two Grand Chaplains, the Rev. Dr. Barry and the Rev. Dr. Coghlan, and was approved by the enormous assembly with a mighty cry of 'So mote it be'. After the furniture had been duly consecrated with corn, wine, and oil, according to immemorial tradition, and after the formula of the obligation for the 'United Grand Lodge' had been approved under the Presidency of Count de Lagardie of the Grand Lodge of Sweden, this was then taken with deep emotion by the entire company, which had joined hands to form a chain. The Duke of Kent thereupon declared his Grand Mastership ended and proposed the Duke of Sussex as the first Grand Master of the United Lodge. The latter was then unanimously elected.

A 'Special Lodge of Promulgation', later 'Lodge of Reconciliation', which had been formed in 1809, comprising nine Past Masters or Worshipful Masters from each group, and which had created the basis for the reconciliation, remained in activity for some years after the Union in order to further the harmonic adjustment of all questions.

That was over a hundred years ago. Since then English Freemasonry has continued to prosper. After the final principles had been laid down in 1813 they were left unaltered. The idea of tolerance was strongly adhered to, as can be seen from the following words of the first Grand Master of the 'United Grand Lodge', the Duke of Sussex, in a Charter for a Lodge in Frankfort chiefly comprised of Jewish brethren:

'Whilst we bow down in all devotion before the Great Architect of the Universe and obey the prescriptions of the Law, we exclude nobody from our Order on account of his Religion or on account of the way in which he worships God, whatsoever be the nature of that worship.'

The Grand Lodge was also far from ready to allow these principles to be watered down by affiliated Grand Lodges. That was clearly demonstrated in the case of the only exciting incident which has occurred in the history of English Freemasonry since the reconciliation between the 'Antients' and the 'Moderns', that is to say, in the case of the breach with the Grand Orient of France. The possibility that the belief in the Great Architect of the Universe might be departed from and that atheists might also be accepted in French Lodges, caused the English to sever themselves from their French brethren. Not, however, because they supposed that the Grand Orient desired to espouse the cause of atheism or

THE NEW LODGE
OF FREE AND ACCEPTED
MASONS,
AT HADLEIGH, SUFFOLK.

Ticket
FOR THE DINNER,
AT THE
SHOULDER OF MUTTON INN, HADLEIGH,
On TUESDAY, the 22d Day of Nov. 1814,
TO CELEBRATE THE CONSTITUTION AND CONSE-
CRATION OF THE ABOVE LODGE.

Wm. Scott, Secretary.

TICKETS 12s. EACH.

☞ The Ceremonies will commence at the Assembly Room,
at 10 in the Forenoon.—Dinner at 3 o'clock.——None will be
admitted to the Ceremonies but upon the production of this
Ticket, nor on any account after the Business is commenced.

(Dorkin, Printer, Ipswich.

LODGE DINNER TICKET, 1814

materialism, but because they regarded the rejection of the 'Great Architect of the Universe' as the removal of the very 'foundation stone' of the whole masonic edifice, as a departure from the 'Traditions and Usages of Ancient and Modern Freemasonry'.[1]

The Grand Lodges of Scotland [2] and Ireland [3] also associated themselves with this letter. The former was founded in 1736 and the latter in 1724, and from the beginning both developed independently of, but concurrently with, the Grand Lodge of England, and have, in the course of time, followed much the same direction; a direction, the aim of which Robert Burns, the Poet Laureate of British Masonry and an inspired writer on Humanity, recorded when he sang:

> Then let us pray, that come it may—
> As come it will for a' that—
>
> .   .   .   .   .
>
> That man to man, the world o'er
> Shall brothers be, for a' that.

[1] As expressed in a letter of the Grand Master, the Prince of Wales, afterwards King Edward VII.

[2] The Grand Lodge of Scotland arose nineteen years after the London Foundation, although Dr. Desaguliers had visited the venerable Edinburgh Lodge as far back as 1721. It was only on the 29th September 1735, that the Canongate Kilwinning Lodge appointed a Commission to study the Grand Lodge question, and after many preliminary discussions the foundation was effected in Edinburgh on the 30th November 1736, St. Andrew's Day, by delegates from thirty-four Scottish Lodges, William St. Clair of Roslin becoming the first Grand Master. According to two ancient documents, the 'St. Clair Charters', originating approximately in 1601 and 1628 respectively, the Lords of Roslin had, since time immemorial, been Patrons and Judges of the Masons in Scotland; but before the election of the Grand Master, William St. Clair renounced this right for himself and all his heirs, but received, nevertheless, every vote.

[3] In Ireland, where, according to Chetwode Crawley (*Caementaria Hibernica*), Freemasonry had gained a firm footing about the year 1688, and had a 'speculative' Lodge at work as early as 1710, Lord Rosse was appointed Grand Master in 1725 by the Masters and Wardens of the six 'Lodges of Gentlemen Masons' assembled in Dublin. This Grand Lodge was reorganized in 1731 by Lord Kingston, who had been Grand Master of England two years previously.

CHAPTER VII

FRENCH MASONRY

WE have already said that, shortly after the appearance of the Anderson Constitution, Freemasonry began to spread to all parts of the world. The first country in which it found a firm footing was France, although the ground on which the seed here fell was of a totally different nature. As early as 1725 a Lodge existed in Paris in the premises of the Restaurateur Hurc, who kept an inn, 'Au Louis d'Argent', in the rue des Boucheries. Nothing further is known about it. A second Lodge was opened on the 17th May 1729, also in the rue des Boucheries, but this time at a different inn. The first Lodge was supposed to have been founded by the Englishmen Lord Derwentwater and 'Lord Harnouester',[1] but the second Lodge had a Frenchman at its head, André François Lebreton, a great benefactor to the poor. In the same year an English lapidary named Goustaud founded the 'Sante-Margeurite' Lodge. In 1732 the 'Loge de Bussy' was founded, and this was the first Lodge under English Constitution and was entered in the London Register as 'No. 90 King's Head at Paris'. The Duc d'Aumont was the first French aristocrat of high rank to belong to it. In 1733 'No. 127 Valencienne in French Flanders'[2] was entered in the London Register, and two years later the Duke of Richmond, and Desaguliers, the latter specially commissioned, formed a further Lodge, which likewise had its home in the rue de Bussy. It was a question here of a very distinguished set of people who had met shortly beforehand in the Château d'Aubigny as guests of the Duchess of Portsmouth. This Lodge was mainly conducted by English peers, amongst whom was the Ambassador Waldegrave, whose son, Lord Chewton, was initiated on this occasion. Prominent amongst the Frenchmen who participated in the forming of

---

[1] Charles Radcliffe, younger brother of the Earl of Derwentwater, who was executed in 1716 for participation in Jacobite affairs, had also been condemned to death, but had fled to France, where he became a zealous follower of James III. He took part in the insurrection of the Pretender Charles Edward, was captured on board one of the rebel ships, and later beheaded in the Tower. Nothing further was ever discovered of Lord Harnouester; he is supposed to be none other than Derwentwater.

[2] 'La Parfaite Union' in Valenciennes.

the Lodge was, according to a report of the London *St. James'
Evening Post* of the 20th September 1735, a man whose
writings were later to revolutionize the intellectuals, the Rt.
Hon. President Montesquieu, who is supposed to have sponsored one of the French candidates, Count Saint-Florentin,
Secretary of State of 'His Most Catholic Majesty'. That is
practically all that is known. If one would obtain a picture of
the initial period, one is dependent chiefly upon a few statements recorded in a 'Mémoire' by the great French astronomer
and zealous Freemason, Lalande, which are to a large extent
reproduced in the article entitled 'Freemasons' in the third
supplementary volume of the great Encyclopædia. The distinguished Paris student of the History of Civilization, Albert
Lantoine, recently undertook, and not without success, the
task of supplementing the scanty material previously available.

At the time when the masonic idea was brought to France
by the English brethren above mentioned, the child Louis XV
was on the throne, following the autocratic régime of Louis
XIV and the subsequent Regency. The elements essential
to the advancement of a society with humanitarian ideals
seemed conspicuous by their absence. There prevailed now,
as before, the most extreme absolutism and the wildest immorality. After the revocation of the Edict of Nantes the
Church was more powerful than ever. The country, crushed
under the burden of a tremendous debt, had been reduced
to a state of poverty. At a time when in England scientific
theories were exercising the minds of the pioneers of progress,
French society manifested its intellect chiefly in the *salons*
by means of sparkling speeches, subtle wit, and clever repartee.
Assemblies were prohibited, and when people desired to hold
meetings these could only take place if strictly confined to
harmless pleasure and under official supervision. There still
existed the constraint of Louis XIV's principle: *Un roi, une
foi, une loi*. In spite of their dire distress the people still
continued to be exploited in the most shocking manner by
debauchers and gluttons, whose thirst for pleasure knew no
bounds. The immorality of the Court, with its insane squander-
ing of money, demanded more and more revenue. The people
heard with the most incredulous astonishment of the liberties
gained by the English. Until this time the desire for a change
in this grossly unfair system had only dared show itself covertly.
If a timid voice drew attention to the fact that the conditions
were untenable, the Royal disfavour was the direct result.

Thus was it with Bishop Fénelon, who had declared: 'Our people lead no human existence, the overflowing measure of affliction is so great that their patience will run out'; and also with Marshal Vaughan.

In these circumstances it was no wonder that it was chiefly the nobility which met in the Lodges. There were, however, a few artists and ordinary citizens. The working was, at the beginning, of a very primitive nature. The men who assembled at the premises of an innkeeper or wine merchant first of all arranged the Lodge in a back room by grouping wax and tallow candles, placing the Bible on a rough table, and arranging a number of arm-chairs around the rectangle, which had been drawn with chalk on the floor, as customary in England. A few white marks in the middle of the rectangle represented the symbolic figures.

The first Grand Lodge was quickly formed. 'Lord Harnouester' has been described as the first Grand Master, but doubts have arisen as to this, because, as already stated, nothing positive has ever become known about this man. The formation of this Grand Lodge did not remain hidden, and a Royal Decree was issued excluding from the Court those members of the nobility who dared to become Freemasons. The King declared also, probably at the suggestion of his Prime Minister, Cardinal Fleury, that any Frenchman venturing to take up the Grand Mastership would be arrested without further warning. On the 14th September 1737 the Lieutenant-General of the Police, René Hérault, proclaimed an 'Interdict' against holding assemblies or forming associations of 'Freys-Maçons'. Restaurateurs, publicans, and owners of inns especially were ordered to permit no assemblies of Freemasons under penalty of a heavy fine and the closure of the premises for the first offence.

But the Freemasons still continued to assemble. The police —excited beyond all measure over the 'English poison'—did their level best to track them down. Chapelot, a wine merchant in the rue de la Rapée, in whose premises a Lodge was discovered, was condemned to pay a fine of 1,000 livres and to have his premises closed for a period of six months. The Court was so suspicious that it expressly directed Chapelot to have the entrance of the premises walled up. The Bull of Clement XII did the rest.[1] Hérault caused a translation of

---

[1] This first condemnation of Freemasonry by the Pope was, in France, not accepted for publication by Parliament, but it influenced the ruling powers to a considerable extent.

an English 'exposure'—*Masonry Dissected*—to be printed and published. The dancer Carton had been able to obtain this document, by trickery, from a Freemason living in Paris, and handed it over to the police authorities. Hérault found a companion-in-arms in the Archbishop of Marseilles, who arranged for a dancing scene to be performed as an interlude in a comic ballet at the Jesuit College in Caen, which poked fun at masonic customs. The Freemason became a very popular figure as a buffoon at the Marionette Theatre in Paris. Thus the same methods were adopted against the Freemasons as in England.

It may be, of course, that the people of whom the Lodges were composed at the beginning of French Freemasonry were not made of suitable material for the standard-bearers of a great idea, and were by no means fully conscious of the magnitude of the Cause which they chose to serve. A significant speech made in 1737 by Andrew Michael Ramsay, the Grand Lodge Chancellor, bears witness to this. Ramsay was a Scottish nobleman, who had been an officer with the English troops in the Netherlands during the Spanish War of Succession, and had then gone to Cambrai full of admiration for Archbishop Fénelon, who had been expelled from the Court at Paris, and was living there. Under the influence of this dignitary of the Church Ramsay became a Catholic. After Fénelon's death he went to Paris, and for a time, was tutor to King James III's son. This activity with the Pretender resulted in Ramsay being banished from his native land. Nevertheless, he was held in such high respect on account of his scientific work and morality that he received from the King a safe conduct to Oxford, in order that he might take the degree of Doctor of Laws. During this stay in his native land he was elected to the Royal Society in London. He was ardently devoted to Freemasonry and was particularly bent on ridding the Society of all those people who sought to use the Lodges for their own selfish and commercial ends. A play by Clément of Geneva of the year 1740, entitled 'Les Frimaçons', in which a penurious poet says the following words: 'I am unemployed; I am looking for a job with the Freemasons', clearly demonstrates that the belief that it was easy to make money with the help of the brethren of the Lodge was widely circulated even at that time.

Ramsay's 'Oration' gave him the opportunity of making important suggestions for the information of French Freemasonry in the true masonic sense. He described 'prudent benevolence' and 'pure morals' as the necessary attributes for admission into the moral Order, and declared as the object of the society 'the revival and propagation of these maxims borrowed from the nature of man.' . . . 'Our ancestors, the Crusaders, gathered together from all parts of Christendom in the Holy Land, desired thus to reunite into one sole Fraternity the individuals of all nations.' They combined with the 'Knights of St. John of Jerusalem', who then, in the West, called themselves Freemasons.

'What obligations do we not owe to these superior men who, without gross selfish interests, without even listening to the inborn tendency to dominate, imagined such an institution, the sole aim of which is to unite minds and hearts in order to make them better, and form in the course of ages a spiritual empire where, without derogating from the various duties which different States exact, a new people shall be created which, composed of many nations, shall in some sort cement them all into one by the tie of virtue and science.'

It will be noticed that Ramsay has made an historical error in his 'Oration' by attributing the origin of Freemasonry to the Knights of St. John and by deriving therefrom the name 'St. John's Lodge'. This caused the unjust reproach to be made against him later that he is to blame for those times of masonic confusion which shortly afterwards set in, and during which numerous Orders of Knighthood arose in many places out of the simple brotherhood. It was also said that Ramsay wished to subject Freemasonry to the Catholics, and that he was inspired with a desire to mix the masonic Ritual with the customs of the Catholic cult, not only for religious, but also for political reasons, as, for instance, in order to create for his erstwhile pupil, Charles Edward Stuart, a phalanx for his endeavours to regain the throne of England; that is to say, a 'Jacobite' Freemasonry, in contradistinction to the 'heretical' English Masonry which supported the House of Hanover. Even to-day the shade of the unfortunate Pretender glides like a phantom through many a book as the 'Secret Grand Master of High Masonry', and as the founder of a Stuartist Masonic Chapter in Arras.

The correctness of these stories has never been proved, however, and the researchers assume to-day, with good foundation, that it was not Ramsay's wish to create anything new, but that, on the contrary, he advocated simplicity.

Ramsay's discourse—which was later attributed to his Grand Master, the Duke of Antin, who took over the leadership of the Grand Lodge in 1738 in spite of all the hostility—contained other much more important statements, but to a large extent this has been overlooked.

For instance:

'Mankind is not essentially distinguished by the tongues spoken, the clothes worn, the lands occupied, or the dignities with which it is invested. The world is nothing but a huge republic, of which every nation is a family, and every individual a child.[1] We desire to reunite all men of enlightened minds, gentle manners, and agreeable wit, not only by a love for the fine arts, but much more by the grand principles of virtue, science, and religion, where the interests of the Fraternity shall become those of the whole human race, whence all nations shall be enabled to draw useful knowledge, and where the subjects of all kingdoms shall learn to cherish one another without renouncing their own country. The Order of Freemasonry was founded to make men lovable men, good citizens, good subjects, inviolable in their promises. . . .

'We have amongst us three kinds of brothers: Novices or Apprentices, Fellows or Professed Brothers, Masters or Perfected Brothers. To the first are explained the moral virtues; to the second the heroic virtues; to the last the Christian virtues; so that our institution embraces the whole philosophy of sentiment and the complete theology of the heart. . . . The Order exacts of each of us to contribute to a vast work for which no academy can suffice, because all these societies being composed of a very small number of men, their work cannot embrace an object so extended. The Grand Masters of other countries exhort all the learned men and all the artisans of the Fraternity to unite to furnish the materials for a Universal Dictionary of the liberal arts and useful sciences, excepting only theology and politics. The work has already been commenced in London,[2] and by

---

[1] In this point of view Ramsay follows his great teacher Fénelon, who, in his *Télémaque*, expresses something very similar.

[2] This refers to the *Cyclopædia* of Ephraim Chambers which appeared in the year 1728.

means of the union of our brothers it may be carried to a conclusion in a few years. Not only are technical words and their etymology explained, but the history of each art and science, its principles and operations, are described. By this means the light of all nations will be united in one single work, which will be a universal library of all that is beautiful, great, luminous, solid, and useful in all the sciences and in all noble arts. This work will augment in each century, according to the increase of knowledge, and it will spread everywhere emulation and the taste for things of beauty and utility.'

This oration was not without success. It was eagerly discussed in the Lodges and many Freemasons pleaded in lectures and in learned societies for the idea which was here born, viz., to create also in France an Encyclopædia which would be so designed as to fill the world with a new spirit. The *bataille de l'Encyclopédie* began; the fight for one of the greatest works of all times. Diderot was the leader in this battle. In 1741, i.e., four years after the 'Oration', he began the work, the first volume of which appeared in 1752. In the end there were no less than thirty-three folio volumes, although the English prototype had only consisted of two.

But other ideas in the great oration deserve attention. Fifty years before the French Revolution it expressed—with a purely spiritual meaning—the idea of a universal democratic Republic and the compatibility of cosmopolitan thought with patriotic sentiment—the idea which Fichte clothed in the following words: 'Cosmopolitan my thought, patriotic my deed.'

That the speech was at that time so understood can be seen from a very rare contemporary booklet, *La Franc-Maçonne*,[1] which states as follows:

'One can very easily guess the secret of the Freemasons when one examines what they do. They initiate without discrimination both high and low and all are placed upon the same level. . . . It is therefore very probable that it is a symbolic Freemasonry, the secret of which consists in attempting to create a universal and democratic Republic, whose Queen will be Intellect and whose Supreme Council will be the assembly of the Wise.'

---

[1] *La Franc-Maçonne ou révélation des Mystères des francs-maçons par Madame . . .* (Bruxelles 1744), quoted in *Louis Amiable et J. C. Colfavru, La Franc-Maçonnerie en France depuis 1725.* New Edition 1927.

We wonder whether the clever woman who wrote that also knew the neat verse which was subsequently sung in the Lodges:

> Nous ne faisons dans l'univers
> Qu'une même famille
> Qu'on aille en cent climats divers
> Partout elle fourmille
> Aucun païs n'est étranger
> Pour la maçonnerie
> Un frère n'a qu'a voïager
> Le monde est sa patrie.

A violent antagonist of Freemasonry, the author of a writing which appeared in 1747, entitled *Les Francs-Maçons écrasés*,[1] in which the assertion was made, for the first time, that Freemasonry had been invented by Cromwell for political purposes, also commented upon the speech, and mentioned Fraternity as one of its principles side by side with 'Equality and Liberty'. That, perhaps, was the first occasion on which mention had been made—and that by an antagonist of the Royal Art— of the great principles which were soon actually to be those of French Masonry, viz.:

'Liberty, Equality, Fraternity.'

At the time of the death of the Duke of Antin, there were more than two-hundred Lodges in France, of which twenty-two were in Paris. On the 11th December 1743 a new Grand Master was elected. This was Louis de Bourbon, Comte de Clermont,[2] under whose leadership French Freemasonry did not progress quite in the way which many of its most honest supporters would have liked. The new Grand Master served for a long period in Flanders as field-marshal and could devote very little attention to the happenings in the Lodges. In the meantime the less aristocratic element had increased in number. The use of swords, which was introduced into the Ritual, served as the symbolization of Equality, as these puny adepts of a

---

[1] The Abbé Perau is generally regarded as the author; however, the book is said to have been written by the Abbé Larudan.

[2] The Comte de Clermont was really a cleric. He could only exercise his profession of a soldier by virtue of a dispensation granted by the Pope. In the beginning he was very zealous. In a report of the Lieutenant of Police, Feydeau de Marville (discovered in the Carnavelet Library by Albert Lantoine), which was addressed to the Minister of the Royal Household, de Maurepas, it is stated of the Comte: 'He is drafting a new Constitution for the Order of Freemasons. . . . He desires to be rid of all those who do not belong to the nobility or who are not good citizens.' Very shortly afterwards, however, he relinquished to others the leadership of the Grand Lodge.

great Mystery understood it. The practice of describing the initiates as 'Gentilhommes', based on the English word 'Gentleman', also served a similar purpose. But a large section of the Freemasons of noble blood were not prepossessed with this equality. An unhealthy desire to count for more in the Lodges, just as they did in private life, made itself manifest. There began that epoch, already mentioned, which has been described as the time of masonic confusion—that period in which the 'Gentilhommes' became all kinds of 'Chevaliers' or 'Knights', simply by setting up above the three original degrees all kinds of still higher degrees and creating an abundance of new masonic systems by making the Orders of Knighthood of the Middle Ages the forefathers of the Freemasons and drastically remodelling the simple masonic symbolism.

We will not go into detail here about these 'Knights of the East', 'Emperors of the East and West', the 'Academy of True Masons', that pretended to teach the hermetic science, nor the 'Elect Coëns', or whatever they all were called; that is to say, we will not deal with that curious mixture of cabalistic and occultistic activities and the fascinating game of playing at knights. That would only lead to by-ways which have nothing to do with the real meaning of Freemasonry but have caused the most grievous ruptures.

It would be doing a great injustice to the French Freemasonry of the eighteenth century were one to judge it on the basis of these manifestations, which were, to a certain extent, the result of enthusiasm and the urge towards things mystical, or to judge it on the resultant schisms. It must, on the contrary, be recognized that although there were always two different camps, which were parted for superficial reasons, very fruitful work was nevertheless performed in the long run.

The 'Grande Loge Anglaise de France' set up a new Constitution in 1756 and became the 'Grande Loge de France.' Any differences of opinion obtaining were glossed over, but only to break out again. At the instigation of the King, the activities of the Grand Lodge were temporarily suspended in 1767. Four years later the Grand Master, the Comte de Clermont, died.

Under the leadership of the men who then took over the reins the revival began, but not through the merits of the new Grand Master, whom Clermont had appointed before his death. This was the Duke Louis Philippe of Chartres, later Duke of Orleans. It is true that he accepted the office which fell into his lap so early, but he troubled himself about the Jewel entrusted to his care little more than his predecessor had done. He appeared now and again at an important function, and that was all. Far greater zeal was displayed by his deputy, the Duke of Luxembourg, who had been appointed Administrator-General of the Order. He was an aristocrat who, by virtue of his birth, could have attained the very highest office in the State, but who preferred to devote himself to the Royal Art. As colonel of the Hainaut Regiment of Infantry he had already founded a Lodge which brought a wonderful spirit into the regiment. Placed in effect at the head of French Freemasonry he devoted his energies to reforming and uniting. The 'Grand Loge Nationale' proclaimed in 1773 was the result of his endeavours. There arose out of this, on the 22nd October of the same year, the Grand Orient de France, for, in spite of all, some were unwilling to collaborate.

A new spirit came into the Lodges. As the previous conflicts and incompatibilities had chiefly arisen out of the fact that once a Worshipful Master had been elected it was impossible to depose him, it was decided to introduce more democratic principles. An excellent Constitution for the Grand Lodge was created, the principles of which were to be found again later, in a very large degree, in the positive work of the Revolution. There was expressed, for example, in a circular letter of the Grand Lodge of 1775 an idea which, sixteen years later, in the *Déclaration des Droits de l'homme et du citoyen* found expression in the sentence:

'The Law is the expression of the Will of the people.'

That the principle on which they worked in the Grand Orient really was democratic can be seen from a 'Mémoire' in which mention is made, with pride, of the 'citizens of the masonic democracy'.

Liberty and Equality as the main pillars of French Masonic work, as the 'precious dowry' of the Freemason, as the 'fundament of the Order' were more and more emphasized. Let us quote Voltaire:

'Les mortels sont égaux, ce n'est pas la naissance
C'est la seule vertu qui fait la différence.'

and also:

'Qu'il ne soit qu'un parti parmi nous
Celui du bien public et du salut de tous.'

That 'Liberty' and 'Equality' were not merely figures of speech is demonstrated by the composition of the Lodges, and by the constant stream of great men of intellect soliciting admission. The encyclopædists and other great people were there. Montesquieu, who had been initiated in England, Diderot and Helvetius, whose work *De l'Esprit* was burned by the executioner in 1761 in a public square, had already been there. Then came Lalande, the great astronomer, member of the Academies of Paris, London, St. Petersburg, Stockholm, Rome, and Florence ; Condorcet, the celebrated mathematician, and Lacépède, the musician and naturalist and, after the Revolution, President of the Senate and Grand Chancellor of the Legion of Honour. They belonged to the 'Les Neuf Sœurs' Lodge, which soon became the meeting-place of the most learned. Lalande was its first Worshipful Master. He was followed by Benjamin Franklin, the veteran of American Freemasonry, who was at that time Ambassador in Paris for the thirteen United States of North America. In this model working-place of the masonic idea the Comte de la Rochefoucauld, who translated the American Constitution into the French language, was to be met, as also were Comte Milly of the Academy of Sciences; the noted advocate Elie de Beaumont, who stood by Voltaire in his fight for justice; Dupaty, whom the latter described as his 'young Socrates from Bordeaux' and who was a great benefactor of Humanity; de Sèze, the most brilliant speaker of the French Bar and defender of Louis XVI before the National Convention; the President of the Provincial Chamber, Dr. Guillotin; the Marquis la Fayette; and Paul Jones, the naval hero of the American War of Independence. Pastoret, the author of the *History of the Legislation of the Ancient Peoples*, creator of the Pantheon and the last French Chancellor, described by Franklin as the greatest scholar of his time; the encyclopædist d'Alembert; the artists Claude-Joseph Vernet and Greuze; the great sculptor Houdon and the poets André Chenier and Roucher worked together in harmony. There were also the Abbé Sieyès, the advocate of the proletariat and the 'Thinker of the Revolution', Camille Desmoulins, Danton, the journalist Brissot, the celebrated chemist Fourcroy, one of the most energetic organizers of public education, and many others.[1] After this 'Philosophers' Lodge', the best known was the 'Loge des grands

[1] Louis Amiable: *Une Loge Maconnique d'avant 1789. La R. Loge 'Les Neuf Sœurs'*. Paris 1897.

seigneurs', with its proper designation of the 'Loge de la rue du Coq-Heron'.

But also in other French Lodges important men, such as Mirabeau, Beauharnais, Beaumarchais, Joseph de Maistre, Baron Holbach, the 'Maître d'Hotel de la philosophie', Robespierre, Massena, Beurnonville, Abbé de Chaligny, Talleyrand and Turpin were performing masonic work. Like the 'Neuf Sœurs' ('Nine Muses'), the Lodges 'Les Amis réunis', 'Loge des 22', 'Les Chevaliers bienfaisants', 'Candeur', and 'Rue de la Sourdière' were the meeting-places of the intellectual élite. The highest thought of the time, e.g., Montesquieu's *Esprit des Lois*, Rousseau's gospel of the 'State of Nature', and the critical theories of Voltaire, was familiar to all these brethren. Freemasonry thus became the centre of enlightenment and culture of the eighteenth century, and it imparted them to the chief members of the *bourgeoisie* throughout the land, to some members of the nobility, and also to many clerics who, in spite of the interdict of Rome, saw nothing in masonic endeavour that was contrary to Christian dogma. To many of these Freemasons in priestly robes[1]—there were noticeably more monks than ordinary clergy—the masonic doctrine of Equality and Liberty seemed indeed to be very closely related to true Christianity.

Even Voltaire, who had meanwhile returned to Paris from his retreat by Lake Geneva, was initiated into the Fraternity. On the 17th February 1778 he was initiated in the Lodge 'Les Neuf Sœurs' (Nine Muses). He was in his eighty-fourth year, and there was an attendance of 250 brethren. Abbé Cordier de St. Firmin, the historian, who with thirteen other priests belonged to the Lodge, proposed the philosopher as candidate. Lalande, Count Straganoff, Chamberlain to the Empress of Russia, and other brethren prepared him for the initiation in an ante-room, in the prescribed manner. After Voltaire, supported by Benjamin Franklin, had entered the Temple, he answered a number of philosophical and moral questions and took the obligation. He was thereupon handed the apron of the late Bro. Helvetius. Voltaire raised it to

---

[1] The Lodge 'Charité sur Loire' was founded exclusively by Benedictines. In the 'Parfaite Union' in Rennes twelve members of the clergy were initiated in 1785 alone. This Lodge supported the works of the Church to no inconsiderable extent. The Lodge in Condon preserves in its archives a letter from a new brother thanking the brethren for supplying him with the priestly robes he required for his first Mass and for taking part *in corpore* in this divine service.

his lips, ran his delicate fingers over the leather, and then tied it on.

Lalande, the Worshipful Master, then gave the solemn address. He glorified the Brotherhood, 'which excludes no Religion or Nation', and praised England as the 'Guardian of Liberty'.

'The English, who are, as it were, the born rivals and enemies of our nation, are nevertheless, as Masons, our friends and brothers and we find amongst them a degree of sympathy which no other consideration would have been able to bring about. In the thick of battle they were often seen to recognize their brothers and more than once to stay the hand of war and extend instead the helping hand of a brother and saviour.

'What society could be strong enough to bind together so closely men who seem to be divided by nature, climate, language, interest, form of Government, morals, politics, and war? Only the Love of Virtue could bring about this union; a love which has bound all noble souls together at all times and amongst all peoples, and has united them with a universal and indissoluble bond. It is just this Love of Virtue which constitutes the basis of our Fraternity. The square which measures and regulates all our actions, the apron which indicates for us an industrious life and useful works, the white gloves which are sponsors for the purity of our motives, for the truth of our words and the honesty of our actions, the trowel by means of which we try to conceal from ourselves the faults of our brothers; all these symbols teach us charity and philanthropy, two attributes which we have long appreciated in Voltaire.' So spoke Lalande, whilst at the Court fanatical zealots decried him as the 'scourge of the century'.

Meanwhile Freemasonry also made itself felt in public life at about this time. Freemasons of consequence attempted to put a stop to the most glaring cases of injustice. The advocate Elie de Beaumont had set the example. Twice did he plead before the judges when Voltaire raised the cry for Justice; the first time in the case of the Protestant Jean Calas who was executed in Toulouse on the false charge of having murdered one of his sons, in order to prevent him going over to the Church of Rome. Robbed of her fortune, Calas's widow fled to Geneva and begged Voltaire to help her. The latter, aided by his friend Elie de Beaumont, intervened, and the honour of the man who had been put to death was vindicated and his property returned to his heirs.

ALLEGED VISIT OF NAPOLEON TO A PARIS LODGE
Engraving by Campagnon, after the Drawing by Seigneurgens

J. M. RAGON

A DISTINGUISHED FRENCH MASON

From the Drawing by Adolphe Ragon

Similar was the case of the Sirven family. Voltaire also raised his voice in this case, and, once again, Elie de Beaumont brought the matter before the courts.

But even greater fame was won by his Lodge brother Dupaty, who risked his all to bring about a reform of the cruel criminal law. He worked on the lines of the Italian Beccaria, who had referred, in a book entitled *Crime and Punishment*, to the barbarous state of the administration of justice. It is true that under the influence of Voltaire's writings some regulations had been moderated, but torture was still the chief feature of the court trials; labour at the galleys had not yet been abolished and even a paltry theft committed by a servant was still pitilessly punished by death. In the year 1785, when three peasants from the neighbourhood of Chaumont were first of all condemned to lifelong servitude at the galleys and afterwards sentenced to death on account of an alleged theft, Dupaty intervened, supported by another Freemason, Legrand de Laleu. In a petition to the king, 250 pages in length, they both clearly demonstrated the monstrosity of the procedure and demanded that a law be drafted which would make such excesses impossible in the future.

Dupaty, supported by his Lodge, brought this document to the eye of the public by selling it for the benefit of the three unfortunates. Proceedings against the two friends were then instituted at the instigation of the Attorney-General, Séguier. Legrand de Laleu's name was struck off the Roll of the legal profession on the ground that he had committed a breach of the regulations of the profession, and the memorandum was burnt by the executioner.

The 'Nine Muses' Lodges now declared itself openly on the side of its members. It caused their portraits to be engraved and distributed to the public. Condorcet, highly respected as Secretary of the Academy of Sciences and member of the Académie française, came to their assistance with several pamphlets.

Dupaty and Legrand were not to be intimidated by their first failure. Within a short time they published six further pamphlets, and, in the end, success was theirs. The triple death-sentence was quashed and the case referred back to the Court of First Instance. Dupaty, although not a barrister, received special permission to plead the case for the wrongly convicted persons before this court. His pleadings, pregnant with the purest masonic spirit, were a flaming indictment of the criminal law of the time and resulted in the acquittal of the peasants. But Dupaty and the Freemasons fighting with him did not content themselves with this success, which was enthusiastically celebrated in the Lodge; they contributed to the triumph of justice in four further trials.

Dupaty went still further. He published his *Letters concerning Criminal Procedure in France*, which summarized all the ideas that had previously been expressed in the pamphlets. A Royal Decree of the 1st May 1788, which held out a prospect of a reform of the Criminal Law, was published shortly after, and some improvements came into force immediately. Dupaty died in the same year, but his work was carried on by the Freemason, Pastoret.

It was somewhat earlier, in the year 1773, when Louis XV was still upon the throne, that a speech which was particularly characteristic of the views prevailing in the ranks of the Fraternity was made at the Winter Festival of St. John of the Grand Orient by Herion de Pensey, afterwards President of the Supreme Court of Appeal, concerning the part played by Freemasonry in the life of the people.

'The true Freemason,' said the speaker, 'is the guardian of morals. Only he who has morals is worthy to rule his equals. . . . Morals and the Law are the pillars upon which the welfare of humanity rests. The possession of morals can make the law superfluous, but where immorality prevails the wisest regulations are worthless.'

Just consider. These words were spoken at a time when immorality at the Court and in many of the highest circles had reached its peak. Thus it can be clearly seen that the obstacles which still impeded the masonic work, i.e., the jumble of high degrees, the occultistic and alchemistic disorder of the many fantastic 'systems' which pretended to be connected with Freemasonry, could not withstand the true spirit of speculative Masonry.

At that time there were 629 Lodges in France, of which 65 were in Paris.[1] Not all of them were of the same quality, but many of them emulated one another in upholding the principles of Justice and Truth, in preaching Equality of Rights, Liberty, and Fraternity in a higher sense and in demanding the removal of unjust privileges, and the emancipation of mankind.

But that does not mean that the French Revolution, which

[1] There were sixty-nine others with Army regiments.

was on the way, was the result of a masonic plot. All investigations which have been instituted with the object of discovering whether a plot to raise the passions of the population to fever heat had been hatched in the Lodges, have all had completely negative results. The work performed by the French Freemasons was of an intellectual nature. They planned merely to assist the adoption of new and more beautiful principles. There was no question of the Lodges wanting to overthrow the régime. The brethren believed that they could reform by constitutional means; they were therefore Royalists and certainly not Republicans. Here is just one more example of their loyalty: in 1782 the Lodge 'La Candeur' sent a circular letter to all its sister-Lodges recommending that a Frigate be equipped from the common funds and presented to the King, so that the latter could place the ship at the disposal of the Americans who were fighting for Freedom.[1] Nothing is more foolish than to think that they would ever have dared to think of killing the King.

One needs only to hear the opinion of so important a Catholic as Joseph de Maistre, who declared, in his *Mémoire à Vignet des Etoles* in 1793, that there probably were Freemasons who had revolutionary tendencies and even isolated Lodges which were composed chiefly of revolutionaries, but that Freemasonry in itself was quite guiltless of the bloody work. On the contrary the revolutionary propaganda had exercised a destructive influence upon Freemasonry. This statement was later completely confirmed by the celebrated Mounier,[2] President of the Constituent Assembly of the 6th October 1789, a non-Mason, in the following words: 'When the rulers ruin the finances, make the Army dissatisfied, bring all sections of the administration into disorder, and then call together a great gathering of representatives of the people and ask for their support, a revolution is inevitable, even if there were not a single Freemason in the world.'

And even that most critical historical expert on the conditions between May 1789 and the 18th Brumaire, Philippe Sagnac,[3] Professor of History of the Revolution at the Sorbonne, answers the question as to whether the masonic teachings of the times had been a doctrine of anarchy:

---

[1] Recorded by Gaston Martin.

[2] Mounier: *De l'influence attribuée aux philosophes, aux francs-maçons et aux illuminés sur la Révolution française.* 1801.

[3] Foreword to *La Franc-Maçonnerie française et la préparation de la Révolution.* 2nd ed., by Gaston Martin. Paris. 1926.

'On the contrary; what they wanted to destroy was anarchy, of which the monarchist government . . . produced so many examples; what they wanted to attain, however, was a régime based on Liberty and Equality of Rights. . . . The theory of a masonic conspiracy is without the slightest historical foundation; it is quite contrary to the facts.'

The very composition of the Lodges would have made it impossible to decide on unanimous action in this respect, for the leading positions in the Lodges were held, not only by the men who afterwards filled the benches of the States-General and of the National Constituent Assembly, and became actors in the drama of the Revolution, but also by priests, aristocrats, and many other people prominent in public life who by no means meditated the overthrow of the throne and the altar, some of whom emigrated and some of whom suffered execution during the years of the Revolution.

It is not widely known that even Louis XVI became a Freemason, together with his brothers, the Comte de Provence and the Comte d'Artois. On the 1st August 1775, a Lodge, 'La Militaire des Trois Frères-Unis' was specially formed for them *à l'Orient de la Cour* at Versailles.

Freemasonry did nothing to organize the Revolution. It could not do so because of its very composition, its membership, and its doctrine. It gave France the theory of human solidarity. Under the direction of Franklin and Lafayette it formulated the rights of citizens and men. 'The ideas of 1789' were fostered under its auspices, ideas which Kant, who was no Freemason and no revolutionary, had expressed; but what followed in 1791 had nothing to do with them, and was in absolute contradiction to all masonic ideals and was a horrible perversion of the intentions which had guided the men of the States-General at the beginning of the Revolution. Freemasons had both place and voice in this assembly in great number; approximately one-half of the deputies would seem to have belonged to the Grand Orient, which does not seem so strange when it is borne in mind that the thinkers, the reformers, and the most popular and esteemed citizens belonged to the Lodges. Probably many constructive reforms were to be found in their *cahiers*, but nothing about abominable, damnable, and all-destroying acts of violence. A parliamentary revolution, perhaps, but not a revolution in the streets.

There would seem to be no prevarication which has not been put into circulation to 'prove' the guilt of Freemasonry for the reign of terror, for the raging of anarchy, for the sea of blood and horror which drowned the deed of 1789 and sounded the death-knell of the ideas of Liberty, Equality, and Fraternity. For instance, it is alleged that a secret committee was constituted, which gave revolutionary instructions to the Grand Orient, and that the latter passed them on to the Worshipful Masters, who had to add to their acknowledgement of receipt the solemn vow that they would adhere strictly to the given order. 'Those who disobeyed were threatened with the dagger and with poison, the *aqua toffana*, which has dispatched traitors into the Beyond since the earliest times.' 'Everything in this Revolution, down to the most horrible deed, has been conceived, planned and decided' by this secret committee.

The unknown rulers of the exalted 'Adepts of the Last Secrets' degree were supposed to have formed this secret committee. They were said to have sent emissaries into all the Lodges, who whispered to the chosen ones the secret watchword: 'Death to the tyrants, *vive la Terreur!*' and commanded them to prepare for the time of the great conflict. It is alleged that the German Illuminati had a hand in it, and also the 'Martinists', the 'Philalethists', the 'Rosicrucians', the 'Knights of the Sun', and the 'Knights of Kadosh'; all those political sanctuaries of Freemasonry, 'with their horrible mysticism and their terrible tests of the courage of the candidates, who were chosen as fratricides and blood hounds'. And all these channels ran into the 'Les Amis Réunis' Lodge in Paris. Here were prepared the loyal political clubs. The Guards who had stormed the Bastille were initiated *en masse* as 'Confidential Masters', and here were fostered by Mirabeau the relations with the Illuminati and the other foreign sects of conspirators.[1]

The propagators of this theory of the Revolution argue that one needs only to read the Rituals to see that these emphasize the doctrine:

'Igne natura renovatur integra.'

Only a fool would believe the official interpretation that this refers to the refining, purifying power of flames. That

[1] In reality, Mirabeau expressed himself not only in his secret correspondence, but also in his description of his journey to Prussia, as being very antagonistically disposed towards the Illuminati.

cannot be symbolic; on the contrary, it means: We have no other God than the element of fire, and this fire, which shall purify the world, is none other than the French Revolution, the bloody rising, the appointed day of which was finally fixed as the 14th July 1789. . . .

That is more or less the line of thought of Barruel, who cried out to the world in 1797 that Freemasonry had been the hotbed of a premeditated conspiracy of the 'Sophists of Rebellion'. But Barruel failed to answer one question: If all these terrible happenings had been premeditated by the Freemasons, who was it then who decreed that so many hundreds of Freemasons would have to go to the guillotine?[1]

At least one person expressed with the utmost clarity that, as far as he could see, the masonic idea of Liberty was not very real. This was the Grand Master, Philippe of Orleans, at the time 'Philippe-Egalité', who gave this as his reason when severing his connexion with the Order and who afterwards issued a public declaration against Freemasonry in the *Journal de Paris*.

If the Grand Orient had really been what Barruel had maintained, then its portals would have stood wide open during the Revolution. However, they were closed in 1792.

The man who opened them again after the cataclysm was Roettiers de Monteleau, who came straight from the dungeons.

The task which he had set himself was by no means light. Freemasonry had suffered tremendously under the Revolution. Many of those who had once been the pride of the Lodges had lost their heads by the guillotine; many had fallen and many had been broken in body and soul in the dungeons of the Commune. When the Grand Orient was brought back to activity by Roettiers, at first only eighteen Lodges answered the call and it was only gradually that life returned to the Lodges. By degrees, the men who represented the old guard of Freemasons, François de Neufchateau, President of the Senate; Fontanes, President of the Legislative Body; Lacépède, Grand Chancellor of the Legion of Honour; Lalande and Pastoret returned. They were joined by the men surrounding Napoleon: his brothers Joseph, Lucien, Louis, and Jérome; his step-son Beauharnais, and his Chancellor, Cambacérès, whose *projet de code civil* became the basis of the Code Napoléon. Twenty-two marshals of France, amongst them Bernadotte, Kellermann, Ney, and Macdonald—as well as Massena and

[1] Of the leaders of the Grand Orient, Tassin was one example.

Beurnonville—were Freemasons. No wonder that the interest at the Court was very active, a circumstance which did not please all Freemasons. Not every one was enthusiastic about a 'Napoleonic' Freemasonry. In the main, however, they were all occupied with a new institution which had been founded in the early years of the century.

In 1803, Count de Grasse-Tilly, a captain of horse, had returned to France from St. Domingo and had brought with him a Patent of the Supreme Council of Charleston (U.S.A.), which had come into being in 1801. This Patent empowered him to introduce into the Old World the 'Antient and Accepted Scottish Rite', a high degree system of thirty-three degrees. Thus, once more, there arose side by side with the Grand Orient a second organization.[1]

On the day following the coronation of the Emperor endeavours were made at Court to restore unity. This object was attained, but only temporarily, for it was soon apparent that two different Rites would continue permanently to exist in France at the same time. Joseph Napoleon now became Grand Master of the Grand Orient, with Cambacérès as his deputy. At the same time Cambacérès became the head of the Scottish Suprême Conseil.

This deep interest taken in the fate of Freemasonry by the people surrounding the Emperor has often aroused speculation as to whether the Emperor himself belonged to the Fraternity.

[1] A fusion had come about in 1799 with the second Grand Lodge of the eighteenth century.

The system of the Antient and Accepted Scottish Rite, which, by the so-called Grand Constitutions of 1786, gave uniformity to a number of older high degree rites, has still a very strong following in Masonry. The 'Supreme Councils', which embraced the Lodges of the high degrees in thirty-six States, all traced their descent from the Supreme Council of Charleston, the seat of which is now Washington and which is at present ruled by Colonel John H. Cowles. These intellectual high degrees (or philosophical degrees) have nothing in common with the confusions of the eighteenth century. They foster the esoteric side of Masonry in a dramatic progress. What uplifts and moves men in the religions and philosophical systems is here made the object of contemplation. Men like the great American Freemason, General Albert Pike, philosopher, poet, archæologist, and a profound scholar of all beliefs and rites, did great creative and formative work, and, in the course of time, the Belgian Comte Goblet d'Alviella and the Dutchman P. G. H. Dop, gave the Rituals of the Antient and Accepted Scottish Rite new shape and new interpretations. All regular Supreme Councils belong to an unfettered association, namely, the Lausanne Confederation, founded in the year 1875, which holds a Congress every five years. After the 1922 meeting, in which Th. R. Marshall, then Vice-President of the United States, participated, the members were charged to work for International Peace and to fight against hatred. A letter addressed to the Congress by President Harding placed the greatest emphasis upon this item of the programme.

This question cannot be answered in the affirmative with absolute certainty, but there are very many signs which seem to prove that Napoleon became a Freemason in one of the Army Lodges. In an official report of the Grand Orient concerning a festival of the year 1805, a speech is reproduced in which it is said that Napoleon 'had sought the Light during his Egyptian campaign and received it in Egypt, the land to which the very beginnings of Freemasonry can be traced'. In 1807, the Milan Lodge—which bore the name of the Empress—toasted Napoleon as 'Brother, Emperor, and King'. There are also preserved in the Lodges of Troyes and Grenoble minutes which suggest that the Emperor was a member. And in the archives of the Grand Orient, Yves de Plessis recently discovered a description of a masonic meeting in Italy, held on the 13th April 1811, 'on the occasion of the birth of the Prince of Rome, first-born of Worshipful Brother Napoleon'. On the other hand, it has not yet been possible to find any register containing a record of the Emperor's membership.

After the fall of Napoleon, French Freemasonry experienced many changes. The 'Suprême Conseil' founded by Grasse-Tilly developed side by side with the Grand Orient. After the Restoration they both became the target of a violent clerical campaign. The Abbé Barruel took up the cudgels, and the ban of the Pope found obedient supporters, a circumstance which would naturally demand resistance and which has contributed in no small degree to the anti-clerical attitude of French Freemasonry, which is peculiar to it even to this day. That it is not correct to say (as it has often been maintained) that antagonism to Religion is the very mainspring of French Freemasonry can be clearly seen from the fact that in 1849, at the instigation of Blanchet, one of its members, the Grand Orient incorporated in its Constitution a regulation stipulating that any person applying for admission had to believe in a personal God and in the immortality of the soul. This was a dogmatic obligation which did not fail to produce a reaction later, and around which there afterwards raged a violent conflict lasting twenty years or more.

Upon its introduction it certainly confounded those attackers who had been preparing to deal the Grand Orient a mortal blow. After the overthrow of the Monarchy in 1848, the leaders of Freemasonry assembled in the Town Hall in order to present to the Provisional Government a vote of sympathy with the Revolution. They were solemnly received by Garnier-Pages and Cremieux, two members of the Government, both wearing masonic regalia. However, after the elections of 1849 the wind began to blow from another quarter, and when, on the 2nd December 1851, Napoleon III's *coup d'état* was successful, it was generally believed that the last hour of French Freemasonry had come. But Napoleon, having an idea that he could use Freemasonry to further his own ends, had other intentions. He forced Prince Murat, son of the one-time King of Naples, upon the Grand Orient as Grand Master. Democratic elements were up in arms at this compulsion, and at the new election in 1861, Prince Louis Napoleon was set up as a rival candidate, and he carried the day. The Emperor, having once made up his mind to bend Freemasonry to his own will, thereupon forbade both princes to take part in the activities of the Order and—acting contrary to every principle —he appointed Marshal Magnan as Grand Master by a decree of the 11th January 1862, although the latter was not a Freemason at all and had to be specially initiated.

Supported by the command of the Emperor, the Marshal called upon the second supreme authority, the 'Suprême Conseil', to place itself under his Grand Mastership, and demanded that it should constitute in future, together with the Grand Orient, a single National Grand Lodge. The poet Viennet, Director of the Academy, who was at the head of the Scottish Rite, offered strong resistance, and declared that the Emperor had no jurisdiction over the internal affairs of Freemasonry.

'What you demand of me is suicide,' he wrote to Magnan. '. . . I might perhaps sacrifice myself, but the Scottish Rite will certainly survive me.'

The answer to this letter was the suppression of the 'Suprême Conseil'. Viennet replied that he would not acknowledge this. And he was right in his courageous attitude. The work of both Lodges went on, and, finally, the most cordial relations prevailed, although there was no fusion. The leadership of Magnan turned out to be by no means unfavourable for the Grand Orient. His régime had been looked forward to with anxiety, for the 'great men of *coups d'état* are not usually over-burdened with scruples'.[1] But Magnan did not misuse his rights as Grand Master; on the contrary, he approved an alteration in the Constitution which materially restricted them.

[1] Louis Amiable in *La Franc-Maçonnerie en France depuis 1725*.

He was followed in office by General Mellinet, and there came again a period reminiscent of that time in the previous century when the Lodges had been the 'States-General of Philosophers'. With the utmost energy the Lodges devoted themselves to the study of philosophical, ethical, commercial, and social questions. The time had again come when the most liberal-minded men, such as Gambetta, Emanuel Arago, Henri Brisson, Jules Ferry, Floquet, Jules Simon, and Anton Dubost poured into the Lodges.

The democratic inclination which inspired them all found expression in the abolition of the Grand Mastership, with all its prerogatives, in the year 1871. In its place they set up a Council which appoints its President from year to year.

The fate of the religio-dogmatical obligation which had been incorporated in the Constitution in 1848 was decided at this time. In 1875 Bishop Dupanloup resigned his member-ship of the Academy as a protest against the election of the great Positivist, Littré, the creator of the *Dictionnaire*. The latter thereupon applied for admission to the Grand Orient as initiate. During his initiation, he was asked whether he believed in the existence of God, and he replied:

'A wise man of ancient times, who was asked the same ques-tion by a king, meditated day after day and never considered himself in a position to answer it. I beg of you not to insist on my answering it, either in the affirmative or the negative.

'No science denies a "prime cause", for nowhere is anything to be found which bears witness either for or against such a thing. All knowledge is relative; we are constantly running up against things and primal laws the cause of which we are unable to fathom.

'He who declares positively that he is neither a believer in God nor an atheist, only demonstrates his lack of comprehen-sion of the problem of the beginning and end of things.'

Two years later the Grand Orient abolished the formula, 'Great Architect of the Universe'. The Protestant Minister Desmons supported the motion proposing the cancellation of the formula by pleading the necessity of expressing, as clearly as possible, the principle of absolute liberty of conscience, and this was expressed in the following words:

'The basis of Freemasonry is absolute liberty of conscience and the solidarity of Humanity. It excludes no person on account of his beliefs.'

CHAPTER VIII

FREEMASONRY ON GERMAN SOIL

FREEMASONRY—in its new symbolic form—appeared in England at a time when the country, after long and heavy storms, finally arrived at the era of Consolidation. It had already spread over France at the time when the insecure foundations of the State began to tremble through the stirring of subterranean forces, which, at some time or other, were bound to appear on the surface with devastating and shattering effects. French Freemasonry was therefore somewhat different to English Freemasonry. The simple form of the English Lodges had undergone considerable changes. The new ideal manifested itself in England in a ponderous, somewhat patriarchial, atmosphere, but in France it appeared in a scintillating and ever-changing setting. Whereas in England the evening in the Lodge stood for personal meditation and sanctuary from the turmoil of the outside world, in addition to the practice of friendly ceremony, the French Lodges were strongly affected by the yearnings and dissatisfactions of everyday life. The wider front of the attacks, the romance of the Knights, the mysticism which was again enjoying a new vogue, the maelstrom of philosophical ideas, the grudges and the fermenting influences of politics, all cast their disturbing and variegated reflections into the masonic Temples.

Therefore, when Freemasonry made its entry into Germany it had already assimilated fragments from both these tendencies. Consequently, it could never be said that the development was of a uniform nature, especially as Freemasonry in Germany, more than anywhere else, was the subject of rumination, speculation, and investigation. First of all, this had adverse effects. Anything new was eagerly welcomed, however much it varied from the fundamental idea. But subsequently reaction set in, and whereas French Freemasons were only the exponents of their philosophers, the German thinkers developed their own masonic philosophy.

The starting-point of the German masonic movement was Hamburg, at a comparatively late period. On the 6th September 1737 the 'carpet' was drawn for the first time on the small floor of a tavern. A handful of men of good standing, by name, Karl Sarry, Baron Oberg, Peter Carpser, the celebrated physician, Dr. Peter Styven, and Daniel Krafft declared a perfect and properly constituted Lodge to be duly formed, to which they first of all gave the French name 'Société des acceptés maçons libres de la Ville de Hambourg'.[1] At first, the officials of the Free City were quite unable to form a clear conception of this new institution; they had heard all sorts of unfavourable things about the 'Indifferentists, Freethinkers, and Libertines' who called themselves Freemasons, and they regarded them as the enemies of public authority and of the Christian Church. The Senate therefore decided to put a stop to their activities by means of a prohibition. This, however, was a fruitless endeavour. About this time the enthusiasm of the few Freemasons of Hamburg was fired to an extraordinary degree, chiefly by a letter which caused no little excitement among them. In July 1739, the Worshipful Master, Oberg, was informed by Major-General Albedyll that the ruling Count Albrecht Wolfgang von Lippe—whom we have already met in England—had expressed to him a wish that a deputation might be sent to Brunswick in order to introduce an *illustre inconnu* into the Fraternity. The Hamburg Lodge expressed its willingness, and four of its members, headed by Oberg, set out on their journey. In Korn's Tavern in Brunswick, a celebrated inn in the Breitestrasse, they met Albedyll and two other Freemasons, Counts Lippe and Kielmannsegge, and with them the candidate—Crown Prince Frederick of Prussia.

The urgent request for this initiation had come about in this way: At dinner one day, during a journey on the Rhine, the candidate's father, King Frederick William, who was so orthodox in all things, adversely criticized Freemasonry. Count Lippe courageously took the opposite view and disclosed the fact that he himself was a Freemason. This made such an impression on the Prince that, after they had left the table, he expressed a desire to become a Freemason also. As the King was to know nothing about it, Brunswick, to which the Prussian Court was to pay a visit during the lively time of the Fair, was appointed as the meeting-place.

The initiation took place on the night of the 14th–15th August. When the Prince's suite had retired to rest he appeared in the room which had been prepared as a Lodge, together with Captain Graf von Wartensleben, who was

[1] Which later became the Absalom Lodge.

J. G. FICHTE

From the Engraving by Friedrich Bury, after A. Schultheis

FREDERICK THE GREAT PRESIDES AT A LODGE, 1740

From an Engraving

initiated after him. The meeting was carried out with strict observance of the English Ritual—the Crown Prince first being made an Entered Apprentice, then a Fellow Craft, and, finally, a Master Mason. This ceremony was followed by a banquet. The Lodge broke up at four o'clock in the morning, and the Crown Prince, who had been pleased beyond all measure by the beauty of the Ritual and the deep significance of the symbolism, then invited Oberg and the Secretary, Bielfeld, to Schloss Rheinsberg in order to found a Lodge there. They both accepted, and Oberg became the first Worshipful Master of the 'Crown Prince' Lodge. After his departure the Crown Prince presided over the frequent masonic meetings himself.

When Frederick came to the throne in 1740 he openly declared himself a Freemason.

Almost immediately after his accession, Frederick issued laws which breathed the very spirit of Tolerance in every regulation, abolished torture and restricted the censorship; but we will not discuss here whether and to what extent this was due to the influence of the Freemasons who, in the early years after the change of sovereigns, formed the King's personal entourage. It is, at any rate, quite certain that the King introduced Freemasonry in Berlin. The carpet was rolled up in Rheinsberg, but the candles were lighted in the Castle of Charlottenburg. Frederick there founded a Lodge which was sometimes called the 'Loge première', sometimes the 'Loge du Roi', or even the 'Court' Lodge. At the first meeting the King personally initiated his brother William. Many of his utterances illustrate his attitude towards the Fraternity. When the King heard that the Empress Maria Theresa was antagonistically inclined towards the Lodges, he said: 'The Empress is quite right, for as she cannot know what goes on in the Lodges she is by no means bound to tolerate them. However, I who do know, can not only tolerate them, but am in fairness bound to uphold them.' In 1741, he wrote the following to Bishop Sinzendorf:

'Humanity should be the first virtue of every man of honour. The voice of Nature, whence all humanity springs, demands that we should love one another and look after one another's welfare. That is my religion.'

The following utterances, which are very bold for the times in which they were spoken, are characteristic of the Freemason Frederick:

'All creeds must be tolerated, and it is for the King's Attorney to see that the one does not harm the other, as it is for each and all of us to find salvation in our own way.'

'False indignation is a tyrant, Toleration is a tender mother. . . .'

About this time a large number of Lodges sprang up in Germany. In Berlin, in addition to the King's Lodge, a second Lodge, called 'The Three Globes,' arose, which, in 1744, became the 'Grand Mother' Lodge, and in Dresden the 'The Three White Eagles' Lodge was founded by Graf Rutowski, a natural son of Augustus the Strong of Poland. The Margrave Friedrich, after his initiation by the King, founded the 'Sun' Lodge in Bayreuth, and there were soon Lodges also in Leipzig, Altenburg, Brunswick, Hanover, Meiningen, Frankfort-on-Main, Breslau, and Vienna.[1]

The Emperor Francis I, husband of Maria Theresa, also belonged to the 'Three Canons' Lodge in Vienna. He had become a Freemason at The Hague in 1731—being the first continental prince to do so—in a Lodge which a deputation from the Grand Lodge of England had set up specially for that purpose. Desaguliers, Lord Chesterfield, and five other brethren initiated him as Entered Apprentice and passed him to the degree of Fellow Craft. Eight months later the Duke— as he then was—visited England and was raised to the degree of Master Mason in the 'Maid's Head' Lodge, Norwich, at a meeting held at the Norfolk country seat of the great statesman Walpole.

He was soon to have an opportunity of assisting the young organization. When, on the death of Gaston de Medici, he took over the government of the Grand Duchy of Tuscany, where, as in France, Poland, Sweden, Spain, and Portugal, persecution of the Freemasons had set in under the influence of the clergy, he prohibited any further acts of violence, liberated many Masons who had been thrown into prison by the Inquisition, and stopped the trials. In the Austrian Patrimonial Dominions and Hungary, however, the Papal Bull, which commanded the clerical and civic authorities 'neither to enter into the Society of Freemasons, nor to propagate it nor to accept them in their houses or palaces' was not published.

---

[1] Freemasonry had been introduced into Austria as early as 1726. Franz Anton Graf Sporck had founded in that year the 'Three Stars' Lodge in Prague. However, some doubt still exists as to the correctness of this date.

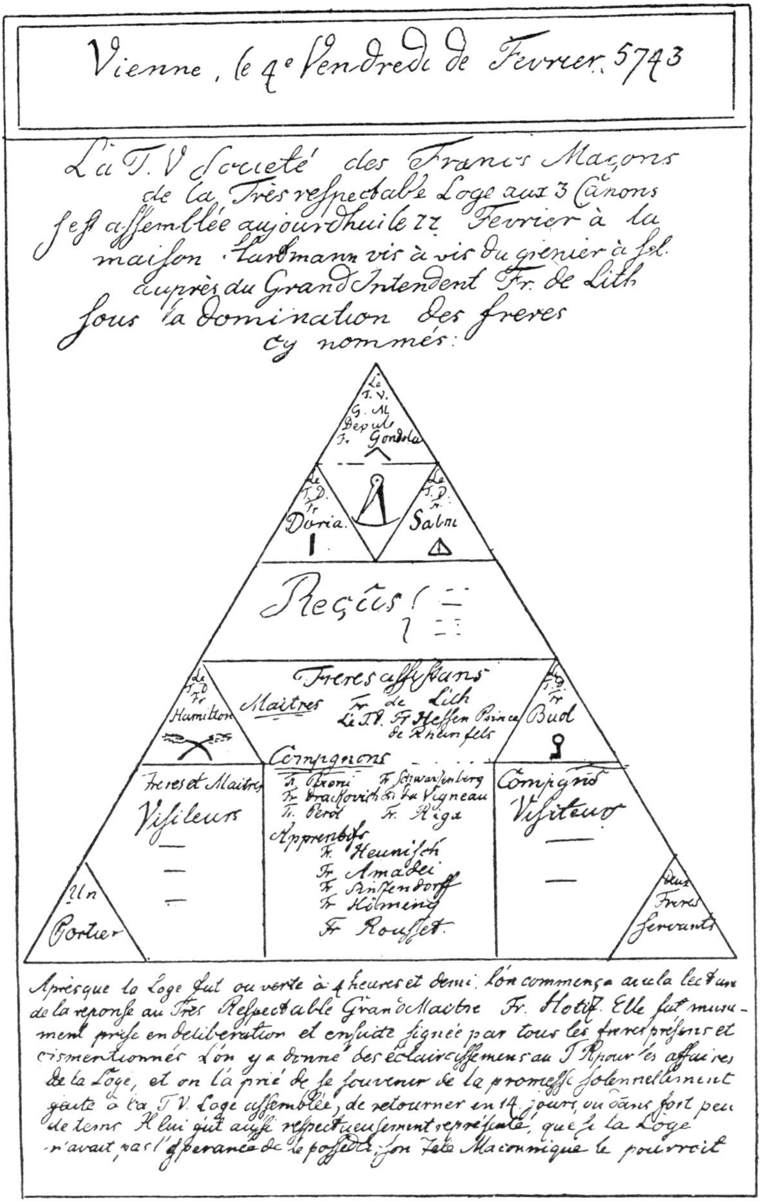

Vienne, le 4e Vendredi de Fevrier. 5743

La T. V. Société des Francs Maçons
de la Très respectable Loge aux 3 Canons
s'est assemblée aujourd'hui le 22 Fevrier à la
maison Hartmann vis à vis du grenier à sel.
auprès du Grand Intendant Fr. de Lith
sous la domination des freres
cy nommés:

Après que la Loge fut ouverte à 4 heures et demi, l'on commença avec la lecture
de la réponse au Très Respectable Grand Maître Fr. Hotif. Elle fut mure-
ment prise en délibération et ensuite signée par tous les freres présens et
cy mentionnés. L'on y a donné des éclaircissemens au T. R pour les affaires
de la Loge, et on l'a prié de se souvenir de la promesse solennellement
faite à la T. V. Loge assemblée, de retourner en 14 jours, ou dans fort peu
de tems. Il lui fut aussi respectueusement représenté, que si la Loge
n'avait pas l'esperance de le posséder, son Fête Maçonnique le pourroit

FROM THE MINUTE BOOK OF THE VIENNA LODGE OF THE
'THREE CANONS', 1743

The nature of the Emperor's activity in the Lodge 'Aux trois canons' (even this one, like most German Lodges of those times, had a French title), which was founded in 1741 by Bishop Graf Schaffgotsch,[1] of Breslau, is not known. However, in the *Journal für Freimaurer* of the year 1784 it was stated that the 'Lodge was held even in the castle itself'. The membership of this Lodge was drawn mainly from the highest ranks of the nobility. The registers record the names of the Princes of Hessen-Rheinfels, Counts Gondola, Hamilton, Bethlen, Wallenstein, de la Cerda, Hojos, Starhemberg, Kaunitz, Trauttmansdorff, Draskovich, Gallas, Zinzendorf, Soerger, Seilern, Salm, the Marquess Doria, and Barons Tinti and Lievenstein, all noblemen closely associated with the Court. All the more excitement was caused, therefore, when, on the 7th March 1743, by command of the Empress, one hundred Bayreuth grenadiers and cuirassiers appeared in the hall of the Margarethenhof at the Bauernmarkt, whilst a Lodge meeting was in progress, demanded the brethren's swords, and declared the whole of the company under arrest. The brethren handed over their weapons to the Worshipful Master, who then laid them down before the officer in command of the grenadiers. The prisoners were subjected to a long examination, at which Cardinal Kollonits was present, but on the 19th March, the name-day of the heir to the throne, they were set free again, thanks to the efforts of 'H.M. the Most Distinguished Mason in Europe', who had stopped the proceedings and declared himself ready to hold himself responsible for the behaviour of the Freemasons and to answer any charges preferred against them. The accusers would have to find better grounds for complaint before the Empress would take further steps in the matter, as that which had been alleged was nothing less than falsehood and misrepresentation.

Various explanations have been given of the reasons which led Maria Theresa to undertake these steps against the friends and brethren of her husband. It is stated in the *Historischen Bildersaal* (Nuremberg 1744), that the inquisitive ladies of the Court had persuaded the Empress because the secrets of the

[1] Count Schaffgotsch was initiated in 'The Three Skeletons' Lodge of Breslau, of which he later became Worshipful Master at a time when he was still an abbot and prebendary of the Cathedral. In spite of the Papal Bull he openly professed himself a Freemason. His canons thereupon declared him excommunicated. Through the agency of the easygoing Bishop von Sinzendorf, the Pope was induced to withdraw the penalty of the Church. However, Schaffgotsch still remained in the Fraternity.

Order had been kept from them; others concluded that the clergy were responsible for the agitation, because the prisoners had been held under arrest in the Archbishop's palace, and it was also said that Maria Theresa was afraid that the Prussian King would, by means of Freemasonry, be able to secure an undesirable influence over her army and her cabinet.

The Lodge could now resume its work once again.

As in the majority of the other German Lodges, the upper strata of society predominated. French was spoken in the Lodges, as it was everywhere else, and anything that came from France was accepted with tremendous enthusiasm; as witness the enthusiastic acceptance of the higher degrees which originated in that country. The Lodges became obsessed with the idea of Knighthood. Labouring under the misapprehension that they had a sacred mission to perform, they snatched at the writings which, based on the misconstrued statements of Ramsay, maintained that Freemasonry had originated in Palestine in the Middle Ages, and that it was necessary to restore its original form, i.e. to bring back to life the Order of Knights Templars which had been destroyed by Philippe le Bel in 1312. They believed, in all sincerity, the legend that the Knights Templars who had escaped destruction before the Grand Master, Jacques de Molay, was burnt at the stake, had, as a most precious bequest, received initiation into the mighty secrets of the 'Exalted Order of the Holy Temple' from its last Grand Master in 1314. Those secrets— so the legend runs—then found refuge in Scotland, where they were preserved in the Gilds of Masons for a period of four centuries.

The whole history of the Templars, which has always been somewhat obscure, was eagerly investigated. Their researches took them back to the beginning of the twelfth century, when nine Knights had founded the Order for the protection of the Holy Sepulchre and of the pilgrims who were flocking towards Palestine, and the King of Jerusalem had allocated to them, for their headquarters, that part of his palace which stood on the ruins of the ancient Temple of Solomon. They waxed enthusiastic about the deeds of the 'poor brethren of the Temple of Jerusalem', as the Templars called themselves. They wished to re-establish the Preceptories which the martial monks had set up in Europe after the collapse of the Crusades. And they sought, as it were, to canonize those men for whom the jealousy of King Philippe and Pope Clement V,[1] who was dependent upon him, had prepared such a cruel fate. Baron von Hund and Alten-Grotkau became the leader of Knights Templarism in Germany. He had become a Freemason in Paris and had returned to Germany as 'Coadjutor of the VIIth Province'. The Lodge of the 'Three Pillars', which was formed by him and met on his estate at Unwürde in Upper Lusatia, and the Lodge of the 'Three Hammers' in Naumberg, the Master of which was Marschall, who, according to Hund, had been installed by the 'Unknown Superiors' as Grand Master of the VIIth Province (of Germany, between the Elbe and the Oder), became the scene of great activity. Surrounded by the greatest secrecy, brethren were dubbed Knights, received Latin names, and pledged themselves to unquestioning obedience to the commands of Hund, of the 'Eques ab Ense'. From this obligation of unquestioning obedience comes the name which the system soon received: it was referred to as the 'Strict Observance,' in contradistinction to the Lodges which adhered to the three degrees of the English system— described as the 'Lax Observance.'

The Strict Observance proved very attractive. When the candidate had passed through the three degrees and that of the 'Scottish Master', and had particularly distinguished himself, he was elevated to the 'Inner Order' in which he first became a novice or 'Chevalier de l'aigle', then Knight Templar, and finally *eques professus*. The Knights of the 'Inner Order' no longer met in Lodges but in Chapters. Over their purple-coloured knightly garb and the gold-embroidered rosettes was thrown the white cloak bearing the red cross of the Knights Templars. The Order aroused their deep enthusiasm, and they threw themselves heart and soul into their work. Those most intimately acquainted with the affairs of the Order whispered that the 'Unknown Superior' was none other than Charles Edward Stuart, who, upon his arrival in Scotland in 1745, had solemnly vowed in Edinburgh Castle that he would re-establish the 'Temple', raise it, and make it more magnificent than it had been in the times of William the Lion.

[1] The Council of Vienna of 1311 confirmed the Bull issued by Clement V for the suppression of the Knights Templars. These were accused, absolutely unjustly, of having betrayed the remaining Crusaders by means of a conspiracy with the Saracens, and it was alleged that they did not recognize the divinity of Christ, that the crucifix was spat upon as part of their religious services, that they indulged in Black Magic, and that they brought children as sacrifices to the devil in the horrible form of Baphomet.

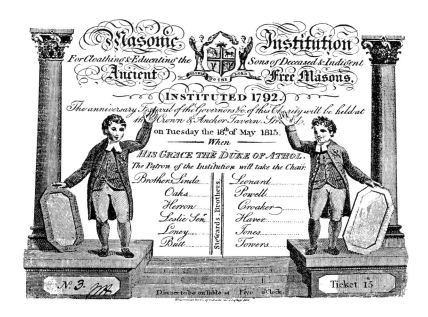

DINNER TICKET
FOR THE MASONIC INSTITUTION FOR BOYS, 1813

A VERY FAMOUS EIGHTEENTH-CENTURY MASON

Engraving by C. West, after the Painting by P. van Dyke

Even so discerning a researcher as Ludwig Keller[1] was convinced, as late as 1906, that the last of the Stuarts had held
the office of Grand Master of the Order, and, consequently,
that the Catholic Church had actually had the designs attributed
to it. He says:

'Upon Charles Edward assuming the office of Grand
Master, the reform, i.e. the connexion of Freemasonry with
the ceremonial of the Crusaders and Knights, which Ramsay
had made possible with such cleverness and success, was
very materially assisted. The outcome all depended upon
whether Charles Edward became King of Great Britan or
not.

'As Grand Master of the Holy Order of the Temple, the
Pretender was, in theory, at the head of all Lodges and of
all Freemasons throughout the world. It was hoped that
recognition of the necessity of the great 'Reform' would
gain ground in all the Lodges, including those that had
temporarily remained outside. Just when the Curia declared,
with all the power at its command, that it was opposed to
the 'Society of Freemasons', there arose, under the promising
protectorship of a Prince who was an ally of the Church of
Rome, a new Order of Knighthood which embraced not only
all the usages of the Masons, but much more besides. Thus,
the overthrow of the existing Patrons of Freemasonry—
who, since 1740, included the King of Prussia, in addition
to the House of Hanover—and the gradual conversion of
the whole organization of Freemasons into a useful body of
Catholic Princes and States and a secular-spiritual congregation, was brought within the bounds of possibility.'

At any rate, the Templars made splendid headway at first.
Then one day there appeared a swindler calling himself Johnson,
a man of fascinating appearance, whose real identity was not
known. He had been forced to flee from Vienna and Anhalt.
In the former place he had convinced the Emperor that he
possessed the secret of the 'Philosopher's Stone'. For years
he had drifted from place to place, always under a new name,
until one day he had struck upon the idea of making money
out of Freemasonry. With the assistance of false credentials
he was able to find his way into a Lodge in Halle.
He bombastically called himself 'Knight of the Grand Lion
of the Exalted Order of Knights of the Temple of Jerusalem',

[1] *Die Tempelherren und die Freimaurer.*

made friends, became a Saxon captain of horse, but indulged again in swindling and was imprisoned. He then reappeared in the service of Prussia, also as a captain of horse, and turned up in Jena in 1763 with a 'princely retinue' of four persons, describing himself as the 'Grand Prior and Emissary of the true Order of the Temple of the real Scottish Superiors'. He produced papers according to which he had been commissioned to organize the Order in Germany and to reform the Lodges in accordance with the Templar usage. He set up a Grand Chapter, created Knights against cash payment, and commanded the Chapter which had been founded by the honest Baron von Hund to show its allegiance to his Obedience. And, strange as it may seem, this command was obeyed. Delegates came from all quarters and handed over their warrants, after the solemn burning of which they were once more initiated into the Novitiate, for which pleasure they had to pay large sums of money, often as much as 2,000 talers. On the other hand, they were then able, booted and spurred, to take part in the 'Knightly exercises' and to indulge the hope of being made acquainted with the art of changing base metals into gold and silver. Even Hund was hoodwinked by Johnson and went so far as to pay homage to him, but he became suspicious and declared him an impostor at an Assembly in Altenberg. Johnson took to flight, but was later arrested and held in captivity in the Wartburg, in the very room which Luther had occupied.

Hund was now regarded as the saviour of German Freemasonry, and was generally recognized as the Provincial Grand Master. The most enthusiastic supporter of the 'Supremus Magister' was the one-time commissariat-officer Johann Christian von Schubart, Deputy Master of the 'Three Globes' Lodge of Berlin, who now travelled all over Germany as an enthusiastic emissary of the Strict Observance and won over Lodges in Dresden, Stettin, and other cities to Hund's system. Conventions were held every year, at which the affairs of the Order were thoroughly discussed. The Convention at Kohlo (1772) was of particular importance. At this Convention the Knights Templars united with another masonic system, known as the Clerical Templars, which had been founded by another enthusiast, Johann August von Starck, a First Chaplain-in-Ordinary and Superintendent-General, who had gone over to the Church of Rome. The members of this Order were an alleged clerical branch of the Knights Templars. Their Ritual, based on the Clerical Orders, was very well conceived. They claimed to possess the latest secrets of occult science and alchemy, and with their insistence upon sacerdotal investiture tended towards Catholicism. Hund remained Provincial Grand Master even after the union. However, Field-Marshal Duke Ferdinand of Brunswick, brother-in-law of Frederick the Great, who had joined the Order in the meantime, was appointed Grand Master of all the Scottish Lodges in 1775, with the title 'Magnus superior ordinis'. It is said that he assumed this position at the instance of the King, who had become aware of the dangers of the troubled water in which a group of Freemasons was so valiantly struggling.

Although the Knights Templars' manner of working was quite a worthy one, interest in this quasi-masonic Order gradually waned. Credence was no longer placed in its mysterious origin, and the members began to lose interest in the pompous ceremonial of the Chapter meetings and refectories and came to the conclusion that the masonic idea was being more and more lost sight of by this Order. The death of von Hund, who departed this life in 1776, and was interred at the foot of the High Altar of the church at Mellrichstadt, was the beginning of the end. The Duke of Södermannland, later King Charles XIII of Sweden, became the next Provincial Grand Master. However, the real leader of the German Freemasons was now, as before, the Duke of Brunswick, who was known amongst his contemporaries as 'The Humanitarian'. When the latter saw that the fall of the system was no longer to be avoided, he called a Convention of German Freemasons at Wilhelmsbad in 1782, at which he hoped to clear up the matter decisively. This Convention was not only intended to reform the Order of the Strict Observance, but also to attempt to regain the ground lost in the meantime to several newly founded Grand Lodges. This attempt did not prove successful. During the thirty-four sittings of the Convention the legend which said that the Freemasons were the successors of the Knights Templars was finally disposed of, but the hoped-for union on a new basis[1] did not materialize. Three of the Grand Lodges which had arisen in the meantime—the National Grand Lodge of All German Freemasons, the Grand National Mother Lodge of the Three Globes, and the English Provincial Grand Lodge of Hamburg—had not even troubled to send delegates.

---

[1] 'Ritter der Wohltätigkeit' (Knights of Charity).

Some months after the Convention a Grand Lodge came into being, in Frankfort-on-Main, which had a decided antipathy to the adulteration of masonic principles. This Grand Lodge was first known as 'The United Lodges for the Restoration of the Royal Art of Antient Freemasonry', but afterwards became the 'Eclectic Union'.

It was so named after a circular letter which resolutely urged that Freemasonry should be put on an eclectic footing.

MEDAL STRUCK IN HONOUR OF DUKE FERDINAND OF
BRUNSWICK

The death-knell of the Strict Observance was sounded when the Grand Lodge of the Three Globes made a declaration formally and solemnly renouncing it. From the very beginning the Frankfort Lodge had refused to receive 'the true Light', and was thereby predestined to be one of the centres of the efforts for the 'restoration of the ancient and true Free-masonry'.

However, this restoration was not solely a question of sweeping away the false system of knighthood; there were other confusions which, having wormed their way into the Lodges, had to be eliminated. In all classes of European society there prevailed a predilection for things mystical. People rejoiced in the metaphysical doctrines of Swedenborg and the Martinists, they pondered over supernatural things and sought to fathom the secrets of Life and the Hereafter.

The New or Gold Rosicrucians gained ground. The brethren of the 'Order of Gold Rosicrucians',[1] which arose about the year 1756, carried the interest in alchemy into many Lodges, where they now searched for the 'Philosopher's Stone' and sought for the secret of making gold. The Rosicrucians also concocted the story of 'Unknown Fathers', from whom the most wonderful revelations were to be expected; revelations concerning happiness on earth and eternal salvation. They perceived in the Lodges suitable ground for their fantasies. Later on their wishes were 'reformed'. They declared then that 'they sought no longer Mammon, but the Kingdom of God'.

But this movement also was soon over. And likewise a third movement, which caused great excitement in Freemasonry and endeavoured to take possession of it by all manner of means, namely, the Society of the Illuminati.

Exhaustive investigations have been made into the part played by, and the significance of, the Illuminati. At all events, no secret society of the eighteenth century has done more harm to Freemasonry than this one, although the Illuminati, at their inception, had absolutely nothing to do with Freemasonry, but worked side by side with the latter quite independently, and only through their enthusiastic apostle, Baron von Knigge, author of the well-known book *Über den Umgang mit Menschen*, did they come into closer association with it.

The Order of the Illuminati was founded by Professor Adam Weishaupt of Ingolstadt. The idea of forming a secret society came to him when he noticed the effect of the Rosicrucians amongst his students. In order to free his young disciples from the gold-making clique, from the ghost-seers, from the dabblers in black and white magic, he formed, with their collaboration, the Society of Perfectibilists, which he later called the Order of the Illuminati, for 'combating moral evil, for improving the morals of the members, and for the higher instruction of humanity'. In his work *Pythagoras oder*

---

[1] The Order had nine degrees, rising from 'Junior' to 'Magus'.

Betrachtungen über die geheime Welt- und Regierungskunst, he describes the object he had in mind as being

'permanently to unite thinking men from all parts of the world, of all classes and religions, in a single society, by means of a given higher interest, without prejudice to their freedom of thought, and in spite of all their different opinions and emotions, and to make them, whether they be inferiors or equals, enthusiastic and responsive to such a degree that the many may act as one and desire and do of their own volition and with the truest conviction, that which no public compulsion has been able to effect since the world and mankind have existed. Such a society is the Masterpiece of human reason, in it and through it the art of government has reached its highest perfection.'

And he declared, apropos of Knigge, that they wished

'to attain, by the finest and surest means, their object of bringing about the victory of Virtue and Wisdom over Foolishness and Malice, of making the most important discoveries in all branches of Science, of improving the members of the society, of cultivating great men and of assuring them, even in this world, of the certain prize of their perfection, of protecting them against persecution and suppression and of tying the hands of despotism in whatever shape or form.'

Weishaupt was certainly inspired by the highest motives, but he employed the wrong means. Although he had been at a Jesuit school he hated the Jesuits like poison, and endeavoured to combat them with his Order, but was not above borrowing many of the principles of his teachers, who had now become his enemies. This antagonism to Jesuitism orginated in the bitter struggle which Weishaupt had been forced to fight for his position in Ingolstadt. He sought connexion with the Freemasons because he believed he would find support amongst them.

Only after the formation of his organization did he enter a Lodge.[1] That this organization was intended to be something quite different to the Society of Freemasons is clear from one of Weishaupt's statements about it: 'What can be done by a secret society which has so little secret that its entire inner constitution is known to the rest of the world?'

---

[1] 'Theodor vom guten Rat', Munich.

Every member of the Order of Illuminati received a Latin or Greek name. Weishaupt named himself 'Spartacus' and Knigge was called 'Philo'. His chief collaborators were Regierungsrat Franz Xaver Zwackh (Cato), the Prebendary of Munich, Hertel, Count von Cobenzl, Provost of Eichstädt Cathedral (Arian) and the Marquis Costanzo (Diomedes). The Order was intended as a kind of learned society, a secret school of knowledge with a definite objective and thereby straightaway contravened the principles of Freemasonry.

However, once having come into contact with Freemasonry, Weishaupt desired to set up Lodges in Athen (Munich) and Erzerum (Eichstädt). Regierungsrat Zwackh had elaborated a plan according to which these Lodges were to be nurseries for the Order. These foundations did not materialize, but, on the other hand, enthusiastic propaganda was made for the Order in Masonic circles. Bode in Weimar and the bookseller and author, Christoph Friedrich Nicolai, in Berlin, were recruiting officers, in addition to Knigge. The Duke Karl August von Sachsen-Weimar (Äschylos), Goethe (Abaris), and possibly Schiller, also became Illuminati. The organization became more and more rigid. At the head of the secret Areopagus stood Weishaupt as Provost of the Order. Every member had his immediate superior, the sponsor who had introduced him into the Order, and to him had to be reported every month what he had performed or learned in connexion with the Order. Certain books had to be read, and each member had to report on certain other members. Detailed reports had then to be made concerning the results of this espionage. So long as the member remained a Novice he was not allowed to become acquainted with any member of the Order except his immediate superior, and throughout the degrees they were bound to render rigid obedience.

But, as in the case of the Strict Observance, the Order of Illuminati may have had form, but hardly an inner content. The progressively inclined Freemasons, who, attracted by Bode, Knigge, and the others, came to the Order of Illuminati, expected to find improved Freemasonry there. They were disappointed, however, and soon withdrew. Weishaupt himself had to confess to Knigge 'that the Order did not exist except in his mind, and that only the lower grade, the nursery, had been set up in some Catholic provinces. For the higher degrees he had collected the most magnificent materials, which he would now hand over to him for elaboration.' Knigge then arranged the Illuminati system in a logical sequence of degrees, which, however, did not all come to life. There were three grades in the new system: 1. Nursery; 2. Symbolic Masonry; 3. Lesser and Greater Mysteries. Before entering the real Order they had to complete the Novitiate, after which they were admitted into the Minerval Degree. At the assemblies of the 'Minerval Churches' the members of this degree wore a green sash with a medallion, upon which was depicted an owl holding in its claws an open book bearing the initials P(er) M(e) C(oeci) V(ident). If they distinguished themselves as Minervals they were promoted to the degree of Minor Illuminatus, after they had been instructed in the theories of Symbolic Masonry. Then came the further degrees of 'Major Illuminatus' and 'Directing Illuminatus', which was supposed to be the gateway to the mystery degrees. The intricacy of the system led to conflicts and, finally, to the breach between Weishaupt and Knigge.

The trouble was chiefly about the Mysteries Priest Degree, which had been described by opponents as particularly dangerous in its ideas. In a book entitled *The latest works of Spartacus and Philo in the Society of Illuminati* (1794), this degree is described.[1] It was composed of 'an invisible assembly' of the Rulers. Here the bitterest criticism of what was then known as 'Enlightenment' was indulged in, it being stated, with more than confused logic, that 'Enlightenment is now spreading with the sole object of cultivating crafty men as a means of satisfying the desire of kings to conquer and subjugate others. In order to prevent such misuse and a return to the previous debasement, Providence has offered, since the earliest of times, a permanent remedy, namely the secret schools of knowledge. These have always been the archives of Nature and of the Rights of Humanity. Through them Man will recover from his fall; princes and nations will disappear from the earth without deeds of violence; the human species will one day become one family and the world the abode of reasonable men. Morality alone will bring about these changes imperceptibly. . . .'

True enlightenment is a necessity.

'If such enlightenment is the work of morality, then enlightenment and mutual confidence progress. Morality, therefore, is the art which teaches man how to attain his

1 Leopold Engel: *Geschichte des Illuminatenordens*. Berlin. 1906.

majority, to rid himself of guardianship and to dispense with Princes and States. If it is not, then what is the use of it?'

Quarrels weakened the Order to such a degree that it was not strong enough to withstand the attacks made upon it, especially by the Catholic Rosicrucians. There was severe persecution in Bavaria. The Illuminati were accused—and with them the Freemasons—of having too little patriotism and too much egotism, of treasonable conspiracy, and of attempts to deliver Bavaria into the hands of Austria. At the instigation of the Jesuit Franck, his father confessor, the Elector Karl Theodor issued a Decree on the 22nd July 1784, levelled 'against all Communities, Societies or Fraternities instituted without the official authority and confirmation of the Ruling Prince'. Without avail the Illuminati demanded a legal investigation. There followed a second and a third prohibition, and although the Order submitted, many of its leaders were severely punished for 'disobedience'. Weishaupt was dismissed from his post and banished from Ingolstadt. Regierungsrat Zwackh, Professor Bader, Prebendary Hertel, the Marquis Costanzo and others were either dismissed from their offices without formal trial or were imprisoned. Weishaupt found protection with Duke Ernest of Saxe-Gotha. But that was the end of the Order of Illuminati; an end which came long before the French Revolution, which the Order is supposed to have stirred up through Mirabeau and Bode. Just as some people had always seen the 'faint shadow' of Charles Edward Stuart sounding the trumpet call for the fight for Catholicism behind all the things which Freemasons did in the sphere of Knighthood, there were now others who declared that the French brethren of the time of the Revolution were the followers of the Anti-Jesuit Weishaupt and his friends. . . .

The question has often been asked how it came about that Freemasonry participated in all these manifestations, which were so contrary to its true nature, which could not contribute to its credit and would be bound to drive away many who had come as enthusiastic neophytes. However, it should never be forgotten that all the schools of thought described, were, when they first appeared in Germany, clothed in the mantle of noble desire and were generally sponsored by idealists of the first water. It would not otherwise be conceivable that so many distinguished Germans should have collaborated in all earnestness. Just as romantic minds imagined that they saw in the Strict Observance the reincarnation of the Order of Knights Templars in all its former glory, that is to say, a new crusade against all the evils of this wicked world, but, at the same time, overlooked the shallow unreality of the make-up which appealed more to the eye than to the intellect, so did they imagine, later, that the Society of the Illuminati was an organization striving solely for the moral purification of the person, and overlooked the above-mentioned superficiality. Freemasons were not the only people who were addicted to meddling with the occult. Many other quite important persons took an interest in it. Thus it came about (just as it does to-day) that the very cleverest people became the prey of charlatans and lent ear to all kinds of swindles which fostered, for the selfish ends of the perpetrators, the belief in the 'true secrets'.

We are already acquainted with the swindler Johnson. A similar figure was the Protestant theologist Rosa, whose real name was Dietrich Schuhmacher, at one time Superintendent of Churches and Schools and Ecclesiastical Commissioner, who, pretending to be able to make gold out of dust glittering in the sunbeams, then procceded to cause all manner of mischief in the system of the Grand Chapter of the Clermont High Degrees, which had been brought to Germany by the French prisoner of war Marquis Tilly de Lernais and Baron von Printzen, W.M., of the 'Three Globes' Lodge in Berlin. He promised 'theological, astrological, cosmological, cosmosophistical, physiognomical, alchemistical, cabalistical and theosophistical knowledge' and carried on his nefarious work chiefly in the 'Philadelphia' Lodge in Halle, but was finally exposed and expelled from the Craft.

Baron von Gugomos also pretended to be an 'Exalted Superior', but, in the end, he also was exposed as a charlatan. He had been a Gentleman of the Bedchamber to the Margrave of Baden and travelling companion to the Prince of Hessen-Darmstadt and had then gone to Wetzlar as a courtier of the Prince von Fürstenstein. In 1776 he issued to the members of the Strict Observance an invitation to a General Convention to be held in Wiesbaden in August of the same year. In explanation of this arrangement he told a strange tale. The previous year, the tale ran, he had gone to the Convention at Brunswick to see whether there really were any Knights Templars among those present. His secret signs had, however, not been understood. He himself had been initiated as a true Knight Templar in a far-off land in order that he might save the German nation, which contained so much good within its soul and strove willingly after perfection. This Wiesbaden Convention actually took place. Gugomos told a most adventurous story and produced an authorization made out by the 'Holy See of Cyprus' and other documents which purported to prove that the attempts to re-establish the Order of Knights Templars had hitherto been on the wrong lines.

The swindler had spared no expense in preparing his forgeries. His 'Commissorium', signed by 'Wilhelmus Albanus Gregorius, Supremus M.T.A.', was provided with an enormous pendant seal of the Order, in a metal casing, with which the document itself was marked. He wore a similar seal of gilt metal on a red ribbon under the waistcoat, and a smaller one on his breast. Both had hieroglyphics on the reverse side. Needless to say all the papers were forgeries. The regulations of the Order, which were attached to the 'Commissorium', displayed a German water-mark when they were later held to the light. From the beginning most of those present at the Convention regarded Gugomos as a swindler. However, he was able, supported by the Hessian Princes and Baron Gemmingen, to encounter the sceptics with the greatest cleverness and declared that 'he could only give instruction in the higher sciences in an *Adytum Sacrum* which would first have to be built, at the consecration of which natural fire would fall from Heaven and consume the innocent offering on the altar'. He would, however, dub knights those who were present, and initiate them into the Order so that, initiated as Duces (leaders), they might approach nearer to the offering through the agency of his teachings. He would explain the plan of the Adytum to two of the initiated, and thereupon journey to Cyprus in order to obtain the necessary implements. The site of the Adytum was to be a castle in Mecklenburg-Strelitz. In order to quieten the many sceptics, who only refrained from leaving lest they should break up the Convention, Gugomos finally undertook the first pseudo initiation in Wiesbaden itself. When they thereupon urged him to start his journey to Cyprus the swindle was discovered. Gugomos was then forced to flee.

Whereas the swindlers mentioned in the preceding pages had devoted their attentions to the Knights, Johann Georg Schrepfer preyed upon those circles of Freemasons in Leipzig whose activities lay in the sphere of occult science. Schrepfer had never been a Freemason, but had stolen identification papers from Prince Georg Holstein-Gotthorp when the latter was staying at an hotel in Leipzig. One fine day Schrepfer came forward with the assertion that he had been sent to found the true Freemasonry. In the billiards-room of the coffee-house carried on by him, he set up a 'Lodge' in which he held spiritualistic séances. He made virulent attacks on the members of the 'Minerva of the Three Palms' Lodge who had correctly sized him up. On one occasion he appeared with drawn sword and cocked pistol at a Lodge meeting, and insulted the Worshipful Master. In spite of such deeds Schrepfer soon gained the reputation of a worker of miracles. When the Minerva Lodge once more took steps against him he smothered the town with libellous pamphlets, and the Patron of the Saxon Lodges, Duke Karl of Courland, considering himself insulted, caused Schrepfer to be arrested by the Governor of Leipzig, and he was soundly cudgelled at the guard-house. Schrepfer thereupon attempted to bring an appeal before the civic authorities, but it was dismissed. He then threatened to publish the masonic Ritual, after which they left him in peace. He proceeded to set up a new 'Lodge' and declared that his activities with the occult science were the chief objects of Freemasonry.

Schrepfer's Lodge-room now became a necromancing chamber in which 'spirits were called from the vasty deep'. His appearance and manner were so confident, and the swindle so cleverly staged, that even his former antagonist, the Duke of Courland, summoned him to his Court to receive initiation into the 'mysteries' at his hands. This apparently went to Schrepfer's head. Upon his return to Leipzig he appeared in a French uniform, calling himself Colonel the Baron von Steinberg, and declared that he had ascertained that he was in reality the natural son of a French Prince. An angry letter from the French Ambassador and, in spite of the ever-increasing donations of his followers, his financial worries subsequently decided him to put an end to his life. One evening he invited four of his supporters, one of whom was the Rosicrucian General Bischoffswerder, to go with him outside the town in order to participate in very special revelations. He came to a halt before a clump of bushes and commanded his companions to wait. They would, he said, hear a supernatural report and they were then to follow him immediately. A report actually was heard. However, it did not come from another world, but from the pistol with which Schrepfer had shot himself.

The 'most remarkable masonic charlatan' of the eighteenth

century, Josef Balsamo, who acquired world-wide notoriety under the name of Count Cagliostro, was also able to make money out of Freemasonry in the course of his wanderings in Europe, though Germany can hardly be said to have fallen a victim to him. This strange person declared himself at The Hague to be a 'Reformer and Founder of Lodges'. He alleged that he had been made a Freemason in London—although his name has never been traced in any register—and maintained the principle that women must also be admitted into the Order. A Lodge which he founded at The Hague, with his beautiful wife, Lorenza Feliciani, as Lady Grand Master, was chiefly intended for women. However, he failed in his attempt to found a similar Lodge in St. Petersburg under the patronage of Catherine II. In Strasburg, where Cagliostro succeeded in worming himself into the favour of the Cardinal Archbishop, Prince Rohan, he confidently asserted that he possessed the secrets of Egyptian Freemasonry (which he invented himself) and formed in Lyons and later in Paris, Lodges according to his 'teaching', which he described as the 'Adoption Mother Lodges of the Exalted Egyptian Freemasonry.' This system, at the head of which Cagliostro stood as Grand Cophta,[1] had ninety degrees and promised 'Perfection through physical and moral *regeneration*' to all who believed.

The notorious affair of the necklace, which brought about the fall of Cagliostro, put an end to this miserable swindle.

[1] See *Der Grosskophta*, by Goethe.

CHAPTER IX

THE REFORMERS

WIELAND, in his application for initiation, spoke of Freemasonry 'in its improved Constitution restored to its former purity and simplicity'. He was friendly with one of the men who were responsible for this reform work. This was Friedrich Ludwig Schröder, theatrical manager of Hamburg, who gave considerable uplift to the German stage as a moral institution, and who should receive the most credit, together with the Frankfort eclectics and Ignaz Aurelius Fessler, for the fact that Freemasonry found its way back to the right path.

Before we deal with these men, let us cast a quick glance into the Grand Lodges existing in Germany about the time of the turn of the century. The Berlin Lodge 'Aux trois Globes,' which was an offshoot from the King's Lodge, had, in 1744, become the Grand Royal Mother Lodge of the 'Three Globes,' of which the King acted as Grand Master. In 1772, under the Grand Mastership of Duke William of Brunswick, this became the Grand National Mother Lodge of the Prussian States called 'The Three Globes'. In the course of the years many subsidiary Lodges had been formed. Other Lodges had been founded by other parties, some of them under English charters. The Lodges had first of all been of the Strict Observance, but had afterwards severed all connexion therewith; many Lodges had, in the past, turned their backs on the Knights Templars and had made themselves independent, and others had never joined them. The remaining systems had also founded Lodges in all parts of the country and had probably attracted to themselves a Lodge here and there. The picture was one of complete confusion, out of which the following groups gradually appeared:

In Berlin, besides the 'Grand National Mother Lodge', there were two other Grand Lodges: the 'National Grand Lodge of All German Freemasons' and the 'Grand Lodge of Prussia, Royal York of Friendship'.

The 'National Grand Lodge of All German Freemasons' was founded in 1770 by Johann Wilhelm Kellner von Zinnendorf.

This man served his country well as Field Surgeon in the Prussian Army during the Seven Years' War and was appointed Surgeon-General and Chief of the Medical Staff of the Army in 1765. He had been initiated very early into a Lodge and, like many other men, strove after the true Freemasonry. Finally, he thought he had found this in Sweden, whence he obtained from the Head of the Order, Friedrich von Eckleff, through the agency of a proxy, all the documents and rituals authorizing him to introduce the Swedish system into Germany. He intended, first of all, to transfer this to the Grand National Mother Lodge, of which he had become the Grand Master, to replace the 'absurd fanaticism' of the Strict Observance, but he shortly afterwards severed his connexion with this Lodge for private reasons and formed his own Lodge according to the Swedish teaching. In 1770, he affiliated this Lodge with the National Grand Lodge. But even this Grand Lodge embraced more than the three original St. John's degrees. Above these were two St. Andrew's degrees and four Chapter degrees, which likewise dealt with the transformation of the Order of Templars into the Order of Freemasons. But the important difference between this system and the other German high degree systems of that period, a difference which, in the course of time, became still more marked,[1] was that the degrees were not set up arbitrarily, but constituted a complete system, based on a uniform idea, the stages of which dovetailed into each other organically; a system in whose teachings the Epiphany took the central place.

The third Berlin Grand Lodge 'Royal York of Friendship' came into being in 1798, as an offshoot of the Lodge 'de l'Amitié', which was founded in 1752 or 1754 by French Freemasons who were scholars, artists and officials resident in the capital of Prussia. In 1761 it was called 'de l'Amitié aux trois Colombes'. When it introduced the brother of the King of England to Freemasonry in 1765 and obtained his patronage, it became 'La Loge Royale de York de l'Amitié'. All these three Grand Lodges possessed royal patents and their position was also outwardly strengthened by the fact that an Edict, issued in 1798 by King Frederick William III, grand-nephew of Frederick the Great, prohibited participation in all secret

---

[1] The Ritual of the National Grand Lodge was likewise redrafted on the basis of revised Swedish texts. The documents upon which this teaching is founded have, from that time, been the subject of violent controversy amongst students of Masonry.

associations or societies in Prussia, but expressly excluded the three Grand Lodges and their daughter Lodges. Thus it was that the activity of other Lodges was not permitted in Prussia; a circumstance which was later to lead to much discord.

Outside Prussia the Eclectic Union in Frankfort (working as an English Provincial Grand Lodge), and also the English Provincial Grand Lodge of Hamburg and Lower Saxony, were at work at the time of the masonic reformation.

The first call for reformation was sounded in the *Eclectic Circular* at the instigation of von Ditfurth, Assessor of the Supreme Court of Appeal of Wetzlar, and Brönner, Master of the Frankfort 'Union' Lodge. The effect of this call for a return to the old simplicity, for the formation of a union whose basic principles would be Liberty and Equality in masonic life, can be judged from the fact that by 1789 no less than fifty-three Lodges in various countries had expressed their desire to be enrolled under its banner. There was also, of course, no lack of opposition. As had so often happened in the past, the mystics asserted that the new foundation was a hotbed of deism, if not of atheism. Frankfort took up the challenge of these attacks and declared war on superstition, astrology and obscurantism of every kind. Only the three St. John's degrees were in future to be recognized as obligatory for the whole of Freemasonry. As for the rest, each individual Lodge was to be left free to superimpose any fancy degrees it might choose.

'In the first degree,' it was said, 'we initiate the Apprentice into the knowledge of himself. In the second degree we direct the Fellow Craft to the knowledge of Nature, and in the third degree we cause the Master Mason to direct his thoughts to the Creator and Originator of All Things, in order that he may obtain a clearer conception of the triad founded on unity and thus find his way to the most secret Wisdom.'

The 'Schröder system' made its entry into the German Lodges in the 'nineties of the century, from Hamburg. Friedrich Ludwig Schröder, who had introduced the works of Shakespeare, as translated by Wieland, into the repertoire of the German stage and who was himself a notable Shakespearian actor, had become a Freemason in the 'Emanuel zur Maienblume' Lodge in 1774. It says a lot for his personality that although he was a 'play actor', i.e., a member of a profession that was not held in the highest esteem in those days, he was accepted without a ballot. What Schröder aspired to in his

GOETHE

Engraved by D. Chodowiecki, after Painting by G. M. Kraus, 1776

JOHANN GOTTFRIED HERDER
From the Painting by Tischbein

reform was a stricter moral sense and obedience, and the abolition of the higher degrees with their control of the St. John's degrees. He maintained that the latter contained everything symbolical that could serve a thinking man helpfully and remindfully, as a guide to moral freedom and brotherly love, from the day of his birth until his last day on earth, and pursued with resolution the idea that the dignity of the Master Mason's degree was the consummation of masonic education. In his endeavours he was confronted by two sources of danger. On the one side there were the gnostic fanatics, and, on the other, the 'innovationists' who would have cast away the gold with the dross and shaken the very foundations of Freemasonry by seeking to banish symbolism altogether from the Temple. With the same impetuosity Schröder attacked those ultra-enthusiastic persons who wished to do away with the language of symbols; that is to say, that which is durable in Masonry; the connecting link which alone makes Freemasonry intelligible to all nations. He also attacked those people who would not part so easily with the occult sciences, cabalism, etc., or who were not disposed to put Masonic republicanism in the place of the hierarchical system. He became a scientific explorer of Freemasonry. He studied all manner of masonic books, rituals and catechisms; in fact, anything he could lay hands on, and he even collected material for a history of Freemasonry, as it seemed especially important to him to put this on the proper footing. He created the 'Engbund', i.e., a 'select circle' for knowledge and research, consisting of brethren who bound themselves specifically to practise, uphold and propagate the principles recognized once and for all as correct, without deriving the right, by reason of their greater interest, to exercise the slightest influence upon the ruling of the Lodges.

All those superfluities which, in the course of time, had been added to the simple symbolism of the English ritual, with all its beauty and depth of meaning, were cast out by Schröder. But before placing the results of his work before the public, he first made Goethe, Herder, and his friend Hufeland, the celebrated doctor and eclectic of the medical science, conversant with the chief characteristics of his efforts for the purification of the system. 'As the Truth is simple, so must the Symbol also be simple', was the motto of the reformer, and, fortunately, he attained a large measure of success. A very large number of Lodges work to this very day according to the Schröder system.

The work accomplished by Schröder in Hamburg was, to a certain extent, accomplished by Fessler in Berlin. In the latter case, however, there was harder work to be done. It is true that the Strict Observance had fallen somewhat into decay after the revolt of Zinnendorf and the severance of the 'Three Globes'. In the State of Prussia, however, the Minister of State von Woellner, chief of the Department for Religious Affairs, remained all-powerful until 1797. In 1788, by his Edict relating to religion and his re-institution of the censorship, this man, who was a zealot and blind fanatic, destroyed almost everything tending towards enlightenment and the spirit of tolerance that had come into the land under Frederick the Great. He also proved very antagonistic to the cause of Freemasonry. Caught in the clutches of the mysticism of the Middle Ages, he was one of the most fanatical supporters of Rosicrucianism and regarded the theory of communion with the spirits as the only true knowledge. As one of the rulers of the Order of the New or Gold Rosicrucians (which now hardly bore any resemblance to that enigmatical secret society which Andrea had conceived) he very nearly made the doctrines of that Order the basis of the ecclesiastical and political systems of Prussia. He was able to do this because he had succeeded, in collaboration with General von Bischoffswerder, who was of the same turn of mind, in placing King Frederick William II completely under the spell of the mysterious haze surrounding the seers of ghosts.

Ignaz Aurelius Fessler took up residence in Berlin in 1796. Although he was only 40 years old, he had a varied and adventurous career behind him. He was born in Western Hungary of a German family, and received from his pious mother a deeply religious education. After studying at the Jesuit College in Pressburg, he took the Capuchin vows in 1773 and travelled on foot from monastery to monastery to complete his education in scholastic philosophy and theology. In Vienna, where he arrived in 1781 and saw the public reforms of Joseph II he became friendly with the supporters of Joseph's liberalizing ecclesiastical policy and was so impressed with the ideas of enlightenment that he stepped into prominence as an innovationist by reason of his literary efforts. He wrote two pamphlets on the sovereign prerogatives of the Emperor in ecclesiastical matters and placed before Joseph II a report of the horrors existing in a monastic prison. The result was that the monastic prisons of the whole country were suppressed and innumerable unfortunate monks and nuns saw the light of day after long incarceration in horrible dungeons. However, this had created much antagonism towards him, and proceedings were taken against him before the Episcopal Consistory Court, and he was condemned; that is to say, he was suspended from all priestly functions for a period of four weeks.

Fessler was then appointed Professor of Oriental Languages[1] and Old Testament Hermeneutics at the University of Lemberg, which had been revived by the Emperor. At the same time, he received the degree of Doctor of Theology. He very nearly did not make the journey, for a fanatical friar known as Pater Sergius made an attempt on the life of the 'heretic', from which he had a very narrow escape.

In Lemberg Fessler withdrew from the Order of Capuchins and became a Freemason. Once again, however, his very existence was endangered when an anti-Jesuit tragedy, 'Sidney', written by him, was denounced as being a revolt against the Church. He fled to Breslau where he was given a post by a Freemason, Prince Schönaich-Carolath, as tutor to his children. He turned Lutheran in 1791. Five years later he went to Berlin, after having finished a work on Marcus Aurelius. He became known there as the founder of a Society of Friends of Humanity, which demanded of its members the strictest morality and honesty, and a high standard of intellectual education. On being admitted into the Royal York Lodge, he at once set about the work of purifying and improving. To be sure, he worked less radically than Schröder, perhaps because he, as a South German, gave more play to his imagination than the sober-minded North German. But he also rid the symbols of the bombastic embellishments, bearing in mind the Antient English Ritual. He converted the (so-called) high degrees into stages of knowledge, gave the symbols an intelligent meaning and the customs and usages a purpose and a foundation of high morality. According to his view, the customs and usages should be nothing more than the outward and visible representation of the nature and objects of Freemasonry. And each one of its disciples should be instructed to propagate these objects to the best of his ability.

There are other reformers who should be mentioned here, who sought, with varying degrees of success, to renew the

[1] Dr. Ludwig Fensch: *Fessler* (Masonic Classical Writers V). Berlin, Wunder.

spirit and Ritual. First of all, we will take Krause, the philosopher, who, although his teachings were based on documents erroneously regarded by him as genuine (the York Constitution of 926, which, in reality, was written at a much later date), painted a vivid picture of the Fraternity of Freemasons as an all-embracing society of humanity which, unfortunately, was not understood by the majority of his brethren. Krause was supported by his friend Friedrich Mossdorf of Dresden, who, as publisher of Lenning's *Enzyklopadie der Freimaurerei* ('Encyclopaedia of Freemasonry'), laid the foundations of the *Allgemeines Handbuch der Freimaurerei* ('General Handbook of Freemasonry'), which is the most important work of German Freemasonry, now, unfortunately, out of print. Material improvements were also made by Zöllner, the Chief Ecclesiastical Councillor of Berlin, as well as by Hofrat Johann Schneider in Altenburg, the latter having opened up new fields of masonic research.

The new spirit which was thus able to assert itself, generally in the face of violent opposition, did not only find expression within the solemn circles of Freemasonry itself, although many of these circles remained entirely unmoved by the refreshing influence; it also found expression in other places. The number of Freemasons who took a leading part in the German liberty movement was large. Not the Lodges themselves, but their best members exercised the most enduring influence on the spiritual re-birth of Prussia at the time of the struggle against Napoleon. Freemasons in all parts of the country contributed to the building-up of German national idealism, which was undoubtedly quite different from the hateful, dreary, and chauvinistic 'Nationals' of to-day. In the times before 1813 it was a question of leading back to glory a nation which was in every respect bleeding to death. Not only was the national existence destroyed after Jena and Auerstädt, not only was commerce at a standstill, but the intellectual and cultural condition of the State presented a picture of the direst decay under the misrule of a body of feudal nobles of limited understanding whose one thought was of their own private privileges. Prussia was described, quite openly, as a 'corpse', as the dead body of a State, the soul of which was missing, and in which lack of character, intellectual lethargy, selfishness, complete absence of social convictions, obstinate rejection of all new ideas, and a dearth of any constructive creative force made themselves felt.

'Ignorance and conceit,' wrote Ernst Moritz. Arndt at that time, 'together with that form of laziness, the most dangerous vice of the mortal being, whose watchword is "What was good enough for my father is good enough for me", destroyed the last German State.'

The many Freemasons who strove for an improvement in this condition, and called for sweeping reforms, were certainly cosmopolitans in the best sense of the word. But it had begun to dawn upon them that, as Fichte thought, cosmopolitanism could indeed be reconciled with a strong national consciousness. In their Lodges they became convinced that the words 'Know thyself, control thyself, ennoble thyself' must also become the basic foundation of the nation's re-birth. The value of the Temples to them as places of sanctuary for all intellectual forces can be clearly seen from the following inspired words spoken by the Preacher Dräseke in the Lübeck Lodge in 1809:

'They could destroy this Temple, but not the edifice of our hearts. They could prevent our meetings, but not our unity in spirit. They could prohibit our calling ourselves Masons, but not our being Masons. . . . I salute thee, O Masonic Temple. When all else beareth chains, thou art the only sanctuary in a devastated world.'

The Freemason Hardenberg, who, in his capacity of Chancellor, undertook the direction of the whole of the affairs of the Prussian State in 1810, recommended Fichte very strongly for an appointment at the newly founded University of Berlin, although he himself was in many respects a man of the old régime. He was fully cognizant of, and enthusiastic about, the education, advocated by Fichte, of the entire nation on a new basis founded on the example set by the Swiss Illuminatus Pestalozzi, the ultimate aim of which was humanitarianism.

Of all those who followed the exhortations of Fichte and came into his camp, we must first mention the Baron von Stein,[1] who regarded the education of the people, the pillars of the Constitution, as the basis of all national reforms. He and his friends perceived in this humanitarianism a new national ideal. Men should no longer be parts of a huge machine; the new State should educate its citizens in such a way that they, as individual units, would act voluntarily for the common weal of the nation.

[1] When he was forced to flee to Austria in 1808, he was stigmatized by the Viennese Government as 'a dangerous Enlightener and Innovationist' and as 'a man imbued with the spirit of Masonry'.

Let us now draw a picture of this new state of affairs. The hereditary serfdom of the peasants was abolished; Stein's laws regulating municipal government, in which the Freemason Frey of Königsberg, in particular, collaborated, freed the Communes from the tutelage of the State to which they had hitherto been subjected, and gave the citizens the opportunity to take part in the management of civic affairs. Under Hardenburg there then followed the institution of the liberty to carry on a trade, the suppression of the monasteries and other religious foundations, and the concession to the Jews of equal rights with their Christian fellow-citizens. The large part played by Freemasonry in this work cannot be denied, nor can it be refuted that men such as Blücher, Scharnhorst, Gneisenau, Councillor of State Theodor von Hippel, who wrote the *Aufruf an mein Volk* ('Call to my Fellow-Countrymen'), the authors Friedrich Rückert and Max von Schenkendorf, General von Kleist; Graf Tauentzien, Hermann von Boyen, Graf Henckel-Donnersmarck, Hiller von Gaertringen, Yorck's aide-de-camp, Christian Gottfried Körner, and many others were not only enthusiastic Freemasons but also strenuously active workers in the cause.

This may be said of Blücher especially, to whom the Royal Art was the very essence of life, and who acted as Worshipful Master for many years. When in September 1813 the allied armies were advancing, the Marshal attended a festival of 'The Golden Wall' Lodge in Bautzen and made the following speech:

'I have borne arms for my Fatherland from youth on, and have grown up with them in my hands. I have seen Death in its most horrible form and have it daily before my eyes. I have seen cottages go up in smoke and their inhabitants rush out naked, and I could not help them. That is the way of this wicked world. The better man yearns to get away from this wild turmoil, and I bless the hour when, with brethren good and true, I can translate myself in spirit into those higher regions where a purer and brighter light shines upon us. Masonry is therefore sacred to me, and I shall remain a faithful member until my death, and every brother will always be dear to my heart.'

However, Metternich's Ambassador in Berlin made bitter complaints to his master at the beginning of the upheaval that the 'heads of the Sect' had seized the reins. And so strong was the flow of officers and volunteers to the Lodges that many of them were forced to exempt the 'applicants' from the period of probation and waiting usually prescribed.

There exists a testimony, which might be described as classical, of the idealism with which these Freemasons were inspired. This is to be found in the reminiscences of the Russian General Alex Iwanowitsch Michailowski-Danilewski, which were published by Theodor Schiemann in the *Forschungen zur brandenburgischen und preussischen Geschichte* ('Investigations into the History of Brandenburg and Prussia'), based upon the diary of this distinguished soldier.[1] The General, who had been initiated in the Russian military Lodge 'Zum heiligen Georg' in Frankfort-on-Main in November 1813, was a regular guest of the Prussian Field-Lodge 'of the Iron Cross' from December of the same year onwards.

'We had,' he wrote, 'very little pleasure during this campaign on account of incessant quarrels with our allies, who wanted to end the war with Napoleon, of whom they had a holy fear. Our chief consolation was the "Iron Cross" Lodge, which was formed in the Prussian Army in 1813. They entertained us Russian guests with the greatest hospitality. We passed there the only pleasant, or rather, happy evenings we had during the French campaign. The speeches made in the Lodge were full of ardent love of country, and when delivered the day after or on the eve of a battle, they filled our souls with the most noble resolves. It is a pity that the people who combat Freemasonry to-day and who, on hearing the news of our victories, probably confine their patriotic feelings to indulging in a dance at some festivity, cannot hear the speeches delivered in the "Iron Cross" Lodge. Every member of the Lodge constantly risks his life for his Fatherland. . . .

'. . . After Paris had been occupied and the frightful struggle had ceased; when Prussia's independence had been gained and the aim thereby achieved, the closure of the "Iron Cross" Lodge was solemnly celebrated. Many brethren were present at the festival, Field-Marshal Blücher amongst them. Once more the speeches touched me to the very heart. The Prussians described the miserable position of their Fatherland before the war and touched upon the holy fight for liberty and the benevolence of the Lodge during the struggle.

[1] See extract from the monthly magazine of the Comenius Society, vol. xxii, 7.

They called to mind how, during the thunder of battle, the members of the Lodge had encouraged one another to bear the hardships of the campaign, and how the words, which had been spoken from the very heart, so full of friendship and love of the Fatherland, had been a true comfort at moments of crisis, and how they had thus broken the fetters which had enslaved the Fatherland, whose glory was now restored. . . .'

They received very little thanks for their deeds, for when the reactionary elements came into power again after the Congress of Vienna the Freemasons were denounced as out-and-out 'Jacobites' and after the Congress of the 'Holy Alliance' (1822) in Verona, the complete suppression of the Fraternity might easily have taken place, but for the resistance offered by King Frederick William III, who declared that he could honestly describe the Freemasons as his best subjects. This was in deliberate contrast to the views of the pitiable Count Haugwitz, who served his Prussian Fatherland so badly that Treitschke thought fit to describe him as a 'disloyal negotiator', and who then entreated the Congress, in a touching memorandum, to put a stop to the workings of Freemasonry, as he was convinced that 'the drama, which began in 1788 and 1789, namely, the French Revolution and the regicide, with all its attendant horrors, had not only been planned by the rulers of the Order of Freemasons, but was the result of the common activity and of the vows taken'.

CHAPTER X

THE PROGRESSIVE PERIOD IN AUSTRIA UNDER THE EMPEROR FRANCIS JOSEPH

THE antagonism towards Freemasonry which found such vehement expression at the Congress of Verona was chiefly caused by Metternich, who, throughout his life, regarded the Revolution as the work of secret societies, and whose character was such that he could not reconcile himself to a Fraternity that dared to speak of Tolerance and Humanity. Even before Metternich came into power the spirit which impelled him had already reached the Court of Vienna, and thus it was that from 1797 Freemasonry had ceased to exist in the Austrian Dominions. Francis II did not actually forbid it in the Austrian States in that year, but he condemned it to death by means of other regulations, although it had flourished previously under Joseph II.

We have already seen, in a previous chapter, that Count Sporck had founded the 'Three Stars' Lodge in Prague and Count Hoditz the 'Three Canons' Lodge in Vienna in the reigns of Charles VI and Maria Theresa respectively.

Franz Anton, Count Sporck, one of the richest Bohemian aristocrats and son of the most famous cavalry general of the Turkish War, was a man of extraordinary stature. An appreciation of science and all works of art went hand in hand with a rare generosity and charitableness. A monastery of the Brethren of Charity, founded by him on his Kukus estate, was endowed with no less a sum than 10,000 gulden. He employed a similar amount for the ransoming of prisoners of war. The Hospital for Disabled Soldiers founded by the Emperor Charles VI was munificently endowed by him, and a book printing-works which he established in Lissa distributed countless works entirely free of charge. Sporck also founded libraries, contributed enormous sums of money for the erection of theatres, churches, monasteries, and hospitals, and summoned painters, chalcographers, and sculptors to the land. But that did not prevent the Jesuits being very hostile to him. They cast suspicion upon him at Court by suggesting that he was an opponent of the pragmatic sanctions and that, by means of his printing-works, he circulated anti-religious and revolutionary writings with the help of money from Karl Albrecht of Bavaria. These accusations were not without their effect. Sporck was thrown into prison in 1729, although he was alsolutely innocent, and was only released through the agency of Francis Stephen after an imprisonment lasting seven years.

The political conditions after the death of Charles VI, the fierce struggles between Bavaria, France, and the Imperialists, and the occupation, siege, and recapture of Prague brought about a schism in Sporck's Lodge, and in 1741 there arose three Lodges, one Austrian, one Bavarian, and one neutral. However, these united in 1743, under the Count Künigl, to form the 'Three Crowned Stars' Lodge, that is to say, in the same year as Maria Theresa caused the 'Three Canons' Lodge in Vienna to be suppressed. The developbment in the Austrian dominions then followed a course very similar to that taken in Germany. Here also Lodges of all kinds of masonic systems were formed; in Vienna the 'Three Hearts' Lodge followed the 'Three Canons' Lodge. There came into being High Chapters according to the Clermont system and offshoots of the Strict Observance and in Prague the Commandery Saint Pölten and the Prefecture Rodomsky appeared. The Imperial States were soon dotted with Lodges, each one of which followed its own particular course, according to the inclinations of its individual founders, but all of which regarded themselves as belonging to Freemasonry. There were plenty of alchemists in high favour at Court, especially with Francis I, and also many Knights Templars, who regarded the Knights who had fought for the Holy Sepulchre as their true Freemasonic prototypes. In addition, there were the Asiatic Brethren, who, according to their Constitution, were 'a fraternal union of noble-thinking, pious, learned, experienced, and discreet men, taking no account of religion, birth, or rank, whose endeavour it is to fathom secrets for the benefit of Mankind from the knowledge of all natural things, according to the methods of the Order', but who, in reality, were a Sanhedrin of the most bewildered minds and of the most confused doctrine.

Although all these by-ways were frequented, life in the Lodges still had its happy sides. There was a number of excellent masonic Lodges in Austria as well as in Hungary (where especially the Lodges of the Croatain Draskovich-Observance [1] did excellent work), in which the most progressive-minded men came together.   Thanks are due to the Freemasons for the fact that enlightenment came to Austria, followed as it was by a marked improvement in the whole system of education, and for the fact that the burden of serfdom was alleviated in Hungary, the lot of the peasants in Bohemia and Moravia improved by the restriction of statute-labour, and the administration of justice rid of many barbarities.   Gerhard van Swieten, the fearless antagonist of all forms of superstition, who was summoned to Vienna as the successor of the cele-brated physician Boerhave von Leyden, in order to become Physician-in-Ordinary to the Empress and Director of Medical Affairs, was also a Freemason.   It was through him that the University became a State institution, and he thus laid the foundations of the fame and standing which medical science at Vienna University subsequently achieved; he was also of great assistance to all other branches of education, and the clinics which he set up in Vienna, Pavia, Budapest, and other places were model institutions of their kind.   Most of the enlighteners who worked with van Swieten, or according to his principles, were exceedingly intellectual men.   There was Gebler, who brought about great improvements in the educa-tional system, who worked for the elevation of the theatre and pleaded for freedom of thought in place of the bigotry which then governed everything.   There was Martini, who instructed the Archduke Joseph in the sciences of law and politics and rendered great service to Austria by 'teaching first the laws of Nature and applying philosophical truths to mankind'. [2]   In this group one must also include Birkenstock, likewise an important educational reformer; Riegger, Professor of Canon Law, who prepared the way for the prohibition of the casting-out of devils and trials for withcraft; his colleague Eybel, the chronicler of 'things connected with Tolerance and the Church',

---

[1] So named after the first Grand Master, Johann Draskovich, a man of uncommonly humanitarian mind, a 'spendthrift of beneficence', and a 'father to all his subordinates', who incorporated in the first Constitution the following phrases: 'In the first place, however, Humanity must be recommended towards persons of lower rank. . . . We were all born alike.   Nature made no distinctions between us.   Those whose lot it is to have subordinates or servants must treat them kindly and do all to avoid aggravating the already hard fate of their class. . . .'

It must be borne in mind that at that time serfdom still existed and that the members of the Croatian Lodges were chiefly large landowners.

[2] Nicolai: *Reisebeschreibung*.

who was put under a ban by Rome on account of his liberal writings; and the book printer, Trattner, who published the *Wienerischen Gelehrten-Nachrichten* with the approval of Maria Theresa.

The most famous of these men, all of whom were Freemasons, was Joseph, Baron von Sonnenfels. Before the Town Hall of Vienna there stands a statue of this son of a small Moravian Talmudist, in the right hand of which there is a scroll which records his greatest achievement, the abolition of torture. It was the enthusiasm of this truly noble man that caused a Proclamation to be posted in all public places in Vienna on New Year's morning 1776, announcing that torture had been abolished. From that day onwards the 'Queen of Trials' ceased to be applied, and the accused were no longer dragged to the rack in order to extort a confession from them, no longer were they maimed, no longer were they tormented with red-hot tongs, nor were their feet forced into Spanish boots.

But Sonnenfels did wonderful work in other spheres. As Professor of Political Science at the University he proved himself a man of constructive leadership to the youth studying there, and he imbued them with his new ideas, which he brought to the knowledge of the public through the medium of his bold and candid periodical *Der Mann ohne Vorurteile* ('The Man Without Prejudices'). 'He stirred up all the inhabitants of Vienna', said a contemporary of this man of universal intellect who conducted a relentless campaign against superstition, prejudice, selfishness, the low level of education, and the plethora of monasteries. Merciless was his cricitism of the low level of the theatre, and he it was who brought about the thorough reorganization of the stage in Austria. How difficult a task that was can be gauged from the words of the Empress: 'These actor people are riff-raff and remain riff-raff, and Herr Hofrat von Sonnenfels could do better than write critiques'. But there were much more severe judgments. The clerical professors at the University held, as Sonnenfels wrote in a letter, 'a council of war' against him, in order to turn him out of his academic chair. 'But instead of overthrowing me, to their consternation, they saw my principles begin to take root.'

Sonnenfels belonged to the 'Perfect Union' Lodge. This was not an ordinary Lodge, but, under Joseph II, was the intellectual centre of Austrian Freemasonry, and perhaps even of Vienna itself. But as long as the Empress lived there were still occasional storms. In 1766 and 1767 prohibitions were issued which were intended to damp enthusiasm, but Free-masonry spread all the more. The Emperor himself might easily have become a Mason had not the masonic groups been so antagonistic towards one another at the beginning of his reign. He went very deeply into the question with the Danish Captain von Sudthausen, who had gone to Vienna in 1776 on private business and had, on that occasion, requested the Emperor, on behalf of the Zinnendorf Berlin National Grand Lodge, to act as patron of a Provincial Grand Lodge which it was proposed to found. The letter of the National Grand Lodge was thoroughly discussed in two long audiences. Sud-thausen explained the principles of Freemasonry to the Emperor, and Joseph seemed inclined to join the Fraternity, but changed his mind when the members[1] of the Strict Obser-vance in Prague immediately implored him, in a letter prefaced by Duke Ferdinand of Brunswick, to become their patron instead.

It is possible that his refusal may have been partly due to the fact that, in 1776, Joseph, as Emperor was still co-Regent with his mother, and still paid attention to her previous decrees. At any rate, he wrote to the Duke of Brunswick that he could not join, as this would be contrary to the laws of the land and would not please his mother. Similarly, he explained to the Prague Lodge that, officially, he ought to speak differently to his mother's subjects, but the confidence they had shown in him deserved his gratitude, and he would therefore point out to them, as fellow-men and beloved citizens, that the laws and repeated regulations against masonic assemblies were still in force; it was neither his place nor theirs to ask why. He could therefore only advise them to exercise the greatest care in all their actions for the time being, which actions, however inno-cent and righteous he might consider them to be, nevertheless ran counter to the decrees of the Empress. As far as he was

---

[1] The men who founded the St. John the Baptist Orphanage in Prague and, later, the Institute for the Deaf and Dumb. The Orphanage, which was established in 1773, under the name 'Verpflegungshaus für arme Kinder' ('Institution for Poor Children'), met with considerable approval from Maria Theresa. In a conversation on the subject with Councillor of State Kressl v. Gualtenberg, she expressed herself in such a way as to make it clear that her views on Freemasonry had not stood the test of time: 'I am convinced that the Fraternity of Freemasons is an innocent friendly society. My late husband, the Emperor, was himself a Maçon, and I am sorry I have persecuted them. That shall not occur again, and I shall endeavour to make up for what has happened in the past.' The Empress then endowed the Orphanage with the sum of 12,000 gulden for twelve orphans and presented 1,000 gulden as a contribution towards the initial expenses.

concerned, they would be left entirely in peace. They would be treated and judged solely according to their actions.

The following letter, however, was sent by Joseph II to the National Grand Lodge:

'A Danish Officer named Sudthausen handed me a letter from a body calling itself the Society of Freemasons in Berlin. Your purpose, i.e., to further Christian Virtue and to be of service to humanity, is highly commendable and is entirely in accordance with my sentiments and wishes. I cannot, however, comply with your request to grant my patronage to a Constitution which is entirely unknown to me, but I assure you that men and societies that act according to these principles need have no fear of my disfavour nor of my inquisitiveness in respect of the secret which they preserve, so long as they continue to do what is really good, and nothing that is wrong. Therefore, let as much good as possible be done in your society. I am firmly resolved to do the same outside. We shall all thereby fulfil the object of our existence.   JOSEPH'

The Provincial Grand Lodge of Austria was set up by Sudthausen. However, in 1781, in view of the Decree of the Emperor, whereby all religious and secular Orders were forbidden to give allegiance or pay sums of money to foreign rulers, it was forced to consider the question of making itself independent of Berlin and of forming a separate National Grand Lodge for Austria.

The 'Perfect Union' Lodge took a very active part in these negotiations. It had sprung from the 'Crowned Hope' Lodge, contemporaneously with which there worked in Vienna round about 1780 the 'Palm Tree', the 'Saint Joseph', and the 'Stability' Lodges. Under its second Master, Ignaz von Born, who had previously been very active as a Freemason in Prague, and was introduced to the Lodge by Angelo Soliman, the noted 'Imperial Moor', son of an African king, the Lodge attained exceedingly high standing. Von Born, a great mineralogist and geologist, had been summoned to Vienna in order to arrange and catalogue the Emperor's natural history collection. He was an outstanding personality and enjoyed an excellent reputation as a benefactor of mankind and a liberal-minded scholar. 'One of the most outstanding, active, and worthy men of imperishable memory of the time of Joseph, appreciated, distinguished, and treated as a friend by the Emperor', as it ran in the *Josephinischen Curiosa* (iv, 201). His Vienna Lodge was intended to be something similar to the 'Neuf Sœurs' Lodge in Paris, that is to say, a Masonic Society of Science, and Academy for the furtherance of Freedom of Conscience and Thought which was now openly approved of by Joseph II. Freemasonry was to be given such a form that it would become useful in the strictest and noblest sense of the word. And that really did come to pass. The first men in Science, Literature, and Art were soon numbered amongst the members of the Lodge 'Zur wahren Eintracht'. In 1784 Born was able to say: 'We are still working according to our original plan. One clever young man after another joins our circle; to secure harmony amongst the clear-thinking minds and good writers of Vienna is still our aim and the dissemination of enlightenment our work. Who can estimate the good which such an affiliation of thinkers must bring about when so many well-prepared men and youths, thirsting for the light, require but a gleam in order to find, for themselves, the way out of the dark regions of superstition and intellectual slavery. . . .'

Other great figures of the times of Joseph belonged to the Lodge besides Born and Sonnenfels; amongst them were the poets Alois Blumauer, author of the travestied *Aeneid*, Joseph Franz Ratschky, to whom we owe the words of Mozart's *Gesellenlied*, and Johann Baptist Alxinger; then there was the Custodian of the University Library of Vienna, Karl Joseph Michaeler, formerly Rector Magnificus of Innsbruck University, who, when reproached that he, a cleric, had become a Mason, in spite of the papal prohibition, replied with a clever essay entitled *Beruhigung eines Katholiken über die päpstlichen Bullen wider die Freimaurerei* ('The Tranquillising Thoughts of a Catholic concerning the Papal Bull against Freemasonry'); Georg Anton Sauter, the professor of philosophy, and Count Ayala, who made a name for himself with his composition *Über Frei—und Gleichheit des Bürgers und Menschen* ('On the Liberty and Equality of Citizen and Man'). One must also include in this list Barth, the anatomist; Hilchenbach, the Superintendent of the Reformed Districts of Austria; Ecknel the founder of scientific numismatics; Koefil, the teacher of political science; Retzer, the censor and author; Schmutzer, the Director of the Academy of Chalcography; Count Kolowrat-Krakowsky, Minister of State; [1] Prince Wenzel Paur, the

[1] Who was later denounced as a member of the Brotherhood by his own son, Stadthauptmann Hofrat Kolowrat, when, during the anti-Masonic régime of Francis II, strong suspicion was harboured against Freemasonry.

Postmaster-General; and Reinhold, the philosopher, who, as a friend of Schiller, took an interest in literature, and had to flee to Weimar because of his liberal views. He there became Wieland's son-in-law and his collaborator in the *Teutsche Merkur*, and finally gave tremendous inspiration to the students of Jena with his lectures on Kant's philosophy. In addition, there was Count Saurau, the future Minister of Finance; Stüz, the Prebendary and Curator of the Court Natural Science Collection; Watteroth, the historian;[1] Count Apponyi, founder of an important library; Georg Forster, the celebrated circumnavigator of the globe; Franz Zauner, the sculptor, creator of the monument to Leopold II and the equestrian statue of Joseph II in Vienna; Adam, the chalcographer; the Abbé Denis, the celebrated bibliographer and literary historian; Count Dietrichstein, Master of the Horse; Artaria, the publisher; Leber, Physician-in-Ordinary to the Empress Maria Theresa; and Professor Pehem, who caused tremendous feeling by his writings on the necessity of reforms in the ecclesiastical orders. It was a galaxy of great names. Scholars, university professors, priests, Knights of Maria Theresa, officers, teachers, high officials, and artists: all these went to form the register of members; not the least important of whom was Joseph Haydn, who was initiated on the 11th February 1785.

The intellectual life of the Lodge manifested itself in different ways. Blumauer propagated masonic ideas in the *Wiener Realzeitung*. Contrary to the practice prevailing elsewhere of laying stress on the secrets, it was explained in the Lodges of Instruction that there was no hidden mystery in Freemasonry. They revolted against the useless enthusiasm for secret societies and for exploring the labyrinth of mysticism, and contributed to the knowledge of true Freemasonry by means of excellent lectures. Any special knowledge was also printed and published in the *Journal für Freymaurer*, which was Sonnenfels' suggestion. This was edited by Blumauer, and contained in its twelve volumes an abundance of interesting essays, speeches, and poems. For a certain length of time another periodical, *Die physikalischen Arbeiten der einträchtigen Freunde in Wien*, was published. Whereas the *Journal* dealt with masonic affairs, the other paper was designed to serve the cultivation and propagation of the mathematical sciences. A huge library and natural history collection, which almost transformed the

---

[1] Who, for a certain length of time, was subjected to persecution on account of 'Voltairianism'.

Lodge-room into a kind of museum, formed the basis for the research work of the Fraternity.

This selfsame circle also gave birth to the suggestion of laying out a botanical garden in the park of Schloss Schönbrunn and of converting the menagerie into a Zoological Garden containing all kinds of exotic animals. Members of the Lodge first of all made an expedition to South Carolina, and then to Africa. The first of these expeditions produced an excellent yield of botanical specimens, and the second brought back from Africa nearly 300 live animals and fifty cases of minerals and geological specimens, together with ethnographical rarities.[1] This may well be cited as a proof of how the Freemasons were at that time bent on raising the standard of education and contributing to the knowledge of the world.

A very good example of how the propagation of new knowledge bore fruit also within their own circle is given by the greatest work which can be attributed to masonic influence, namely, the masonic opera of Mozart, 'The Magic Flute'. Born's lecture in the Lodge on the Egyptian mysteries, which was afterwards published in the *Journal für Freymaurer*, undoubtedly inspired this imperishable musical representation of the conflict between Light and Darkness. It cannot be said that Mozart belonged to Born's Lodge the 'Perfect Union' itself, but he became a member of the 'Benevolence' Lodge in the autumn of 1784, probably at the instigation of Baron Otto von Gemminen, and he later joined the 'New Crowned Hope' Lodge, but he was a regular guest of the brethren of the 'Union' Lodge. These latter also passed him to the degree of Fellow-Craft on the 7th January 1785, and he was present a month later at the initiation of Haydn. It is open to doubt whether the fact that this, of all years, was Mozart's 'Haydn year' can be attributed to this Lodge-friendship. The celebrated six quartets which were composed in 1785 are dedicated to the composer of the Austrian national anthem, the words of which were written by the poet Haschka, who, by the way was also a Freemason. Mozart, who was distinguished as a musician by his exceedingly fine and rich spirituality, and by his enthusiastic appreciation of natural beauty, and who possessed goodness of heart and *naïveté* of mind in such large measure, found great stimulation in the masonic circle, where earnest intellectual conversation was the order of the day. He also

[1] Abafi: *Geschichte der Freimaurerei in Österreich-Ungarn*, IV. Budapest. 1893.

introduced his father to the brotherhood. A competent judge, Bernhard Paumgartner, Director of the Salzburg Mozarteum, who was not a member of the Fraternity, wrote as follows:

'The benevolent and liberal efforts of Freemasonry, its fight against superstition and narrow-mindedness, the idealistic principles of mutual assistance and fraternal equality of rights, undoubtedly had a strong effect on Mozart's sensitive disposition. His inclination for cheerful society, the necessity which he felt for more profound conversation amongst intimates, and his mind which was open to all humanitarian ideas and which, in spite of genuine faith, was always subconsciously striving to rid itself of all that which is strictly dogmatic in matters of faith and ethics, all these things must have made him appreciate the Fraternity of Freemasonry as a revelation after the repressing narrowness of his Salzburg environment. The mysterious ceremonial of the Order and the important part played by solemn music at all their festivities and ceremonies completed the hold of Freemasonry on Mozart's artistic imagination.'

Many compositions were evolved in this masonic environment: 'Die Gesellenreise', the cantata 'Maurerfreude' (composed in honour of Born),[1] the song 'Brüder reicht die Hand zum Bunde', the 'Maurerische Trauermusik', and the 'Kleine Freimaurer-Kantate', the last work which Mozart completed and conducted. Mozart's love of Freemasonry and the earnestness with which he regarded its doctrine are demonstrated in all these works. His funeral music illustrates this best of all. It expresses what Mozart wrote to his father shortly before the the latter's death:

'As Death (strictly speaking) is the ultimate destiny of our lives, I have, in the last few years, made myself so well acquainted with this, the best friend of mankind, that his picture not only holds nothing terrifying for me, but much that is soothing and consoling, and I thank God that He has granted me the good fortune to make for myself an opportunity (you understand me) of getting to know Him as the key to our true happiness.'

[1] Born was very much in the limelight at this time owing to a scientific discovery, a new method of fusing, which earned for him the rank of Knight of the Empire, and also on account of a keen polemico-satirical writing, *Naturgeschichte der Mönche*.

What Mozart here hints at, which is the same thing as Goethe's 'Stirb und Werde', is taught by Freemasonry in the symbolism of its most beautiful degree. To the Freemason, Death is not destruction, but the dawn of Eternal Life. He leaves the narrow confines of this corporeal life in order to take up the spiritual. The brilliant light of the 'eternal East' guides him across the darkness of the grave.

'The short adagio of Mozart's funeral music, inspired with a wonderful solemnity and easy transfiguration, also sounds like a highly-personal acknowledgment of the mysteries of Death. Even the outer form of the perfectly-finished piece of music, the extremely careful choice of instruments and their exquisite technical handling, and also the peculiar setting of the solemn march round the melody of a Gregorian chant, very similar to the treatment of the sacred canto fermo in the second finale of the 'Magic Flute', give to the whole a unique, peculiar and significant place amongst the entire works of Mozart. Although composed in July 1785, that is to say, six years before the 'Magic Flute,' which was the brightest jewel in the crown of all Mozart's compositions inspired by Freemasonry, the 'Maurerische Trauermusik' ('Masonic Funeral Music') reveals features which are closely related both to this opera and to the Requiem. Here sounded, perhaps for the first time, the new, highly-personal tones, replete with sweet melancholy and tenderness, so characteristic of the last works of the master. It is very important that this should be recognized, for it is particularly in this work of a masonic nature that one perceives more clearly the early traces of a significant change of style, in the formation of which the spiritual and cultural influence of the Order played an undeniable part on Mozart's creative impulse.' [1]

Schikaneder, the librettist of the 'Magic Flute' and Giesecke, who is said to have assisted him, also belonged to the Lodge with Mozart. Their original intention was probably to write one of the much-loved 'Zauber' operas (fantastic operas), but the result of their efforts was something quite different. It was the highest expression of a passionately felt ideal of the purest love of mankind, a glorification of the humanitarian idea, the 'befriending of antagonists': an opera, the text and music of

[1] Bernhard Paumgartner: *Mozart*. Berlin. Volksverband der Bücherfreunde.

which are interwoven with masonic symbols, with allusions to the 'fashioning of the Ashlar', to the 'peregrinations' and 'trials,' and in the final chorus of which the pillars of the Temple of Humanity are seen erected: 'Es siegte die Stärke und krönet zum Lohne die Schönheit und Weisheit mit ewiger Kröne.' The characters of this opera were soon construed as follows: Tamino, a prince, 'still better, a man', who is seeking Light in the Darkness, is the Emperor Joseph; Pamina is the Austrian nation; Sarastro, the Dispenser of Light, is the spiritual head of Viennese Freemasonry, Ignaz von Born; the Queen of the Night is Maria Theresa; and Monostatos represents the clergy who stirred up a storm of passion against Freemasonry after the death of Joseph.

Egon Komorzynski,[1] who sought to discover the spiritual home of the 'Magic Flute' in his very conscientious work, considers it possible that the first sketch, which was in a lighter vein, received its depth of feeling at Born's death-bed; that is to say, from Born, who, right up to his very death, took a vivid interest in the creations of his brethren. He regards the wise Sarastro as an artistic monument which Mozart erected to the memory of the beloved Master—a monument of Love in its most beautiful and sublime form, a love which, free from all self-interest, does good by sheer force of example and seeks to encompass fraternally, and make happy, the whole of mankind, whether friend or foe.

However, when the 'Magic Flute' was produced in public for the first time Austrian Freemasonry was no longer what it had been ten years previously. The luxuriant growth of all kinds of systems had, it is true, caused Joseph II[2] to place Freemasonry under his own personal protection in 1785, but, at the same time, to restrict the number of Lodges. The number of Lodges in Vienna was restricted by an edict to two, or, at the most, three; the same applying to the provinces. In return for this the Government agreed to grant full recognition, protection and freedom to Freemasonry in all places; never to force their way into the interior of the Lodge or interfere with the Constitution, which was still entirely left to them, and to refrain from any form of inquisitive examination or investigation. 'In this way, the society of Freemasons consisting as it does of many individuals personally

---

[1] 'Der neueste Stand der Zauberflötenfrage' in the *Alt-Wiener Kalender,* 1926. Amalthea-Verlag. Vienna.
[2] At Born's suggestion.

known to me as honest men, can become useful to the State.'

In accordance with this decision the six Lodges of Vienna were reduced in 1785 to two: the 'Truth' and the 'New Crowned Hope'. Two other Lodges, the 'Saint Joseph' and the 'Stability' were dissolved. Born was placed at the head of the 'Truth' Lodge. That such a highly esteemed and celebrated scholar should publicly associate himself with Freemasonry in such an emphatic manner, at the time of the Bavarian persecutions of the Illuminati, caused a great deal of excitement in scientific circles. He made this public avowal when, as a protest against these oppressions, which—as the Decree of the Elector says—were also directed against 'the infamous Masonic Craft', he returned his diploma of Fellow of the Electoral Academy of Science and Scholars' Society in Burghausen, accompanied by a letter in which he declared that he regarded the fact that he was a Freemason as redounding to his credit. And when his request for cancellation was not acceded to he repeated his desire in an angry letter to Chancellor Freiherr von Kreitmayr, the President of the 'Court of Inquisition in respect of Free-masonry'. In this letter he said, *inter alia*:

'. . . I do not think I am adopting the wrong course when I turn to you with the request that you will instruct the Electoral Academy to comply at once with my wishes. In your praiseworthy zeal for the welfare and honour of your Fatherland, Your Excellency has found ways and means to remove from Munich and Bavaria several of your country's most sensible and enlightened men, and to deprive others of office and living, all on account of Freemasonry. How could you possibly object to rendering this same service to a stranger, especially as I frankly confess that I do not regret that I am a Freemason? To this confession, which is perhaps somewhat offensive to your ears and to those of the Right Reverend P. Frank, I would like to add, with that frankness peculiar to me, that I regard Zaupser's poems concerning the Inquisition as the most beautiful products of Bavarian intellect; that I read . . . all good books; that I am an open enemy of ignorant monks . . . to whom the education of youth should not be exclusively entrusted; that I consider Jesuitism and fanaticism as synonymous with perfidy, ignorance, superstition, and foolishness; in short, my way of thinking is the very antithesis of what is desired in Bavaria.'

The death of Joseph II, shortly followed by that of his successor Leopold II, ushered in bad times for Freemasonry. It is true that there arose, under the latter, a new Lodge 'Love and Truth', which, of Rosicrucian nature, met with the approval of the Emperor, and that the Lodge 'Saint Joseph' was revived. But lethargy came with the reign of Francis II. The false allegation of a masonic conspiracy which led to the French Revolution was also circulated at the Court of Vienna by the enemies of the Fraternity, who were now encouraged by new hopes, and the monarch believed them blindly. This conviction came from his very soul. From the day of his coronation onwards he lived in fear of the 'machinations of secret societies' and, particularly, of the Freemasons.. Immediately after the death of his father he ransacked all the chests and tables in search of insidious writings relating to Freemasonry and similar things, and, locking them in huge portfolios, took them into his safe keeping. Even the secret trial in connexion with an alleged Jacobin conspiracy, which to this very day has not been entirely cleared up, and in which, amongst hundreds of other accused persons, a few Freemasons were involved, was regarded as evidence of their 'dangerousness.' It was therefore not by accident that, in the year 1795, the 'Magic Flute' was also stigmatized in the *Geheime Geschichte des Verschwörungsystems der Jakobiner in den österreichischen Staaten* ('Secret History of the System of Conspiracy of the Jacobins in the Austrian States'), published on behalf of the Government, as it was regarded as an allegorical glorification of the French Revolution.

In the following year a still more violent attack was made on masonic endeavours. There appeared in 1796 a memorandum entitled *Die zwei Schwestern P. . . . (Paris) und W. . . . (Wien) oder neuentdecktes Freimaurer- und Revolutions-System . . .*' ('The Two Sisters Paris and Vienna, or a Newly-discovered Masonic and Revolutionary System . . .'), the authorship of which was attributed to the notorious informer, Professor Leopold Alois Hoffman, whose endeavours had, for years, been directed towards persuading the Emperor to take energetic action against the brethren of the Lodges.[1]

We live in 'evil times,' he wrote, 'in which one hears so

---

[1] In the description of these events we follow the statements of Professor Viktor Bibl, a Viennese historian, who, founding his assertions on material of extraordinary interest, explains them for the first time in his excellent work entitled *Der Zerfall Österreichs*. Vienna. Rikola. 1922.

much of regicides either attempted or actually committed.' Freemasons were united throughout the world and were therefore extremely dangerous to the State; their building of the Temple consisted of nothing but 'pretended mysteries', and referred to nothing less than the destruction of all religions and of all great personages. Their benevolence was only a swindle; merely a cloak for activities dangerous to the State. It was clear from the principles of the 'Perfect Union' Lodge, that Vienna was 'the true sister' of revolutionary Paris, and therefore it was possible that the overthrow of the State Constitution and the murder of the king might indeed become fact. The preliminary work seemed to have been done already. The sudden death of Emperor Leopold II proved, he alleged, that he had been disposed of by assassins.

Other books contained similar statements. They were eagerly devoured by the Emperor and placed by him in his collection of books, which is to-day the Fideikommiss Library in Vienna. Every kind of brochure, police report, or pamphlet against Freemasonry that it was possible to lay hands on were assembled there, and, especially, all that was written in the *Wiener Zeitschrift* and in various books by Professor Hoffmann. The majority of these books were published anonymously, the most widely circulated being the *Briefe eines Biedermannes an einen Biedermann über die Freymaurer in Wien*. ('Letters from one Honourable Gentleman to Another Regarding the Freemasons in Vienna'). He was a typical renegade, of whom Leopold II once said: 'Der Kerl ist ein Esel, ich weiss es, aber er leistet mir als Spion sehr gute Dienste' ('The fellow is an ass, I know, but he renders me good service as a spy').

The feeling against the Lodges became so antagonistic that they were forced voluntarily to suspend their activities, fearing that it might become worse. However, for the time being, they were not formally suppressed by the Government. It was in 1797 that a proposal was first put before the Emperor to forbid all secret societies and to warn all officials not to join them. This proposal met with the approval of the Emperor, but with the proviso that 'they should not proceed too harshly, but with becoming moderation, since, otherwise, more harm than good might be done in the matter'.

The procedure 'with becoming moderation' consisted of the police commissioners being instructed to have the Freemasons spied upon and to report fully on their doings. After the Peace of Lunéville more severe measures were enforced, and officials were strictly forbidden to belong to secret societies. The servants of the State had to confirm this obligation by means of a sworn undertaking, which, in the beginning, had to be renewed every year.

The Emperor's fears afterwards led to an increasingly absurd system of espionage. Police spies were especially active in Prague, as they feared that Bohemia might also be attacked by the 'contamination of enlightened ideas' from the adjacent Dresden and Leipzig, which were the home of the book trade. Secret police officials, as, for instance, Police Commissioner Preissler, received the 'imperial command' to apply for admission as initiates, either in Dresden or in another German town, and to report to the Emperor after they had been admitted. These reports of the *faux-frères*, as this select company of spies was popularly named, contained the most absurd nonsense, as has been discovered by the Vienna Hofrat, Ludwig Brügel, from various documents in the State Archives of the Ministries of the Interior and Justice in Vienna. The most important duty of these 'police brethren' was to deliver up to the competent authority a list of the members of the Lodges, in order that steps might be taken against these Austrian 'conspirators'.

Although the majority of the reports stated that there was no question of 'ramifications' existing between German and other Freemasons, that the former followed tendencies entirely different from those followed by the French Masons, for instance, and were 'quite harmless' as far as Austria was concerned, this system of espionage continued for a period of thirty years. The Chancellery of the Cabinet of Vienna was inundated with confidants and informers bringing disclosures and information, and there was even an official who specialized in this subject, a retired Government clerk named Feldhofer, who, during a period of fully twenty years, concocted all kinds of fantastic fairy-tales for the Emperor. These tales were all on the same lines. For instance, he would report that 'the mysterious Jacobins have aimed at dethroning the Monarch and at skinning him alive'. With malicious persistence he appeared in the Chancellery of the Cabinet whenever a crisis occurred in the imperial family, in order to state that the secret Vehmic tribunals had once more had a finger in the pie. If he happened to be refused an audience of the monarch—such refusals were always conveyed to him with expressions of great appreciation —he immediately accused the persons attending the Emperor of implication in masonic affairs. He excluded neither the worthy Cabinet Minister Colloredo nor Count Wrbna, the Lord High Chamberlain. However, one day when doubts regarding his 'authority' arose in the mind of the Emperor, von Haan, the Lord Chief Justice of Lower Austria, received orders to investigate the matter and to report whether Feldhofer's denunciations were true or false. When von Haan reported on the result of his investigations, he declared that Feldhofer's statements were 'delusions and absurd imaginings', and closed his report with an appeal to the dignity of the Emperor to rid himself of Feldhofer. But Francis still had great faith in this tale-bearer and Feldhofer continued to make his reports for another ten years. Whenever a book well-disposed towards Freemasonry fell into the hands of the Emperor, he immediately dispatched the dangerous piece of literature to the censor, who naturally decided on its suppression. The Emperor even went so far as to instruct his spies to ascertain whether it would be possible to foment the quarrels already existing in German Freemasonry, in order thus to give the Craft the *coup de grâce*. One of the informers was so enthusiastic about this idea that, on the 30th September 1821, he wrote to Count Sedlnitzky, President of the Court Police Department, as follows:

'If this weapon of the promotion of quarrels is vigorously employed there will be a possibility that those States in which Freemasonry has prevailed up to now, may finally rid themselves of it, or so restrict it that it will never again become troublesome. . . . Until Freemasonry is suppressed and the Protestant Universities are restricted and placed within the bounds of strict scientific methods, and until the loathsome, heartless, and sober Protestantism is incorporated in, or brought nearer to, Catholicism, by means of the elevating forms, there will be neither lasting quiet nor true contentment amongst men. . . .'

In such circumstances it was impossible to contemplate a continuance of masonic life. Only now and again was it able to make a timid movement. During the Napoleonic occupations of 1805 and 1809 meetings of French Field Lodges were held in Vienna, and in 1810 a Lodge, 'The Three Blue Heavens', arose for a short time in the suburb of Hernals, but in 1812 a Lodge in the vicinity of the Town Hall was suppressed by the police. At the time of the Congress of Vienna, first the

Prussian, then the French, and finally the Italian Freemasons attempted to revive the Royal Art. But they were always merely short-lived attempts which had no lasting success. It was not until 1841, after the death of Francis II, that a more vigorous effort for a revival was made. But Metternich dealt quickly and effectively with this Lodge, which met in the Dorotheergasse. All the officials who had joined it were transferred to the provinces as a punishment and many foreign members were deported.

The 'Saint Joseph' Lodge, reopened by Professor Dr. Ludwig Lewis in the days of the Revolution in 1848, did not last much longer. The Berlin National Grand Lodge had renewed the Warrant after permission to hold Lodge meetings had been granted by the Minister, Doblhoff, and a solemn installation took place,[1] for which purpose the brethren assembled on the 5th October in the house of Count d'Harnoucourt in the Teinfaltstrasse. That, however, was the only meeting. When Vienna was declared in a state of siege, Lewis could receive no further authorization, and twenty years passed by before regular masonic activity could once more take place.

[1] By the Provincial Lodge of Silesia.

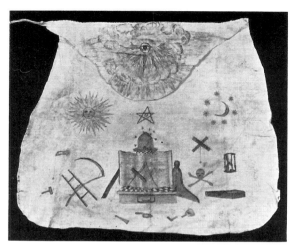

EARLY ENGLISH LAMBSKIN APRON, HAND-PAINTED

VERY EARLY EIGHTEENTH-CENTURY LAMBSKIN APRON,
HAND-PAINTED

SCOTTISH APRON

LATE EIGHTEENTH CENTURY

FRENCH APRON

CHAPTER XI

ITALY

THE history of Italian Freemasonry begins about the year 1733, and it is one of the few branches of Freemasonry that have come to an abrupt stop for the time being. Even its very beginning was attended by a terrible case of persecution: the trial by the Inquisition of the Florentine poet Tomasco Crudeli.

The masonic idea was first propagated by Lord Sackville amongst the Englishmen who, at that time, visited the academies of Florence. Lord Sackville is supposed to have founded a Lodge, at the head of which stood 'Monsiù Fox', probably Henry Fox, later Lord Holland, George III's Secretary of State and father of the statesman Charles James Fox, the great rival of Pitt. From the beginning, the Englishmen joined together with Italian friends, chiefly learned scholars of the Accademia del Cimento and the Accademia Botanica. For a time they worked in peace and harmony, but a few years sufficed to usher in the period of the edicts against Freemasonry. A Lodge at Leghorn, in which Catholics, Protestants, and Jews had found it possible to work together in harmony, aroused the pious rage of Rome. It was declared that such harmony amongst several confessions of faith could have no good result. Here surely must unbelief prosper. The threat of excommunication was designed to avoid this evil, but the Freemasons were not to be intimidated, and, in spite of all the decrees, Lodges were soon founded in Milan, Verona, Padua, and Venice; there was also a Jacobite Lodge in Rome.

They were not intimidated by the execrations of Paolo Ambrogio Ambrogi, the Inquisitor of 'Heretical Depravity', nor by the denunciation of the Resident Minister of Lucca, who said: 'The Freemasons are accused of having no faith, of not observing Friday as a day of fast and of declaring openly that no cultured person should have prejudices, and that only idiots can believe blindly.' Nor were they upset when the poet Goldoni asserted in his oft-played comedy 'Donne Curiose', in which a Lodge is represented, that the Freemasons hated light.

The higher clergy, however, would not be quietened. A painful trial should put the atheists in their proper place. An opportunity soon presented itself. A member of the Lodge in Florence, the Abbot Octaviano Bonaccorsi, was in the habit of relating to his friend Bernardino Puppiliani, with great enthusiasm, interesting things about the work in the Lodge; how they discussed theological and philosophical questions, the movement of the earth, the immortality of the soul. But Puppiliani repaid him very badly for this confidence. When he went to the confessional during the Easter of 1739 he confessed to Father Guadagna, his confessor, that he knew something of the masonic secrets. They had been waiting a long time for such a 'material witness'. Puppiliani was forced to make another confession; this time to the Inquisitor's Vicar, the Jesuit Benoffi. Amongst the names mentioned to him by Puppiliani was that of Crudelli, who was already under the suspicion of not taking his religion too seriously, and who had been accused of heresy by another informer. The agonies of torture which Crudelli was made to suffer undermined his health and, although he was soon released through the influential intervention of Duke Francis Stephen, he died of hæmorrhage of the lungs in 1745, at the early age of forty-three.

A period of very irregular development then followed. An advance in many cities was offset by the decline brought about by the measures taken against Freemasonry. The Royal Art reached its highest state of perfection in Naples. Intellect and culture competed with each other in the Lodges. No restrictions were put upon their activities by Charles VII, and even very small towns had their 'loggia'. There were Lodges in Capua, Messina, and Gaeta, and masonic *canzonette* were sung that sounded like Neapolitan folk songs:

> Su fratelli, allegramente
> Qui passiam tranquille l'ore
> Nel felice ozio innocente
> Di un' amica società.
> Regna ognor nel nostro core
> Amicizia e fedeltà.

And even in the schools the children recited a naïve masonic epic poem of the Abbate Antonio Jerocades entitled 'Paolo o dell' Umanità liberata' which described the ritual actions in the form of prophecies and introduced St. Paul as a philosopher

ITALIAN VIGNETTE

FRONTISPIECE TO 'DICHIARAZIONE DELL' ISTITUTO, E SCOPO DE'
LIBERI MURATORI', 1749

who had received the masonic Light and who, in Heaven, had recognized St. Peter as a Brother:

> . . . o dì beato e caro
> Quando l'amico, al segno a lui sol noto
> Riconosce l'amico al volto ignoto.

But this singing soon came to an end. Hatred and slander made their appearance here also. A violent offensive against Freemasons started in the time of Ferdinand IV. The King and his minister Tanucci were very antagonistic to them. At the festival of St. Januarius in 1776, when the people were awaiting the miracle of the blood and this refused to liquefy, as it was expected to do, hired women ran through the streets shrieking that the saint had refused to perform the miracle because the city was contaminated by the masonic pest. It was only with the greatest difficulty that the incensed multitude was restrained from indulging in violence against the Freemasons. Ferdinand, however, now had a 'reason' for intervening. A large number of brethren were thrown into jail. Jerocades amongst them.

These brethren received unexpected help from Ferdinand's wife, Queen Caroline, daughter of the Emperor Francis I. She was extraordinarily interested in Freemasonry, whose head, at that time, was Prince Di Caramanica. She therefore caused the edict of Count Tanucci to be rescinded, cut the ground from under his feet, and would willingly have seen the King become a Freemason. However, this weakling would not join for a very remarkable reason. He was afraid of the trial during the initiation ceremony, concerning which someone had told him that the courage of the candidates was put to a severe test. In a letter to the Pope he complained about his spouse:

> 'Freemasonry is patronized by my wife, who wants to rule in all matters of importance.'

However, the Queen's favour suddenly disappeared when the French Revolution demanded the head of her hapless sister, Marie Antoinette. A hatred of all Liberal thought took possession of her, followed by a strong antipathy to the Lodges. . . .

When Napoleon made his entry into Italy the military Lodges appeared with him, and, shortly after, two Grand Masters, Prince Eugene Beauharnais, who, in Milan, became the head of the Freemasons combined in a Grand Orient, and

Joachim Murat, who became at the same time King of Naples and Grand Master of the Order there. At that time there were already a goodly number of Freemasons in Milan. In Austrian times the Lodge 'De la Concorde' (1785–1787) had united the Visconti, Trivulzio, Beccaria, and Castelbarco with the heads of the Viennese bureaucracy, the Wilczeks and Künigls and others. During the Napoleonic rule Italian Freemasonry became exactly similar to its French sister. Marshals, Knights of the Legion of Honour, Senators, and Deputies dominated the Lodges. At about this time a peculiar movement began to stir, especially in Southern Italy. Secret sects with Radical political tendencies sprang up all over the country. The most Radical amongst them was the Carbonari, the charcoal-burners, whose usage was in many respects, very similar to that of Freemasonry, and who, in isolated cases, probably regarded the Lodges as the most suitable place for their own purposes. Instead of meeting in 'Lodges', the charcoal-burners assembled in 'huts', in which the 'good cousins', as the members were called, were charged with the most holy duty of fighting against tyranny, or, as the Carbonari expressed it in their symbolic language, 'hunting the wolves in the forest'.

It is because of this similarity that it is often asserted that the Carbonari were identical with the Freemasons; but that is not the case. The identity of Freemasonry with the politically active Italian secret societies has never been established.[1] Even the accusers themselves have withdrawn this assertion. Whereas Pius VII, in his Bull of the 13th August 1814, still declared that the 'Carboneria' was a new name for Freemasonry, it was described in the Bull 'Ecclesiam' of September 1821 as 'perhaps an offshoot or certainly an imitation of Freemasonry.' Some Freemasons, of course, did belong to this movement for liberty, which must not be regarded in the same light as the Mafia, or Camorra; for instance, there was the great Italian patriot Mazzini, who founded 'Young Italy' and dreamed of a third Rome. For at that time Freemasonry had in its fold 'the first intellects, the most fiery hearts, the proudest men of will and the boldest characters.'[2] But the difference between Freemasonry and Carboneria became quite clear. Whereas Freemasonry served an abstract idea, Carbonarism represented

[1] This is corroborated by an antagonist of Freemasonry. Alessandro Luzio, in *La Massoneria e il Risorgimento italiano*. Bologna. Zanichelli. 1922.
[2] Michael Bakunin : Entire Works, vol. ii. Berlin. 1923.

the definite will to revolutionary action. Attempts have been made to gloss this over by asserting that the Carbonari were really a 'lower department' of the society, a kind of national Masonry which translated idea into deed, the abstract into a concrete plan, and the discussion of principles into their employment in public life. This, however, is not viewing it in its correct perspective. Had the Freemasons really wished to play an active part they would not have found it necessary to go the roundabout way of setting up a new foundation with strange and complicated rituals.

However, Italian Freemasonry had one thing in common with the Carboneria: both—later only the Lodges—were, to a large extent, instrumental in inculcating in the the population of the Italian States the feeling of national unity and freedom, and the idea of a greater Italy. If we look at a list of the men who contributed to this rebuilding, we shall find the names repeated in the registers of the Italian Lodges. This is borne out by the following extract from one of Buscalioni's works: [1]

'The Expedition[2] of a thousand volunteers was inspired by Br. Mazzini and elaborated by the brethren Crispi, Bertani, and Lafarina. They travelled in two ships which the Freemason Fauché had placed at their disposal. Bros. Lafarina and C. M. Buscalioni provided the money. Garibaldi, the Commander-in-Chief, Bixio, his lieutenant, and also the officers and volunteers were nearly all Freemasons. They were secretly supported by Br. Cavour. . . . This heroic expedition, which has no parallel in history, represents one of the most glorious pages of Italian Freemasonry.'

In this connexion, a member of the clergy, Fra Giovanni, should be mentioned. He was a Lecturer in Philosophy at a Franciscan monastery and placed himself at Garibaldi's disposal as chaplain to the expedition. After the successful campaigns of his hero he applied for admission into the Lodge 'Fede Italica'. In his application for admission he wrote: 'Profession: Priest. Adherent of the universal priesthood of the Freedom of Nations.'[3]

[1] 'La R. . . . M. . . . L.: *Ausonia e la Spedizione de 'Mille'*. Turin. 1915.
[2] The heroic expedition of Garibaldi and his supporters to Marsala, where they landed on the 11th May 1860 in order to gain control of the island in the name of Victor Emanuel.
[3] Giuseppe Leti: *Carboneria e Massoneria nel Risorgimento*. Genoa. 1925.

After the capture of Palermo, Garibaldi himself became the ruler of Masonry.[1] One evening he took the whole of his General Staff with him to the Lodge in order to introduce these officers to the Fraternity, of which he said enthusiastically: 'Freemasonry will take mankind forward. The constant application of its holy principles must lead to a fraternal alliance of all nations.' On another occasion he wrote in a letter dated the 18th May 1867:

'The Freemasons are a chosen part of the Italian nation. They rise above profane everyday emotions and thus, imbued with the wonderful mission which the great masonic institution has placed in their hands, they will found the ethical unity of the nations.'

And also in a further letter:

'That Freemasonry represents the incarnation of everything that is honourable and noble, and yearns for the elevation of mankind—is that not a task worthy of the greatest of the communities serving humanity?'

Similar observations were also made by Mazzini, who, in numerous letters to the Grand Lodge in Palermo and the Lodges 'Lincoln', 'Stella d'Italia', and 'Ragione' expressed his enthusiasm for the masonic cause, in whose activities he perceived the most beautiful form of expression of the ardent love of liberty inspiring his endeavours.

At Mazzini's funeral on the 17th March 1872, Rome saw masonic banners in its streets for the first time. The members of the Grand Orient of Italy, which, after the capture of Rome, had been transferred from Florence to the capital, made their way in solemn procession from the Piazza del Popolo to the burial-ground.

To the above-mentioned names of those who adopted this gospel of the unity of Italy and the union of nations, many others may be added. There was Giovanni Bovio, the philosopher and brilliant orator; Aurelio Saffi, the Roman triumvir; Giosuè Carducci, the poet; Joseph Mazzoni, one of the Tuscan triumvirs of 1848; and Ettore Ferrari, the sculptor, who created the Rome memorial to Giordano Bruno, the martyr of Free Thought; they were all active Masons.

---

[1] He was elected Grand Master, *ad vitam*, of the Masonry which had arisen from the fusion of several systems.

The democratic spirit which inspired these men was the spirit of Italian Freemasonry until the day when Fascism brought an end to its activities. Freedom of conscience in each and every respect, and a democratic State, were the demands which were constantly being made with the utmost emphasis. The Grand Orient of Italy, which was the supreme authority in masonic affairs, even though other masonic groups existed at the same time, was a centre of the most progressive thought under the Grand Masters Mazzini, Petroni, Frapolli, Adriano Lemmi,[1] Ernesto Nathan,[2] Ferrari, and Torrigiani. The fact that this progressive thought expressed itself with marked determination in an anti-clerical sense and often appealed to the Italian nation by means of speeches, placards, and other means, always earned for the Grand Orient the reproach of indulging in political activity, but, in view of the circumstances, it is not at all surprising that this was done. It was repeatedly explained that 'although ours is a patriotic society, it is non-political'.

'We Italian Freemasons are not anti-Catholic, for we respect every religious conviction, and nothing is more false than to say that we are the antagonists of religion. For if it were true, how could we incorporate men of each and every faith in our chain; men from whom we demand but one thing: that they shall respect the eternal law of progress. Never have we attacked a religion, but we are the sworn enemies of the clerical parties, that is to say, those parties that make use of religion in order to throw Italy into bondage once more. We are the enemies of all who wish to subject religion to exclusive interests, but we have, as ever, no prejudices as to any form of religious conviction. We are neither the instigators of certain political schools of thought, nor are we the advocates of certain political groups. Our political conceptions have nothing to do with those schools that tie the intellect to doctrine nor with those groups that fight for power. We are always, and above all, Italians.

---

[1] This exceedingly active Freemason, who was known as the 'Banker of the Revolution', was a particularly ardent advocate of unrestricted freedom of thought and action. The unveiling of the Giordano Bruno Monument on the Campo di Fiori took place during his term of office, as also did a mighty masonic procession to the grave of King Victor Emanuel, and this, in view of the Bull 'Humanum genus', which had been issued shortly before, was of great significance.

[2] Subsequently Burgomaster of Rome.

In serving our Fatherland with all devotion we believe we are serving the whole of Humanity.'[1]

In a word: the Grand Orient—which every year on the 20th September celebrated the anniversary of the liberation of Rome by Garibaldi—regarded itself as the school of freedom, tolerance, and public education, and as the preserver, entirely free from party influence, of the best liberal traditions.

This was not merely its own opinion; the same view was held in wide Italian circles and was often expressed in official quarters.

[1] From a Speech of the Grand Master Ernesto Nathan, the basic principles of which recur in all the public statements of the Grand Orient.

CHAPTER XII

RUSSIA

THE keen anti-masonic feeling which found expression at the Congress of Verona made a strong impression on one of the monarchs present; the author of the Holy Alliance, Alexander I of Russia. After ascending the throne in 1802, he had proved himself to be a very liberal-minded ruler. He had carried out very important reforms in the sphere of education, he had prohibited corporal punishment, and had done away with the 'secret expeditions,' that fearful proceeding by which persons in ill favour were thrown under suspicion without the slightest evidence, and subjected to barbarous tortures, and sent to the dungeons or to Siberia. According to many statements he had himself become a Freemason. Twenty years later, however, he was the most embittered antagonist of the cause of freedom. He was a sick man, shy and retiring, a 'recluse upon the highest throne in the world', whilst his mind was clouded by a hazy mysticism. Immediately upon his return from Verona in 1822 he issued an edict prohibiting Freemasonry as being bound up with 'philosophical sophistry and its attendant sorrowful results', after the Fraternity had experienced a very changeful fate during the ninety years of its existence on Russian soil.

It has often been written that Freemasonry was first brought to Russia by Peter the Great, whom Sir Christopher Wren had initiated in a London Lodge. That, however, is hardly in accordance with the facts, but it would be correct to say that the first Freemasons in Russia were foreigners, who, attracted by the liberal economic policy of the Czar, came to Peter's new capital. In 1731, Captain John Phillips was appointed Provincial Grand Master for Russia by the Grand Lodge of England. In 1740 the same dignity was conferred upon James Keith (a cousin of the English Grand Master John Keith, Earl of Kintore) who was then serving in the Russian Army, and who later became a Prussian field-marshal. This Scottish nobleman was one of the most remarkable personalities of his time. 'A hero whose knightly and human qualities presented a high ideal and example for imitation and attainment.' A follower of the Stuarts, he had been forced to go into exile and had been recommended by Phillip V to the Russian Court. No further particulars exist concerning the Lodge founded by him in his new environment. It is known, however, that, together with English mariners and merchants, a large number of Russian aristocrats were members. In any case, it would probably not have achieved widespread activity in those days, when the Empress Anna, who was ill-disposed to all spiritual things, was upon the throne. Only Lorenz Natter can be described as the real propagator of the masonic cause. He was a celebrated chalcographer and lapidary to the Royal Houses of Europe and was of Swabian birth. He went to St. Petersburg from Florence, where he had been an intimate friend of Lord Sackville, the supposed founder of the first Italian Lodge. According to Boris Telepnef,[1] there is reason to believe that Czar Peter III was a Mason.

The many different systems which were flourishing in Germany at that time then made their entry into Russia. An important part was played by the masonic Rosicrucian organization, which had at its head Professor Johann Eugen Schwarz of Moscow and the eminent author Nicolas Novikov, the founder of Russian journalism,[2] two enlightened men who not only did much for Masonry, but also had a strong influence on the whole of Russian intellectual life. Schwarz, Professor of the German Language and Philosophy, and Chief of the St. Petersburg Pedagogic Institute of the University, founded elementary schools and training colleges for teachers, published text-books, and built hospitals. Novikov likewise considered that the object of his masonic system was to fight against illiteracy and to raise the population from their dreadfully low level. He published scientific and religious pamphlets in huge, popular editions by means of a printing-works founded and directed by himself. A magnificent lending library was at the disposal of all classes of the community. His friends made generous contributions for the education of poor children who showed promise. Novikov completed in grand style what Schwarz, who died at an early age, had begun. New elementary schools and hospitals were built and a society was formed with the object of supplying bread and provisions to the inhabitants of vast districts when they were threatened

[1] *An Outline of the History of Russian Freemasonry.*
[2] Ernst Friedrichs: *Geschichte der einstigen Maurerei in Russland.* Berlin. Mittler. 1904.

with starvation owing to the failure of the crops, a thing which occurs so frequently in Russia. When one considers the times, one realizes what an immense undertaking this was.

However, as time went on, Novikov's efforts to bring light into the Russian darkness met with violent opposition. The fanatics of 'intolerance', or the 'true believers', who rose up against the Freemasons in all countries, did the same thing in Russia also. Novikov was accused of disseminating false doctrine amongst the population, and was imprisoned in the fortress of Schlüsselburg for four years. His enemies had succeeded in influencing the Empress Catherine against this man of fiery spirit, whom she herself had been instrumental in diverting from the career of an officer into the service of the Chancellery. This was the same Catherine who, at the beginning of her reign, had not been able to do enough to stress her enthusiasm for the writings of the French Encyclopædists.

The Empress, who carried on so lively a correspondence with Voltaire and was so enthusiastic about the pedagogic principles of Rousseau, was, fundamentally, no enemy of the Fraternity and, at first, permitted it to spread over the whole of her dominions. In order to give an idea of how the society worked at that time, in spite of all the confusion of systems, we may well quote the following from one of the best-known literary histories:

'Masonry produced many enlightened and noble personalities, who proved themselves highly useful workers in the various branches of the Russian State.'

In 1776, the two systems that had previously rivalled one another—the English and the Swedish systems—were united. The latter had been chiefly promoted by Reichell, the Director of Science of the National Cadet Corps of Nobles, whilst at the head of the English Provincial Grand Lodge was the Senator and Privy Councillor, Johann Elagin, who became the leader of the new Provincial Grand Lodge, which soon styled itself the 'National Grand Lodge'. In this and other obediences that remained independent, aristocrats such as Count Roman Voretzov, one of Catherine's favourites; Lieutenant-General Melissino, founder of an original masonic system; Baron Ungern-Sternberg; the Princes Alexander and Nicholas Trubetzkoy; Gagarin; Dolgoruky; Galitzin; Netvitzki, and others were the leaders.

Although many of Novikov's companions concentrated chiefly upon making their own system supreme, they did wonderful work in Moscow. The Prussian Hofrat Fischer, publisher of *Eleusinien des* 19 *Jahrhunderts*, relates the following in an essay on Masonry during the reign of the Empress Catherine II:

'A number of rich brethren, imbued with the idea of serving humanity, had formed themselves into a great institution with a multiplicity of objects. First of all, they purchased handsome palaces with gardens adjoining, which they dedicated to their institutions. The first idea was to erect an Educational Institute, but this did not materialize as they were afraid that they would be classed with the Jesuits, or that their intentions would be misinterpreted. They thereupon procured a licence for a Dispensary, which they furnished in the most perfect and up-to-date manner. The medicine was sometimes provided at a small charge and sometimes entirely free. When there was a famine they purchased large quantities of cereals from afar and then either sold this foodstuff at low prices or gave it to the poor. . . . In addition to this they worked for the furtherance of enlightenment, and this, their most important business, they carried on on a magnificent scale. Two brethren of this society, Major Kutozov, a Russian, and Baron von Schröder, a native of Mecklenburg, were constantly on journeys, especially in Germany, in order to report upon all notable, useful and appropriate innovations for the common good and, especially, to collect and send in the latest and best works for translation into Russian. The translation of foreign writings that furthered the cause of enlightenment was the chief object of the society, and they pursued it according to the measure of their own degree of culture. As they owed their own enlightenment to the celebrated authors of France and England, they gave preference to these in the form of translations, as the chief means of furthering enlightenment amongst their own countrymen. Their choice therefore fell chiefly on Voltaire, Rousseau, Montesquieu, Hume and the like. Some learned scholars lived in the Institute itself as translators and correctors but they also made use of several of the professors attached to the Universities of St. Petersburg, Moscow, and Kieff. As the persons supporting the enterprise were content with a low rate of interest on their capital, they were able to print colossal editions and sell the books at the price of ordinary prayer-books. The printing-works consisted of some thirty presses.'

But an end was soon put to these activities; when the Institute, the greatest of its kind ever undertaken by Free-masons, had grown only to about half the size the founders hoped it would reach, both it and they were overtaken by sudden disaster. The widespread operations of the Moscow nobility aroused the jealousy of the Court nobility in St. Petersburg; they therefore declared that the dissemination of enlightenment was dangerous to the State, and maintained that the Freemasons of Moscow had hoarded up in their cellars a store of weapons for the equipment of an army. The Chief of the Moscow Police received the order to surround the whole of the Institute with a guard, to seal everything, and make a thorough search for arms. Of course, they found nothing there, but the Institute was suppressed notwith-standing this, and some of its chief members were exiled to Siberia, whence they were only allowed to return under Paul I.

Kutozov's fortune was confiscated, but he managed to escape banishment because he happened to be in Berlin at the time of the raid. Novikov, however, was thrown into a dungeon in the fortress of Schlüsselburg.

But Catherine was influenced against Freemasonry by an entirely different cause, namely, by the fact that Cagliostro had then just founded one of his Egyptian Lodges in Mitau and had cast a powerful spell over Count Friedrich von Medem and his poetess daughter, Countess Elisa von der Recke, who was friendly with Goethe, Gottfried August Bürger and the two Counts Stollberg. Nevertheless, this clever authoress dis-covered the swindle and warned the Empress when Cagliostro made his way to St. Petersburg. And thus it came about that, during the course of a séance, he was exposed as a swindler. This caused Catherine to write three satirical comedies: 'The Siberian Magician', "The Deceiver', and 'Deluded', in which she applied the swindles of Cagliostro and other deceivers to the whole of Freemasonry.

Then, after the French Revolution, when the accusations of the Abbé Barruel also found their way to Russia, they did not fail to have an effect on the Empress. Although she did not forbid the working of the Lodges, she made the great personages of her Empire feel that their membership was regarded with disfavour. Masonic activity was, in consequence, very much restricted. Under Paul I, in 1797, it was prohibited altogether, but it was once again permitted by Alexander I in 1803, owing to the influence of Böber, the Director of the St. Petersburg Cadet Corps. Once again Lodges began to be formed in large numbers, and such people as the Grand Duke Constantine, Count Stanislav Potocki, Count Ivan Voronzov, Alexander von Württemberg, the Lord High Chamberlain Alexander Narischkin, and many other courtiers joined them. In the Lodge 'De la Palestine', the Greek champion of liberty, Prince Alexander Ypsilanti, developed an intensive activity, whilst Boieldieu, the eminent operatic composer, wrote the songs for its festivals. An enthralling description of the manner in which the Lodges worked at the time has been given by no less a person than Leo Tolstoy in *War and Peace*.[1] Amongst the leaders of Russian Freemasonry in 1809, we also find Fessler, the German reformer, who, in the meantime, had gone to St. Petersburg as Professor of Oriental Languages at the University. Here again he spared no effort in abolishing all that was superfluous.

The activity of the Freemasons during the following ten years was, in spite of many an internal quarrel, so beneficial, that in 1822 the Czar's inhibition was not at first understood. They had, of course, become more and more conscious of the way in which Metternich's reactionary policy was gaining increasing effect upon Alexander, and of how 'he finally had no other will than that of the first Minister of the Austrian Court'. But they had not thought it possible that he could so completely belie his past.

Alexander's successor, Nicholas I, renewed the prohibition in 1826. It is believed that he did so because Freemasons were supposed to have participated in the Decabrist rising in December 1825, an unsuccessful revolt of Guards' officers united in the 'Brotherhood of the Common Weal', which aimed at obtaining a more liberal Constitution for the Empire after the death of Alexander. However, this revolt only resulted in their being mown down with shot before the Winter Palace of St. Petersburg, together with their troops. There were indeed some Freemasons amongst those who suffered death upon the scaffold, or who, in heavy iron chains, were forced to make their

---

[1] The author's characterization of the Freemasons encourages the view that he regarded them as the best elements in Russian society, which was in a very bad way at the time of the Napoleonic Wars.

weary way to Siberia, whence few ever returned. However, one of them, Lieutenant-Colonel Batenkov, recorded in 1863, when he was a septuagenarian, the following beautiful sentences about his Freemasonry:

'During my twenty years' solitary confinement, during the whole of my youth, without books, without the society of a living being—which is enough to make one commit suicide or at least lose one's reason—I had absolutely no help in my cruel mental torture until I renounced all worldly things and lost myself in things spiritual. I then employed the methods of the Freemasons to survey and organize the new world which had risen up before me. In this way I reconciled myself and survived the many attacks of Despair and Death.' [1]

Freemasonry in Russia thus died out. At a later date there still glimmered in small, obscure circles a modest masonic light, and Pissemsky, in his novel entitled *The Masons*, writes minutely about it. Especially in the western provinces is Freemasonry said never completely to have disappeared. According to statements of Boris Telepnef,[2] there were always Lodges in Kieff, Poltawa, Odessa, and Schitomir, as well as other Ukrainian towns. In 1900 there was some talk of forming a Ukrainian Grand Lodge. It was eventually established in Proskurov, but not until 1919, and then only for a few months, during the short life of the independent Ukrainian Republic.

A new masonic movement began to stir in Moscow and in St. Petersburg in 1906. Kedrin, a Member of the Duma, his colleague, the Moscow Professor Maxim Kovalevsky, and Professor Nicholas Bajenoff, and about fifty other prominent Russians, mostly members of the Constitutional Democrats' Party (Cadets), who had become Masons in France, set about founding Lodges in Czarist Russia as well. The 'Polar Star' Lodge in St. Petersburg and another, the 'Regeneration' Lodge in Moscow, were consecrated with the utmost precaution. The leading members of the *bourgeois intelligentsia*, consisting of members of the Duma, scientists, lawyers, and authors, joined these and other Lodges. One of the Lodges consisted exclusively of progressive-minded officers, another entirely of deputies. However, their activity was discovered by the Russian Secret Police as early as 1909. The brethren consequently

[1] Friedrichs, a. a. O.
[2] *The Freemasons*, vol. lxviii, No. 3103. 1928.

decided to restrict their work once again. Nevertheless, one of them had the courage to publish in Moscow, in 1912, a pamphlet entitled: *Who are the Russian Freemasons and what are their aims?*

During the Great War the supervision became less strict, and in 1917 there existed in the whole of Russia some thirty Lodges embracing solely plebeian elements. These disappeared again, however, as soon as the Soviets, who immediately adopted an anti-masonic attitude, came into power. Proof of this is given by the following resolution of the fourth Congress of the Communist International:

'It is absolutely necessary that the leading elements of the party should close all channels which lead to the middle classes and should therefore bring about a definite breach with Freemasonry. The chasm which divides the proletariat from the middle classes must be clearly brought to the consciousness of the Communist Party. A small fraction of the leading elements of the Party[1] wished to bridge this chasm and to avail themselves of the masonic Lodges. Freemasonry is a most dishonest and infamous swindle of the proletariat by the radically inclined section of the middle classes. We regard it as our duty to oppose it to the uttermost.'

There are also people who call Freemasonry the international vanguard of Bolshevism. It would do them good to see the men who assemble in the Russian Lodges and clubs of London, Berlin, Paris and Cairo. They have all, without exception, had to flee their country. And amongst them are to be found brethren such as the Shuvalovs and Lobanov-Rostovskys, whose forefathers were numbered amongst the most brilliant members of Russian Freemasonry at the time of its greatest splendour.

[1] In France.

CHAPTER XIII

SPAIN AND PORTUGAL

THE fate which has overtaken Freemasonry in Italy and Russia has often threatened the Fraternity on the Iberian Peninsula. In Spain and Portugal the masonic cause has produced thousands of martyrs—brethren who held their heads high as they walked into the Valley of Death for their ideal. In both these countries, however, the most bloody oppression could not silence the crusaders of the idea of Humanity. As early as 1740, members of a Lodge in Madrid were apprehended in their Temple and thrown into the dungeons of the Inquisition. A Royal Decree of Ferdinand VI caused all Freemasons to be banished from the country as traitors, so that it was only under the more liberal-minded Charles III (1759–1788) that it was possible to form a Grand Lodge. But a reaction soon set in: the Grand Master, Count Aranda, was banished by the reactionary Prime Minister Goday, and further meetings prohibited. It was only after the French invasion of 1807 that it again became possible. The fall of Napoleon ushered in a new era of persecution. Hardly had Ferdinand VII come to the throne than the Craft was again outlawed and the Inquisition reinstituted. The Marquis de Tolosa, the learned scholar Mariana, Dr. Luque, Physician-in-Ordinary to the King, and General Alava, who had been aide-de-camp to Wellington for six years, were tortured and imprisoned.

This cruel oppression without the slightest cause explains why, in Spain, the Freemasons became more and more the champions of liberty, the leaders of democracy, and the pioneers of liberal thought. All the achievements which this country has to record are largely attributable to them, and the Inquisition was all the more relentless against them. Freemasons who had never taken part in political activities were subjected to torture merely because they belonged to the Brotherhood. Although the Infante Francisco de Paula de Bourbon became the head of the masonic organization in 1823, Ferdinand VII intensified the measures against it in the following year. He alleged that the Freemasons had participated in the Revolution of 1820 and that General Ballesteros,

156

in the days of the rule of the Cortes, had released all the brethren who had been languishing in the dungeons of the apostolic Junta. According to the new edict all Freemasons had to report themselves as such and give up their Lodge certificates within thirty days under penalty of arrest and execution without trial. That was no mere threat. In pursuance thereof—September 9th 1825—a Lodge having been surprised at Granada, seven of its members, chiefly officers, were given short shrift and executed, whilst a candidate for admission was let off with eight years' hard labour. In the years that followed other citizens also were put to death 'as they had been guilty of connexion with Freemasonry and had not declared themselves as such'. Brother Antonio Caro, who had been condemned to die on the gallows, still had the spirit to cry, 'Long live Freemasonry', although the noose was already round his neck. Perhaps it was for this reason that, after the execution, his right hand was cut off and his body buried in unconsecrated ground.[1] The same fate overtook the Worshipful Master Lieutenant-Colonel Galvez in Barcelona in 1829, and his friends were sent to the galleys.

After Ferdinand's death, Lodges at once sprang up again. They were left in peace for a certain length of time, but after a while the insinuations of the clergy gained the day and Freemasons were again proceeded against. In 1853 the members of a Lodge in Gracia were arrested, bound and gagged like dangerous criminals, conducted to Barcelona under a strong escort, and sentenced to imprisonment.

The Revolution of 1868 made Duke Amadeo of Savoy, second son of King Victor Emanuel, the ruler of Spain. He was himself a Freemason, and, right from the very beginning of his reign, he had to cope with the greatest difficulties. He occupied the throne for three years only, and upon his departure from the country the Republic was proclaimed. During the period that followed, Freemasonry was able to develop freely. Several central authorities came into being, including a 'National Grand Orient' and a 'Grand Orient of Spain', and for several decades the Brotherhood enjoyed comparative freedom from persecution. It was not until the 'nineties of the last century that persecution once again became prevalent. The revolutionary occurrences in Cuba and the Philippines, which led to the United States of North America declaring war on Spain, were unjustly blamed upon the Freemasons, and the archives of

[1] Arthur Singer: *The Fight of Rome against Freemasonry*. Leipzig. 1925.

the National Grand Orient were confiscated, and one of the Grand Masters was arrested, together with his junior officers. They were released after ten months' imprisonment without having been tried, as it had proved impossible to find the slightest evidence upon which to base a trial. On the 30th December 1896, however, a Freemason named Rizal faced a firing-party in Manila for alleged participation in the disturbances. That was indeed a judicial murder. The administration of Spanish justice in the Philippines intentionally confused Freemasonry with the Catipunan, a secret society with revolutionary tendencies to which Dr. José Rizal had never belonged. Although he was only twenty-seven years of age, he had already made a name for himself in the Far East as an oculist, naturalist, and philologist. An antagonist of the all-powerful monasticism, he was banished to the Island of Mindanao, where he devoted himself to the education of the youth of the locality. When the insurrection of the Philippines broke out they dragged Rizal before a court martial, declared that he had been the spirit behind the revolution and sentenced him to death. He faced the firing-squad on the plain of Bagumbayon, and, a month later, ten other Freemasons, whose only crime had been their activity in the Lodge, were executed on the same blood-stained field at a mass execution carried out by Spanish riflemen with their Remington breech-loaders.

Rizal is to-day the national hero of the Philippines, and the anniversary of his death is the greatest national festival of the populace.[1]

With the coming of the twentieth century the troublous period of Spanish masonic history was not yet at an end. Whenever liberal sentiment is proceeded against in Spain, the police also force their way into the Masonic Temples, especially since the régime of the Dictator, Primo de Rivera. They know quite well to-day that present Spanish Freemasonry is only active masonically, and that neither the Grand Orient nor the Grand Lodge of Spain—the two Obediences now working— have anything at all to do with the oppositionist parties.[2] But merely because those schools of thought that are opposed to the idea of the Dictatorship have supporters also

---

[1] Leo Fischer-Manila in his address at the decennial jubilee of the Grand Lodge of Vienna. 1928.
[2] The Police Headquarters in Barcelona are situated directly opposite the premises of the Grand Lodge.

amongst Freemasons, it has been found expedient to make use of the weapon of demagogism and to vilify Freemasonry on every possible occasion. In November 1927, when the Prime Minister, General Primo de Rivera, in a note to the newspapers, spoke of 'Freemasons, Communists, and professional politicians who are capable of wavering in their love of Spain', Esteva, the Grand Master, answered him with a strongly worded letter in which he declared that there was no sentiment stronger in the bosom of Freemasonry than love of the Fatherland.

'I assure Your Excellency, in all earnestness, that you have done a gross injustice to our Institution by describing it as unpatriotic. . . . Our injured dignity compels us to protest against it. . . . From no one, and in no circumstances, will we tolerate our love of country being doubted. . . . That we are not more often prominent may be attributed to the fact that our society is compelled to live under a toleration, which, to be sure, recognizes our right to exist, but is by no means constituted in accordance with our merits. . . . The international character of Freemasonry is based upon the Christian belief in the necessity of bringing together all men of good intention to work for the creation of an *entente* between all nations, so that the spilling of further blood in fratricidal struggles may be prevented. It is actuated by the desire to attempt everything that will secure the essentials for that state of universal peace amongst mankind that will enable it to devote its energy solely to the betterment of social conditions. The future world, in which, we hope, true brotherly love will prevail for the good of all humanity, can only be formed in such a way.'

No answer was received to this letter.

The formation of the Spanish Republic in 1931 resulted in a revival in Freemasonry. Since the advent of the Republic the anti-masonic Press has spoken not infrequently of a 'Masonic Republic'. Captain Fermin Galan, the martyr of Taca, who sacrificed himself for the idea of the Republic, was admittedly a Freemason, and there are also many members of the Fraternity in the Government, but it would be quite incorrect to assume, on that account, that Freemasonry, as such, has had a decisive influence upon the happenings from day to day. Free masonry has never had anything to do with attacks upon monasteries and churches. That was the work of frenzied anarchists.

On the 10th May 1931, the Grand Orient of Spain (there is also a Grand Lodge, both Obediences having their headquarters in Madrid) expressed its joy at the birth of a régime 'that is the expression of the Will of the Nation'. At the same time, however, the Grand Orient stressed the fact that Freemasonry was conscious of its independence of all partisan tendencies, and pointed out that its object was to propagate chivalry and tolerance.

Portuguese Freemasonry has suffered vicissitudes of fortune very similar to those of Spanish Freemasonry, the only material difference being that the brethren in Lusitania had a still more agonizing, blood-strewn path to follow.

'Through evil-smelling dungeons, through the torture-chambers of the Inquisition, it led to ghastly charnel-houses, to the iron collar of the garrotte, to the flaming stakes of numerous *autos-da-fe*, to the galleys or to exile on some Devil's Island.'

Freemasonry, which was introduced into Portugal in 1735 by a Scotsman, George Gordon, under a Charter granted by the English Grand Master, the Duke of Montagu, had been carrying on its cultural work for less than ten years when the first of its members met a martyr's death. A Provençal Dominican friar, Bonnet de Meautry, confessor to the French Ambassador, a fanatic and informer, modestly calling himself 'carnassier de Notre-Seigneur', denounced seventeen brethren to the Grand Inquisitor, Don Pedro de Silveira, for conspiracy and heresy, and demanded the prosecution and exemplary punishment of the *Pedreiros livres* (Freemasons). King John V, seized with religious fervour, gave his consent to a summary trial, and, without troubling to obtain the approval of the Cortes, issued a decree declaring that any person proved to be a Freemason would be condemned to death without the right to appeal. Hardly had this edict been issued than the Lodge 'Virtud' in Lisbon was raided by police and musketeers on the 8th March 1743. Three members of the Lodge, the two aristocrats Damiao de Andrade and Manoel de Revelhos and the serving brother Christoph Diego, a baptized Mohammedan, were forced to mount the scaffold on June 1st, after the most terrible tortures of the third degree had been unable to wrest from them the names of their fellow Lodge-members. Nevertheless, the police, assisted by the disclosures of an informer, succeeded in tracing some of their quarries. These, however, were three foreigners: Thomas Braslé and Jaques Mouton, who were French subjects, and Johann Coustos, a Swiss from Berne. The first-named were jewellers, whilst the latter was a lapidary and cameo-artist. The wife of one of their competitors had denounced them to the Inquisition as Freemasons. It was an actual fact that Coustos had founded a Lodge. The three prisoners were severely maltreated in the open street and were delivered up at the Palace of the Inquisition covered in blood. No less than nine times within three months they were subjected, in the presence of the Grand Inquisitor, Cardinal de Cunho, to 'painful interrogation', i.e. they were stretched on the rack until their limbs were dislocated, tied together with chains and burned in the pit of the stomach and under the armpits with pitch torches. Time and again they were clumsily patched-up by surgeons in order to undergo further torture. But no 'secret' could be extracted from them. Thomas Braslé succumbed as a result of the torture, and the day which saw the execution of the above-named Portuguese brethren also saw Coustos, wrapped in a shroud of sacking, complete with caricatures of the devil and tongues of flame, conducted in public procession to the *auto-da-fe* in the Church of the Dominicans, in order there, in the presence of the King and the entire Court, to hear his sentence. He was condemned to four years at the galleys and was excommunicated, but he was released and permitted to go to London in the following year after the British Ambassador had intervened on his behalf. But two other brethren who came under the *auto-da-fe* at the same time as Coustos, the portrait artist Macedo and the solicitor Dr. Jorge da Silva, a Jew, had to suffer death by burning as the penalty of their membership of Freemasonry.

When John V died in 1750, he was succeeded by his son, José I. The latter's mother, Marianne, daughter of the Emperor Leopold I, recommended him to award the post of Prime Minister to the then Portuguese Ambassador at the Court of Vienna, Dom Sebastiao de Carvalho e Mello, who, before he went to Vienna, had been Ambassador in London and had been admitted into a London Lodge by the Grand Master of England, Frederick, Prince of Wales, on St. John's Day 1744. In Vienna he had repeatedly visited the 'Three Canons' Lodge. His activity as Prime Minister was really wonderful. He issued an Edict of Toleration, gave the country a

Liberal Constitution based on that of the English; he created new branches of industry and an extensive system of canalization; he built large harbours, abolished the Inquisition, torture, and the prerogatives of the privileged classes, and thus transformed what had been an exhausted and impoverished land into a flourishing State. The King expressed his gratitude to Carvalho by creating him Marquez de Pombal; and this name still occupies a prominent place in the history of Portugal as belonging to one of her greatest sons.

It is quite evident that Pombal favoured the revival of Freemasonry; Lodges sprang up in all parts of Portugal and her colonies. These Lodges then proceeded to create large public libraries and important institutions for the public welfare. On All Saints' Day 1755, when tidal waves destroyed two-thirds of Lisbon and 30,000 souls, the Portuguese Freemasons earned the thanks and appreciation of the nation by their self-sacrificing participation in the rescue work and other services.

However, the death of José I put an end to Pombal's work. Queen Maria I, José's daughter, in spite of the magnificent reforms of Pombal, ranged herself on the side of his deadly enemies, the hidalgos and the clergy, and, especially, the Jesuits, who had been turned out of Portugal in 1759. Pombal was condemned to death after a grotesque trial. He was then pardoned, but was expelled from Lisbon in his seventy-eighth year. How violently he was hated by the clergy is illustrated by a funeral oration, pronounced by the Barnabite priest, Don Alexander, in an important Viennese Church on the occasion of Pombal's death five years later: 'The notorious and sacrilegious Pombal is dead at last. And now, after having received here below the just deserts of his wicked deeds, through the punishment of Heaven, he can enjoy himself to his heart's content in the infernal regions, with his worthy brothers Luther, Calvin, and other blackguards'—an obituary which caused the Emperor Joseph to remark: 'Really a lucky man, this Pombal, that even his most deadly enemies wish him, *post mortem*, such excellent company.'

Queen Maria renewed the Decree of her grandfather against the *Pedreiros livres*, and a new and unhappy period opened for Portuguese Masonry. The most eminent men of the country only escaped the Inquisition by taking to flight. One of these was the poet Frc. Man. do Nascimento, who went to France, and to whom Lamartine, under the title 'Gloire d'un poète

JOHN COUSTOS Aged 43 Years,
A Sufferer during 16 Months in ye Inquisition
at Lisbon for Being a Free Mason.

JOHN COUSTOS
From the Engraving by Truchy, after Boitard

CAGLIOSTRO RECEIVED AT A LODGE
'Drawn by a Brother Mason, a witness of the scene'

exilé', dedicated some of his most beautiful poems; and, amongst others, there were the doctors Ribeiro Sanches and d'Avelar Brotero and the Abbé Correa da Serra, who had actually been arrested, but broke away from the police on the way to prison. On the other hand, da Cunha, the mathematician, languished in the dungeons of the Inquisition from 1778 until 1780. The French Revolution was taken as an excuse for even more severe persecution. In 1792, the Governor of the Island of Madeira received a command to deliver up to the Inquisition as many Freemasons as he could lay hands on, since they were the 'authors of the Revolution'. A number of Freemasons learnt of their great danger from the Governor's wife and they were able to persuade an English sea-captain, Walter Ferguson, himself a Freemason, to grant them a passage on his two-decker *Good Hope*, which was lying in the roads of Funchal. Sixty-four Freemasons and their families went on board this vessel, which took them safely to New York after a long voyage. The vessel entered New York Harbour flying a white flag, bearing the inscription: 'Asylum quaerimus' ('We seek asylum').

The American brethren gave the refugees a very warm welcome. The Grand Lodge of Pennsylvania invited them to Philadelphia, and a frigate of the Union Fleet conveyed these victims of persecution to the Delaware River. In the presence of thousands, George Washington greeted them in the name of the Union and granted them citizenship.

But Lodges still continued to be formed in their mother country, Portugal, in spite of all the persecution. For quite a long time they met on ships lying at anchor in Portuguese harbours. Particularly celebrated was a British guard-ship, the frigate *Phœnix*, the personnel of which consisted almost exclusively of Freemasons. In the year 1797 a meeting was held every Friday evening in this floating Lodge-room. The meetings were attended by ships' captains, British and Portuguese officers, and French Royalist refugees. There were often as many as 140 brethren present at the 'Royal Navy Lodge Phœnix', and it even became a mother-lodge, for it gave birth to the highly respected Lodge 'Regeneraçao' of Lisbon, and this Lodge, in its turn, gave Light to five other Portuguese Lodges.

This 'masonic frigate' was, of course, not unknown to the Government and they demanded that the English Ambassador, Sir John Partridge, should have it recalled; but without success. The Chief of Police, Diego Marrique, then took more vigorous measures. He first made it compulsory for all Freemasons to wear a badge, and then declared them 'fair game'. In a memorandum to the Prince Regent John, son of Queen Maria, who had become insane, Marrique poured forth the vials of his wrath upon the 'godless riff-raff'. A police spy, he alleged, had declared on oath that, through a hole in the wall of the Lodge-room, he had seen the Masons kick a picture of the Saviour, which had thereupon spilt a quantity of blood and emitted sorrowful sighs. The edicts dating from the year 1773, which provided the death penalty for every Freemason, were then re-promulgated. The prisons filled up once again, and although the Government did not dare to execute Freemasons, many of them disappeared for ever into ghastly dungeons. When French troops advanced into Lisbon under General Junot in 1807, they found in an underground prison nine skeletons in chains. In Marrique's reign of terror, during which he gave full rein to his violent rage, there were numerous examples of the most heroic espousal of the masonic cause. In 1798 nearly 200 masonic brethren assembled in the valley of Alcantara for a kind of masonic Grütli,[1] and, on bended knees, they swore to endure the most horrible torture rather than renounce Freemasonry. A committee of six ('Commissiao do expediente') was formed to direct the work of the Lodges and to protect them, as far as possible, from persecution. They were even bold enough to form a Grand Lodge, and elected Sebastio Sampejo de Castro (brother of the Marquis de Pombal), Counsellor of the High Court of Justice, as Grand Master of Portugal. That, however, was only a gesture, for the persecution did not stop. In 1816 the Grand Master, General Gomez Freire d'Andrade, together with eleven other brethren, was arrested at the instigation of Lord Beresford, an Englishman, who was the commander-in-chief at that time. As supporters of the constitutional monarchy they were not prepared to submit to foreign domination. They had to pay for this with their lives, and on the 15th October 1817 they were hanged, after which the corpses were burned and the ashes scattered in the sea.

After the counter-revolution of 1823, an Edict of John VI threatened all Masons with five years' banishment to Africa. In the following year the Usurper, Dom Miguel of Braganza,

---

[1] Historic meeting of Swiss subjects to form the Swiss League against Austria.

issued a decree concluding with the words: 'Long live the King! Long live Roman Catholicism! Death and destruction to the sacrilegious Freemasons!' The same night a proclamation of Cardinal Souza, Archbishop of Lisbon, inciting the populace against Freemasonry was distributed in the streets, and this led to the murder of seventeen brethren. 'Portuguese blood must flow in streams, as previously did that of the Jews, for the Infante has sworn that he will not sheath his sword until he has dealt with Freemasonry. I am eagerly longing to steep my hands in blood', preached the REVEREND Father Joao Marianno. At the order of the Grand Master the Lodges were closed, and for a time masonic activity was limited to the island of Terceira in the Azores and to Brazil.[1] But after the capitulation of Miguel at Evora, when the young, legitimate Queen Maria came into power, Freemasonry was once again able to spread over the whole kingdom.

From the various foundations, which, in the course of a century, now merged into one another and now parted company, a single organization has in recent times been formed once more. This is the Grande Oriente Lusitano Unido ('United Grand Lusitanian Orient'), whose head, Dr. Sebastiao Magelhaes-Lima, was formerly Minister of Education and is one of

---

[1] Freemasons had played a leading part in founding the South American Republics, which were created in the nineteenth century. They were responsible for the emancipation from selfish exploitation which mocked at the very dignity of man; for the development of a large number of these States, and, especially, for the Declaration of Independence of the provinces of Rio de la Plata, Chili, and Peru from the pitiless Spanish policy of privileges. General Francisco Miranda, the great Venezuelan champion of liberty, who had become a Freemason in Cadiz, founded the 'Lautaro' Lodge in London in collaboration with other young South Americans, and many of the members of this Lodge rendered magnificent service to their home-country, as, for instance, General San Martin, Argentina's greatest hero, the Washington of South America, who was Worshipful Master of the Lodge when it was set up in Buenos Aires in 1812. Champions of liberty also came together in the first Lodge to be founded in South America itself, the Lodge 'San Juan de Jerusalen,' which was consecrated in Buenos Aires in 1807. However, it did not occur to them to set up a state within a state; they were all true sons of their nation. But this did not deter their clerical-monarchist opponents from describing their actions as the effluence of sheer wickedness, so that when the troops of General San Martin marched into Lima a cry of horror ran through the country: 'The Freemasons are coming!' This went on until the ignorant populace learned from experience that these 'fiends in human shape' were, in reality, unselfish men who brought them freedom. Freemasonry rendered great service to Brazil, which had arisen out of a Portuguese colony and became, first of all, an Empire, and at no time called for any very severe struggles for freedom. For a certain length of time the Brotherhood was ruled by the Emperor Don Pedro, and did great work in the struggle for the abolition of slavery and in the fight against intolerance.

the most eminent men in Portugal. He once expressed his masonic creed in the following words:[1]

'There is only one lasting law in the world, and that is the Law of Love. Not only that love which manifests itself in kindness and in infinite beauty and in profound sympathy for every living creature, but also the love which may briefly be described as a love for all mankind; as the ardent desire to live for others. It is love for the young, for the humble and for the oppressed of this world. This love fraternizes, illuminates and makes for solidarity; it is the Freemason's love.'

[1] These words were uttered during a visit to the 'Kosmos' Lodge in Vienna in 1912.

CHAPTER XIV

MASONRY AT THE TIME OF WASHINGTON

THE space at our disposal does not allow us to take our readers along all the paths by which Freemasonry wended its way through the world in the first half of the eighteenth century. In almost every case the advance with flying banners was short-lived. There is scarcely a country in which prejudice and hatred did not quickly attempt to destroy the edifice in course of erection. We have also demonstrated the remarkable fact that even the most violent persecution was only able to repress Freemasonry temporarily. It is true that Lodges and Grand Lodges were obliged to stop their meetings, but they never failed to recommence their activities within a short time, in spite of the internal strife which rent them and the persecution from external sources. There were differences of opinion as to the system, the interpretation of the 'Charges', and the concrete form to be given to the Great Idea. And it was not as though the initiative for this rebuilding of destroyed Lodges came from new blood. It was not like a broken chain in which a new link might be skilfully fitted by some clever hand. In most cases the links had to be forged anew from the old material. The pages of masonic history contain the record of much martyrdom and self-sacrifice, not theatrical, but calm, resigned heroism sustained by enthusiasm for a distant ideal, only dimly perceived by the mental eye.

It can safely be said that, even before 1750, Freemasonry had become active in all parts of the world.

As early as 1730 there was a Provincial Grand Master in England's American colonies. He was Daniel Coxe, to whom the English Grand Master, the Duke of Norfolk, had granted a charter for New York, New Jersey, and Pennsylvania. Coxe was probably the first to elaborate a plan for the confederation of the various colonies, but he was not the first American Freemason. It was in 1704 that Jonathan Belcher of Boston, who later came into prominence as Governor of several States of New England, had been initiated in a London 'Society of Masons'. The official entry of Freemasons into America was announced by the Press. The founding of Lodges 'in this

Province' was announced to the population of Philadelphia on the 8th December 1730, by Benjamin Franklin, in his *Gazette*, as an item of news of special interest. He was also the first to publish the Anderson *Book of Constitutions* in America, for his edition appeared in print in 1734. In the same year, Franklin, the indefatigable promulgator of the idea of the United States, became Grand Master. He was followed by Henry Price in Boston (Massachusetts), who had, even earlier, received an English charter for 'His Majesty's Dominions of North America.' Under him Franklin accepted the dignity of Provincial Grand Master for Pennsylvania.

For a time the propagation of masonic thought followed a normal course. The Lodges which had been formed in Boston, Montserrat, Philadelphia, Savannah, Charleston, Portsmouth, New York, etc., had the same schismatic development as those of the mother country; they were divided into 'Ancients' and 'Moderns'. But more disruptive changes appeared with the coming of the revolutionary epoch, when the elements striving for independence began to be a force to be reckoned with. Life in the Lodges suffered in many places because of the citizens' ever-increasing interest in politics, but in others it had the very opposite effect. The schism according to the two English systems—even if not actually expressed in words and universally applied—resolved itself into a division as to conviction. The Lodges of the 'Moderns', the officers of which were such people as Governors and high officials, were recruited chiefly from the Tories, or those who had no wish for a breach with England. On the other hand, the 'Ancients', who were much greater in number, were composed principally of merchants, technicians, and craftsmen, amongst whom were to be found most of the people striving for independence. In the ranks of these 'Ancient' Freemasons the idea of the U.S.A., of which they were the originators, now began to take definite shape. In colonial times Freemasonry was the only institution which enabled the leaders of the various colonies to meet on common ground. Thus it was that the United States of America were conceived in the Lodges, although the meetings did not develop into political discussions. When Freemasons of opposite convictions met in Lodge, they made every effort to adopt towards one another an attitude as fraternal as was possible in those days when feeling ran high. On such evenings the Temples became meeting-places in which political passions lost much of their bitterness.

GEORGE WASHINGTON AS A MASON
From the Engraving by A. B. Walter

BENJAMIN FRANKLIN

From the anonymous Painting, in the National Portrait Gallery, after the Portrait of 1782 by J. S. Duplessis

But the spiritual leaders of Freemasonry were to be found chiefly in the Independence camp. The large majority of the men who rendered the country such memorable service at this time wore the masonic apron, and it has been computed that out of the fifty-six men who signed the Declaration of Independence, so magnificent in its liberal conception and of such great importance to Europe, no less than fifty-three were Freemasons. In the 'long room' of the Green Dragon Tavern in Boston, which was later described by many historians as the headquarters of the struggle for independence—it actually was the meeting-place of a large number of political clubs and 'sons of liberty'—a Lodge, the 'St. Andrew's' Lodge, also had its Temple, which was attended by the most eminent men of the city and many of the most prominent patriots. With three other Lodges it had received from the Grand Lodge of Scotland the right to set up a Provincial Grand Lodge. Its first Grand Master, General Joseph Warren, was later—at the battle of Bunker Hill—the first to lay down his life in the cause of freedom.[1] Warren was also the spiritual force behind the 'Caucus Pro Bono Publico' Club, whose members were Freemasons, which conceived the idea of the 'Boston Tea Party' and many other plans that actually brought about the American Revolution.

Of the many Freemasons whose names are inscribed on the Roll of Honour of the American War of Independence, let us here mention the following: George Washington, Benjamin Franklin, James Otis, who, when only a young Boston advocate, was the first to plead for the inalienable natural rights of man in a brilliant speech before the Court; Samuel Adams, the man of the people, whose words at the Boston Town Meeting: 'This assembly can do nothing more for the deliverance of the country' acted like an alarm signal and led to the storming of the tea ships lying in the harbour; Alexander Hamilton who, as a member of the legislative body of New York, drafted the Constitution of the United States and created the foundations of the public treasury; Patrick Henry, the 'orator of the revolution'; John Marshall, not only the highest, but also the greatest, judge of his time; James Madison, who, with the latter and Hamilton, built up the new political structure; Washington's heroic generals and fellow-combatants Nathaniel Greene, Lee, Sullivan, Lord Stirling, and the two Putnams,

---

[1] When the British General Gage received the report of Warren's death, he said that his death meant more than if 500 other rebels had fallen.

the German Baron Steuben, who, having served and received his training under Frederick the Great, made the army ready to take the field again after many defeats; Lafayette, Montgomery, Jackson, Gist, Henry Knox, Ethan Allan; and also Paul Revere, the Spanish Grand Master of Massachusetts, who, when the Freemason John Pulling caused the signal lights to blaze up on the tower of the ancient North Church of Boston to announce the landing of the English at Cambridge, threw himself on his horse and gave the alarm to the patriots on his daring ride through the night from Charlestown to Lexington, a deed to which the following lines of Longfellow were dedicated:

'A hurry of hoofs in a village street,
   A shape in the moonlight, a bulk in the dark,
   And beneath, from the pebbles is passing, a spark
Struck out by a steed flying fearless and fleet.
   That was all: and yet, through the gloom and the light,
   The fate of a nation was riding that night;
   And the spark struck out by that steed in his flight
Kindled the land into flame with its heat.'

Most of these men were active Masons like Benjamin Franklin, and notably Washington himself, who was initiated in the 'Fredericksburg Lodge No. 4' in Virginia, and later became the Worshipful Master of the 'Alexandria Lodge No. 44' in Alexandria. One of his biographers, Sidney Hayden, wrote of the General:

'The key to Washington's public and private life is to be found in his character as a Freemason. Through his whole life is discernible the practice of the sentence coined by himself: "The virtues that ennoble mankind are taught, nourished, and fostered in the halls of the Freemasons; they encourage domestic life and serve as a standard for the highest duties of the State."'

When Washington became Commander-in-Chief of the Army, he immediately surrounded himself with Freemasons. Lafayette had said of him that he was very unwilling to grant independent commands to officers who were not brethren. Meetings were held regularly in the Field-Lodges. There were Lodges both in divisions and in army corps. The soldiers used to snatch an hour in order to go to a barn in which a block of wood represented the altar. They stepped into the oblong rectangle and formed the fraternal chain which, as battle followed battle,

WASHINGTON'S APRON
EMBROIDERED BY THE MARQUISE LAFAYETTE
In the possession of the Grand Lodge of Pennsylvania

FRONTISPIECE TO THE 'AMERICAN BOOK OF CONSTITUTIONS', 1792
DEDICATED TO GEORGE WASHINGTON
Drawn and Engraved by Seymour

became significantly smaller. The Army Lodges proved of great value. They served as a bond of rare strength for the motley host of warriors fighting for liberty. The simplest soldier belonging to the Lodge felt himself fraternally one with the Commander-in-Chief and his masonic generals and officers. The 'American Union No. 1' became the most celebrated Field-Lodge. Its seal bore a chain of thirteen rings, each one of which represented one of the thirteen States participating in the struggle. In the unhappy battle of Long Island a large number of its members were killed, and many were taken prisoner, but the survivors rescued the working tools of the Lodge, carried them with them on the adventurous retreat from New York, and, on Christmas Eve, amidst the roar of battle, they arranged the candlesticks of the Lodge in a rudely constructed workshop behind the new line on the Delaware.

Whenever it was possible Lodge meetings were held between the battles. Washington appeared first in one Lodge and then in another. Amidst the distress and privation of the terrible winter camp of Valley Forge, the Lodge meetings were the only solace for those so anxiously praying for victory. Lafayette is supposed to have received the Light under these conditions.

There were many Military Lodges on the British side also, and, consequently, when troops were taken prisoner, it often happened that Freemasons fell into the hands of brethren. Many a soldier owed his life to this. On the British side, it was chiefly Joseph Brandt, an Indian of the Iroquois tribe, and Chief of the Indian warriors allied with the English, who repeatedly rescued brethren of the opposing camp from death. The same spirit, however, was also demonstrated by the Colonists. It often happened that property of English Masons was amongst the spoils of war, and Washington issued an order that such articles were always to be returned. When the members of the English Field-Lodge No. 227 were forced to leave their Constitution and all the emblems behind them on a certain retreat, Washington sent everything back under the escort of an officer and a guard of honour. When the guard of honour entered the British camp showing the flag of truce and bearing the Lodge Chest, they were at once received with full military honours. An English regiment took up parade formation and presented arms to the deputation from the enemy camp.

On another occasion—on the 23rd July 1779—the Lodge of

the 17th Foot, after an unsuccessful battle, lost its Warrant
and Constitution. General Samuel H. Parsons, an officer of
the 'American Union Lodge', sent them back, with an accom-
panying letter which read as follows:

'BRETHREN!
'When the ambition of monarchs or jarring interests of
States call forth their subjects to war as Masons we are
disarmed of that resentment which stimulates to undis-
tinguished desolation, and however our political sentiments
may impel us in the public dispute we are still brethren and
our professional duty apart ought to promote the happiness
and advance the weal of each other.
'Accept, therefore, of the hands of a brother the Constitution of the Lodge Unity No. 18 to be held in the Seventeenth
British Regiment which your late misfortunes have put in
my power to return to you.
'I am Your Br. and
'obedient servant,
'SAMUEL H. PARSONS'

After Philadelphia had been evacuated by the English and
the General Congress of the Colonies once again assembled in
the 'Independence Hall', which was founded by Freemasons,
Washington, at the Festival of St. John the Evangelist, headed
a solemn procession of 300 brethren to Christ Church, where
a masonic divine service was held. And later, after Independence had been gained, when each State had its own national
Grand Lodge, Washington still remained an ardent Freemason.
When performing his office as Worshipful Master of the
'Alexandria Lodge' he used to wear an apron which had been
presented to him by Lafayette as a gift from his wife. At
Washington's installation as first President of the United States,
the Secretary of State, Livingston, Grand Master of the Grand
Lodge of New York, used the Volume of the Sacred Law of the
'St. John's Lodge' for the swearing-in ceremony, and, on the
18th September 1793, at the laying of the foundation stone
of the Capitol in Washington, which had recently been chosen
as the capital of the Union, the President appeared on this
ceremonious occasion in the regalia of an Honorary Master
of his Lodge.
Thus Freemasonry seemed to have taken firm root in North
America. Numerous new Grand Lodges sprang up, and the
growth of the Union was accompanied by a rapid advance in

masonic institutions. But in 1826, there occurred an incident which, in many States, offset years of masonic progress. This was the Morgan affair, which was never properly cleared up.

Fellow-citizens and Brothers,
of the Grand lodge of Pennsylvania

I have received your address with all the feelings of brotherly affection mingled with those sentiments, for the Society, which it was calculated to excite To have been, in any degree, an instrument, in the hands of Providence to promote order and union, and erect upon a solid foundation the true principles of government, is only to have shared with many others in a labour, the result of which let us hope, will prove through all ages, a sanctuary for brothers and a lodge for the virtues. —
Permit me to reciprocate your prayers for my temporal happiness, and to supplicate that we may all meet thereafter in that eternal temple. Whose builder is the great Architect of the Universe

G. Washington

LETTER FROM GEORGE WASHINGTON TO THE GRAND LODGE OF
PENNSYLVANIA

A rumour had become current that William Morgan, a stone-mason in the small town of Batavia in New York State, intended, with the help of a printer named Miller, to publish a work about Freemasonry and to give the most detailed information as to its doctrine, ritual, symbols, and signs of recognition. The Freemasons of this small town, who were

not aware that disclosures of a similar nature had been published as much as a hundred years before, and still continued
to appear with great regularity, became wildly excited about
it. They issued a warning to Morgan in the Batavia newspaper,
The Spirit of the Times, but he merely replied that the book
would be published. Feeling became more and more intense,
and this culminated in certain persons being somewhat carried
away by their excitement. They came to an infinitely foolish
decision, namely, to take Morgan into safe custody in order
to persuade him to abandon his project. And Morgan was
actually abducted. He was arrested on a charge of theft,
but was released the following day and taken by his 'liberators'
in the direction of Fort Niagara in Canada. However, he
disappeared *en route* in a most mysterious manner. It was, of
course, at once asserted that he had been shot or thrown into
the Niagara. This has since proved to be false. Morgan
turned up again in Smyrna in 1831, but as this was not known
in 1826, the affair created a tremendous sensation. The
abductors received terms of imprisonment as punishment.
But this was not the end of it. All those people who were in
any way prejudiced against Freemasonry—clerical partisans,
Baptists, Mennonites, Schwenkfeldians, Quakers, and other
sects—made the very utmost of this escapade of high-spirited
young people. Meetings of protest were advertised everywhere.
'Anti-Freemasonry' became a programme at the State and
Presidential elections. William Wirt, it is true, failed in his
candidature for the Presidency; but in New York and Vermont,
Governors were elected on this platform. This fierce agitation
naturally had its effect on the Lodges; many brethren withdrew, for they were not prepared to submit to the vituperations
of the public, who called them murderers, nor were they
anxious to figure in any criminal drama. Sensation was at
its highest when, in October 1827, a body was washed ashore
in the neighbourhood of Fort Niagara. Although this body bore
not the slightest resemblance to Morgan, his wife and Miller
swore that it was his body. They even convinced the authorities
as to its identity, and a murder trial might easily have resulted,
had not the corpse been recognized, when the first excitement
had barely died down, as that of Timothy Munroe, from the
Canadian district of Newcastle, who had disappeared a month
previously. The anti-masonic papers that had suddenly
sprung up kept this knowledge from their readers and agitated
for a commercial boycott, for the social ostracism and discharge

of Freemasons from all public posts.   Never had America experienced such a campaign.   Teachers and clerics lost their positions, the children of Freemasons were excluded from schools and their fathers from church congregations.   It frequently happened that the sacrament was refused to the most respected of citizens, as soon as their membership of the Brotherhood became known.   Families became divided against themselves.   Prohibition of masonic activity was clamorously demanded, and, although this was never attained, many Lodges closed down of their own accord.   The Grand Lodge of New York, which in 1827 had counted 227 Lodges, had only 41 in 1835.   The Grand Lodge of Vermont held no meetings over a period of many years and the whole of Masonry had to suffer bitterly for the tragic mistake of a few, who believed that the disclosure of the Ritual, which in any case had been done long before, would shake the Brotherhood to its very foundations, and had sought to avoid this by their foolish act. [1]

But reason gradually gained the upper hand.   The general public began to realize that they had been suffering from a form of mass-psychosis and had allowed themselves to be led into excesses of hatred by unscrupulous persons who, behind their campaign against Freemasonry, concealed another, a political, object.   And they began to be ashamed of their mistake, especially as they could not fail to notice that, during the most stormy years, many of the best men in the land had remained true to the masonic banner.   President Andrew Jackson was a great advocate of Freemasonry.   During the election for the presidency he was taxed with being a Freemason.   He did not attempt to deny it and wrote the following words: 'Freemasonry is an institution whose object is the welfare of mankind, and I am convinced that it will flourish also in the future.'   The opponents of Freemasonry were anxious to use their campaign of agitation to assist Henry Clay, his opponent, but he returned a categoric refusal to their unfair suggestion. And the celebrated Stephen van Rensselaer, who, when the decline was at its greatest, was elected Grand Master of the Grand Lodge of New York, made the following declaration:

'If I were to question my own personal feelings I should have to decline the great honour offered me, but when I see how the Order is so unjustly blamed and the brethren

---

[1] It is significant that Woodrow Wilson makes no mention of this sad episode in his *History of the American People*.

persecuted, I regard it as my duty to accept, if this step can in any way usefully serve our cause.'

And so began the revival. In New York, where the number of members had fallen from 20,000 in 1826 to roughly 3,000 ten years later, a new development set in about the year 1838, and, in the 'forties the times of severe crisis were regarded as past history. The same might also be said of the other States. Several new Grand Lodges were founded, the number of candidates rose by leaps and bounds, and the 'anti-Freemasons' were soon out of business in the United States of America.

PART II

PRESENT-DAY FREEMASONRY IN VARIOUS
COUNTRIES

CHAPTER I

ENGLAND

IN the preceding chapters we have attempted to give a rough outline of the development of Freemasonry in the most important centres. We shall have to do the same in regard to present-day Freemasonry in order to obtain a clear idea of it, for it would be futile to select at random any one of the national masonic organizations and endeavour to derive therefrom a conception of all the others. We should arrive at entirely false conclusions. The peculiarities of the most important groups must be carefully considered because, as we have sufficiently indicated in our outline of history, these are frequently extremely marked and give rise to great dissimilarities, in spite of the common fundamental idea, identical symbols, and, to all intents and purposes, the same Ritual.

The United Grand Lodge of England, the Mother Grand Lodge, is still, as in the past, the real upholder of tradition. This mighty organization, with more than 300,000 members (exclusive of Scotland and Ireland), is governed by thoroughly conservative principles which have remained unchanged since 1813. It is borne in mind at all times that all classes of society and all opinions and beliefs are represented. A tenacious adherence to tradition is considered of paramount importance.

To anybody who has been in England it must seem incomprehensible that Freemasonry should ever be spoken of as a secret society. For the Grand Lodge itself, which has so often been described as the headquarters of the masonic 'system of conspiracy', is practically a public affair. Every occurrence in the Lodges, every election of a Worshipful Master, every festivity and every jubilee, is faithfully recorded in the newspapers, together with the names of all present, under the heading 'Freemasonry', and anybody who wanders by accident into the back rooms of any of the best London restaurants catering for the meetings of clubs and societies, will, in all probability, find Lodge Temples there also.

It is often said in the mother country of Freemasonry that it is really an antiquated thing, and that 'the Freemasons are people who wear funny aprons, cling to antiquated ceremonies, arrange splendid balls and excellent dinners, and, at the same time, contribute a bit to charity', but this view is disproved by the fact that, especially in the ten years following the end of the War, the Grand Lodge of England has increased to an unprecedented degree.

This influx of new members into the Lodges is, of course, favoured by the fact that opposition to Freemasonry makes itself felt but little in England and her Dominions. And many may have been attracted solely by the fact that five members of the Royal House and many of the highest dignitaries of the Crown and of the Empire, are members of the Fraternity. But that alone can by no means explain the large increase in the number of new brethren.

How large it is may be seen from the following figures: from the end of 1913 until the end of 1930, more than 300 new Lodges were founded in London alone. During the same period the number of Lodges in the Provinces increased from 1,749 to 2,600, to say nothing of several hundred Lodges in overseas possessions, and it would perhaps be appropriate to mention here that, like Scotland and Ireland, almost every British Dominion has its own Grand Lodge, which works in the same spirit, however, so that if we were to regard the Freemasonry of the British Empire as a whole, we should arrive at quite different figures. In the last Year Book of the Grand Lodge of New York, which, in its Grand Historian, Ossian Lang, had at its disposal one of the best-informed masonic statisticians, Great Britain is credited with roughly 6,120 Lodges and nearly 486,000 members. In 1913, 14,800 new brethren were admitted by English Lodges, while the increase amounted to 27,722 in 1922 and rose still higher in the following years.

As we have already said, members of the Royal House play leading parts in the Grand Lodge. The Grand Master is the Duke of Connaught, uncle of the present King. He took over this office in 1901 as successor to his brother, King Edward VII, who, before ascending the throne, i.e. as Prince of Wales, had acted as Grand Master for 27 years. That this is no mere formal dignity is demonstrated by the Rule contained in the Constitutions of the Grand Lodge, according to which no innovation may be introduced, and no resolution may come

THE DUKE OF CONNAUGHT, K.G.,
AS GRAND MASTER OF THE GRAND LODGE OF ENGLAND

KING EDWARD VII AS PRINCE OF WALES
GRAND MASTER

into force, without first having received the approval of the Grand Master.

Although the present King of England is not a Freemason, he is the Patron of masonic charitable institutions. Three of his sons, however, are active members of the Fraternity. The Prince of Wales and the King's second son, the Duke of York, are Provincial Grand Masters. A few years ago they acted as sponsors for their brother, Prince George, at his initiation in the 'Royal Navy' Lodge, which is exclusively for officers of that Service. Prince George was subsequently, in 1933, appointed Grand Senior Warden. The Earl of Harewood, brother-in-law of the princes, and their cousin, Prince Arthur of Connaught, are at the head of Provincial Grand Lodges. The Pro-Grand Master, Lord Ampthill, late Viceroy of India, deputizes for the Grand Master. It is the rule of the Grand Lodge that the office of Pro-Grand Master must be held by an English Peer of the Realm, just as it has been the tradition in many Provincial Grand Lodges, for a hundred years and more, for the leadership to devolve, by inheritance, as it were, upon the highest families in the country.

A casual glance through the long lists of high officials of the Grand Lodge of England and of the Provincial and District Grand Lodges reveals the names of the most exalted aristocrats, privy councillors, great statesmen, governors, generals, prominent judges and clergymen, but also the names of many men who occupy no leading place in every-day life. Every form of belief is represented in these institutions. There are Jews, Mohammedans, Parsees, Buddhists and followers of Confucius. And even differences of political opinion have no significance. Only a few years ago, when the one-time Liberal Lord Chancellor vacated his office of Grand Warden, an active Conservative Lord Chancellor was appointed as his successor. Even amongst the clergy serving as officers in the British Grand Lodges there is scarcely a religious denomination that is not represented, always, of course, excluding the Roman Catholics. Numerous bishops and other dignitaries of the Church of England belong to the Grand Council of the United Grand Lodge. A Lodge almost exclusively consisting of members of the clergy meets under the shadow of Westminster Abbey, and there are two Lodges, one in London and the other in Manchester, which have only Methodists as members. In view of the composition of English Masonry, it is obvious that the working rules of English Lodges must be very strict. Any subject that might give offence or upset even one of its members is barred. Because of this the practice of the Ritual, the study and assimilation of the symbolism, the cultivation of friendship and charitable activity play the most important parts.

The fact that English Freemasons may, contrary to the practice in many other countries, belong to more than one Lodge favours the formation of class Lodges. That such class Lodges are constantly springing up is yet another proof of the uncommonly strong spiritual bond forged by Freemasonry. If this were not so, would it be possible for men who are constantly rubbing shoulders in every-day life to feel the need of imparting the masonic blessing to their association? There are Lodges for the members of certain professions and religious denominations; Lodges for Teetotallers, Rotarians, members of the Young Men's Christian Association, and Old Boys of the great public schools; Lodges for collectors, bibliophiles, officers and regiments. Two London Lodges only admit high officials of the City Corporation as members; the Worshipful Master is nearly always the Lord Mayor of London in office. There are numerous Lodges designed to knit closer the bond existing between the Colonies and the Mother Country, Lodges meeting in London which are visited by brethren coming to the capital from overseas. The English Colonials always were very fervent Freemasons. It was once said, apropos of Britain's vast colonial possessions that 'England's greatness is the work of the Freemasons'. This, of course, was an exaggeration, but it is true, nevertheless, that wherever English pioneers set foot, a masonic Lodge was quick to arise, and that many detachments of soldiers took their Lodge with them, and, wherever they served, whether in the primeval forests of Africa, in the jungles of Asia, in town or village, they set up their pillars and altar so that the brethren might attend the Lodge after their hard service in the field. And it is the same to-day. Every British colonial soldier who is a Mason carries his apron with him in his knapsack; that badge of which the Ritual says: 'It is more honourable than the highest Order'.

Rudyard Kipling, the celebrated poet, winner of the Nobel Prize for literature, who has also written a number of masonic compositions, gives us a very good idea of these overseas Lodges in his clever poem 'My Mother-Lodge', which he dedicates to the Indian Lodge 'Hope and Perseverance' in Lahore.

H.R.H. THE PRINCE OF WALES
AS PROVINCIAL GRAND MASTER OF SURREY

THE RT. HON. THE LORD AMPTHILL, G.C.S.I., G.C.I.E.

PRO GRAND MASTER UNITED GRAND LODGE OF ENGLAND

Painting presented to him by the English Craft, taken from the original by Sir Arthur Cope, R.A. The presentation picture was from the brush of Dorofield Hardy

MY MOTHER-LODGE

There was Rundle, Station Master,
An' Beazeley of the Rail,
An' 'Ackman, Commissariat,
An' Donkin' o' the Jail;
An' Blake, Conductor-Sergeant,
Our Master twice was 'e,
With 'im that kept the Europe-shop,
Old Framjee Eduljee.

Outside—'Sergeant! Sir! Salute! Salaam!'
Inside—'Brother,' an' it doesn't do no 'arm.
We met upon the Level an' we parted on the Square,
An' I was Junior Deacon in my Mother-Lodge out there!

W'd Bola Nath, accountant,
An' Saul the Aden Jew,
An' Din Mohammed, draughtsman
Of the Survey Office too;
There was Babu Chuckerbutty,
An' Amir Singh the Sikh,
An' Castro from the fittin'-sheds,
The Roman Catholick!

We 'adn't good regalia,
An' our Lodge was old an' bare,
But we knew the Ancient Landmarks,
An' we kep' 'em to a hair;
An' lookin' on it backwards
It often strikes me thus,
There ain't such things as infidels,
Excep', per'aps, it's us.

For monthly, after Labour,
We'd all sit down and smoke
(We dursn't give no banquets,
Lest a Brother's caste were broke),
An' man on man got talkin'
Religion an' the rest,
An' every man comparin'
Of the God 'e knew the best.

So man on man got talkin',
An' not a Brother stirred
Till mornin' waked the parrots
An' that dam' brain-fever-bird;
We'd say 'twas 'ighly curious,
An' we'd all ride 'ome to bed,
With Mo'ammed, God, an' Shiva
Changin' pickets in our 'ead.

Full oft on Guv'ment service
  This rovin' foot 'ath pressed,
An' bore fraternal greetin's
  To the Lodges east an' west,
Accordin' as commanded,
  From Kohat to Singapore,
But I wish that I might see them
  In my Mother-Lodge once more!

I wish that I might see them,
  My Brethren black an' brown,
With the trichies smellin' pleasant
  An' the hog-darn passin' down;
An' the old khansamah snorin'
  On the bottle-khana floor,
Like a Master in good standing
  With my Mother-Lodge once more.

Outside—'Sergeant! Sir! Salute! Salaam!'
Inside—'Brother,' an' it doesn't do no 'arm.
We met upon the Level an' we parted on the Square,
An' I was Junior Deacon in my Mother-Lodge out there!

Again, a fair number of English Lodges devote themselves seriously to masonic research. The most celebrated of these is the 'Quatuor Coronati' Lodge, the active membership of which is restricted to a select body of the most eminent historians, but the correspondence circle of which is comprised of many thousands of masonic students and researchers in all parts of the world. The publications of this Lodge are of the greatest scientific value to the Craft, and their infinite number demonstrates the enormous creative activity of the association.

The charity work of English Freemasonry would make a chapter in itself. Year in, year out, the Fraternity renders services that could hardly be exceeded in magnitude. The United Grand Lodge supports many philanthropic institutions on an extensive scale. These include two large schools for masonic orphans, one for boys and one for girls; an institution for old people and widows; the Royal Masonic Hospital, which was formally opened by the King in 1933, etc. Every year immense sums of money are placed at the disposal of these institutions, many thousands of pounds being subscribed at a single annual festival.

This same generosity manifested itself when the plan was put forward to erect in London a monument worthy of the greatness of English Freemasonry which would, at the same time, be regarded as a memorial to the British Freemasons

RUDYARD KIPLING
AUTHOR OF 'MY MOTHER LODGE'

MASONIC PEACE MEMORIAL
FREEMASONS' HALL, GREAT QUEEN STREET, LONDON
DEDICATED BY THE DUKE OF CONNAUGHT, K.G., 19 JULY, 1933
Designed by H. V. Ashley and Winton Newman, FF.R.I.B.A.

who fell in the Great War. This Memorial takes the form of a new Masonic Temple of gigantic proportions. For the erection of this edifice in Great Queen Street, no less a sum than one million pounds was required, but the money was subscribed within a short time and the foundation stone was laid in July 1927. At this ceremony the M.W. Grand Master used the same wooden mallet as that used by Sir Christopher Wren, the greatest architect England has ever known, for the laying of the foundation stone of his crowning achievement, St. Paul's Cathedral.

The official dedication of the new Temple took place on the 19th July, 1933. The exquisite and bold design of this new building will give a fresh countenance to that part of the great metropolis in which it is situated.

CHAPTER II

UNITED STATES OF AMERICA

WHILST the monumental landmark of English Freemasonry has only just been erected, American Freemasonry, so closely related to it, already boasts of hundreds. It would be impossible nowadays to conjure up a picture of a large American city without its towering masonic Temples, which are frequently amongst the most important pieces of architecture of the city. These take the form of 'sky-scrapers' which tower into the heavens and compete with those devoted to commerce, etc. These colossal buildings of the most extravagant splendour give some indication of the numerical strength of the American Craft. A glance at the statistics at our disposal shows us that they constitute the great majority of the world's Freemasons. Every one of the North American States has its own Grand Lodge. Excluding Canada, they embrace no less than 16,750 Lodges, with three and a quarter million members, that is to say, almost 82 per cent. of all Freemasons.

These figures demonstrate clearly the tremendous progress that Freemasonry has made in the United States. There are Lodges everywhere; they exist in the most out-of-the-way places in the mountains, in the middle of the broadest prairies, in outpost blockhouses in which small detachments of soldiers keep their lonely vigil, in the stony wastes of the Rocky Mountains, and even in the inhospitable prospectors' camps and icy wastes of the extreme North. And in the midst of a forest it is possible to come across a rectangular clearing containing a primitive Lodge, roughly constructed of logs. There are not only Lodges, but also clubs and associations, and innumerable Chapters of all kinds of masonic Rites, which, in themselves, are organizations with hundreds of thousands of members. Amongst these are the Scottish Rite, the 'Knights Templars' and the 'Nobles of the Mystic Shrine'. The latter Order incorporates no masonic system, but is intended to serve as the playground of the Brotherhood, and the endeavour of its members is to lay stress on the brighter side of life, whilst at the same time dispensing charity.

Discord of all kinds in Freemasonry has already been mentioned many times in these pages. The fact that there are forty-nine Grand Lodges in North America has nothing to do with these differences of opinion. It is true that they all go their own sweet way, but, even in their independence, they live in truly beautiful harmony. Wherever differences in the working are to be found, they can always be explained by the environment. The number of central authorities arises solely out of the masonic law of territoriality—'A Grand Lodge for each State!' which has been rigidly adhered to in the United States. Almost all of them have one thing in common with their mother, the Grand Lodge of England, i.e. a constant and rapid growth that is, perhaps, still more marked in the States than in England. While Freemasonry in other countries has exhibited no inclination to deviate from the principle of strict selectivity, the Americans have for a long time past declared for the theory of 'number'. The Lodges there hold the view that a society designed to serve the idea of 'Fraternity' must, of necessity, admit every free man of good report who is capable of assimilating and acting upon this idea. And they act in accordance with this point of view. It can safely be said that every tenth American of full age is a Freemason, though naturally this popularization of Freemasonry finds as many opponents as champions.

There is no lack of voices declaring that American Freemasonry must be raised to a higher intellectual level. It is necessary, they claim, to use the Lodges more as places for the study of philosophical, ethical and social questions. But the general tendency is quite contrary to this line of thought. The majority of the leaders of American Freemasonry maintain that it is by no means a question of intellect, but rather of cultivation of sentiment as a means of inspiring the brethren with the idea of Fraternity. Men, they argue, must be educated to the consciousness of their interdependence and be guided in the direction of Unity, and Freemasonry is an excellent means to this end.

This urge towards Fraternity has been demonstrated by very many American Freemasons in a most striking manner. This, no doubt, makes itself felt less in the wild rush of the metropolis than in the smaller towns and in the country, but there are brethren everywhere to whom the Lodge, or the Freemasons' Club, is a place of refuge where the deadly struggle and the flurry and scurry of every-day life may be forgotten, and where they can be men amongst men. The desire to cultivate masonic friendship with members of the same profession is very marked. There is probably no trade or profession which has not its Lodges or circles that are models of true fellowship. Doctors and lawyers, policemen and merchants, arctic explorers and firemen, teachers and engineers, soldiers and craftsmen— all have their masonic organizations. And this applies even to actors and journalists, who can only commence work on 'the rough ashlar' after their 'daily work' is finished (long after midnight); it is the same with the film people who, in the Hollywood '233 Club', have created an association in which the merest 'super' rubs shoulders on terms of equality with the most celebrated 'stars' (almost all of whom are Freemasons); there are seafarers who put on their regalia and 'stand to order' when on the high seas, and there are long-distance fliers who, like Lindbergh, Byrd, Balchen and Floyd Bennet,[1] affix their Master Mason's certificate to the aircraft that is to carry them over the Atlantic, or hoist the masonic banner on the Polar ice.

As we have already seen, there was a time when the aims of American Freemasonry were confined within extremely narrow bounds. That was in the times of George Washington[2] and Benjamin Franklin.

What these Freemasons thought of the State they founded— their democratic, political, and social ideals—is incorporated in the Constitutions of the various States and other documents of the time. The following beautiful passage, which obviously originated in masonic philosophy, was prominent in the Constitution of the State of Massachusetts and played an important role in the abolition of slavery in that State:

'. . . All men are born free and equal, and have certain natural, essential, and inalienable rights; among which may be reckoned the right of enjoying and defending their lives and liberties; that of acquiring, possessing, and protecting property; in fine, that of seeking and obtaining their safety and happiness.'

At that time the Lodges of the patriots were by no means overburdened with members. Nowadays, it is explained,

[1] The heroic pilot who died as a result of an illness brought on by his flight to the extreme north of America in order to render aid to the German ocean-flyers Köhl and Hünefeld.

[2] On a hill at Alexandria a tower is now being erected by all the American Grand Lodges as a monument to Washington, and this is to become a place of pilgrimage for all Freemasons.

Freemasonry is a much more widely spread organization than in the days of the War of Independence; hence larger and larger circles are introduced to the Fraternity and masonic life is to a large extent enacted in public. Freemasons usually take a leading part in the parades which fill the avenues with colourful splendour at all great American festivals, and they march in the processions wearing their aprons. When the foundation stone of a new masonic Temple is to be laid, it is a matter of interest to the whole city, as if it were an ordinary public building. Congresses of many of the numerous masonic associations attract hundreds of thousands, and such an assembly hardly ever takes place without messages containing masonic instruction being broadcast over the whole Union by the radio stations; messages preaching brotherly love and attacking that form of intolerance which is gaining ground in many circles under cover of the slogan 'One-hundred per cent American'. The majority of the American Grand Lodges have declared themselves particularly antagonistic to the outrageous Ku-Klux-Klan secret society, and most of them have declared membership of this organization to be a serious masonic offence. The Grand Master of Kentucky decreed in 1923:

'We cannot subscribe to the theory that any number of men have the right to form an invisible empire and under the cover of darkness attempt to regulate their fellowmen. An organization which appeals to religious prejudices and racial hatred is unmasonic, and if any member thinks more of the invisible empire than of Freemasonry, he should be dealt with by having the severest penalty known to Masonry inflicted upon him or them. The Jew and the Gentile have equal rights, and all mankind should be permitted to serve God according to the dictates of his own heart.'

Br. Tompkins, the Grand Master of New York, expressed himself even more vigorously in a speech in 1924, in which he censured as unjust, un-American, and un-Christian the endeavour of the Klan only to admit to the Government white people of Protestant faith.

Masonic Divine Services are often arranged in the churches of the various denominations. Members of the clergy who belong to the Fraternity wear masonic regalia over their vestments, and, attended by brethren of their congregation, preach on masonic ideals. Underlying all this is obviously the idea of bringing the doings of Freemasons before the eye of the public as much as possible, in order to demonstrate that Freemasonry is not an institution which flourishes underground. That this is recognized by the civil authorities is demonstrated by the fact that not only were a great many of the past Presidents of the United States Freemasons (MacKinley, Roosevelt, Taft, and Harding in our own time, as also the present President, Franklin D. Roosevelt), but that even those who did not belong to the Fraternity seldom missed an opportunity of meeting the official personalities of Freemasonry. And on more than one occasion, newly elected Presidents have taken the oath on the volume of the Sacred Law of the New York 'St. John's Lodge No. 1' on taking up office at the White House. It was this Bible that was used at Washington's inauguration ceremony.

A wonderful tribute to Freemasonry was paid by President Warren G. Harding, who died in the year 1923. A few months before his passing, he used the following words at a great masonic assembly in Washington:

'No man has ever taken oaths and entered into solemn obligations more conscientiously and after deeper reflection than I did on taking the various degrees in Freemasonry, and I say after ripe consideration: I have never, in Freemasonry, come across a doctrine or heard expression given to an obligation, which could not be broadcast to the whole world.'

On another occasion in Birmingham, Alabama, he said:

'The fraternal spirit is one of the finest in our country. I want to see more of the fraternal spirit among nations.'

Harding attempted to translate this truly masonic ideal into practice by convening a Disarmament Conference in Washington. That the results of this conference did not come up to his expectations is quite another matter. This fiasco, however, did not shake the President's belief in the eventual victory of the masonic idea. Even on his death-bed he dispatched an address to Hollywood which concluded with the words:

'I am full of optimism that the fraternal spirit will continue to grow and that the obstacles in our path will be successfully overcome and the barriers dividing the nations in the world will be torn down. . . .'

It is the special endeavour of the Grand Lodge of New York to work for the removal of any such barriers standing between Freemasons. Since the end of the war this Obedience, which has also found it possible to establish friendly relations with the Catholics of its State, sends a mission to the European Grand Lodges every year, in order to give proof of its desire for collaborative activity. On these journeys the Historian of the Grand Lodge, Ossian Lang, always acts as deputy for the Grand Master in office. These missions have naturally not remained unnoticed in antagonistic circles and self-styled 'well-informed observers' have been whispering of late that the 'centre of world conspiracy' has recently removed its abode to New York.

The traditional association of American Freemasons with the spirit of the American Constitution makes it unavoidable that American Freemasonry should, to a certain extent, regard itself as the guardian of this constitutional document. In addition to that, enthusiastic work on educational problems plays an important part in the activities of many Grand Lodges. American Freemasonry was always intent on allowing the idea of interdependence to illustrate itself first in the schools. It was Freemasonry that fostered the national schools, that is to say, those schools which must be attended by every child irrespective of class, religion, or birth. Thus it was that the first school in New York City to abandon the system hitherto in force of segregating the children according to their religions, was founded by Freemasons and was for many years supported entirely by them. The desirability of having one school only for rich and poor members of all the various religious denominations was first propounded with success in America.

The important material effects that this interest in education can have is illustrated by an endowment of very recent date. No less a sum than one million dollars has been placed at the disposal of the University of the Capital of the Union by the Supreme Council of the Scottish Rite in Washington, represented by its Grand Commander, John H. Cowles—an endowment which was designed to provide a chair of National Economy and Diplomacy, and this useful sum has subsequently been considerably increased by further masonic donations. That money for philanthropic objects should flow abundantly from masonic circles is, as in England, taken as a matter of course. But there are many branches of charity-work in which the benevolence of Freemasonry has attracted public attention

even in America. The care of orphans by the Fraternity of
Pennsylvania, the many hospitals for crippled children, perhaps
the best-equipped in the world, which owe their existence to
the masonic association of the 'Shriners', many sanatoria for
tuberculosis, the great New York Freemasons' Hospital and
many other institutions are private creations of no ordinary
kind.

CHAPTER III

FRANCE AND BELGIUM

As compared with the Anglo-Saxon Freemasons, who are, of course, in the majority, continental Masons are few in number. Consequently, the various shades of masonic thought which exist on the Continent are thrown into greater relief and the pulse of individualism throbs all the more strongly in many of the Grand Lodges. This individual and intellectual outlook is to the fore in Latin Freemasonry, and, in this category, the French are outstanding.

French Freemasonry has developed very uniformly since, in the 'seventies of the last century, the Radical elements of the community returned to the fold in such a decisive manner. The struggle between the systems then, to a certain extent, ceased; the 30,000 Masons of the Grand Orient, imbued with an extremely liberal spirit, work in harmony with the 15,000 members of the Grande Loge de France, which arose out of the Suprême Conseil of the Scottish Rite in 1879. However, the latter organization has not carried the principle of Tolerance so far away from the English conception as did the Grand Orient in 1877, and the words 'Great Architect of the Universe' still stand at the head of its Ritual, whereas the Grand Orient, even after sixty years, still holds the view that this constitutes dogma to which it cannot subscribe. At the Convention of 1877, which was of such great consequence, the Protestant Pastor Desmons cried out to his brethren:

'Leave it to the theologians to discuss dogma. Freemasonry must remain what it is. It must never enter the arena of theological discussion; it must take care never to try to become a church, a council, or a synod.'

And Arthur Groussier, the President of the Council of the Order and a former Vice-President of the Chamber of Deputies, repeated this at the Convention of the year 1927. To a statement published shortly before by an authoritative Dutch Freemason named Gonsalves, in which he reproached the Grand Orient and asserted that the principle of Freemasonry was definitely religious inasmuch as the Brotherhood is deeply rooted in its belief in the existence of a spiritual and moral system in the world that enables mankind to progress, Groussier replied:

'It is true that we are not imbued with the marked religious spirit of the Anglo-Saxon Lodges. But even if, in the course of time, we have developed in such a way that we profess absolute freedom of thought, have not other Obediences also, to a certain extent departed from the wonderful principles of Tolerance, Morality, and Fraternity which are embodied in our Constitution, and have they not also drawn near to one of the recognized creeds? We do not reproach them in any way; we respect their belief completely. We have not the slightest adverse criticism to make against any Rite; we demand only that those of a different mind should remember that Tolerance is one of the chief virtues of Freemasonry. Let them retain their dogma if their creed so demands, but let them also allow us, for our part, to deny the infallibility of the dogmas. . . . True, in this twentieth century, materialists do exist within our ranks. But even in the eighteenth century prominent members of this school of thought were members of our Lodges. Is it surprising, therefore, that those people who, in particular, are mercilessly persecuted by the various religious bodies, should seek sanctuary in the Temple of Freedom of Thought?

'Even downright Spiritualists are to be found in our Lodges, for the Grand Orient preaches no dogma; that is to say it teaches neither atheism nor materialism nor deism. It takes care neither to instruct its members to recognize certain principles nor to reject others; it merely exhorts its brethren to be thinking men.'

The Grand Orient is not expected to abandon this attitude' despite all efforts to induce it to teach a better one in the interest of International Freemasonry. It clings to the conviction that 'Freedom of Conscience' should rid the individual of the social obligation to profess any form of creed. It is, however, as already stated, ready to regard any religious man who recognizes this standpoint and is able, consistent with his creed, honestly to conform to it, as a person of the same conviction, and to open its portals wide for his reception; and it believes that it has thus correctly interpreted the tenet that all men are the sons of one father, that is to say, that the human race constitutes one single unit.

Now let us consider the position of French Freemasonry in regard to politics. Nowadays it has become a very common thing to speak of 'French political Freemasonry'. 'The Grand Orient secretly directs the League of Nations' is one view; 'It finances the anti-fascist machinations' is a second; and 'Dark ways lead from the Paris headquarters of Freemasonry into the world of political intrigue' is a third. Here again we will let President Groussier have his say. To the accusation 'You take active part in politics! In exactly the same way as Rome, you are striving for political power!' he replies:

'Ethical power?' Yes!

'Political domination?' No!

'Our Order aspires as little to power as it would submit to it. It defends ideas but categorically refuses to satisfy ambitious desires.'

These are the facts: If by 'politics' one understands interference with the shaping of the internal life of other nations, or participation in party struggles, then neither the Grand Orient nor the Grand Lodge have anything to do with politics; it is expressly forbidden in the Lodges to interfere in electoral struggles. That must be so even for practical reasons, quite apart from the question of principle. For although not every political camp is represented in the Lodges, as in England,[1] French Freemasons, to which a large number of the 'intellectuals' belong, is, nevertheless, composed of members of all kinds of democratic and republican, but not reactionary, groups, and is by no means exclusively made up of Socialists and Radicals, as is generally supposed by non-Masons. But, no matter to how many camps these men may belong, they are, nevertheless, united in regarding it as their common task to discuss everything connected with the intellectual and social progress of mankind. Thus it is that there are few new ideas that do not have an echo in the Temples of French Freemasonry. Although socialistic views do not preponderate, the brethren grapple with the problem of the rational alleviation of human suffering, and, without preaching antagonism to religion, they advocate the separation of the schools from the Church. They endeavour, as far as possible, to consider with an open mind all proposals for the general good and for mutual understanding. And they have also recorded their views regarding the position occupied by French Freemasons in the life of the nation.

[1] With the exception of the Communists.

'The special position of French Freemasonry has become quite clear under the Third Republic. Its history records an important part of the mighty struggle that led to the re-birth of the French nation. Freemasonry has borne a burden that has perhaps damaged it and left its mark on it, but it has thereby rendered its country a service of inestimable value.'[1]

French Freemasonry especially, although so often stigmatized as a secret society of the deepest dye, furnishes proof again and again of how absurd it is to believe in a conventicle of unknown rulers, who, amidst mystical forms of adjuration, make world-revolutionary decisions in the mysterious gloom of their Temple and pass these on to the responsible statesmen to be put into effect. All decisions made leave the Lodges in the form of resolutions which are handed to the Press, or in pamphlets setting forth the results of the discussions, or in public measures. Every week thousands of men, and often women, are to be seen in the great hall in the rue Cadet and in the crypt in the rue Puteaux—the two great assembly rooms of the Grand Orient and the Grand Lodge—where they are informed of the aims of Freemasonry by eminent orators. These public meetings are known as 'Tenues blanches', and, very often, public leaders who do not belong to the Fraternity are given the courtesy of the platform. Never does one hear party affairs discussed at these assemblies, or in the more intimate circle of the Lodges. Whenever French Freemasonry takes any active interest in public affairs it is always in respect of questions of a higher order. At the time when it was a question of rescuing the whole country from the machinations of General Boulanger, who was consumed by a deadly hatred of Germany and an antagonism against the Republic, the Freemasons were at their posts. The same was the case when the public mind was so excited by the terrible injustice of the Dreyfus affair,[2] and when the question of the parting of Church and State arose. Their intervention is always in defence of the thought of national democracy and cultural liberalism.

[1] C. N. Starcke: *Die Freimaurerei, ihre geschichtliche Entwicklung und kulturelle Bedeutung bei den verschiedenen Völkern.* Hamburg. 1913.
[2] For instance, the heroic Col. Picquart, whose sense of justice led him to suffer tremendous persecution, expulsion from the Army, and arrest, in order to prove the innocence of Captain Dreyfus, was an ardent member of the Brotherhood.

FRENCH PRISONERS OF WAR JEWELS

DERISIVE PICTURE

FRONTISPIECE TO 'LES FRANÇS-MAÇONS ÉCRASÉS', 1747

Engraving by S. Fokke

The question whether the idea of tolerance is to be reconciled with the marked anti-clerical tendencies of the French Brotherhood has often been investigated. Anyone who knows of the relentless war which the Church has waged against Freemasonry for more than a century need not look far for the answer. The anti-freemasonic Papal Encyclicals of the nineteenth century have given birth to widespread organizations whose sole object is to fight the 'wicked sect' without mercy. It is very difficult indeed to give an adequate description of the severity of these attacks. Even the schoolchildren were taught to fear and loathe Freemasons. They were slandered in the newspapers. Their names were placarded, and attempts were made to ruin them in business, to make their lives impossible for them in the Army and in the Government, and to brand them as anarchists and agitators.

'Freemasons disturb the peace of countries and work for the subjection and destruction of nations of the orthodox faith. Their activity is a plot against society, their liberalism has undermined the principle of authority and leads to chaos. Theirs is the most criminal of all secret societies. The whole burden of blame for the most wicked and murderous attacks against the Fatherland falls upon them.'

Such statements can be read almost daily. And it is not surprising that these denunciations emanating from Rome should call forth resistance, from sheer necessity and lead to the attitude towards militant Catholicism that is so peculiar to the French Obediences. They are faced with the necessity of fighting a defensive action, but for some considerable time past this has been carried on with marked passivity. Other problems have come to the fore: the combating of epidemics of disease, educational reform, and, above all, the question of Peace. Unlike the Anglo-Saxon Grand Lodges, whose members, generally speaking, entertain uniform views in regard to the execution of the masonic tasks, because of their fundamentally narrower sphere of activity, opinions in France are frequently at absolute variance. Hardly two Lodges are alike. Many are places of assembly for the keenest intellects, others resemble humanitarian clubs; to many the Ritual is the living embodiment, to others it is the inner meaning of their work on the rough ashlar. But since the end of the Great War, unanimity has reigned on one point. They feel themselves bound to march at the head of all those who are filled with the desire to make up the quarrel between France and Germany,[1] to get rid of the mania of hatred and to make the whole world conscious of the interdependence of mankind.

'Freemasonry is either universal or it is nothing!'

That is the theory impressed upon every newly admitted Freemason. For many years past the possibilities of abolishing the horrors of war and creating an atmosphere of peace have been discussed. The *rapprochement franco-allemand* has, again and again, been one of the subjects passed on to the Lodges for discussion by the Conventions of the Grand Orient and the Grand Lodge, which are held in the autumn of each year. Long before Thoiry and Locarno, at a time when political violence was the order of the day, the view was expressed that there should be one French policy only—that of reconciliation, and a 'Comité Fraternité-Réconciliation' was founded. It was declared that the Peace Treaty was unjust and that the occupation of the Rhineland should be ended as quickly as possible. At the 1924 Convention, a member of the Grand Lodge said that the Treaty of Versailles[2] 'ferments hatred and is a disgrace to its authors, who wish to throw a nation into bondage in the twentieth century'. And a resolution of the Convention approved of disarmament in a military, moral, economic, and financial sense, and the education of nations to be peace-loving. The view was also expressed that it is the main duty of France to fight against the hatred incited by the War and 'to proclaim Peace in the world'.

'We should not threaten but conciliate; we should not thump the table with our fist, but offer the hand of friendship.

'Germany should be offered a Court of Arbitration without conditions and without reservations. Her entry into the League of Nations should be worked for energetically. (At that time, Germany had not joined the League.)

'The withdrawal of the army of occupation in the Ruhr should be accelerated.

[1] Even before the Great War this desire prevailed. At the beginning of 1914, the Grand Lodge studied the 'chimera' of a friendship with the German Reich and was thereupon accused of entertaining unpatriotic views; the Grand Orient brought about the meeting of German and French parliamentarians at Bern, with the object of creating better relations.

[2] 'The Peace Treaties are the temporary triumph of boundless egotism. Instead of eliminating, or at least reducing, all sources of future conflict, they have perpetuated them,' said Camille Savoire, one of the highest officers of the Grand Lodge, at Belgrade in 1926.

'The agreement with Germany must preclude every military alliance with other States.

'Customs barriers, the chief causes of war, with all its misery, must be abolished as far as possible.

'Everything that can further the mutual, intellectual, and ethical intercourse of the two races, whose respective cultures are mutually complementary, is to be supported.

'Chauvinism and provocative methods are to be attacked with the utmost vigour.

'Youth should be made conscious of the interdependence of mankind, and anything that might possibly promote hatred must be eliminated from the educational curriculum. Germans and Frenchmen must be made to realize the infinite suffering and fratricide they have endured since the splitting of Charlemagne's Empire in the eleventh century. They must begin to learn that every transgression committed by the one nation against the spirit of peace must be followed by a similar transgression by the other.

'Every Frenchman must know what European culture owes to the Germany of the Renaissance, the romantic poetry, the spirit of Weimar and the great German philosophers.

'The German language must be taught in the schools, for without this the German soul can never be properly understood.

'The exchange of students and schoolchildren should be effected on the largest possible scale. Only thus can the children help to lead the older generation, who still cling to their inveterate hatred, back to consciousness of the duties of civilized man.'

Thus resolved the Grand Lodge; and the Grand Orient likewise. And they acted accordingly. They organized assemblies in which the antagonism—unfortunately not yet eradicated—was traced back to its true causes, whereby very valuable work was done. Public opinion was lastingly influenced by demonstrations advocating Peace; and the work is being continued. No Convention has been held since 1923 [1] which has not

[1] In this year 1923, when the post-War anti-German national policy of Poincaré's *bloc* had reached its zenith, a speaker at the Grand Banquet of the Grand Orient criticized this in strong terms: 'What shall we say to this Government which, by its irresponsible behaviour, does not allow the world to settle down. Is it not sheer madness to penetrate into the territory of a neighbouring country in times of peace? Such action . . . is a crime! Millerand and Poincaré and the *bloc* hinder the understanding with Germany that we so much desire. They goad the people on and deceive them.' At

expressed its wish for peace and its deep desire for an understanding between the two races.

André Lebey, one of the leading Freemasons of the Grand Orient, has coined a phrase for this persistence: 'No Utopia, no illusion can remove our conviction that if mankind does not destroy war, war will destroy mankind. Ideals do not materialize, and are never realized, if they are not advocated time and again.' And Maurice Monier, Grand Master of the Grand Lodge,[1] issued the watchword in 1927: 'The only task of present-day Freemasonry is to work for Peace!'

French Freemasonry would naturally like to perform this work in collaboration with the German Grand Lodges. It has therefore made many attempts to bring about a revival of the intercourse which had been completely stopped by the War, but, up to the present time, the results have been negative. On one solitary occasion—in February 1927—at the suggestion of the French, an informatory conversation took place at Frankfort-on-Main between Herr Ludwig Ries, Grand Master of the Eclectic Union, Senator Brenier, at that time President of the Grand Council of the Grand Orient, and M. Doignon, Deputy Grand Master of the Grand Lodge.

Herr Ludwig Ries took the opportunity of raising several questions touching upon the occupation of the Rhineland and the matter of 'responsibility or guilt' for the war. Both French Obediences,[2] however, were obliged to express their regret that they were not in a position to intervene in the political adjustment of questions of an international character existing between France and Germany.

about the same time, the Grand Lodge drew the Government's attention to the way in which anti-German songs were being tolerated in cabarets and café concerts. And the Verdun Lodge urged reconciliation with the words, 'From the devastated ground of Verdun, from this blood-drenched city, shall go up the first cry for moral disarmament.'

[1] Whose head, for the period 1928–1931, was Lucien Le Foyer, the most active of French pacifists.

[2] In addition to these, a third Grand Lodge, the 'Grande Loge Nationale Indépendante et Régulière', has been working since 1913; the membership of this is, at the moment, still quite small. It was brought into being by two Grand Orient Lodges, the ancient 'L'Anglaise' Lodge in Bordeaux (founded 1732), mainly composed of English Freemasons settled in France, and the Paris Lodge 'Centre des Amis', which two Lodges were joined in 1914 by a new foundation, the English 'St. George' Lodge of Paris. This Grand Lodge, which is based entirely upon the principles of the English Brotherhood and is therefore recognized by the Grand Lodge of England and Anglo-Saxon Freemasonry, has founded a number of daughter Lodges since the War. They number 27, as compared with the 425 of the Grand Orient and over 200 of the Grand Lodge.

When speaking of Freemasonry in Latin countries, mention must also be made of the Grand Orient of Belgium, whose head, until 1929, was the President of the Senate, Charles Magnette, who, until 1927, was President of the Advisory Committee of the 'Association Maçonnique Internationale' [1] and one of the most important of Belgian Liberal parliamentarians. This masonic organization, with its marked intellectual character, is closely related to French Freemasonry, but it goes further than the latter in its intensive cultivation of ritual and symbolism. Like Magnette, many Belgian Freemasons, such as Count Goblet d'Alviella, ex-Minister of State, a brilliant scientist and prolific author; Senator Lafontaine, the winner of the Nobel Prize for Peace; Emil Vandervelde, the statesman; Pierre Tempels, the great eclectic, and the lawyers Fernand Levêque and Raoul Engel (Grand Master since 1928), have rendered valuable service to international Freemasonry, or have done great work for the systematic inculcation and propagation of its principles.

For decades Belgian Freemasonry was also the object of a fanatical resistance from clerical circles. Hardly had Baron van Stassart, President of the Senate and Governor of Brabant, accepted the dignity of First Grand Master of the Grand Orient in the 'thirties of the last century, than the Archbishop of Mecheln (1837) put the whole of Belgian Freemasonry under a ban, in spite of the fact that very many faithful Catholics were to be found in its ranks; the example of the Bishop of Liège, who held Lodge-meetings in his own palace, still being before their eyes. Two years after the great ban, persecution became the order of the day. The names of the brethren were published, and whosoever became known as a Freemason was threatened with material loss of business and social ostracism of the most rigid kind. The President of the Senate, the Governor of Brussels, and many other officials lost their posts. For a certain length of time the Brotherhood was powerless against these onslaughts, although even King Leopold I was a Freemason. But after a while the defenders began to gain in strength. Both in the Chamber and in the Senate masonic parliamentarians took up the fight with the greatest vigour and determination against this persecution that had such a cruel effect upon the private lives of the brethren. The threatened ideals were fought for with the utmost ardour, and time and again the masonic view was

[1] See chapter 'The Beginnings of an International Organization.'

defended from the parliamentary benches by the Liberal leaders van Schorr, Tuisseaux, and Verhaegen.

In this way great service was rendered to freedom of thought which had (and still has) a sanctuary in the Brussels Free University ('Université libre'), which was founded at the suggestion of Pierre Théodore Verhaegen, sometime Worshipful Master of the Lodge 'Les Amis Philanthropes', and, subsequently, Grand Master.

The Grand Lodge of Belgium has on many occasions arranged international masonic congresses. Its desire for peace has often been manifested, an outstanding instance of this being the demonstration in connexion with the Tripoli War. At the Congress of 1910 (the year of the World Exhibition) M. Sluys, the Deputy Grand Master, expressed the desires of Belgian Freemasons in the following terms:

'1. Freedom of conscience is the fundamental principle of Freemasonry. It joins the masonic authorities of the world fraternally for the purpose of joint endeavour; yet they preserve complete autonomy and adhere to the regulation that the admission of new members shall never be prohibited on the score of religion, nationality, or race.

'2. The Constitution forbids the Lodges to engage in politics or religious matters; this prohibition, however, is not to be interpreted in the sense that the impartial discussion of religious, philosophical, social, or political questions is excluded, since any theory may be subjected to elucidation and unrestricted criticism within the bosom of the Lodge, provided that the freedom of conscience of the members of the Lodge is in no way prejudiced by the creation of majorities or minorities by voting.

'3. It is the duty of each and every Mason to intercede in everyday life as much for the freedom of thought of his fellow-citizens as for his own, to bring this about by any legal means, and to help to cultivate it where it does not exist, and to defend it when it is threatened. Each brother himself determines the manner in which he shall perform this duty; the Lodge makes no suggestion in this respect.

'4. The Fraternity of Freemasons, as such, abstains from all political action; it is left entirely to the free will of the members whether they engage in politics in everyday life or not, and no instructions are given as to voting at elections.'

CHAPTER IV

GERMANY

GERMAN Freemasonry, with its multiform systems, is not so easy to analyse as that of other countries. The strong intellectual characteristics which have struggled for expression since the appearance of the reformers in the various systems; the efforts made to create a masonic philosophy; the cultivation of technology; the enthusiastic endeavours of eminent thinkers and authors to solve all kinds of problems; and the numerous peculiar points of view that have resulted from the development of life in the Lodges, which, right from the beginning, was so multicoloured in Germany, have caused the contours to stand out all the more sharply and have created more clearly defined divisions than were to be found elsewhere. Since 1918 these had become even more marked. For since the Great War a somewhat new situation had arisen, which had been brought about by the great catastrophe, by the results consequent upon it, and by the necessity of self-protection against certain groups which used the Fraternity as a scapegoat and attempted to blame it for all the distress that had fallen upon Germany. These groups also accused the German Fraternity of having had treacherous friendships during the War and assigned to it the blame for Germany's collapse and her subjection to a Jewish anti-national yoke that undermined the Christian faith and subverted every patriotic sentiment. These accusations have long since been refuted and, in normal times, would have vanished beyond recall, but, at a time when the whole German nation was in a state of ferment, they could not fail to have a certain effect upon those people who were groping so hysterically in the dark for the 'guilty parties'.

From a superficial point of view the Freemasonry of the German Reich might, until the commencement of the Hitler régime, be divided into two groups, comprising ten Grand Lodges.[1]

[1] An eleventh Grand Lodge—the 'Freemasons' Union of the Rising Sun'— which was formerly located in Nuremberg, but was subsequently directed from Hamburg, was not recognized as regular. It was founded as a 'Reform Grand Lodge' on a monistical basis, published valuable writings and carried on a determined fight against hatred between nations. The manner in which it came into being, however, by no means conformed to the conditions generally associated with the founding of a new Grand Lodge.

One group comprised humanitarian Masonry based on the old English usage, which only recognized the three St. John's degrees and asked no questions as to the creed of the candidate, valuing him according to his personal merit. To this category belong the following seven Grand Lodges:

The Grand Lodge of Hamburg,
The National Grand Lodge of Saxony at Dresden,
The Grand Lodge 'Sun' at Bayreuth,
The Mother Grand Lodge of the Eclectic Union of Free-masons at Frankfort-on-Main,
The Grand Lodge 'Concord' at Darmstadt,
The Grand Lodge 'German Fraternal Chain' at Leipzig, and
The Symbolic Grand Lodge of Germany.

The other group comprised the Christian Masonry of the three old Prussian Grand Lodges, which made admission into their Lodges dependent upon Christian faith and which had added high degrees to the St. John's degrees or, at least, had incorporated stages of knowledge. These Berlin Grand Lodges were as follow:

The Grand National Mother Lodge of the 'Three Globes',
The National Grand Lodge of all German Freemasons (a German-Christian Order), and
The Grand Lodge of Prussia of Friendship (formerly 'Royal York').

The Swedish system of the National Grand Lodge 'still contained the strongest traces of legendary chivalric culture, and, with its high-degree Ritual and symbols of a pronounced and positive Christian character, it was the most exclusively Christian of all the various systems of these three Obediences. The high degrees of the Grand National Mother Lodge might also be described as positively Christian in principle, but in the case of the Grand Lodge of Prussia the transition to the more general masonic view could already be clearly seen.'[1]

This positive Christian outlook was, for example, expressed in the General Principles of the Grand National Mother Lodge in the following words:

'The Brotherhood perceives in the doctrine and life of the Master from Nazareth the greatest revelation of God. It

[1] Gotthilf Schenkel: *Die Freimaurer im Lichte der Religions- und Kirchengeschichte*. Gotha. 1926.

attacks no ecclesiastical dogma; it has indeed adopted no dogma, but bases itself on Christ's teaching.'

The National Grand Lodge, however, which, by the way, also adhered strictly to the Order-like character of its system, described the latter[1] in the following sentences:

'It is a method, tested by the practical work of centuries, of leading men of good intention back to that which man so easily loses in life, namely, the consciousness of his being a child of God. And only He who called Himself the Son of Man, but Who, nevertheless, spoke of God, in a special sense, as 'His Father', can be the Leader in this. Thus it was that the manifestation of Christ became the central point of the work of our Order. . . . Not only His teachings, but also His manifestation. . . . In our highest degrees the certainty that complete and conclusive revelation of God is given in His person and teachings, stands out in bold relief.'

In order to demonstrate this difference between humanitarian and ancient Prussian Freemasonry, we must once again cast a glance back on the history of German Masonry. Frederick William III's Edict of 1798, which only sanctioned in Prussia the activities of the three Berlin Grand Lodges, enabled the extension of Freemasonry to take a course somewhat parallel with that of the State groupings; the formation of Grand Lodges followed the example set them in the realm of politics,[2] and the Grand Lodges formed in the nineteenth century avoided all that which had previously been the object of strife. One question, however, did for some time play an important part in all these bodies; a question which, with the exception of the three northern States, has scarcely made an appearance in any country, namely, the Jewish question. According to the idea of Tolerance as laid down in the 'Antient Charges' of 1723, neither race nor creed can form a ground for exclusion from the Fraternity of Freemasons. Thus there were 'Jews and Christians' in a London Lodge as early as 1723, for in the Home of Freemasonry there has never been any restriction as to creed, with the exception of the rejection of atheism.

In Germany it was different. The admission of persons

---

[1] *Die Grosse Landesloge von Deutschland in ihrem Werden und Wesen.* Berlin. Mittler. 1929.

[2] The 'German Fraternal Chain' arose much later; it resulted in 1924 from the 'Freie Vereinigung' of five highly respected, ancient and independent Central German Lodges.

professing religions other than Christianity was naturally impossible in the case of the Templars of the Holy Sepulchre, and the same applied to those who were swept along by enthusiasm for Christian mysticism, both of which held sway for decades. Many people held the view that the idea which led in 1723 to the formulation of the 'universal religion' was that of a Christian Church according to the conception of Comenius, that is to say, a reconciliation of the various Christian denominations that were at loggerheads with one another. Those who made use of Comenius's name had a very scanty idea of his views, for his Brotherhood of Humanity was also designed to exclude nobody, to be all-embracing. Did he not say, in his Panegersia, of the spiritual edifice he had in mind:

'Mother Earth bears and feeds us all. The air fills our lungs and refreshes all mankind. The same heaven is above our heads. The same sun by day and the same stars by night light us all alternately. The same spark of life glows within us. We are all fellow-citizens of one world. Why should we not then join together in a single Commonwealth under the same laws?' [1]

This point of view, the only proper conception of the idea of Tolerance, has always been represented in the Freemasonry of almost every land: 'We certainly regard all Masons as Brothers, be they Christians, Jews or Mussulmen; for Freemasonry is universal and not restricted to any particular creed, sect or mode of worshipping God,' said a speaker in an English Lodge in 1757. And this conviction, which was also held by Desaguliers and Anderson, and which on one occasion only—in 1738—seemed temporarily to disappear, when mention was made in the second edition of the *Book of Constitutions* of a 'catholic', instead of a 'universal' religion, has, since that time, suffered no change.

In Germany, however, the Worshipful Master of the 'Three Globes' Lodge declared in 1763 that only Christians could become members of the Order. Other Lodges acted in the same way without a 'Jewish question' arising. This Jewish question first arose when a number of Germans of the Jewish faith, who had been initiated in France, applied to the Grand Orient of France, together with a number of Protestants, for a Charter to set up a Lodge in Frankfort-on-Main. This application

[1] See *Allgemeines Handbuch der Freimaurerei*, 3rd edition, vol i, p. 513. Leipzig. 1900.

being granted, the Lodge received the name 'L'Aurore nais-
sante' ('Nascent Dawn') and began to develop rapidly. Ludwig
Börne, the much-praised political author; Bertrand Auerbach,
the poet and a passionate supporter of the idea of German
unity, who was condemned for his membership of the 'Bur-
schenschaft'; Gabriel Riesser, the successful champion of the
Jews in their struggle for equality of civil rights, and other
important men were subsequently members of this Lodge.
It was in this circle that Börne made his glorious speech,[1]
many quotations from which have passed into recent rituals:

> 'Masonry is the holy fountain where faded beauty finds
> once more its adoration; where obscured wisdom regains
> its light, where weakened strength revives. It is the haven
> of intimidated loyalty, the balm for injured innocence,
> the requiter of selfless love. . . . It destroys the barriers
> which Prejudice has set up between man and man; it with-
> draws the golden robe that decks the soulless body. It
> brings heart to heart, spirit to spirit, strength to strength. . . .
> It teaches us to value the tree for its fruits and not for the
> soil that bears it, nor for the hand that planted it.'

In a number of German Lodges the masonic reforms then
gradually began to have the effect of dismissing the problem of
creed, and, in proportion as the Lodges re-approached the
original English conception, the idea of tolerance regained the
character it had in the minds of the founders of the London
Grand Lodge. A very interesting situation was created when
the Grand Lodge of England, acting contrary to the view of
its Provincial Grand Lodge in Frankfort, now granted a Charter
to the 'Nascent Dawn' Lodge, which had seceded from the
Grand Orient of France for political reasons. During the discussion, it expressed its wish once again that the 'universal
religion' should suffer no restraint. The Grand Master, the
Duke of Sussex, whose views on this subject we have indeed
already learnt,[2] expressed himself to German Freemasons
with extraordinary clarity.

On one occasion he said to a representative of the 'Royal
York' Grand Lodge:

> 'Masonry is a beautiful bond that binds together men of
> all religions. Although this principle does not apply in all
> cases, it is only a question of time, for we are approaching

---

[1] Complete Works, Vol. 2, xxxix.   [2] See chapter 'The Reformers.'

this wonderful aim. All the power at our disposal must be employed to reach it, and the sooner the better. I am a great believer in the emancipation of the Jews and it is to be regretted that many Lodges are still closed to them. Masonry should not close its doors to any educated man, whatever his belief may be, so long as he has been found worthy. Even when it is maintained that Masonry is a Christian institution and has nothing in common with other religious beliefs, we are nevertheless taught by religion to love our neighbours, and we humans are alike in the sight of God. The Creator embraces His creatures with the same love, and why should we weak humans wish to make exceptions? It is probably because we are weak that it happens. Although the manner in which other nations recognize and worship God may be different, it is our God whom they worship, and it is always weakness on our part when we believe that we are better than they. The right which we believe we possess, and which often makes us intolerant, belongs also to those against whom we fight. Only when we have rid ourselves of all prejudices, and one bond only, the bond of universal, pure, and unfeigned love, surrounds us and warms our hearts, will Masonry become a real Brotherhood and its ideals be fulfilled. Love is supposed to be the watchword that guides us; but how often is this beautiful word misused, how often the word lacks the pure and noble deed, the very spice of life!'

The Grand Master impressed upon the delegates of the 'Nascent Dawn' Lodge that:

'Not only in Frankfort but in the whole of Germany do I want to make an Epoch with this Constitution, for I perceive that instead of making progress there, enlightenment is on the decline. I do not ask whether this Constitution pleases the other Lodges very much. . . . The other Lodges have certainly no cause to be ashamed of what the Grand Lodge of England, the first Mother Lodge of all, recognizes.'[1]

The first Grand Lodge that subsequently gave the Light to Jews was that of Hamburg. This was followed by the Grand Lodge of Hanover,[2] which was founded in 1828, but subsequently ceased to exist; then by Saxony and Bayreuth. In

---

[1] Friedrich Kneisner: *Geschichte der deutschen Freimaurerei in ihren Grundzügen.* Berlin. Unger. 1912.
[2] Its first Grand Master was Prince Ernest Augustus, Duke of Cumberland, afterwards King.

1844 the humanitarian principle carried the day even in Frank-fort. It was prescribed in 'detailed explanations' to the Lodges that

> 'the Mason must be a believer and worshipper of the only God, as this creed is the only one in which all men can agree. Every Mason may entertain his own opinions and religious convictions.'

The 'Praeceptor Latomorum Germaniae,' the distinguished writer of Freemasonic History, Johann Georg Kloss, Grand Master of the Eclectic Union from 1836, contributed very largely to this change of view. His writing *On the Inadmissibility of the Attempt to Introduce Positive Christianity into Freemasonry*, which clearly defined the boundaries between the Christian and the humanitarian standpoint, caused a lasting sensation.

On the other hand, the ancient Prussian Grand Lodges persisted in their standpoint, with the exception of the 'Royal York' Grand Lodge, which admitted Jews from 1872 onwards, but returned in 1924 to the old principle under the severe pressure of the anti-masonic campaign. Nevertheless, these Prussian Lodges admitted visiting brethren to their Lodge meetings irrespective of creed, so that no member of a regular German Lodge was excluded from participation in the assemblies of another Lodge.

It should also be mentioned that even authoritative persons in the ancient Prussian camp had, in earlier years, repeatedly considered following the humanitarian principle. The Federal Board of the Grand National Mother Lodge repeatedly put forward this proposal, which, on each occasion, failed to be accepted; not because it was impossible to obtain a majority in favour of it, but because the prescribed majority of two-thirds was not forthcoming.[1] In a letter from the 'Three Globes' Lodge addressed to the Dutch Grand Orient in 1881, the following view was expressed:

> 'We recognize, as you do, the principle that the exclusion of the Israelites from admission into our Lodges is irreconcilable with the basic principles of Freemasonry, and we earnestly hope that these barriers will disappear from our Order in the not-too-distant future.'

[1] In 1874 out of 110 Lodges 65 voted for and 43 against the elimination of the paragraphs making the admission of Non-Christians impossible; in 1876 the ratio was 88 : 57.

In view of all that has happened since the War in the social life of Germany, there is little prospect that this hope will be quickly realized.

A man of uncompromising humanitarian conviction was the Grand Master of the 'Royal York' Grand Lodge, Prof. Dr. Hermann Settegast, of Berlin, who resigned his office in 1892, when feeling against the admission of Jews again began to make itself felt in many Lodges of his Obedience. He also withdrew from the Grand Lodge and founded his own central authority in Berlin, the Grand Lodge of Freemasons in Prussia, 'Kaiser Friedrich zur Bundestreue.' This, however, was not such a simple matter, for the Edict of 1798, under which foundations in Prussia not emanating from the ancient Prussian Grand Lodges were prohibited, was still in force. The Berlin Chief of Police thereupon declared that there was nothing against the Society as such, but that the description 'Grand Lodge of Freemasons' was inadmissible. The result was a sensational lawsuit conducted first before the District Court and, finally, before the Supreme Court of Appeal by Dr. Hugo Alexander-Katz, which ended in victory, in consequence of which numerous Humanitarian Lodges arose in Berlin and other Prussian cities. However, Settegast's Grand Lodge disappeared in 1900, when it became a Provincial Grand Lodge under the Grand Lodge of Hamburg. Before the Great War there was no lack of eminent Freemasons who, time and again, suggested to their brethren that there was a superfluity of systems in Germany and inquired whether there was no possibility of arriving at unity. Even at the time of the formation of the German Reich the creation of a single National Grand Lodge, or, at least, a 'United Grand Lodge of Germany', was enthusiastically suggested. Johann Kaspar Bluntschli, a celebrated lecturer in Constitutional Law at Heidelberg, and the President of the Association of German Freemasons, Robert Fischer of Gera, and many others, were enthusiastic supporters of this idea, as also was Prince Frederick William of Prussia, afterwards Kaiser Frederick. The latter's father, who had been admitted into the Brotherhood as Prince of Prussia in 1840, and who was also Protector of the three ancient Prussian Grand Lodges,[1] had awakened his interest in Freemasonry. Both of them regarded their membership not in the light of a dignity, but as a mission. Frederick William's initiation took place in a spectacular manner, just at a time when a

---

[1] He retained this office even as King Emperor.

stormy agitation against Freemasonry was again being raised in Berlin by a narrow-minded orthodox Protestant, to wit, the theologian Ernst Wilhelm Hengstenberg, and in Dresden by an ex-lawyer, Eduard Emil Eckert, whose romantic ideas ran away with him.

Hengstenberg, to whom tolerance was repugnant in any shape or form, and who believed from the bottom of his soul that any view other than the orthodox constituted a grave danger to Christianity, is responsible for the phrase: 'The basic principle of Freemasonry is deism, antipathy to specific Christianity.' This phrase, and varying modifications of it, recurred constantly in his *Evangelische Kirchenzeitung* and several other books. He attempted to emphasize his prophecies of disaster by continually whispering in the ears of similarly intolerant high officials in the Government that they should do all possible to 'smoke out the monster so closely related to the Devil'.

Eckert also bombarded them with denunciations. He was, however, not particularly well disposed towards the Prussians, because the 'Prussian Eagle had started the revolution in Dresden in 1848', but he regarded it as his mission to 'eliminate the high-sounding names from the Society of Crime'. He was the Ludendorff of his time, on account of his method of carrying on the campaign. 'I alone have been fighting the revolution since the spring of '48', he wrote to Fürst Schwarzenberg.[1] He added that he regarded the destruction of Freemasonry as his object in life. This endeavour might seem foolish to many people, 'but a man of vision, education, and energy may accomplish much'. One person at least really believed Eckert's flights of fancy in his *Magazin der Beweisführung für Verurteilung des Freimaurerordens* ('Magazine Stating the Case for the Condemnation of the Order of Freemasons') and his *Tempel Salomonis oder Generalcharte des Arbeitsplanes des Revolutionsbundes* ('Temple of Solomon or General Chart of the Plan of Action of the Revolutionary Society'). It was Count Kuefstein, the Viennese Ambassador in Dresden, who triumphantly handed over to Kempen von Fichtenstamm, Austrian Minister of Police, the 'juridical proof of the dangerous nature of the Order of Freemasons and its incompatability with the Law of the Land'.

By his application for initiation, which was open for all to see, Prince Frederick William showed himself in sympathy with his father, who had not merely remained unaffected by

---

[1] Dr. Josef Volf, Prague, in the *Vienna Freemasons' Journal*, 1927.

these attacks, but offered active and determined resistance to them. This was of all the greater consequence as Protestant clericalism was particularly powerful at the Court of Frederick William IV. Although William had caused a sensation by arranging his own programme on a visit to Solingen, going straight from the railway station to the Lodge-room in order 'thereby to demonstrate the love and respect in which he holds Masonry and by this step and his warm interest in the affairs of the Order put right the wrong conception of Masonry', it was nothing to the amazement excited in initiated circles by the letters [1] he wrote to the Magdeburg Superintendent-General Möller, an enthusiastic follower of Hengstenberg, who had declared in Erfurt that he would do everything in his power to induce all the clergy of his diocese to withdraw from the Brotherhood. The following paragraphs from two of the letters are of special interest:

'*10th November*, 1855.

'. . . A decision of such importance made by a man as eminent as yourself can only be based on a profound knowledge of the subject and a thorough study of the conditions. That this is only possible when one is oneself a member of a corporation, which one urges one's subordinates to abandon, is comprehensible. Although I was not previously aware that you belonged to the Order of Freemasons, but must now assume from the foregoing that this is the case, I request you to be good enough to inform me, with all speed, of the observations you have made in the Order that have led you to the conviction that both your further association with the same, and that of your subordinates, is undesirable. As I am Protector of this Order it is naturally of the greatest importance to me that I should not hold a misconceived view, for I have hitherto failed to perceive, by my own observation, anything which would justify your view in the slightest degree. However, should you not belong to the Order, I must then ask you how you can reconcile with your otherwise conscientious actions the condemnation of a Corporation which, as it shrouds itself in a veil of mystery recognized by the State and is viewed by the outer world solely through the eye of writings of a very spurious character, must in its inner nature still be entirely unknown to you?

[1] Published by Dr. Johannes Schultze in the *Hamburger Fremdenblatt* of the 3rd October 1928.

If you wish for enlightenment as to the expediency of clergy becoming or remaining members of the Order, then you should ask men of your own rank and calling who do belong to it, why they fail to withdraw from it in spite of the ease and possibility of so doing, if it does not agree with, and is not reconcilable to their views, religious obligations, and wishes? And you should investigate the work of your brothers in office in order thereby to form an opinion as to whether any detrimental effects are discernible in their activity that might be attributed to their membership of the Order. Only after such an impartial investigation can I acknowledge the passing of judgment, which in any case would be a rash one unless you yourself belong to the Order. The Order should, moreover, be above all suspicion, seeing that the two Heirs Presumptive to the Prussian Throne are at its head, and that their positions both in State and Church are likewise above suspicion.'

'18th November, 1855.

' . . . I regret to see from your letter that your knowledge of the Order of Freemasonry falls into the second category mentioned by me, that is to say, you are not a Mason, and consequently are only acquainted with the Order from hearsay. Indeed, you go so far as to confess: "that you have never applied for enlightenment from members of the Order, that you have never studied the literature on the subject, and that the judging of the case, so far as it concerns public and social life, is beyond you; but that the Order is deserving of confidence from the ethical point of view because of the people who are at its head."—As you thus admit that you have a very superficial knowledge of the Order of Freemasons, how can you conscientiously maintain with such conviction that your subordinates: "are hardly doing themselves any good by seeking and cultivating such association". I concede that you set your mind at rest about this claim of yours by reason of the fact that your superior officers entertain a similar conviction, but I am carrying on the same quarrel with those gentlemen as with yourself, as they also possess absolutely no knowledge of the Order and have just as little justification as you for looking askance at, and passing judgment on, members of the clergy who belong to it. You quote the principles acknowledged by you in respect of religion, its exercise and cultivation, and assert that in addition to this Blessed Mystery the preservation of no other mystery should be tolerated. This means, perhaps, that every mystery is prohibited. Is it not rather rejection of invented mysteries such as those set up by the Roman Catholic Church as part of its cardinal doctrine, in addition to the aforesaid Blessed Mystery, and for which it demands the same adoration as we Protestants pay only to the Mystery just mentioned? Since you have yourself acknowledged that every mystery is prohibited, how can you say that "there are, however, many worthy and honourable men of your State who are worthy of honour, although they belong to the Order." Would any competent authority with your conception of a mystery be justified in allowing a member of the clergy who is a Mason to remain in office another twenty-four hours? As no such action is taken, it is perhaps sufficient proof that the authorities are exceedingly shy of going forcibly to work, because they do not know enough of the subject and do not wish to commit an injustice. And this is the correct standpoint for those outside the Order. As, however, the first requirement of a Prussian Freemason is that he should profess one of the creeds acknowledged by the State, and as piety, morality, and brotherly love, without detracting from duty towards the State, Church, and Family, are the characteristics of the Order; as loyalty to the King is the chief law of the same, and as, on the other hand, all discussion of religion and politics in masonic lectures is prohibited—I ask you what objection there can be to such a Brotherhood, in which there is no other mystery than their work, ceremonies, and signs of recognition. A man's Christian religion does not change when he becomes a Mason; in Masonry it rests on the same foundation as that which you accept; how can one priest persecute another in face of such truths? The times when Freemasons were credited with conjuring up spirits, with dabbling in alchemy, magic, and all sorts of other rubbish are, I hope, far behind us! I shall never deny that all things are capable of misuse; but in order to indulge in misuse it is quite unnecessary to join a Brotherhood. In these times this is demonstrated almost every day, both in ecclesiastical and in public life. . . . I give you my solemn word as a Prince that Prussian Freemasonry indulges in no misuse. . . . Now in all truth. Why should not members of the clergy be Freemasons?'

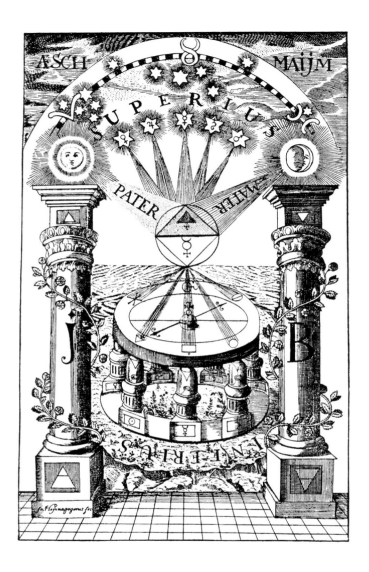

FRONTISPIECE TO BIRKHOLZ' 'COMPASS DER WEISEN', 1779

ENTRANCE TO A TEMPLE

In view of such a conception, it is no wonder that Bismarck [1] said of the Emperor William : 'He fulfils his duties towards the Brethren with almost religious devotion.'

His son Frederick William, who was Grand Master of the Grand National Lodge from 1860 onwards, was, as already mentioned, filled with zeal for the idea of unity in German Freemasonry on a humanitarian basis. The chief task he set himself was to rid his Grand Lodge of all legends and traditions that might fan the flame of prejudice between the various systems. On the 24th June 1870 he stepped into the limelight with a most remarkable speech, on the occasion of the centenary festival of the National Grand Lodge, in which he put forward emphatic demands for unity throughout Freemasonry, for thorough historical research and for the recognition of the fundamental significance of St. John's Freemasonry.

'. . . In my opinion there is only one Freemasonry, although it appears in different forms. . . . Let us cling in future to the consciousness of the unity of Freemasonry and of the homogeneity of the various systems. Let each one of us give up the vanity of believing that we alone possess the whole and real truth and alone employ the genuine and correct form for the truth. May each of one us in the future treat even those of different opinion with brotherly esteem and appreciation and so let the next century really become a new era. . . . The Grand National Lodge has in recent times been the object of violent attacks, some of which have been very spiteful. The more these attacks demonstrate that the antagonists are only acquainted with isolated fragments of the history and of the doctrine of the National Grand Lodge and that even these they do not know thoroughly, the less chance they have of misleading us. . . .

'We can accept a competent judgment on the National Grand Lodge only from those who are thoroughly acquainted with its doctrine, practices and history. . . . We are now confronted with the demand that we should separate the history of the origin and development of the National Grand Lodge from the history that is so closely associated with the symbolic actions and mysteries of the various degrees of our Order, and that we should set forth the former so that it may be examined by all in the Brotherhood. . . . Whereas in earlier times the authority of tradition was

[1] *Gedanken und Erinnerungen*, I, S. 204.

sufficient, investigations into the history have to-day
become critiques of such force that they defy even the most
holy of traditions. . . . My endeavours have, therefore, been
directed for a long time towards a thorough investigation and arrangement of the historical documents. . . .
Historical truths can only be established by historical investigation. . . . We must bring increasingly into prominence the idea that the St. John's Lodge must be the chief
aim of Freemasonry and must attain the most significance.'

The Conservative elements predominating in the National
Grand Lodge were, however, by no means enamoured of the
humanitarian revival which the Crown Prince had in mind.
A conflict soon arose with Archdeacon Gustav Adolf Schiffmann,
who, at the instigation of Frederick William, made a thorough
investigation into certain doubts entertained by the latter in
respect of the alleged ancient origin of the Swedish system, and
thereupon declared certain traditions to be erroneous. In consequence of this quarrel, the Crown Prince resigned his office of
Grand Master of the Order, but remained Deputy Protector of
the ancient Prussian Lodges. But his interest in Freemasonry,
the pillars of which, he declared, were religious freedom and
tolerance, progress, and not stagnation, remained undiminished.

His early death put an end to all hopes of the idea of unity
being fulfilled. A meeting of German Grand Masters certainly
did take place and was followed by the formation of a Union
of German Grand Lodges, but its only aim was to ensure co-
operation between the Lodges in Germany and to secure a
common attitude towards Grand Lodges outside Germany.
Nevertheless, it laid down remarkable principles. When negro
Grand Lodges arose in America, it declared, for instance, that
neither race nor colour could form a barrier to recognition.[1]
In 1877, when the Grand Orient of France 'in view of the fact

---

[1] On another occasion it declared, on the proposal of Prof. Diedrich Bischoff,
Leipzig, that anti-Semitism cannot be reconciled with the character of Freemasonry. Bischoff was President of the 'Verein Deutscher Freimaurer',
('Union of German Freemasons'), an excellent organization embracing approximately 25,000 members in eight Grand Lodges, which rendered wonderful
service to the intellectual life of German Masonry. During its existence, the
Union of German Freemasons lived up to its motto of 'Durch Arbeit zur
Einigkeit' ('Through Work to Unity') by the publication of the third edition
of the *Allgemeines Handbuch der Freimaurerei* ('General Handbook of Freemasonry'), the magnificent Wolfstig Bibliography and other works, by
organizing prize-competitions and arranging an annual interchange of views
between members of the various German systems. These conversations were
of a very high standard and laid stress upon the common idea.

that Freemasonry is not a religion and has therefore, very logically, not included any doctrines or dogmas in its Constitution', abolished the symbol of the 'Great Architect of the Universe', the Union of German Grand Lodges replied:

'The Masonic Brotherhood demands of its members no particular dogmatic belief in God, and the admission of individual brethren is not made dependent upon a religious creed. The masonic symbols and rituals, however, refer expressly to God and, without God, would be incomprehensible and absurd. The principles and history of Freemasonry teach of and bear witness to God. Freemasons worship God as the Great Architect of the Universe. The moral law sacred to Freemasons has its deepest and strongest root in God. If Freemasonry were to renounce the idea of God its striving for ideals would lose its enduring force and its highest aim, and it would become lethargic and impotent. Therefore, the conference of German Grand Lodges, in the name of the Brotherhood of German Freemasons, expresses its conviction that a masonic Lodge that questions or denies the existence of God, is not to be regarded as a true and perfect Lodge and that an atheistic Freemasonry ceases to be Freemasonry.'

This resolution had no practical effect upon the Grand Orient of France, as relations had been broken off since the Franco-Prussian War. Only after a period of thirty years had elapsed were they resumed. In 1907 the recognition of the Grande Loge, which had come into existence in the meantime, was proclaimed, and in 1909 relations with the Grand Orient were revived. When the Grande Loge constituted the German Lodge 'Goethe' in Paris, this was regarded as the promising beginning of a new friendship. On this festive occasion the representative of the 'Royal York' Grand Lodge expressed the wishes of the Germans in the following words:

'We congratulate you on your undertaking, which we hope will turn out to be a step forward in the direction of a Franco-German understanding, and we also earnestly hope that the day may soon dawn when the work of reconciliation will be crowned with success and that the two nations, which, to be sure, are very different, but which, for that very reason, form such a wonderful complement to each other in character, thought, sentiment, and deed, may go forward hand in hand!'

A year later the World War broke out. And when it had passed by the antagonistic feeling between the nations was more intense than ever before.

In 1923 the ancient Prussian Grand Lodges withdrew from the Union of Grand Lodges. That is to say, at a time when, thanks to unscrupulous agitation, the word 'humanitarian' had become synonymous with 'hostility to the State' in the minds of many misguided persons. It is unnecessary to say that nothing could be more false than this imputation, and it need hardly be said that the whole of German Freemasonry was on a national foundation, that its brethren loved their country, that they regarded the Lodge, with its religious characteristics, as an academy of German idealism in which the legacy of the intellectual classics was cultivated and propagated. Up to 1932, not one of the German Grand Lodges had resumed relations with the former European enemy States. However, this did not mean that all the Grand Lodges took the view that they must remain henceforth in 'splendid isolation'. Even the ancient Prussian Freemasons recognized that Fichte's words regarding love of country and world citizenship must be acknowledged. Hans Wilhelm Pinkow, late Chief Editor of the *Kölnische Zeitung*, one of the most brilliant German Lodge orators, who, although strongly patriotic, clung nevertheless to the ancient watchword, 'World citizenship and humanity', explained his idea in one of his speeches, as follows:[1]

'The way in the world and round the earth can only be made via one's own country, via the Fatherland. Only those peoples with a strong national feeling are respected amongst the nations of the earth and only such nationals dare harbour a thought of internationalism without damaging their honour or their souls. We German Freemasons who are called upon to co-operate in finding a new spirit for our race, can, and should, assiduously attempt to break down, via the individual brethren of the individual nations, the hatred which has been incited, and make room again for a sensible humanity. . . . If we want to rise up again, we must not remain scowling and sulking in some corner of the world; we must combat the power of Force with the power of Work, and this chain, which should girdle the Earth, may also be followed by the chain of Masonic Brotherhood and Masonic Thought.'

[1] Hans Wilhelm Pinkow: *Macht und Einfluss der Freimaurerei, Vera-Verlag*. Hamburg. 1922.

Pinkow might very well have made use of the words of
Stresemann, the late German Minister for Foreign Affairs, also
a Freemason: 'Whosoever wishes to hinder the international
exchange of Culture forfeits his membership of the International
Commonwealth of Culture'. Or Goethe's words:

> So ging es mir! Mög es euch so ergehen,
> Dass aller Hass sich augenblicks entfernte,
> Und wo wir noch ein dunkles Wölkchen sehen,
> Sich alsobald der Himmel übersternte,
> Es tausendfach erglänzte von den Höhen
> Und alle Welt von uns die Eintracht lernte.—
> Und so geniesst das höchste Glück hernieden
> Nach hartem äussern Kampf den innern Frieden.

The view of the German Grand Lodges, however, was that
renewed relations, especially with the French Freemasons,
could certainly not be considered until the question of 'War
Guilt' had been cleared up, or whilst foreign troops remained
in Germany. No doubt the questions appertaining to the
occupation of the Rhineland raised at the meeting between
Ries, the Grand Master of Frankfort, and the French Brethren
originated in this attitude.

As the spirit of Germany became more radical and more
nationalistic, the more did this radicalization have its effect
upon a large number of Lodges. A gradually increasing number
of the members wished to make a complete break with tradition
and take refuge in a German National Christian Freemasonry
having absolutely no connexion with Freemasonry in other
countries. This 'new Freemasonry', they advocated, should
abandon the idea of masonic universality and reject pacific
ideology as a weakness and a physicial degeneration inimical
to the State.

There were, however, very many brethren who did not share
these views, and who advocated grasping the hand of the
French Freemasons, who were fighting against 'concert hall
patriotism', or the patriotism of hatred, in order to collaborate
in bringing about an understanding between France and
Germany, an understanding on which the peace of Europe
ultimately depends. Amongst these brethren were many of
those who, since 1925, had been called upon to speak at the
Congresses of the Universal League of Freemasons, the international association of individual members of Lodges,[1] who

[1] Especially eminent in this respect was Dr. Leo Müffelmann of Berlin, who
also in Parisian Lodges made speeches imbued with the spirit of reconciliation
which were received with great acclamation.

esteemed it their solemn duty, in the strictest interpretation of the Antient Charges, to serve the patriotism of Love; to follow the star which, high above this world of confusion and conflicting interests, points to the place where Deliverance from Hatred and Animosity becomes incarnate;[1] who desire to forget the Past, in order to bring about friendly co-operation and build bridges that will lead out of an era of violence into a time of understanding. Such work, they declared, is not Utopian pacifism, but merely the conscientious acknowledgment of the tremendous task which the times have called upon Freemasonry to undertake.

'The personal bond of similar conviction and common endeavour must be stretched from man to man, from an ever-increasing number of brethren to a very host of brethren, if a time of annihilating hatred and barbarous violence is to be replaced by an epoch of solidarity, truth and justice.'[2]

As a result of strenuous efforts made in 1932, friendly relations were at last resumed between the three humanitarian Grand Lodges (Hamburg, Frankfort, and Bayreuth) and the United Grand Lodge of England. But the joy evoked by this first step was short-lived. The whole outlook was changed at one stroke by the advent of the National Socialist ('Nazi') régime in Germany. Although Hitler and his Government subsequently prohibited Freemasonry in Germany, it may be said that it ceased to exist as from April 1933.

From the very beginning, National Socialism was ill-disposed towards Freemasonry. A person applying for membership of the National Socialist Party was required to sign a declaration to the effect that he was not a Freemason (and this applies even to-day). Alfred Rosenberg, the well-known Nazi expert on foreign affairs and Chief Editor of the *Völkischer Beobachter* is a particularly active antagonist of Freemasonry, and he has written several newspaper articles and pamphlets attacking masonic ideals. In these writings he speaks of a 'Romanic-Anglo-Saxon Lodge policy against Germany' and describes Freemasonry as 'anti-national' and 'liberal-plutocratic', and classes it as 'out-of-date trumpery like the other ideas of the eighteenth century which were still further coarsened in the nineteenth century'. Rudolf Hess, Hitler's secretary, now his deputy, wrote in 1930, on his leader's instructions, that the

[1] The Rev. Ernst Klein, Frankfort, *Leuchte*, 1925.
[2] Prof. Kraft, Dresden, at the Conference at Basle in 1925.

'German Lodges had never opposed in a proper manner the oppression and unfriendly acts of Germany's antagonists', and, in accordance with the established principle, every Nazi was still 'forbidden to be a member of a secret society, including Freemasonry'. Similar declarations were also made subsequently from time to time. When the elections of March 1933 made Hitler the master of Germany, the German Grand Lodges anticipated Government measures by either dissolving or falling into line. Three Lodges took the former course (Frankfort, Bayreuth, and the Symbolic Grand Lodge); the remainder transformed themselves into Christian National Orders. They changed their names, abandoned the terms 'Freemasonry', 'Freemason', and 'Lodge', released the members from all oaths, compelled non-Aryans to withdraw, abolished all secrets, and removed from the Ritual everything that savoured of the Old Testament and the medieval Steinmetzen. The members of the Orders now recognized by Hitler no longer work on the erection of the Temple of Universal Love of Mankind, but swing the Hammer of Thor and wield the Sword of the Valiant. Their symbolism seeks to find a basis in the ancient Nordic Wotan cult.

These Christian German Orders have therefore ceased to be masonic organizations. The flame of Freemasonry that once burned so clear and bright in the German Reich has now been extinguished to the last glimmer.

CHAPTER V

AUSTRIA

AUSTRIAN Freemasonry is one of those in which the work for peace has become a clearly defined aim, and, ever since the Grand Lodge of Vienna was founded on the 8th December 1918 it has constantly endeavoured to make its members active pacifists. Not pacifists who live in the clouds, but pacifists in close touch with reality; pacifists whose universalism arises from their humanitarian views, whilst at the same time losing nothing of the consciousness of their duty to their own nation. Not men whose patriotism becomes lost in the mist of a Utopian World Republic, but men whose unswerving loyalty to their own country, impoverished and enfeebled by the World War, inspires them to serve the highest ideals of Humanity.

'Nobody in the whole world was quicker to realize the insanity of war, and nobody abhors it more than the Austrian Fraternity, and this feeling imbued them with an ardent desire for peace, which was expressed in the recognition and appreciation of men of all tongues and all creeds without discrimination. By espousing the cause of cosmopolitanism with ever-increasing determination, and by their steadfast refusal to regard a Brother from one of the formerly hostile countries as an enemy, or even as an antagonist, they made for themselves their programme',[1]

were the words of a splendid message from the Grand Master of Vienna, Dr. Richard Schlesinger.

The fact that it was not possible to establish the Grand Lodge of Vienna until after the readjustment of European affairs was due to the conditions prevailing in Austria, which have already been described in an earlier chapter. The men guiding the country's destinies have always found a way to keep alive the erroneous belief that Freemasonry is an institution inimical to State and Church alike, which should not in any

[1] Preface to *Die Gegenwartsmaurerei: Gesicht, Geist, Arbeit,* festive presentation of the Grand Lodge of Vienna on the occasion of the tenth anniversary of its foundation. Vienna. 1928.

circumstances be tolerated. These accusations were often made in spite of better knowledge, for—since 1871—no objection has been raised to the existence of Freemasonry in Austria under another name. Although no Lodges were permitted, 'non-political associations' were tolerated, in spite of the fact that it was known that masonic activity, supposedly so dangerous, was being carried on on Hungarian soil—first in Neudörfel and then in Pressburg. Consequently, for reasons of state, they fostered, as it were, the 'mystery' which they pretended so determinedly to combat, and presented the world with the strange picture of the Emperor of Austria prohibiting what he permitted as King of Hungary.

For since the political division of 1867 normal Lodges existed again in Hungary. The consecration in this year of the 'Unity in the Fatherland' Lodge in Budapest was followed by further consecrations in Temesvar, Ödenburg, Pressburg, Arad, and other cities and, in 1871, a St. John's Grand Lodge came into being under Franz von Pulszky, the brilliant orator and energetic Secretary of State of Kussuth, the leader of the Hungarian Revolution.[1] In addition to this, a Scottish Grand Orient arose in the following year. The founders of this Grand Orient were also patriots of the Hungarian struggle for freedom, and, amongst them were General Stefan Türr, who was obliged to take to flight in 1849, fought in the Crimean War, and against Russia (with the Circassians) in 1856 and then became one of the bravest of Garibaldi's Thousand from Marsala who struggled for the freedom of Italy; Georg von Joannovics, Grand Master, a martyr to his Liberal views;[2] General Georg Klapka, who so valiantly defended the fort of Komorn in the War of Independence of 1848–49; and Count Theodor Csaky, leader of the Prusso-Hungarian Legion. The Viennese Lodges were able to unite themselves with these two Obediences, which in 1886 became one—the Symbolic Grand Lodge of Hungary. The first was the 'Humanitas' Lodge in 1871. The founders of this Lodge had made many applications to the Austrian Government for a permit for their proposed masonic activity. Their first intention was to revive the 'St. Joseph' Lodge, but their proposal was rejected. They

[1] Count Julius Andrassy (the elder), who, after the overthrow of the revolution of 1848, was hanged in effigy, but who later became the celebrated Foreign Secretary of the Austro-Hungarian Monarchy, was also a Freemason. He became a member of the 'Mont Sinai' Lodge in Paris in 1854.

[2] He was sentenced in 1854 to twelve years in the dungeons, but was pardoned in 1857.

thereupon made application in respect of a new Lodge, but were once again unsuccessful. However, when it occurred to them to apply as 'a non-political association' the permit was granted. Lodges were only allowed to exist on the other side of the Leitha, that is to say, two hours' railway journey from Vienna. This association was constituted on the 9th March 1871 in Neudörfel on the Austro-Hungarian frontier, under a Hamburg Charter. The minutes recording the foundation were signed by twenty-five Viennese brethren who had belonged to the Ödenburg 'Fraternity' Lodge.

Official circles in Vienna were fully aware of all this, for after the Hungarian Minister for the Interior had granted permission for its foundation and had set his 'Láttam', Vidi, to the Statutes, the Dean of Neudörfel made angry protest. He was enthusiastically supported in this by the *Wiener Kirchenzeitung* (an ecclesiastical journal), which wrote:

'The Royal Hungarian Ministry of the Interior has committed a serious offence by interfering with the autonomy of the parish, as the local dean, in conformity with the Papal Bulls, has forbidden the founding of a Lodge of Freemasons there.' [1]

But Vienna apparently regarded this solution as extremely clever. Officially Austria had no Freemasonry, and if it were there, then the Royal Hungarian Government had to bear the responsibility for all that might come. [2] Consequently, all attempts to alter the situation were abortive. A proposal by Herr Foregger, a member of Parliament, to permit Freemasonry in Austria was rejected by the Austrian Imperial Council in 1873. At the beginning of the twentieth century the formation of an association, the 'Grand Lodge of Freemasons in Austria', was forbidden, and in 1905 an appeal against this prohibition put forward by the Freemasons, Ernst Viktor Zenker and Dr. Emil Roth, was dismissed by the

---

[1] Essay of Dr. Adolf Kapralik: *Wege und Ziele der Freimaurerei in Österreich*, a pamphlet issued by the 'Schiller' Lodge in Vienna. 1925.

[2] The Lodge meetings on Hungarian soil and the assemblies in Vienna were nevertheless strictly and secretly watched. Ludwig Brügel, the Viennese investigator, discovered amongst the 'Acta secreta' of the official archives which, since the revolution, have been open to his gaze, many reports from the secret police concerning journeys made by Viennese Freemasons. It was reported regarding the consecration that a tremendous sensation was created, and that Count Heinrich Zichy, the great landowner, had at once placed the sum of 6,000 Gulden in the hands of the Primate for the creation of extensive agitation against the Fraternity.

Supreme Court. At a kind of Austrian anti-Freemasonic Congress in Vienna in 1897, after those present had discussed the activities of the Viennese Freemasons throughout the day, Count Ferdinand Zichy, a member of the House of Magnates, cried out in a sarcastic tone: 'The State cannot and dare not permit the association of Freemasons, unless it wishes to abdicate in its favour.'

This state of affairs lasted for forty-five years. Austrian neophytes were initiated in Hungary, the date and hour of these festivals being known to every one, and they were then able to carry on their excellent benevolent activities in Vienna, Prague, and other cities. A large number of philanthropic institutions arose either out of their exclusive efforts or mainly as the result of their work. Children's Homes, holiday camps, trade schools for juveniles, a convalescent home, institutes for the blind and sanatoria for the tuberculous were the result of their initiative. There were few undertakings for the common weal that were not supported by Freemasons, and scarcely any cultural work which was not assisted by the Fraternity.

Fourteen Lodges were working in Vienna in 1918 and their constitution as a Grand Lodge was approved by the authorities of the new Republic at the beginning of 1919. Since that time the number of Austrian Lodges has increased to twenty-six. Freemasonry in its original form is practised in these Lodges; that is to say, in exactly the same form as laid down by the 'Antient Charges', which is the very essence of their extensive activity, and which, without losing itself in the welter of every-day politics, embraces a study of the most varied subjects. Austria has a Freemasonry that avoids all bias and seeks to serve its cause by allowing all the various intellectual talent from the numerous schools of thought represented in the Lodges to give free expression to its views and by spurring the Lodges on to collaborate in a number of important cultural institutions, the furtherance of which lies within the sphere of the Grand Lodge of Vienna. Amongst these there is not a single organiza-tion which is guilty of a religious bias, and not a single one of those associations flies the banner of 'Religious Hatred'. Austrian Freemasonry fights against Hatred in whatever form it may appear.[1] The chief aim of the Grand Lodge: the further-

[1] The attempt of Dr. Friedrich Hergeth, in his study *Aus der Werkstätte der Freimaurer und Juden im Österreich der Nachkriegszeit* (Graz, 1927), to put Austrian Freemasonry down as an organization of Jewish-Socialist-Latitudi-narian shock-troops was a very abortive affair.

ance of internal and external peace, has already been briefly outlined.

The fundamental pacific ideal of the Grand Lodge has on various occasions found expression outside the country. It was represented at the World Peace Congresses, it supported the propagation of the pan-European idea, and at the commencement of the occupation of the Ruhr, addressed an exhortation to all the affiliated Grand Lodges to do all in their power to rectify this unjust state of affairs with the utmost dispatch, as such oppression would only nourish a desire for revenge and a thirst for war. This appeal did not fall on deaf ears as far as the French Freemasons were concerned. Frequent opportunities have also arisen on subsequent occasions for the Grand Lodge of Vienna to make clear to its Lodges that only through the blessings of an assured peace can that fraternal chain for which Freemasonry strives be created. This ardent desire, with which the whole of Austrian Freemasonry is imbued, finds expression above all in the sphere in which it is most likely to meet with success: Vienna brethren are in the forefront of the endeavours directed towards creating the international chain. They work on the lines laid down by Alfred Hermann Fried, winner of the Nobel Peace Prize, who fought and suffered in their ranks, and whose views, which are also theirs, are roughly as follow:

The social world is in a state of sickness—a sickness in which peaceful periods alternate with crises and in which conditions of apparent peace are followed by violent convulsions. These crises and convulsions are wars.

However, the state of latent sickness cannot be described as peace. The absence of war is far from being peace! Peace is world organization, understanding between nationalism and internationalism. And this must come! For war means the reverse of divine world order. It can never be in harmony with it, for it means clamant discord. On the other hand, an assured peace that unites mankind in work for the common good is the condition precedent to social welfare.

CHAPTER VI

CZECHOSLOVAKIA

THE Grand Lodge 'Lessing of the Three Rings in the Czechoslovakian Republic', founded on the 23rd October 1920 is very much akin in its views and progressiveness to the Grand Lodge of Vienna. It numbers round about 1,000 members, and is composed chiefly of German Lodges and a few others in Slovakia, working in the Hungarian language, which lost all connexion with their Hungarian mother Grand Lodge through the readjustment of international frontiers after the War. This Freemasonry, which is on a very high intellectual plane, also aspires to international understanding without prejudice to national individuality and cultural collaboration, together with the free development of national characteristics. And really exceptional opportunities to realize this aim are afforded in a country in which two great national cultures come into close contact, and have done so for centuries, and where the national frontiers overlap one another.[1] True to the prescriptions of the Antient Charges, the members of the Grand Lodge 'Lessing' consider themselves loyal citizens of their State; its Constitution lays stress on the charge that each Freemason is to do all in his power to maintain internal peace. Particularly in this Grand Lodge is it clearly shown that to think thus and to act thus, calls for no sacrifice whatsoever of individual patriotism. The German, as well as the Hungarian, brethren of the Grand Lodge are devoted to their nationality. They are fully conscious of the words of Felix Dahn: 'Man's greatest asset is his nation', and they regard their Freemasonry in the first place as a fundamental art. In short, Freemasonry to them is

'work on one's own nation, and, therefore, primarily national, in order to be able to become international. The Freemason has to demonstrate to his own people whether he properly understands the building operations on the Temple of Humanity'.[2]

[1] Message of the Grand Master, Girschick, on the 28th October 1928 (*Die drei Ringe*, 4th year, No. 10).
[2] Oskar Posner: *Am rauhen Stein*. Reichenberg. 1925.

227

That is to say, active participation in the work which cul-
minates in the removal of all barriers that still stand in the
way of understanding. It is just this impeccable national
feeling, however, that enables the members of the Grand Lodge
'Lessing' and the Czech and Slovakian brethren, who have
their own Obedience, the National Grand Lodge, to meet in
harmony in the desire for common cultural work. This desire
has repeatedly been expressed by both sides.[1]

In this respect special significance attaches to a meeting of
the German Lodge 'Harmonie' in Prague in February 1928, at
which Dr. Benesch,[2] the Czechoslovakian Minister for Foreign
Affairs, spoke on 'Freemasonry and the World Crisis', a fact
that called down upon him from the chauvinistic Press the
reproach that he had sold himself body and soul to the German-
speaking nations. An absurd suggestion. For, to make use
of the excellent words of the artist Mucha, one of their leaders,
which were also addressed to the Czech Freemasons, the nation
is an altar to which they bring the most beautiful fruits of
their labour. 'But they have also to give to the nation proof
of their love of peace and give her men who fulfil their national
tasks, not with the sword, but with truth and perfection'.
These tasks are: to cement democratic liberal thought, and to
strive for national reconciliation.

The National Grand Lodge regards itself, above all, as the
guardian of the rich legacy of Comenius, undoubtedly one of
the greatest apostles of love of mankind, much of whose magnificent work has been brought to light in recent years by the
endeavours of the Prague Freemason Vonka. The first Czech
Lodge which arose in Prague out of the frontier Lodge 'Hiram'
in 1919, therefore bears the name 'Jan Amos Komensky'. And
also in the Ritual of the 'Lessing' brethren there is the beautiful
passage:

'We will now make a solemn agreement with one another:
firstly, that we have but one aim in view: the welfare of
mankind, by ridding the world of party spirit, destruction,
compulsion and acts of violence, by leading every one back
to universal happiness and prosperity, by returning to simple

[1] 'One of the most important tasks of Freemasonry in the Czechoslovakian
Republic will always be the creation of an internal understanding between the
nations forming the State,' said Johann Urzidil, Prague, in an article in the
Jubilee Book of the Grand Lodge of Vienna, 1928.

[2] Dr. Benesch, a member of the Czech Lodge 'Komensky,' delivered his
speech in the German language.

WILLIAM PRESTON
AUTHOR OF 'ILLUSTRATIONS OF MASONRY'

WILLIAM HENRY WHITE
GRAND SECRETARY OF UNITED GRAND LODGE
OF ENGLAND, 1813–1856

ENGLISH LODGES IN 1735

Engraving by I. Folkema, after L. F. du Bourg

truth and to infinite peace in all things. Secondly: that we will discuss without artifice, sophistication or tumult every-thing that concerns the welfare of humanity. Further: that in the whole work we will have no consideration other than the common weal. The prestige of persons, nations, languages, or sects is here entirely ignored. Neither love nor hatred, nor envy nor contempt towards another shall interfere. Are we not all citizens of one world, all of one blood!'

The activity of the Czechoslovakian Grand Lodge is also influenced by other outstanding men. It is very much inspired by the influence of Peter Chelčicky, the fifteenth-century pacifist, who, after the horrors of the Hussite war, protested against all forms of violence and pleaded for love, equality, fraternity, and tolerance. It has named a Lodge after the noble Bernhard Bolzano, the Liberal German theologian of Italian descent at the University of Prague, who, persecuted by Rome and Metternich's absolutism, propagated humanistic and national-idealistic thought amongst the Czech people, and who lost his Professorship of Religious Science in the revolution of March 1848 because, according to the imperial decree,

'He had failed in his duties as priest, teacher, and good citizen by his teachings which ran as follows: "The time will come when war, that nonsensical procedure for proving the right of the sword, will have been universally abolished, as also will the time when the thousand and one differentiations as to dignity, and the various class barriers between men, will have been sufficiently broken down so that each may see in the other a brother. And the day will finally dawn when such violent misuses of power as are now the order of the day will no longer be permitted—a day when nobody will continue to regard it, in all seriousness, as an honour to scrape together as much of this world's goods as would suffice to satisfy the needs of thousands." '

The work of the Czech brethren is inspired by the ideas of the clerical Freemason Dobrowsky, the 'Blue Abbot', but more especially by the spirit of Masaryk,[1] whom even the people of other nations, who previously opposed him, to-day honour as a truly great philosopher and statesman.

[1] The President of the Czechoslovakian Republic is not a Freemason.

CHAPTER VII

THE NEUTRAL COUNTRIES

How great a need there is for active work in the cause of Peace is illustrated by the fact that although it is now more than fifteen years since the Great War came to an end, it is still possible to speak of the 'neutral countries', not with the idea of constantly stressing the fact that these countries did not allow themselves to be drawn into the ghastly struggle, but in order to suggest that even to-day each one of them constitutes in many respects a happy island on which the people are less affected by the evil circumstances that elsewhere gnaw at the very hearts of men. Consequently, there devolves upon the Freemasonry of these countries a special role, although the Grand Lodges of the 'neutral' States do not necessarily on that account all present the same aspect.

The Swedish, Norwegian, and Danish Freemasons are neutral in the strictest sense of the word; or, to put it more clearly, they lead their own secluded life in the sphere of Masonry also. Freemasonry in all these countries follows the Swedish system, the strictly Christian and mystical system, which was also that of the National Grand Lodge of Freemasons of Germany. This system, which is so bound up with the symbolic representation of religious events, is based upon the pure doctrine of Jesus Christ as presented in the gospels, so that the Bible, which contains these books, is not merely the symbol of religion, but is, in reality, 'the greatest of all lights'. This system,[1] a revival of the Christian mysticism of the Middle Ages cloaked in masonic forms, consists of a systematically articulated edifice of eleven different degrees, divided into three classes: I, 'St. John's' Lodges, comprising the Craft; II, 'St. Andrew's' Lodges, the Scots degrees; and III, The Chapter degrees. Christ is proclaimed as the true Master and Knight. The 'St. John's' brethren are guided into a mystical and speculative line of thought beginning with the knowledge of the Divine Spirit as it manifests itself in the material world, and aspires, through the knowledge of the Divine Spirit in Humanity, to a knowledge of God Himself. In the higher degrees these

---

[1] Founded in 1756 by Count Eckleff.

mystical interests become an endeavour to press onwards, through the Christian religion, to the true religion, to make faith in the Saviour really strong in their hearts and to understand the true meaning of the Trinity. The methods of the system show many indications of having been influenced by Swedenborg, the great Swedish 'seer' of the eighteenth century, who was mathematician, naturalist, and theosophist: 'Many conceptions contained in Swedenborg's *Arcana Cœlestia*, his interpretation of the Revelations and his representation of the New Jerusalem, recur in the Swedish high degrees'.[1]

The exceedingly close connexion with the Royal House gives Swedish Masonry a 'cachet' all its own. There is no country, England not excluded, where the Brotherhood has been so actively assisted by the monarchs themselves. As early as 1752, King Adolphus Fredrik undertook the office of 'Master of all Freemasonic Associations in the Kingdom'. Fredrik Adolphus became National Grand Master in 1779. It was said of Gustavus IV that, upon ascending the throne, he declared all Swedish princes to be born Freemasons. This, perhaps, may be connected with the fact that his father had placed the Red Cross of the Tenth Degree in his cradle. Charles XIII, who came to the throne in 1809, was inspired with a tremendous enthusiasm for the Royal Art. As Master of the Order, he changed the Red Cross, 'in honour of the Virtues that are prescribed by no statute' into an Order of the State, the Order of Charles XIII, which, since that date, has always been bestowed upon Swedish princes at birth, but the insignia of which they are only allowed to wear when they have become Freemasons and have attained the Tenth Degree.[2] This official Freemasonic Order, which is to be regarded as the zenith of the system and is always presided over by the reigning monarch, is restricted to twenty-seven secular and three clerical members, exclusive of the Royal Princes.

There is an established rule that the King of Sweden (at present Gustav V) is always the Master of the Order, or Vicarius Salomonis, whilst the Crown Prince undertakes the office of National Grand Master. They are assisted in the direction of the Order by a Sanhedrin composed of nine secular and nine clerical officers.

In the course of time, conditions took the same turn in

---

[1] Starcke, C. N.: a. a. O.

[2] *Allgemeines Handbuch der Freimaurerei*, vol. ii. According to C. N. Starcke the highest masonic degrees also carry with them the ennoblement of their holders.

Denmark, whose Freemasonry (introduced in 1740) joined the Swedish system in 1858, under King Frederick VII. The latter was succeeded as Grand Master by King Frederick VIII, who died in 1912. Forty years long had he been the brilliant ruler of Danish Freemasonry, and the present King, Christian X, as Master of the Order, is also deeply interested in the Brotherhood.

The Freemasons of Holland and Switzerland are neutral in an entirely different sense. Both of them (the Grand Lodge 'Alpina' in Switzerland, and the 'Grand Orient of the Netherlands') have always—and not merely since the World War— regarded it as their task to act as mediators between the various masonic central authorities and to work for the universality of Freemasonry and, in this way, for the improvement of relations between nations.

On the 15th March 1915, that is to say, in the early months of the World War, the Dutch Grand Master, Hugo van Gijn, signed a circular letter in which the Freemasons all over Europe were exhorted, even in the midst of the fearful struggle, and during the destruction of so many young lives and of so much moral and material worth, not to forget that, when peace came back again, it would be the task of Freemasonry to remind mankind, which at that time was running amok, of the Ideal of Humanity now disfigured beyond recognition. It was the duty of the Fraternity of the neutral States, he said, to do everything within their power to prepare the way for this work for a new humanity.

Dutch Freemasonry, which in its early days was subjected to all kinds of attacks—as early as 1735 a Lodge was raided by a fanatical mob that plundered the building of all they could carry off and destroyed what they could not—afterwards followed a somewhat even course of development. Even here quarrels about the system were not to be avoided, and the ever-changing situation in the country's foreign affairs (Republic, union with Belgium, and the separation of the Southern Provinces) did not remain without its effect upon the extension and development of Dutch Freemasonry. But it was spared the tremendous fluctuations which occurred in other countries. At all times Dutch Freemasonry has been prominent because of its important acts of benevolence. The magnificent Institute for the Blind in Amsterdam is the work of Freemasons. It was erected in 1808 at the expense of the Amsterdam Lodges, which numbered only four at that time, and it is not without interest to note that the municipal authorities categorically refused to contribute to this splendid undertaking. Many other important foundations speak for the benevolence of the Fraternity, which, by the way, possesses one of the most celebrated freemasonic libraries in the world, the 'Klossian Library'. This was founded by the German historian Kloss and purchased by Prince Frederick of the Netherlands, who presented it to Dutch Freemasonry, which he led in an exemplary manner for several decades.

Dutch Freemasonry—and there are also many enthusiastic Lodges in the Dutch East Indies and South Africa[1] working under the Grand Orient—inclines strongly toward the Anglo-Saxon view of the nature of the Fraternity. The religious consideration is prominent in their work, in their cultivation of the ritual, in which they stress the following: The spiritual striving of the Freemason finds expression in the endeavour to create a greater feeling of happiness in mankind. In order to demonstrate this desire man must regard himself as an active and living part of the universe and feel himself consciously responsible for that which he, in contemplation of the universe, may or may not do. Freemasonry is a state of mind, a spiritual form of life. To be a Freemason means to conduct oneself in accordance with it. This art of life must of necessity lead to religious perfection, for Freemasonry, as 'recognition of the unity of the finite and the infinite', is the striving for unification between the personal ego and the living environment. It is the task of religious perfection to find a solution for the conflicts that arise in the spiritual life of mankind and thus to arrive at a new and higher unity, that is, according to the precepts of the Grand Orient of the Netherlands 'a higher spiritual and moral development'.

Freemasonry is based upon the confident belief in 'a spiritual and ethical world system that enables men and mankind to progress'. This certainty of being bound in our state of life, our ideas and our actions to a spiritual and moral form is the religious principle of Freemasonry, which it symbolizes through its work 'in the Name of the Great Architect of the Universe'. The Freemason cannot therefore be a 'man with a dead soul'. He has to regard as leading principles: the high value of individuality; independence of the individual in the search for truth; the moral responsibility of the person for his

[1] They are combined in a Provincial Grand Lodge.

conduct in life; the equality and fraternity of mankind; the duty to work for the happiness of mankind in general.[1]

The obligation to work for the world chain, which has always been most emphatically demanded by the leaders of Dutch Freemasonry, follows from these principles. They also demand, however, that this spiritual, but, nevertheless quite undogmatic view, should be the basis of every international freemasonic union or society. This has led the 'Grand Orient' into differences of opinion with the 'Grand Orient of France' which we will touch upon later.

Finally there comes Swiss Freemasonry, which came into being as early as 1736.[2] For a long time past it has placed in the foreground the obligation to work in a practical manner for understanding between the nations, and seeks to open up new channels for this and to produce pioneers in this sphere. The Swiss Lodges of the three nationalities had passed through many vicissitudes and these Lodges, with their varying outlooks on cultural matters, were united in 1844 in the Grand Lodge 'Alpina', in which there were always many men who devoted the whole of their energy to creating a useful basis for the thought of world Freemasonry, and thus sought to serve the cause of universal peace.[3] Let us bear in mind the words of its first Grand Master, Johann Jakob Hottinger, the historian, spoken on his death-bed:

'But the most beautiful thing of all is active love.'

Another eminent Swiss who, with Hottinger, was one of the original members of the 'Alpina', was the magistrate Dr. Jonas Furrer, whose fellow-citizens showed their confidence in him by electing him to be the first President of the Swiss Confederation. There was also Johann Kaspar Bluntschli, later Professor of Law at Munich and Heidelberg, at that time still a member of the Federal Council and one of the greatest German-speaking jurists. At the same time, his was one of the most enthusiastic and fertile intellects ever to serve the Royal Art.

[1] E. L. Faubel in 'W.F.Z.', 9th year, 1927.

[2] The first Lodge was founded, at the instance of George Hamilton, in Geneva in 1736, by Englishmen resident in that city. Owing to a Decree of Abolition issued by the Council of the Two Hundred this Lodge declined shortly after its foundation. Three Lodges were still in existence in 1744, although citizens were forbidden to join Lodges under penalty of a fine of 100 ducats and imprisonment. The first Grand Lodge on Swiss soil was founded in 1769—also in Geneva—and this was followed in 1822 by a Provincial Grand Lodge of the Grand Lodge of England, which were joined by governing bodies in Zurich and Basle and/or Lausanne.

[3] One of the most enthusiastic was the poet Heinrich Zschokke.

These men were followed by many others who combined 'the work on the rough ashlar' with excellent work for the community by educating the nation and by training the youth, and whose range of vision was not confined within the limits of their native frontiers, but who, as apostles of the true meaning of life which they experienced in the Lodges, undertook the mission of awakening the conscience of the world. In the spring of 1928, the whole civilized community celebrated the centenary of the birth of Henry Dunant of Geneva, the winner of the Nobel Prize for services in the interests of Peace, in whose heart was born, on the battlefield of Solferino, the idea of the Red Cross. Dunant was a Mason, as was also Elie Ducommun, who likewise received the Nobel Prize, in 1902, for his vigorous and international work in the cause of Peace. Dr. Haeberlin, the Zurich physician, and Herr Bucher-Heller of Lucerne, have also played an important part in the movement for universal peace.

However, in the sphere of international Freemasonry, the Grand Master Quartier-la-Tente was particularly prominent. He created the Bureau for Masonic Relations, the international freemasonic bureau, and was the organizer of a number of international transactions. This Councillor of State of Neufchâtel regarded the self-sacrificing struggle for the universality of Freemasonry as his life-work, and he carried it on until his last day. No disappointment or opposition could distract him from his work, which was modestly crowned by the formation of the 'Association Maçonnique Internationale'[1] in 1921.

From that time onwards the Grand Lodge 'Alpina' has continued its earnest endeavours to bring about a *rapprochement* and to adjust all quarrels under the auspices of this association of Grand Lodges. The former Grand Master, Dr. Fritz Brandenberg, is an excellent mediator and it devolved upon him, at the Freemasonic Congress at Belgrade in 1926, to elaborate a programme for international activity in the cause of Peace.

Like the 'Association Maçonnique Internationale', another international freemasonic group has arisen on Swiss soil, namely, the Universal League of Freemasons,[2] which is every

[1] See chapter entitled 'The Beginnings of an International Organization.'
[2] The Governing Committee of the Universal League of Freemasons meets at Basle, the central office being in Vienna. It maintains, amongst other things, an international masonic press bureau. Dr. Fritz Uhlmann, Honorary Lecturer at Basle University, Dr. Chr. Rothenberger, one of the greatest advocates and champions of the Swiss Social Insurance, and Lafontaine, the Belgian Nobel Peace Prize Winner, etc., are amongst its leaders.

day gathering more and more Freemasons into its folds, and which, designed originally as an association of Esperantists belonging to the Fraternity, has, since 1925, made very vigorous endeavours to organize all Freemasons throughout the world to work for universal peace. It does not appeal to the various Obediences but solely to individual Freemasons who are prepared, of their own free will and from inner conviction, to devote themselves to this work, the one object of which is to promote the universal welfare of mankind. The Congresses of Basle (1925 and 1927), Vienna (1928), Amsterdam (1929), Geneva (1930), Paris (1931), and The Hague (1933), bear witness to the good work and splendid results already achieved by the League.

CHAPTER VIII

YUGOSLAVIA (THE SARAJEVO ASSASSINATION)

W HENEVER the question of a 'masonic conspiracy' is discussed it has, in recent times, become the habit to refer to particularly close relations between the French and the Belgrade Grand Lodges; relations which are alleged to have been in existence long before 1914 and to have led to the Sarajevo assassination and, consequently, to the World War.

The Yugoslavian Grand Lodge, or, to give it its full name, the 'Grand Lodge of the Serbs, Croats, and Slovenes of Yugoslavia,' was founded in 1919. There were previously a few Lodges of the various systems in Belgrade, which united in 1912 to form a Supreme Council; in 1919 this united in its turn with the 'Yugoslavian Grand Mother Lodge of Charity' in Zagreb, which arose, immediately after the termination of the war, out of the Croatian Lodges working under the Grand Lodge of Hungary. From its inception this young Obedience had to submit to vigorous attacks from foreign quarters.

The suggestion of a connexion between Serbian Freemasonry and the murder of the heir to the throne and his wife was made in a Croatian publication even during the War. An article then appeared in Berlin in 1918, as a supplement to *Archives for Penal Law and Criminal Procedure*, about the prosecutions of the assassins of Sarajevo 'based on the official shorthand notes of the case, written by "Professor Pharos" '. What seemed to give this publication an authentic character was the introduction, written by Josef Kohler, a well-known professor of Berlin University, which said, in so many words, that it had been proved that the Grand Orient of France had greatly assisted the Serbian propaganda against Austria-Hungary, in order to strike a blow at the vital nerve of the German-speaking nations. It was alleged that the Serbian 'Narodna Odbrana', in which all the avowed enemies of the monarchy had combined, was controlled by Freemasons, and that the brains behind the Sarajevo outrage, Tankosić and Kazimirović, had been very popular in Parisian Lodge circles, and that the conspirator, Ciganović, who supplied the money, the bombs and revolvers for the murder, had also belonged to the Fraternity.

These allegations, coupled with the shorthand report of 'Pharos', were 'classical material' for Wichtl, the passionate Austrian anti-Freemason, who shortly afterwards published the passages referring to Freemasonry in his notorious and sensational writings [1] and thus created for them the widest possible circulation.

According to 'Professor Pharos's' representation, the hearing of the case on the 14th August 1914, took the following course:

The representative of the Lodge in the matter of the murder plot was Radoslav Kazimirović, a Serb, already mentioned; regarding whom the accused bomb-thrower Nedjelko Čabrinović made the following declarations:

Čabrinović: 'He (Kazimirović) is a Freemason; in fact, to a certain extent, he is one of its heads. He went abroad almost immediately afterwards.' (After they had offered to undertake the assassination.) 'He journeyed all over the Continent. He went to Budapest, Russia, and France. Whenever I asked Ciganović what the position was in regard to our affair, he would reply: "When he (Kazimirović) comes then. . . ." Ciganović told me also at that time that the Freemasons had already condemned the heir to the throne to death two years previously (1912), but they had no one to carry out the sentence. Afterwards, when he gave me the Browning and the cartridges, he said: "Our friend returned from Budapest yesterday." I knew that he had made the journey in connexion with our affair and had conferred abroad with certain circles.'

President: 'Is that not pure fabrication?'

Čabrinović: 'It is the absolute truth and a hundred times truer than your documents from the "Narodna Odbrana".'

In another passage:

Counsel for the Defence (Dr. v. Premuzić, to Čabrinović): 'Have you read Rosić's books?'

Čabrinović: 'I have read his treatises about Freemasonry.'

Premuzić: 'Were these books distributed in Belgrade?'

Čabrinović: 'As a typesetter, I have set them up.'

Premuzić: 'Tell me, do you believe in God or in anything else?'

Čabrinović: 'No!'

Premuzić: 'Are you a Freemason?'

Čabrinović (becomes confused and hesitates. The silence

[1] Dr. Friedrich Wichtl: *Weltfreimaurerei, Weltkrieg, Weltrevolution* ('World Freemasonry, World War, World Revolution').

lasts a long time. He turns towards Premuzić and looks at him): 'Why do you ask me that? I cannot answer the question. . . .'

Premuzić: 'Have you heard in Belgrade that Austria is reproached with being a Catholic State?'

President: 'One moment, that is a leading question.'

(*To Čabrinović*): 'Were you aware that the Archduke was a pious man?'

Čabrinović: 'Father Puntigam, who is here present, was his adviser.'

Premuzić: 'Is Voja Tankosić a Freemason?'

Čabrinović (again embarrassed, remains silent): 'Why do you ask me about that?' (After some hesitation): 'Yes, and Čiganović as well. . . .'

President: 'How do you know that?'

Čabrinović: 'By the fact that Tankosić wrote an article in the 'Piemont' against the Government, because they had handed over to the authorities in Skoplje a Russian anarchist who wanted to murder the Czar.'

President: 'From which it follows that you are also a Freemason. Only a Freemason can prove another man to be a Mason.'

Čabrinović: 'Please do not ask me that. I shall not answer it.'

President: 'Silence implies assent.'

And at another afternoon sitting:

President: 'Tell me something more about the motives. Was it known to you before you decided to commit the assassination that Tankosić and Čiganović were Freemasons? Did it have any influence upon your decision that you and they were Freemasons?'

Čabrinović: 'Yes.'

President: 'Explain that to me. Did you receive orders from them to commit the assassination?''

Čabrinović: 'I received orders from nobody to carry out the assassination. Freemasonry is connected with the assassination in as much as it was through Freemasonry that my resolve was strengthened. Freemasonry permits killing. Čiganović told me that the Freemasons had already condemned Francis Ferdinand to death a year before.'

President: 'Is there not a certain amount of fabrication in that? Where was he condemned?'

Premuzić: 'I will furnish proof of it.'

President: 'Did he tell you that at once or only after you had told him that you wished to carry out the assassination?'

Čabrinović: 'We spoke about Freemasonry much earlier, but he said nothing to us about this death sentence until we had finally decided on the assassination.'

On the same day the examination of the chief actor in the Sarajevo assassination, Gavrilo Princip, was continued.

President: 'Did you speak to Čiganović about Freemasonry?'

Princip: 'Why do you ask me about that?'

President: 'I ask you because I should like to know. Did you speak to him about it or not?'

Princip: 'Yes. Čiganović told me he was a Freemason.'

President: 'How did he tell you he was a Freemason?'

Princip: 'When I turned to him for the means of executing the assassination, he told me and laid stress upon it, that he would speak to a "certain man". He would obtain from him the means of carrying out the assassination. On another occasion he mentioned to me that the heir to the Austrian throne had been condemned to death by Freemasons in a Lodge.'

President: 'And you? Perhaps you also are a Freemason?'

Princip: 'Why this question? I shall not answer it.' (After a short pause:) 'No! I am not!'

President: 'Is Čabrinović a Freemason?'

Princip: 'I do not know! Perhaps. He said on one occasion that he would join a Lodge. . . .'

Opposed to these 'authentic' statements, solely circulated by 'Professor Pharos', there is the fact that the official reporters of the Sarajevo trial had no knowledge of all the foregoing. There is, moreover, the important consideration that the Sarajevo murderers were still much too young to be members of a Lodge when they committed their ghastly deed.

Consequently, Father Hermann Gruber, S.J.,[1] a prominent enemy of Freemasonry, in response to Wichtl's assertion that 'it is quite clear from the foregoing that the plan for the assassination was hatched by the Freemasons', gave expression to his serious doubts in the following words:

'. . . Not one of the assassins had attained his twentieth year at the time of the assassination. It is, however, a universal principle of Freemasonry that only candidates of full age, or "free men of good report", that is to say, people who hold a fairly independent position of good standing in society, can be admitted as members of the Brotherhood of Freemasons. The lowest age at which candidates are admitted is generally accepted as that between the twenty-first and the

---

[1] *Stimmen der Zeit*, vol. xcvi, Part ii, November 1918.

twenty-fourth completed year. It is quite possible that the two assassins who declared themselves to be Freemasons, were deceived into believing that they were Masons.'

This, however, was not enough to satisfy those people who sought to establish Freemasonry as the chief instigator of the World War. An Englishwoman, Miss Edith Durham, came to their assistance. This lady, who had travelled a great deal in the Balkans, also supported the absurd story about Free-masonry in her book *The Sarajevo Crime*. She cited as her authority another English author, H. C. Norman, according to whom the Grand Orient of France had prepared the way for closer relations with the notorious Russian 'Ochrana' in 1906, and she also made reference to 'documents' published by Horatio Bottomley, the notorious English politician who has been exposed and condemned as a swindler of the lowest order. These 'documents' dealt with a plan, drawn up in the Spanish language, for the murder of the Archduke Francis Ferdinand. The Spanish language was used, according to Norman's assertions, because the communications between the Grand Lodge of France and the Balkan States were carried on in that language.

It appears incomprehensible that sane people can base concrete accusations upon such flimsy evidence. Never has the Grand Orient of France discussed plans for an assassination in the Spanish or any other language, and never were the youthful Sarajevo murderers, nor the instigators of the terrible crime, Freemasons. At the critical time of the year 1914, the Belgrade Lodges were mainly composed of people who took absolutely no part in active politics. Even Pasić, who has often appeared in anti-masonic books as a 'Brother', complete with masonic apron, was not a member of a Lodge.

It has been established, however, that Voja Tankosić, leader of the Komitatschi, organized the assassination; that he dis-tributed bombs and revolvers to Princip and his accomplices; that he handed these youths over to Milan Ciganović, the rail-way-man, in order that he might instruct them in bomb-throwing and revolver-shooting, and that he finally made it possible for them to cross the Serbian frontier and take the weapons to Bosnia. Tankosić was an exceedingly unruly, restless and rough type of man, a ruthless insurgent with iron nerves. He was a born terrorist who had enjoyed for years the reputation that the police were unable to get him within their grasp. As a young lieutenant he had taken part in the conspiracy against King Alexander and, on the night of the murder, had had Likola and Nikodija Lunjević, the brothers of Queen Draga, slain by his soldiers. Always dissatisfied and bitter, he retired from the 'Narodna Odbrana' in 1911, as, in his opinion, it was too moderate. With seven of his friends he founded another society, the secret terrorist organization 'Unity or Death', sometimes known as the 'Black Hand'. The assassination of the heir to the throne and his consort was planned by members of this group, mainly by Tankosić and the chief of the organization, Colonel Dragutin Dimitrijeivić-Apis. This has recently been admitted by a former member of the 'Black Hand', Dr. Oskar Tartaglia.[1] At the same time, however, he makes it quite clear that neither the assassins nor the instigators had anything to do with Freemasonry, including Apis, in whose brain the idea of the assassination was born.

This testimony of a man who was in the closest touch with the conspirators is no doubt worthy of implicit belief. The value of his statements is enhanced by the fact that he has now cleared up the mystery of 'Professor Pharos', who linked the Freemasons with the Sarajevo crime. 'Pharos' is none other than Father Puntigam, the leader of the Jesuits in Sarajevo. In other words, the same Reverend Father who induced the President at the murder trial, Counsellor of the Court of Appeal Luigi von Curinaldi, to lay aside his secular robes and to don those of the religious order of the Society of Jesus. Father Puntigam did not exactly invent the 'statements' of the youthful assassins but in his account their declarations are invested with a character which is not their own. For it was quite clear that the assassins had no knowledge of Freemasonry, but having been given a hint by the counsel for the defence, they grasped the idea as a drowning man grasps a straw, in order to divert the trial into a false channel.

The 'masonic' murder of Sarajevo belongs just as much to the realm of fable as the no less grave 'reports' that appeared in many newspapers in 1926 when relations between Yugoslavia and Italy were seriously strained; 'reports' to the effect that Yugoslavian Freemasonry was urging war against Mussolini, that their Grand Master had financed the purchase of bombs and gas-masks and that delegates of the Belgrade Lodges had held a secret Conference in Paris with Czechoslovakian Freemasons, with the object of promoting an insurrection in Albania, with the assistance of catholic Beys.

[1] In the Sarajevo newspaper *Večerna Pošta*, No. 2182, 3rd October 1928.

CHAPTER IX

THE SYMBOLIC GRAND LODGE OF HUNGARY
(NOW DISSOLVED)

THE unwarrantable agitation against Freemasonry has fallen on fertile soil in two States since the Great War: in Hungary and Italy. In both these countries masonic Lodge meetings are no longer permitted. The temples have been closed and the columns, once the emblems of a splendid activity, now gather dust in lumber-rooms.

The light of Hungarian Freemasonry flickered and died at the same moment as the proletarian dictatorship was proclaimed in Budapest. On that black Friday evening—it was the 21st March 1919—the Budapest Lodge 'Comenius' had celebrated another initiation. On the following day the Council of the Peoples' Commissars declared the dissolution of Freemasonry, together with all other civil associations, and Red soldiers seized the Grand Lodge Buildings in Podmanicky Street. After the 121 days of the Communist reign of terror, the house once more came into the hands of the Grand Lodge but the Rumanian occupation of Hungary and, later, the clamorous anti-masonic campaign of the counter-revolutionaries made the revival of meetings an impossibility.

On the 24th May 1920, the Grand Lodge building once more served as a military billet. Without any previous agreement being arrived at, two officers, accompanied by a company of soldiers, forced their way into the premises and declared house and furniture confiscated. They were not in a position to show any kind of warrant from the authorities, but this high-handed procedure was legalized the very next day. The Budapest authorities granted a lease of the premises, complete with furniture, to the 'Move' Officers' Association.

Three days later a Decree of the Hungarian Ministry of the Interior was issued declaring both the Symbolic Grand Lodge and its dependent Lodges illegal, and suppressing them.

This decree was worded as follows:

'Royal Hungarian Minister of the Interior
    'Number 1550, Reservat.
    'Re: Dissolution of Masonic Associations.
'To all Municipal Commissars of the Government.

'The masonic associations (Lodges, etc.) were formed from their earliest beginnings for the realization of humanistic and social aims. It has come to my notice, from the lamentable events of the immediate past, that instead of working for the realization of the aims and tasks defined in their Constitutions and sanctioned by the Government, their activity has been directed towards influencing politics and the seizure of power.

'It is a well-known fact that the Freemasons have been engaged in constant intrigues. These intrigues, which began with their instigation of the War, continued during the War and have been carried on since its unfortunate end for our country, have been directed towards fostering defeatism and the general destruction, the stirring-up of revolution and the promotion of Bolshevism. It is impossible for me to disregard the unanimous view entertained against Freemasonry by Hungarian society, by the Press and by the individual municipalities, and, by virtue of my legal powers of control over the activities of associations and societies, I hereby finally dissolve all masonic associations (Lodges, institutions) within the boundaries of Hungarian territory, whatever be the names under which they are carried on and whether or not the associations concerned possess Statutes approved by the Government and whether they are active at the present time or not, and this I do with the immediate object of taking steps to prevent Freemasonry—which has renounced Fatherland, religion and nationality, and still continues to conspire—from continuing this its wicked work in the future.

'In the execution of this my Decree I confer upon the Government Commissars of the respective Government authorities the powers of ministerial commissars.

                                    'DR. MICHAEL DÖMÖTÖR.
    'BUDAPEST, 18th May 1920.'

These are terrible words that stigmatize Hungarian Freemasons as traitors of the vilest kind! Words that carried all

OLD ENGLISH LODGE MEDALS

PIERCED LODGE JEWELS

the more weight since the country, in those days, was still sore from the thousand wounds that war, revolution and communistic councils had inflicted upon it. The people were entitled to think that such an official condemnation of several thousands of Hungarian citizens had been preceded by a thorough investigation or, at least, that discoveries of a startling nature had been made. But such was not the case! No investigation had taken place, and the Decree was probably merely issued for the purpose of justifying, after the event, the confiscation of the Grand Lodge building by a group closely associated with the Government of the time. This assumption is supported by the manner in which the whole affair was handled. In 1920, when the 'Move' received the palace with its magnificent halls, its library and its museum, they were instructed, as 'tenants', to make an exact inventory of its costly contents and to preserve them intact. But this was not done. No inventory was made, and vast quantities of valuable exhibits from the Masonic Museum, masonic jewels, and even the Grand Master's gavel disappeared, only to turn up again later in a second-hand-dealer's shop. In September 1923, the building was transferred by the Ministry of the Interior to the Health Insurance Fund under the Ministry of Public Welfare. Even then the 'Move' did not vacate the premises, which it described in all its official letters as 'its' house. In 1927 the Minister of Public Welfare leased the house anew to the officers' association for a period of 16 years.[1]

The leading members of the dissolved Symbolic Grand Lodge of Hungary naturally did all in their power to vindicate their honour, which had been so unjustifiably besmirched, and to regain their rights. Within a few days of the enforced closing of the Lodges, they lodged a petition with the Regent, Admiral Horthy, and with the Prime Minister, Count Paul Teleky, in which they demanded an enquiry and the restitution of the Grand Lodge building which had been confiscated without justification. They could not only state that the official accusations against Hungarian Freemasonry were entirely untenable, but that—even in times when political trials were the order of the day—not a single trial had been instituted against a Freemason in respect of any one of the charges made against the Fraternity ('treasonable acts against the State', 'high treason', and 'revolutionary activity').

They received no redress, although the petitions were

---

[1] *Wiener Freimaurer-Zeitung.* No. 10. 1927.

renewed at every change of Cabinet, and there set in instead, as seems to happen everywhere in such cases, a systematic anti-masonic propaganda in the Press, in social circles and in all public institutions. The agitation in respect of the 'unanimous view of Hungarian Society' had to be created retrospectively in order to counteract the many voices raised in protest against such a violent misuse of power. In the following year, however, the Government did not hesitate to place themselves in official communication with the leading members of the dissolved Grand Lodge in order to request them, with a view to the speedier repatriation of Hungarian prisoners of war still languishing in Russia, to take the matter up with foreign Grand Lodges. But the Government in power still turned a deaf ear to their plea for justice. On one occasion, to wit, in 1922, Count Klebelsberg, who was Minister of the Interior at the time, promised to set up the enquiry for which application had been made. But this never took place, for he was succeeded in the same year by a new Minister, Stefan Rakovszky, who declared that, in point of fact, an enquiry had already taken place, the results of which had been recorded in a book published in the previous year, namely, *The Iniquities of Freemasonry*. That was a very clumsy evasion, for no official functionary of any kind whatsoever had participated in the alleged 'enquiry' and not a single Freemason had been examined. What really happened was that two anti-masonic journalists, one of whom was Karl Wolf, a fanatical type of conservative, 'investigated' the matter and wrote a book in two volumes, which was chiefly designed to cause a sensation and which omitted none of the usual accusations contained in the general run of anti-masonic inflammatory literature. Hungarian Freemasonry was naturally not prepared to acknowledge 'proceedings' of this nature and has demanded time and again that justice be done. In spite of the fact that Hungarian Government circles to-day regard the matter in an entirely different light to that of 1920, there has, up to the present time, not been the slightest question of instituting the enquiry demanded, nor of rehabilitating the Grand Lodge, nor of restoring the confiscated building.

Up to the moment of its dissolution the Symbolic Grand Lodge of Hungary was one of the most active in Europe. Especially in the sphere of benevolent activity did it render magnificent service to humanity. The institutions it created were models of their kind. Especially well known were its institution for the distribution of free bread, its children's welfare centres, and its work for down-and-outs and discharged convicts. During the war the Grand Lodge building became the most magnificent of hospitals for wounded soldiers and, following this example, all the Lodge houses in the provinces became military hospitals.

In those days Hungarian Freemasons had other opportunities of demonstrating their patriotism, and the fact that the Hungarian Prime Minister, Count Stefan Tisza, frequently made use of the services of Freemasons for negotiations with foreign countries, proves that this was appreciated. Clear proof of this is also to be found in the collection of the Count's letters published by the Hungarian Academy of Sciences.

On the 28th August 1914, Count Tisza wrote the following words to Count Johann Forgach, the Departmental Chief of the Royal and Imperial Ministry for Foreign Affairs:

'I intend to make use of your suggestion regarding Freemasonry and I hope to be able to report progress within a day or two.'

Some days later, on the 1st September 1914, Count Tisza addressed the following letter to Count Czernin, the Ambassador at Bucarest, who afterwards became Minister for Foreign Affairs:

'DEAR FRIEND,

'In accordance with a suggestion from the Ballplatz,[1] I have proposed to the leaders of the Freemasonic Lodges of this place that, through the agency of Rumanian Freemasons, they should bring pressure to bear upon the Press of that country, so that the war news may be published at least impartially and in accordance with the truth. The bearer of this letter, Herr Jenö Csukássy, is travelling to Bucarest on behalf of these gentlemen and on his arrival he intends to get into communication with the most important journalists.

'In recommending to you this capable and trustworthy man I request you to be good enough to help him in every possible way in the execution of his patriotic task.

'Yours very sincerely,

'TISZA.'

[1] Ministry for Foreign Affairs, Vienna.

Jenö Csukássy, the Deputy Grand Master, thereupon departed for Bucarest, accompanied by a prominent Viennese journalist, and did all that it was possible to do there in view of the critical position. In spite of the fact that success was no longer to be attained, the Hungarian Government had recourse to Freemasonry on a later occasion.

The following letter, dated the 18th January 1915, addressed by Count Tisza to the Departmental Chief Forgach, may be quoted in this connexion:

'DEAR FRIEND,

'The Freemasons here are sending the enclosed letter to one of the leaders of the Lodge in Naples with the request that we allow the letter to arrive at its destination without being censored. As it is a question of an action taken on our initiative, and at our desire, I am forwarding the letter with the request that you will allow it to pass to its destination through our Consul in Naples.

'With kindest regards,
'Yours sincerely,
'TISZA.'

As early as August 1914, Dr. Rudolf Temesváry, an eminent physician of Budapest, entered into correspondence with an Italian friend of his, a university professor who was also a member of Parliament and a very influential politician. The Hungarian physician expressed the opinion that the Italian attitude towards Austria-Hungary and Germany constituted a breach of the terms of the Treaty. The answer he received was exceedingly short and the correspondence was broken off. However, on the 6th April 1915, Dr. Temesváry received a telegram from Genoa which invited him to go to Italy as quickly as possible. The situation was critical and no friend of both nations could fail to do anything that was likely to maintain the friendly collaboration of the two countries. Dr. Temesváry communicated with Tisza and at his pressing request set out on the journey to Italy.

On the 21st April, he had an interview in Rome with Signor Sonnino, the Minister for Foreign Affairs, in the presence of his Italian friend. The proposals made by the Minister were, of course, unacceptable, and an idea of them may be obtained from the letter which Sonnino wrote to Tisza:

'The spirit of the Italian people is in every way sympathetic to Hungary and to the Hungarian nation. In my desire to inaugurate a policy beneficial to Hungary, I find that there is not only no hindrance as regards my own nation for such an endeavour but, on the contrary, there is encouragement. I picture the execution of this policy on the lines that the Hungarian Government, after having established close relations with the Hungarian Croats and Rumanians—especially the latter—might take the initiative for the creation of a lasting peace between the nations of Europe. Consequently, the Hungarian Government would have to make all preparations in order to be able to declare that it desires peace. Italy is in every respect disposed to act morally, and has every interest in furthering the creation of a Greater Hungary, free, as far as possible, from German influence, and it would be exceedingly easy to arrive at a secret agreement between Hungary, Italy and Rumania whereby the specific interests of these countries would be served. That would be the only possible way of solving the tragic problem of the present hour.'

On his return, the Hungarian Freemason made a full report to Tisza regarding his conversations with Sonnino. Tisza said exactly what Dr. Temesváry had declared in Rome from the outset: that such unreasonable demands could not even be discussed.[1]

It may well be assumed from the foregoing that, as far as Count Tisza was concerned, it was not a 'well-known fact' that the Freemasons played such a prominent part in the instigation of the war and during the war . . by fostering defeatism and the general destruction. . . .'

It might also be asked whether there is anything in the suggestion of 'constant intrigues . . . in the stirring up of revolution and the promotion of Bolshevism'. In this respect also Hungarian Freemasonry can hold its head high. There was, to be sure, in some of their Lodges, for example, the Lodge 'Martinovics', a number of Radical elements who were of the opinion that it was the duty of Freemasonry to perform progressive work. But they were at no time able to influence the Symbolic Grand Lodge in the direction of supporting revolutionary endeavours.

During the October Revolution, two Freemasons, Oskar Jászi and Paul Szende, became Ministers in the Károlyi Government. They were both men whose good intentions and

Bakonyi Kalman: *A magyar szabadkömivesek igazsága.*

unselfishness would not be denied even by their enemies. However, Hungarian Freemasonry did not follow their lead, and of this there is decisive proof. In the wildly exciting days of October there belonged to Freemasonry a Secretary of State of Károlyi's Cabinet. He appeared one evening at a masonic assembly, described with much enthusiasm the political situation, and demanded the support of Freemasonry for the new Government. But it was refused! This Radical Secretary of State, who thereupon withdrew from the Fraternity, was none other than Stefan Friedrich, the reactionary agitator, who subsequently became the first Prime Minister of the counter-Revolution.

The 'information' as to the connexion with the Bolshevist tragedy may also be put down as fable. Otherwise the Communist Dictator, Béla Kun, would hardly have been in such a hurry to chase the Freemasons out of their temples and forbid every one of the activities. In so far as the Social Democrats supported the Communist Councils, not one of them was a Freemason; in fact, during the war, the Social Democrats forbade members of their party to belong to the Fraternity.

But all reference to these facts fell on deaf ears.

As Hungarian Freemasons were unsuccessful in their plea for the institution of an enquiry, endeavours were made on many occasions from other quarters to enlighten the Budapest Government as to the true state of affairs. After the attention of the representatives of the various Grand Lodges had been drawn to the sad plight of Hungarian Freemasonry by the Grand Lodge of Vienna at the first Convention of the Association Maçonnique Internationale at Geneva, Robert H. Robinson, the Grand Master of the Grand Lodge of New York, addressed a letter to the Hungarian Prime Minister, Count Bethlen. On the recommendation of Count Bánffy, the Hungarian Minister for Foreign Affairs, who had been sounded in Geneva, Reverchon, the then Grand Master of the Swiss Grand Lodge 'Alpina', and Ossian Lang, the Historian of the Grand Lodge of New York, had an interview in Budapest, in the autumn of 1921, with the Minister for the Interior, Stefan Rakovszky.

The latter's father had previously played an extraordinarily important part in Hungarian Freemasonry. He had been Grand Master of the Symbolic Grand Lodge. Even the twin brother of the Minister had belonged to the Fraternity at its dissolution; he was, in fact, an enthusiastic member of the oldest Hungarian Lodge, the 'Corvin Mátyás'. The two masonic leaders made reference to this when they protested against the reproach of disloyalty to the Fatherland being levelled against the Hungarian Brotherhood. In the course of the discussions the minister put forward the suggestion that the Freemasons should form a new benevolent association. In the event of its activity receiving the approval of the Government and society, the members would, in the course of time, again receive the right to hold masonic meetings. Reverchon and Lang then passed on this suggestion to the former leaders of the dissolved Grand Lodge, who declared, however, that Hungarian Freemasonry was unable to take up its work again, in any shape or form, until it had been given an opportunity of vindicating itself, in the eyes of the public, of the charges of high treason and atheism of which it had been officially accused.

Even in the Hungarian Parliament reference was repeatedly made to the shocking injustice suffered by the Freemasons. For instance, in May 1928, when a large Hungarian delegation had returned from New York, where they had taken part in the dedication of the monument to the greatest Hungarian patriot, Ludwig Kossuth. Like the other national heroes, General Türr, General Klapka, and Count Andrássy, he was also a Freemason. The money for the erection of the monument was subscribed mainly by Hungarian members of American Lodges. The Hungarian Government had consequently invited even the outlawed Freemasons to send delegates to New York, and the leaders of the Hungarian delegation thus came into contact with American Freemasonry. The impression they gained was summed up in a speech made before the National Assembly by M. Lukács, a former Minister of Education and a member of the Government Party, in which he said: 'I believe that the time has arrived when, owing to the altered circumstances, the attitude towards the Freemasons adopted by the Government in recent years may at last be subjected to a revision!'

CHAPTER X

THE DESTRUCTION OF ITALIAN FREEMASONRY

L IKE the Hungarian Grand Lodge, Italian Freemasonry, which was at one time so strong, has been dissolved. Under the iron rule of Fascism there remained in the long run no chance of existence for it, although its members fought heroically to defend its ideals.

The trouble began within a few months of the March on Rome. The theme 'Fascist Party and Freemasonry' was first discussed on the 13th February 1923, by the Grand Fascist Council under the presidency of Mussolini. After a long debate the following resolution was passed:

'The Grand Fascist Council resolves:
'In consideration of the fact that recent political events and the attitude and certain resolutions of Freemasonry have given just cause for the assumption that Freemasons pursue a programme and employ methods contrary to those which inspire the whole activity of Fascism, the Council calls upon those Fascists who are Freemasons to choose between membership of the National Fascist Party and Freemasonry. For there is only one discipline for Fascists, that of Fascism; there is only one hierarchy, that of Fascism; and there is only one allegiance, absolute and humble allegiance to the Duce and the other leaders of Fascism at all times.'

What had preceded this?

In the early days of February the General Assembly of the Symbolic Rite of the Grand Orient of Italy[1] had revised its Constitution in close sympathy with the Constitution of the Anglo-Saxon Grand Lodges, and, at the same time, discussed the problem of Fascism, in respect of which the following report was made:

[1] As the Fascist campaign against Freemasonry mainly concerned the Grand Orient, we are ignoring in our account of the development of events a second group of Italian Freemasonry, the 'National Grand Lodge' of the Scottish Rite, also known as the 'Freemasonry of the Piazza Gesù' after its headquarters. Finally, this group followed the same fate as the Grand Orient.

'Under the presidency of the Grand Master, Torrigiani, the General Assembly discussed the question of how the words "national duty" were to be interpreted in this significant moment of the national life. The very searching and fruitful debate, in which brethren in high political positions participated, demonstrated, as the Grand Master put it in his summing-up, that Freemasonry can never become a political party, and that, in the interests of national thought, it must be above all parties. Also at this hour, which shows, quite comprehensibly, all the signs of a revolutionary movement, the Fraternity of Freemasons cannot and must not depart from its traditions, which are based on the conviction of the sovereign power of the people as the unshakable foundation of our civil life.'

This *communiqué* was in all probability the real cause of the action taken by the Fascists fourteen days later.

Hardly had the proclamation of the Supreme Fascist Council been published than the governing council of the Grand Orient assembled in order to consider the newly created situation. The result of this consultation was the following lucid resolution:

'The Fascist Brethren have full freedom to break off all connexion with Freemasonry in order to give further loyal service to the Fascio. Those who do so will demonstrate by their action that Love of Country is the supreme commandment impressed upon them in the Lodge.'

And the result?

Many of those who belonged to both groups left the Fraternity. These were naturally Fascist functionaries, and young stormtroopers fired with the enthusiasm which the movement inspired in the hearts of the greater part of the youth of the country. But by far the greater number turned their backs on Mussolini, and renounced all the chances that the party which had just come into power had to offer to its loyal supporters, and these men, faced with the choice between Fascism and Freemasonry, remained true to the ideal of democracy.

Perhaps the most eloquent expression of this loyalty was to be found in the interchange of correspondence between General Luigi Capello and the political leader of the Roman Fascio. The latter had called upon the General, who had been one of the leaders of the March on Rome, to renounce Freemasonry. The answer was a letter containing his resignation from the Fascist Party.

Shortly afterwards the Grand Master, Torrigiani, published a grey book (*Massoneria e Fascismo*. Rome. 1923), in which he placed the whole of his material before the public under the title *Freemasonry and Fascism.*

Among the various letters published in this brochure there were many that aroused the greatest interest. Perhaps the most interesting of them all was a circular letter dated the 19th October 1922, i.e. before the victory of Fascism, sent out by the Grand Master to the various Lodges, in which he informed them of his attitude towards the Fascist movement. In this letter he first of all drew attention to a circular of the 21st December 1921, in which he had declared that forcible procedure could never be approved of, for force, which may be necessary when it is a question of resisting force, must never in any circumstances become a normal political method. . . . In its beginnings Fascism had been a necessity and a work for freedom, for it was then a matter of opposing conditions of anarchy and the threatened dictatorship of the proletariat. Numerous Freemasons were then to be found within its ranks who were certainly not forbidden to remain in the Fascio, but they must regard it as their duty to take care that its activity did not degenerate into a Terror.

In October 1922, Torrigiani added the following remarks to this reminder:

'A man can only be a Freemason when he is really devoted to the idea of Fatherland and Liberty. No particular political creed is thereby implied. There is room in our ranks for the most varied schools of political thought. . . .'

'Just as we always have the welfare of the Fatherland in mind in all our activities, so it is with us in our attitude towards Fascism. Our endeavour was directed towards removing the venom from political feuds, towards combating acts of violence and towards the pacification of Italy. We wished to propagate the idea of Humanity and the consciousness of the brotherhood of the nations. Those are the general lines of our work to-day. And, therefore, let us hope that the Fascist theories will not take such forms as will strike a blow in the face of all the conceptions of democracy and freedom, and amount to an oligarchy.'

Some months then passed without anything apparent happening. Only occasionally did there appear, here and there, an attack on the Grand Orient in one of the new Fascist newspapers that were springing up like mushrooms. But suddenly—at the end of 1923—the Fascist troops began to indulge in excesses against the assemblies of their political opponents, and a considerable number of Masonic Lodges fell victims to this new 'activism'.

The Temple of the Lodges 'Giuseppe Mazzini' in Prato and 'Ferruccio' in Pistoja were wrecked. The priceless library of the 'Ernesto Nathan' Lodge in Termoli was destroyed. The Lodge in Monteleone was attacked by soldiers during a festival. The furniture was broken up, and pictures of Mazzini and Garibaldi, and Lodge emblems, insignia, etc., were carried off as 'trophies' to the headquarters of the Fascio. Even the home of the two Grand Orient Lodges in Lucca were visited by a similar band. They took down the great triangle from above the Master's chair and threw it into the Piazza Napoleone.

The next morning the police took the insignia to the Town Hall. The Fascist burgomaster expressed his strong disapproval of the perpetrators, apologized in the name of the commune to the Worshipful Master of the Lodge 'Francescho Burlamacchi' and ordered the stolen articles to be returned. The Worshipful Master thereupon sent him the sum of 1,900 lire for ten poor familes of the city, at the same time drawing attention to the necessity for peace in matters of politics and religion. This letter drew forth sympathetic comment from all quarters of Italy, and in all circles.

Nevertheless, within a few days another act of terrorism occurred in San Severo. The Temple of the Lodge 'Luigi Zuppetta' was completely demolished, the archives destroyed and the furniture first broken up and afterwards burned.

Finally the rooms of the Turin Lodges were broken into during the night of the 23rd–24th January 1924, and the furniture and archives of four Lodges were carried off on motor lorries.

Torrigiani thereupon applied to the Minister of Justice for redress. The extent of his 'success' may be judged from a letter he wrote to the Prime Minister, Mussolini, in the autumn. In this courageous letter he said:

'I am turning to your Excellency in the name of the many Italians belonging to our Order, amongst whom there is not a single one who does not regard love of country as his first duty.

'I applied to the Minister of Justice at the beginning of the year on this same matter. On the 31st January I wrote to him as follows: "Our Lodges have been subjected to sudden attacks for several months past. This is something new in our country, where the national and cultural merits of Freemasonry and the faithful and heroic services it has rendered to the re-birth of Italy for more than a century are well known." I have reported to the Minister of Justice the acts of violence which have befallen Lodges in Turin, San Severo, Foggia, Monteleone, Termoli, Lucca, Pistoja, etc., within the course of a few weeks, and have requested him to issue strict orders to the guilty parties in order that such raids may not be repeated.

'The Minister replied to me, on the 3rd February, to the effect that he had requested the competent judicial authorities to report to him without delay. Since that time, however, these attacks and acts of terrorism have occurred with even greater frequency, and I now find myself obliged to apply to the head of the Government himself, for the good reason, Your Excellency, that immunity from punishment in respect of these acts of violence has naturally acted as an incentive to further excesses. In the last few days it has become worse and worse: Milan, Bologna, Venice, Leghorn, Perugia, Foligno, Spoleto, Forli, Bari, Tarent, Andria, etc., have, to the horror of the population, witnessed deeds that scorn all the beautiful traditions of Italy, scenes more reminiscent of the Middle Ages, scenes that are foreign to our national character. Why? You know yourself, Excellency, that our Lodges and their members have never failed in their loyalty to the Fatherland and that in every one of the towns mentioned patriotism has its very home in the Masonic Lodges. Have I to remind you of Aurelio Saffi, Carducci, De Meis and countless others?

'But we will not pursue that subject. More important is the conviction that such numerous acts of destruction and devastation, in which the same methods are always employed, must represent the execution of an extensive plan.

'We are well aware of the prejudice that has been worked up against us in the last two years. It would be interesting, but would lead too far, to record what lies behind the campaign directed against us. It is sufficient to adhere to the consequences it has brought with it. Have we not even lived to see "heroic" Fascist Members of Parliament marching at the head of the bands that stormed our Lodges?

'Your Excellency will probably still remember the untiring work we performed during the War, when, in the days of Caporetto, defeatism raised its head. At that time great praise was showered upon us and we earned this also when—again for the welfare of the Fatherland—we resolutely combated, during the severe post-War crisis, those people who were preparing to set up the dictatorship of one class, when we opposed our ideals of Freedom and Democracy to these destructive ideas with all the strength at our disposal. Surely we have won the right to be still respected to-day by the men who are now at the helm! That which we have always preached, namely, respect for every honest conviction, toleration of the views of others, humanity and kindness to our fellow-men—must apply to the Government also in the days when party quarrels are staining the streets with blood.

'It is maintained that we are not popular because we are in the clutches of an international association that places foreign interests above our national interests. This is, of course, absurdly untrue, and can be disproved with the greatest ease.

'We willingly plead guilty to the "offence" of being the guardians of the ideas that have made Italy great—the ideas of Freedom, of the sovereign power of the people, the autonomy of the State as against every ecclesiastical hierarchy and equal rights for all. But this point of view should naturally not prevent your Excellency from taking care to see that the law is also applied in our protection.

'Your obedient servant,
'DOMIZIO TORRIGIANI,
'Grand Master.'

Behind the official scenes, however, events had previously taken the following course:

After the declaration of incompatibility of the 13th February 1923, Messrs. Rossi, Balbo, and Acerbo, members of the Grand Fascist Council, who were Freemasons, had resigned from the Grand Orient.

On the 5th August 1924 the Grand Council again discussed the question of Freemasonry, on which occasion Signor Caprino, a Member of Parliament, demanded that the attitude of Fascism towards Freemasonry should no longer be confined to platonic protests and mere resolutions. The suppression of secret societies was necessary, for their existence could be traced back to a too liberal constitution. Bodrero's motion was thereupon adopted, in the following form:

'1. Fascists may no longer join the Masonic Brotherhood.
'2. Fascists who are still Freemasons are to withdraw from the Brotherhood immediately.
'3. Fascists who can give the Government information as to masonic elements attempting to sabotage the activity of the Government must not fail in their duty of disclosing such information.'

It can be clearly seen from this resolution that Torrigiani's letter to Mussolini was of no avail.

The Grand Orient now adhered strictly to the Fascist prohibition. It also insisted that the brethren must choose between Fascism and Freemasonry, and in consequence of this, Signor Dudan, a Member of the Grand Fascist Council, who had merely regarded the declaration of incompatibility from an academic point of view, was excluded from his Lodge.

But the acts of violence still continued.

The authoritative governmental organs declared their indignation at these acts of terrorism on the part of 'irresponsible elements', and promised redress, but within a few days the trouble started again. The pillaging of the beautiful Lodge building in Florence caused indignation the whole world over, but this did not prevent the continuation of shameful deeds in Genoa and Leghorn (where a bomb was exploded outside the Lodge building), Pisa, Venice, Perugia, Bologna, and Palermo, to name but a few. The Palazzo Giustiniani, the headquarters of the Grand Orient in Rome, was frequently subjected to nocturnal raids. Only by calling out a large number of armed soldiers was it possible to prevent the Fascists, who, armed with revolvers and knives, arrived at the scene of 'battle' in motor-lorries, from destroying everything. On the 1st January 1925, at 3 o'clock in the morning, the Bologna house of Eugenio Jacchia, a Member of the Council of the Order, was officially searched. He wrote the following letter to the Minister Federzoni:

'I am making no complaint. I only wish to place on record that when I was prosecuted by the former Austro-Hungarian Government in the year 1889 for implication in Irredentist conspiracy, I received much more lenient treatment from those authorities than I have to-day received from my own countrymen.'

The fact that no repressive measures were taken by the authorities in respect of these occurrences strengthened the belief that an attack was being planned in official quarters, and this was not long in coming. A commission was entrusted with the task of collecting 'information' concerning Freemasonry. The memorandum they published—by order—regarding their investigations was more than weak. Its chief aim seemed to be to prove that Freemasonry had, in fact, had nothing to do with the great Italian national movement of the nineteenth century—the so-called Risorgimento. (An assertion diametrically opposed to the truth.) And a systematic persecution of the greatest severity then began.

The *Roma Fascista*, a weekly newspaper of the Fascist Right wing, sent a circular letter to its political partisans in Parliament asking for their views on Freemasonry. The answers, of which tens of thousands of copies were distributed were mainly inspired by a fanatical hatred of 'Massoneria,' but contained very little else.

Despite all these shadows of coming events, the brethren of the Grand Orient were not to be influenced in their attitude. They steadfastly pursued their opposition to the idea of a dictatorship, and, after the murder of Matteotti, General Capello was one of the first to declare publicly that a stop must be put to violence. Time and again it was emphasized that the constitutional order of Italy must not be based on terrorism, but solely on democracy.

About the middle of December 1924, Torrigiani made a speech in Milan to many hundreds of brethren, in which he referred to the incompatibility of Fascism with Freemasonry and stated that Fascism constitutes an intellectual and moral retrogression for Italy. Fascism was a return to the methods of political crime.

The Fascist Council thereupon attempted to give their campaign against Freemasonry a more active form by forbidding even non-Fascist officials and officers to belong to Lodges. And this affected a large number of members of the Army and the bureaucracy.

The great blow which had been expected was struck on the 10th January 1925. An Anti-Masonic Bill was introduced in Parliament by the Cabinet on the proposal of the Minister for the Interior. This Bill was outwardly directed against associations of all kinds, but, in reality, was chiefly levelled at the 'snake in the grass'.

Article I of this Bill decreed that all societies, corporations, and institutions working in Italy must lodge with the police their memoranda of association and statutes, as well as a list of members and persons occupying any kind of official post. In addition, associations were required to supply to the police, on demand, information as to their organization and activity. This information had to be supplied by the persons in authoritative central or local positions within two days. Any person contravening this regulation was to be liable to a penalty of not less than three months' imprisonment, and a fine up to 6,000 lire. Any persons wilfully making false or incomplete statements were to be punished by not less than one year's imprisonment and fined up to 30,000 lire, with forfeiture of the right to occupy any official position for a period of five years. Associations might also be dissolved for giving false or incomplete information.

The most important paragraph is the following:

'No State, Provincial or Parochial officials, or officials of institutions subject to the control of the State, Province, or Parish may be members of secret societies or such societies as demand the oath of secrecy. The penalty for contravention is dismissal. All officials must comply with the regulations within fifteen days from the date of the entry into force of this Act.'

This general attack on Freemasonry was accompanied by violent onslaughts from the Fascist newspapers. The *Idea Nazionale* declared that Freemasonry had lost its civil rights once and for all. On the other hand, certain prominent newspapers, including those which generally supported the Government, expressed strong disapproval of the proposed restrictions. Even the ministerial *Messaggero* took the part of the Freemasons, 'the rough treatment of whom might lead to painful results'. No less disapproving was the attitude which the *Tribuna*, an authoritative journal, adopted towards the Bill.

Mussolini's faithful followers brought all sorts of new charges against Freemasonry to offset this criticism. They even went so far as to suggest that the crash of the lira was the result of a masonic plot.

In order to attenuate the distressing impression created abroad, Mussolini endeavoured, in an interview he granted to the celebrated American journalist Karl H. von Wiegand, to convey the idea that Italian Freemasonry had conspired with French brethren against Italy.

'I asked Mussolini,' wrote Wiegand at the time, 'why he was taking action against the Freemasons.'

'The Bill is not solely directed against the Freemasons, but against all secret societies that constitute a danger to the peace and quietness of the State,' answered Mussolini. 'In England, America, and Germany, Freemasonry is a charitable and philanthropic institution. In Italy, however, it is a secret political organization, but what is worse, it is completely dependent upon the Grand Orient of France. I should be glad if Italian Freemasons were what the English and the Americans are—a non-political fraternal association for mutual benefit.'

Even before the Bill had been passed by the Chamber and Senate there were further instances of official antagonism to the Grand Orient. Their organ, the *Rivista Massonica*, was suppressed.

The officials of the Grand Orient then discussed the steps to be taken to deal with the new situation. They decided, first of all, to play a waiting game and to grant the Grand Master, Torrigiani, the widest powers. However, the President of the Supreme Council, Ettore Ferrari, addressed a circular letter to his brethren in which he implored them to stick to their posts.

On the anniversary of the foundation of Rome, Torrigiani published an appeal to all Freemasons in Italy, in which he made a strong protest against the measures the Government proposed to take against Freemasonry.

The appeal declared that Freemasons had been prepared to make known to the authorities the names of their members. But the matter had now assumed a totally different aspect, in view of the severe persecution and restrictions to which they were exposed. In the event of the proposed measures becoming law, Freemasons, amongst whom there were many citizens who had rendered inestimable service to the Fatherland, would have to choose between severing their connexion with the Brotherhood, which was so dear to their hearts, and the greatest hardship for themselves and their families. But in view of the shocking state of affairs sacrifices were not to be recommended.

The Anti-Masonic Bill came before Parliament for debate in

May 1925. From the very first it was clear that it would finally be passed by Parliament, which was entirely under Mussolini's sway. But even these politicians were not prepared to give easy passage to a law that was a barefaced violation of traditional rights. The first vote of the Chamber had to be ignored as 'by some unfortunate chance' the requisite number of members did not happen to be present. Only after the refractory members had been threatened with punishment were they able to obtain the 'unanimous' adoption of the Bill with 307 votes: 'unanimous' since the 200 and more members of the Opposition, who, in spite of Mussolini's electoral law of 1925, were still members of the Italian Parliament, had, for more than a year, no longer attended the sittings of the Chamber.

Nevertheless, this division of Parliament was preceded by a vigorous campaign. A few days before the debate, whilst the Judicial Budget was being discussed, the Minister of Justice made a speech in the Senate in which he expressed his deep regret that it had come to his knowledge that some of the Judges belonged to Masonic Lodges. This was 'all the more regrettable since Judges could not be members of secret societies of an international character without seriously prejudicing the performance of their duties'.

It was also made known that the Committee of the Chamber had made the Government's Bill even more strict. The nature of the new regulations was such that they could only result in the complete suppression of Freemasonry.

At the first of the two sittings of the Chamber the House was crowded. Naturally, the main feature of the proceedings was Mussolini's speech.

He described his mode of campaign in the following words:

'First of all I break the bones of the enemy, and then I take him prisoner! . . . My principle is: all that is good for my friends, and all that is bad for my enemies. I shall therefore oppose Freemasonry to the uttermost.

'This Bill illustrates the essential consistency of my whole life. Fifteen years ago I belonged to the Socialist Party and even then I could follow the trend of masonic activity. Then, as now, I set little value on democracy, liberalism, and the so-called immortal principles. To the horror of the Socialist leaders of that time I preached the necessity of mass action and a mighty revolution. That was the old youthful impulse of Italian Socialism. To extol it after the War was sheer megalomania. . . . During the time I have been in office I have found that the Freemasons have planted their followers in all spheres of Italian life. Without a doubt the most important institutions of the State: justice, education, and the army have been under the influence of Freemasonry. That is intolerable and must stop. The Bill will demonstrate that Freemasonry is out of date and no longer has the right to exist in the present century. As Freemasonry opposes us and seeks to break us up, we have the acknowledged right to defend ourselves and to attack, since attack is the best form of defence. Yesterday perhaps we were still floating with the current, but to-day we are swimming determinedly against it. Whatever harm this Bill can cause us has already been done. Moreover, the Freemasons on the other side of the Alps and across the seas will not sacrifice their own interests.'

Despite Mussolini's resolute language, he was unable to command a large number of the votes of his own followers when the division took place. Farinacci, the chief Fascist Whip, devoted two whole days to winning over 'disloyal' members, and the Bill, in its more drastic form, was 'unanimously' adopted at its second reading.

It did not come into force at once, however, for it had not yet been passed by the Senate, but many Lodges stopped all activity immediately. However, the Grand Orient itself still carried on. A General Assembly took place in the Palazzo Giustiniani on the 6th September, at which more than 400 delegates were present. As the *Messaggero*, which was decidedly not a pro-masonic journal, put it, the extremely difficult position in which Freemasonry found itself had caused a much larger number of delegates to be present than was usual. Domizio Torrigiani was once more elected Grand Master for a period of six years, and his special powers were confirmed. In his opening speech Torrigiani declared that in no circumstances would Italian Freemasonry allow itself to be prevented from raising up its voice in protest against the illegal dictatorship that corrupted the Italian people. 'Freemasonry,' he declared, 'must defend the moral treasure of the Order with the utmost vigour as long as it is possible to do so.'

Within two days of this assembly its repercussions made themselves felt. Two high officials of the Chamber, Cav. Di

Francia and Cav. Cacciolli were dismissed from their posts in disgrace. A sensation of which the Fascists had never dreamed arose from this action. The Fascist Press first of all circulated the story that it had come to light that the discharged officials, together with a large number of employees of the Chamber who belonged to the Fraternity of Freemasons, had been indulging in the most evil corruption, and that Fascism had consequently done its duty in removing such vice.

Then came the first disappointment. A grave error had been made in punishing Staff-Inspector Cacciolli, as he was not, in fact, a Freemason; or, to be quite exact, he had been struck off the rolls in 1915. On the other hand, he was an enthusiastic Fascist, having participated in the march on Rome and done everything in his power to secure the dismissal of his colleague, Di Francia, by denouncing him as a Freemason! It was really rather a tragi-comedy that he of all persons should, through a mistake, also fall a victim to the very fate he had prepared for his colleague.

Di Francia, the Freemason and victim of discipline, had not been indulging in secret activity, but had quite openly applied to Cacciolli for leave of absence for a few hours in order to attend a meeting of the Grand Orient. Cacciolli at once hastened to give this information to Farinacci, the Secretary-General of the Fascist Party, and this, the most rabid of all Italian anti-Freemasons, had immediately done 'the necessary.'

One can imagine the astonishment created in Italy when, within forty-eight hours of disciplinary action having been taken against Di Francia, the following paragraph suddenly appeared in one of the few opposition newspapers still in existence:

'Farinacci, the great "idealist", is an out-and-out political opportunist; even his campaign against Freemasonry does not spring from idealist motives—for he was himself once a Freemason!'

At first Farinacci denied this assertion most emphatically, and maintained that the contrary was the case; that he had always opposed the Freemasons and was proud of having repeatedly given the command to pillage and burn Masonic Lodges. But the 'calumniators' and 'liars' stood their ground and the *Voce Repubblicana* published original documents which proved beyond a doubt that, in 1915, Farinacci had joined the 'Quinto Curzio' Lodge in Cremona. This Lodge, it is true, had not rated him very highly upon his return after his

War service and had given him to understand that his presence, as a 'rebel', was hardly desired. Then, scenting the advent of Fascism, he had turned his back on the Lodge and become one of the most violent opponents of Freemasonry.

The 'revenge' for this disclosure followed immediately. They returned once again to the methods favoured by Farinacci, whose newspaper, the *Cremona Nuova*, demanded that lists of members of the Lodges should be obtained with all speed so that the Freemasons might be 'shot *en masse* as traitors'.

The *Idea Nazionale* began the new campaign by publishing bogus documents attempting to prove that the Italian Freemasons were guilty of high treason in that they received orders from abroad. The Grand Orient at once published a counter-declaration in which they defended the patriotic traditions of Italian Freemasonry and strongly repudiated the assertion that the Grand Orient demanded the intervention of foreign powers contrary to the interests of the country; and maintained that the Grand Orient had repeatedly offered to place evidence before the Government in order to disprove such calumny.

Mussolini answered in the *Popolo d'Italia*:

'Freemasonry is opposed by the Fascists because it is an international organization which pursues its activity in Italy according to orders from abroad. It is possible to be a good son of France, as well as a Freemason, because the Free-masonry of the rue Cadet (Headquarters of the Grand Orient in Paris) is an excellent French propagandist, espe-cially in the Mediterranean, the Danubian countries, and the Balkans. It is possible to be a good Englishman and at the same time an active Freemason, because English, as well as American, Freemasonry makes Anglo-Saxon world propa-ganda in a pietistic and humanitarian sense and also in the sphere of commerce.

'It is not possible, however, to be a good Italian and a Freemason at the same time, because the Palazzo Giustiniani obeys foreign orders. The Freemasonry of the Palazzo Giustiniani has always been opposed to Italian action in Abyssinia, Lybia, Dodecanes, Dalmatia, and Albania. It supported our participation in the World War because of an international criterion, but it debased the victory. It wanted the war, but hindered our reaping the legitimate and holy fruits of military triumph. . . .

'In view of this servitude, and since the Palazzo Giustiniani represents an Italian organization that is under the influence of international powers, Freemasonry must be opposed until it has been completely eradicated. . . .

'Farinacci, the faithful warrior, has an opportunity here to add fresh laurels to his crown.'

This called forth the following from the *Giornale d'Italia*:

'The Fascist Press accuses Italian Freemasonry of being in foreign pay. It is very easy to disprove this assertion if only for one reason, and that is that many Fascists and very many of their leaders (Mussolini excepted) belonged to the Fraternity, and they would not have done so, in view of their high patriotic spirit, if they had been of the opinion that Italian Freemasonry was a tool in the hands of enemies or of foreign opponents of Italy. Let us say, in all honesty, that there is only one reason for the campaign against Freemasonry, namely, that it is democratic; the question of foreign entanglements plays no part in it at all.'

Such protests were of no avail. Although it was proved that the 'documents' published by the *Idea Nazionale* were forgeries, the tremendous campaign of certain newspapers that vociferously demanded the 'hunting down of Freemasonry' was sufficient to bring the feelings of the people to boiling-point. Indeed, when it was reported that Freemasonry regarded the crash of the lira as the grave of Fascism, riots broke out again in various places; in Florence, Brindisi, and a number of other towns, Freemasons were taken from their offices and counting-houses and maltreated, businesses were wrecked and Lodge property destroyed.

The authorities of the Fascio in Florence quite openly encouraged acts of violence, as may be seen from the following appeal:

'Neither Freemasons nor Freemasonry should remain a single moment unmolested from to-day onwards. The destruction of Lodges has become a farce. Freemasons, their interests and their goods must be destroyed without mercy. They must be chased out of office. . . . Not a single one should be spared. Good citizens should denounce every Freemason to the police. They must be isolated, like lepers, under the pressure of our power. We declare war on this association of cowards and will fulfil our duty by ridding Italy once and for all of these, her worst enemies.'

This declaration of war was posted during the night on the shutters and windows of businesses belonging to Freemasons, and it created the desired impression. For four days a regular battue of Freemasons was carried on in Florence. Many of them were bullied into leaving the town. More than fifty brethren were violently assaulted, businesses belonging to alleged Freemasons and Socialists were plundered and municipal and State officials were forced to resign their posts at once. A publican named Ariento, two officials called Milanesi and Pezzini, and Burroni, a market inspector, were taken by the ambulances of the 'Misericordia' to the Santa Maria Nuova Hospital suffering from serious injuries.

On the 26th September, some young people forced their way into the Palazzo Vecchio, flogged the district officials who had not yet yielded and forced them to resign on the spot. They made reference to the fact that Farinacci had declared that he would 'obliterate the twenty-four hours during which he himself was a Freemason by a vigorous campaign against them', and they described themselves as the tools carrying out this intention. The *Battaglie fasciste*, one of the wildest partisan papers, said:

'The end justifies the means. Purifying fire must follow upon the breaking of windows. Let those who belong to the sect note that from now onwards they will have to live the lives of outlaws. . . . We know that the improvement in the financial situation of Italy has aroused their anger, and that they have only one aim: to filch riches from the corpse of Italy and to serve the plans of Paris.'

On the evening of the 3rd October the house of the sixty-year-old State official and Worshipful Master Brandinelli, was visited by Luporini, the Vice-President of the Florentine Fascio, with three other Fascists, who requested him to go with them to the Fascist headquarters 'for the purpose of giving information as to Freemasonry'. Brandinelli refused, probably knowing that he would be severely mishandled. The Fascists thereupon attempted to drag him away by force. His friend and neighbour Bacciolini (who was not a Freemason) then went to his aid. During the struggle he drew his revolver and shot Luporini, probably in self-defence. He was unsuccessful in his attempt to flee and was arrested and beaten. The Fascists then broke up everything in Bacciolini's dwelling, set the house on fire, and proceeded on their way to further acts of violence.

The whole night through the fire brigade had to work to extinguish the fires. Freemasons arrested for their own protection were dragged from the soldiers and literally torn to pieces. During these few hours Neciolini, a railwayman, Pilati, a former Member of Parliament (a war invalid who had been decorated with the silver medal for valour), and a lawyer named Console, were killed, amongst others. These shocking deeds were perpetrated in the light of the 'purifying fire'.

The persecution was continued even on the Sunday, and only came to an end when Mussolini telegraphed ordering the cessation of all 'reprisals', the horrors of which had resulted in eighteen deaths and forty cases of serious injury.

The Government did not decide to intervene until riots had broken out in Rome also. The party headquarters in Florence were closed down and General Balbo was entrusted with the direction of the Fascio there. But the Grand Master of the Grand Orient now decided to safeguard Freemasons against such acts in the future, and, consequently, he declared the cessation of masonic activity in Italy.

But this did not put a stop to the tragedy.

A few weeks later, during the evening of the 4th November, the world resounded with the news that Zaniboni, the Socialist, had planned to murder Mussolini at the instigation of General Capello and the Grand Orient.

CHAPTER XI

THE CAPELLO TRIAL

THE Capello case constitutes the darkest chapter in the story, so full of black pages, of the struggle between Fascism and Freemasonry.

General Luigi Capello had sealed his fate when, exercising his right as a citizen, he adopted the attitude that he did towards the Matteotti case. They had not forgiven the gallant officer, who had led an Italian army corps at Görz during the World War, for having decided in favour of Freemasonry when he was called upon to choose between that and Fascism. At the same time, however, they wished to strike a blow at Italian Freemasonry in general, in order finally to crush 'the snake in the grass'.

On the 5th November 1926, the *Agenzia Stefani* published that notorious *communiqué* in which it was stated that Zaniboni, the one-time Member of Parliament of the Opposition, had been arrested in the Hôtel Dragoni, in the immediate vicinity of the Foreign Ministry in Rome, just when he had everything prepared for the execution of a criminal conspiracy. And it went on to say:

'In connexion with the investigations made at the same time, General Luigi Capello was arrested in Turin as he was about to depart for abroad.

'Federzoni, the Minister of the Interior, immediately ordered the occupation of all Masonic Lodges connected with the Palazzo Giustiniani, including those in the colonies. It is said that other prominent members of the Grand Orient are implicated in the conspiracy.'

The arrest of the General took place on the accusation of a journalist named Quaglia. As soon as it was known that the latter was mixed up in the affair there was only one opinion: that it had been engineered by the machinations of an *agent-provocateur*. Quaglia stated before the examining magistrate that Capello had handed over to him, on behalf of the Grand Orient, a large sum of money for Zaniboni. The *Epoca* did not hesitate to state the amount at once—500,000 lire. The money was to be employed for the purpose of organizing the rebellion of armed groups against Fascism.

Torrigiani, the Grand Master, once more made a public declaration:

'A Rome newspaper has accused Freemasonry, of which I am the head, of having paid Zaniboni directly, or through the agency of General Capello, the sum of 500,000 lire in order that he might stage a conspiracy against Mussolini or assassinate him.

'I shall request the authorities investigating the matter to hear my case at once, so that this calumny may be seen in its proper light.

'I shall merely state to-day that Freemasonry regards the life of every single person as sacred, that this high conviction would be confirmed on oath by every single one of our brethren, and that Freemasonry abhors nothing so much as the spilling of human blood.'

For the time being, however, Torrigiani was not examined, but the Lodge buildings in the hands of the authorities, especially the Palazzo Giustiniani in Rome, were 'thoroughly searched for evidence'. Documents and objects connected with the Ritual and, especially lists of members, were confiscated. Many Freemasons whose names came to light were arrested or turned out of office, and riotous excesses broke out afresh. Lodges in Rome and other cities were demolished, but the activities of the Black Shirts were at their worst in Trieste. The whole of the furniture and fittings in the villa of the Advocate Ahrer and the Parish Councillor Samaja were smashed to pieces.

In the midst of all these events the law against Freemasons was passed by the Senate, but not, however, without some speakers of the Opposition expressing their grave doubts. The former Minister of Education, Senator Ruffini, otherwise a consistent opponent of Freemasonry, stated that the law was the first link in a chain of laws designed to revoke all those typically traditional rights which the Constitution safeguards to Italians, and he also made references to the isolation Italy would have to face in the Liberal-Democratic civilized world of our time. If Italy were to renounce all the achievements of Liberalism, then, of all the civilized nations, only Russia would remain at her side. She would then have to break the ring of the other Liberal countries, either by means of propaganda or by force.

Benedetto Croce, the celebrated man of letters and former Minister of Education, declared emphatically that the spirit of the Bill proposed by the Government was so un-Liberal that he could not give it his approval. Mussolini retorted brusquely that the Fascist régime could not do without this law.

Immediately after the adoption of this Bill the Grand Master, Torrigiani, published a proclamation stating that all Lodges were to be regarded as dissolved.

Italian Freemasonry had ceased to exist. . . .

Meanwhile every one was waiting for the trial of General Capello, who had protested his innocence from the very first. The investigation lasted eighteen months, the trial being postponed several times. General Sanna, President of the Special Court of Jurisdiction which had come into existence in the meantime, resigned his post because he was convinced of Capello's innocence. But the latter was not the only one to be dealt with. The authorities hoped to find incriminating documents during the examination of the Lodge archives and the searching of the houses of the Grand Master Torrigiani and other officials, in order to be able to put several other prominent Freemasons in the dock at the same time. But this was a vain hope. The trial did not develop into a trial of the Grand Orient and, consequently, it was in no way a trial of Free-masonry. Not the slightest evidence of a conspiracy was discovered.

At long last, Capello came before the judges, in the spring of 1927. The bill of indictment against the General and Zaniboni was based entirely on the statements of Quaglia, the *agent-provocateur*, who created the worst of impressions in Court. 'He is the only shady and sordid figure in the trial,' said the correspondent of the conservative Basle newspaper the *Nachrichten*.

Capello passionately and indignantly denied the accusations made against him, and stated that he himself had first been a Fascist and had afterwards gone over to the Opposition, but had always kept within legal bounds in his political activity. In 1925, he had undertaken to deputize for the Grand Master of the Grand Orient, Torrigiani, in his absence. Some days later Zaniboni had requested him for an interview and, on that occasion, had demanded the sum of 100,000 lire in order to concentrate anti-Fascist troops in Rome. Zaniboni had seemed so agitated and excited that Capello had done all in his power to calm him. Not a single word was spoken about an attempt on

Mussolini's life nor of anything like it. He had attempted to dissuade Zaniboni from his idea of an insurrection, but there had not been the slightest discussion of details. If Freemasonry really had approved of the plan to depose Mussolini he could have obtained the sum of 100,000 lire demanded by Zaniboni with the utmost ease. He had, however, merely lent Zaniboni 300 lire on one occasion, to be exact through Quaglia, who always begged for money for Zaniboni whenever he met him.

'I should never have been so foolish,' said Capello, 'as to have supported such a mad plan. As an old General with the experience of fifty years' service, I had no reason to assume that the military would join forces with the rebels.'

Zaniboni, who admitted that he really did intend to shoot Mussolini, also stressed the fact that Capello had had absolutely nothing to do with his intention; he alone—may the whole world know—was entirely responsible for the plan.

But this definite declaration did not satisfy the Public Prosecutor. With every means at his disposal he attempted to obtain the conviction of Capello, and, through him, of Freemasonry, for participation in the alleged attempted murder. Time and again he put the pointed question: 'Then where did Zaniboni obtain money?' And when Capello shrugged his shoulders, he brought forth his trump-card by calling Quaglia, the 'witness for the Crown,' in spite of the fact that the police had not dared to deny the shameful role he had played. The former Chief of Police of Rome refused to answer when questioned as to whether Quaglia had been an *agent-provocateur*.

The spy directed his rehearsed statements towards incriminating Freemasonry, of which, he said, Zaniboni was the willing tool. According to him, Zaniboni had been assured by Capello, as early as September, of the support of the Freemasons. The General had not been able to give him any money then, however, 'as the Grand Master had refused to finance an undertaking which was not yet concrete and for which no preparation had been made'. On the 3rd October, Capello had requested Quaglia to persuade Zaniboni to hold up his plan of assassination. But he (Quaglia) had advised Capello, in view of Zaniboni's excited state, to speak to him personally and to dissuade him from his project. Capello had thereupon contented himself with asking: 'Do you think Zaniboni could succeed?' He had then considered it necessary to advise the authorities of the plan. Capello had been Zaniboni's evil spirit throughout. 'He knew,' said Quaglia, 'that only a military dictatorship could result from the general chaos, and that he, as a General and one of the leaders of Freemasonry, would have the reins of Government in his hands.'

General Capello described the statements of Quaglia as wicked invention; likewise Zaniboni, who jumped up from his seat in the dock in a state of great excitement and exclaimed, raising his hand as if to take an oath: 'Capello had nothing to do with all that. By the head of my daughter, which is the one dear thing left to me in life, I swear that on the morning of the 4th November Quaglia begged of me, in the room of the Hôtel Dragoni, the honour of shooting at Mussolini at the same time as I.' And as Quaglia, deadly pale, denied it, Zaniboni stood once more erect and said: 'If there were a God that punished liars then you would drop dead here and now.'

Never was there such a sorry picture as that of the man who had been elected to destroy Freemasonry by his evidence.

But as Capello's 'guilt' had to be established in any case, there was another witness for the prosecution at hand. This was Giuseppe Alberto Mascioli, who turned out to be one of Quaglia's associates and to have taken part in all he did and always to have informed the police. Mascioli naturally knew how to tell a good tale about the 'masonic conspiracy'. The Grand Master, he asserted, had personally promised Zaniboni a large sum of money, and had then gone back on his word, whereupon Capello had given Quaglia 1,000 lire out of his own pocket to facilitate Zaniboni's flight after having carried out the assassination. This money was handed over to Quaglia on the 2nd November on the Cavour bridge. . . .

This story was the prominent feature of the great speech for the prosecution made by Noseda, the Attorney-General, who carried on just as if—quite contrary to the evidence—Freemasonry had been found guilty.

He was, it is true, obliged definitely to admit that the investigation had not brought to light the least evidence against Torrigiani, so that to prosecute him also was out of the question. Nevertheless, said the Attorney-General, there is not the slightest doubt that money from masonic sources had played a part in the conspiracy. Capello wished to set himself up in a military dictatorship, and Freemasons had supported him in this scheme. As the cat's-paw of the Grand

Master, the General had conspired with Zaniboni and provided him with money. He should therefore be found guilty.

The speech in defence of Capello was made by his counsel, Petroni. A breathless silence reigned in court as he rose to make his speech.

'I undertook the defence of Capello,' he said, 'at a difficult moment; I did it because I was completely convinced of his innocence. And I repeat that I still have the same conviction. . . .

'Capello never had designs upon Mussolini's life. Never did he approve or support Zaniboni's plan for an assassination. He likewise never had the intention of setting up a dictatorship; nor did he intend to become a dictator himself.

'To think of such a thing in October 1925 would have been sheer madness, for even if the attempt on Mussolini's life had been successful, the situation, as far as political power was concerned, would have remained unaltered. Capello could not fail to know that such a terrible act would have caused the nation to rise up, not against Fascism, but against the conspirators themselves.

'What motives then could have inspired Capello to indulge in madness such as that now attributed to him?

'It has been asserted that he acted in blind obedience to the commands of the Grand Master, Torrigiani. But this assertion has been refuted in such a way that even the Prosecutor himself has had to let the matter drop.

'If, however, Capello had been a man seeking his own personal advantage, as has also been suggested, then he would have acted quite differently in 1923, when he was faced with the choice between Fascism and Freemasonry. He had become a Fascist in 1922 because he was convinced of the absolute necessity of the movement. Chosen by Mussolini for the highest dignities, he remained true to Freemasonry when an attempt was made to control his outlook. Just at that time Fascism had achieved tremendous triumphs. Rome had been taken and Mussolini was a hero and a victor. Any one with personal ambitions could find satisfaction only in the ranks of the Fascists.

'But Capello refused to become War Minister or leader of the military. He stuck to the banner of Freemasonry, which was so sacred to him. That, if it may be so called, is Capello's tragic guilt.

'The daring suggestion has also been made that Capello

received a bribe for crossing over to the Opposition. That is a miserable calumny! It is admitted, and has never been denied, that Capello worked for the Opposition in the year 1925, but he retired even from this as early as August of the same year.

'But what happened between August and the 4th November, the day of the planned assassination? At the time when the plan for the murder took shape in Zaniboni's mind the political connexion between him and Capello had already been severed. That was why Zaniboni also attempted to obtain money from Senator Frassati, Director of the "Stampa" in Turin. Frassati was just as definite in his refusal as Capello had been. If this Senator was not reproached for not having given information to the police about Zaniboni, can Capello be blamed for remaining silent?

'In his financial embarrassment Zaniboni went to Friaul, and as he received nothing there from his friends, he went abroad. Then he returned to Rome, where he had his notorious conversation with Capello on the 21st October, during which the assassination was supposed to have been decided upon. Zaniboni narrated his foolish plan to storm the Palazzo Chigi and to seize the person of Mussolini. He did not mention any intention to murder the Duce. As he was about to go into further detail about his ideas, Capello interrupted him: "That is enough. I don't want to hear any more! If you are in debt and need money I will help you out; I can lend you 5,000 lire, but nothing more!"

'A most remarkable thing is that although this conversation was described as decisive by the prosecution, Capello was the only one to speak of it, and neither Quaglia in his minutely detailed reports to the police, nor the latter in their communications to the Minister of the Interior made mention of it.

'Quaglia's eloquent silence in this respect is the proof of Capello's innocence.

'This conversation of the 21st October is the vital factor in the whole trial. If it cannot be proved that Capello then knew of the plan for an assassination, the whole case collapses. And I hereby solemnly declare that the Attorney-General has not been able to produce the slightest evidence! He has propounded a theory without being able to support it.

'The conversation was followed a few days later by a letter from Capello to Zaniboni, who had, in the meantime, travelled to Urbignacco. This letter also was a point-blank refusal!

'That Zaniboni understood it as such is evidenced by the fact that he then went with Quaglia to Milan, in an endeavour to obtain money from Senator Albertini, the proprietor of the *Corriere della Sera*.

'Capello, however, regarded the matter as entirely finished with, but on the evening of the 1st November a young man knocked at his door; it was Quaglia. He brought a letter from Zaniboni, who once again begged for money, which led to the much-described scene on the Cavour bridge, reminiscent of robber stories, where Capello, watched by the second spy, Mascioli, handed Quaglia the ominous envelope containing 300 lire for Zaniboni. Attempts have been made to convert this envelope into a huge packet; but even Mascioli only dared speak of "about" 1,000 lire.

'Consequently, there is not the slightest circumstantial evidence of the alleged guilt of Capello. All the statements prove his innocence. The suggestion that he was guilty of conspiracy and had also drawn up the strategic plans for the projected armed revolt may be countered by the question: where, then, are the men who were to assist him? Where are the arms? Quaglia has stated that they planned to disarm the Fascist Militia and thus get possession of arms. But to believe such nonsense of Capello is to go too far!

'As early as the summer of 1925, Capello had perceived that, in view of the sentiment of the nation, it would not pay to expend money on an electoral campaign. And yet he was supposed to have conceived such a childish plan as that related by Quaglia!

'Take care, Gentlemen of the High Court of Justice, not to commit a terrible miscarriage of justice! You are Fascists and men of honour! The Duce has put you in office so that you may administer justice. Fascism is strong. It is the State. And a State is only great when it also deals justly with its opponents. I demand justice for this man who, in war and in peace, has always had the welfare of the Fatherland at heart. I do not ask for leniency, I demand an acquittal!'

When the counsel for the defence closed his speech the unexpected happened: a loud burst of applause, which only ceased after the President had made repeated and determined demands for silence, broke from the Fascist public.

But the convincing words of counsel for the defence made no impression upon the President or upon his fellow-judges.

'Thirty years imprisonment, with solitary confinement for

the first six years,' was the amazing and horrifying sentence. Thus was judicial murder committed!

Strange as it may seem, the accused had expected the Court to adopt a different view:

'When, for the purpose of hearing the passing of sentence, they were brought, fettered to a long chain, into the dock, in which ten soldiers had taken up position,' wrote the *Neue Zürcher Zeitung*, 'cheerful confidence was written on their faces; perhaps the defending counsel had given them a ray of hope. This soon completely vanished, however, when the President, who had become very severe and grim, read the sentence. They heard their fate in silence. Hardest hit of all was Capello. After the six hours of clever and masterly pleading by his defending counsel the situation of the old General had seemed, if not completely reversed, certainly improved. The faint smile he had worn before judgment was pronounced faded from his parched lips.'

That this sentence can only be described as judicial murder is a view shared by many who cannot be accused of serving the 'sect'.

One of the most anti-masonic newspapers of Europe, the ecclesiastical *Germania* of Berlin, the chief organ of the German Centre (Catholic) Party, felt that it was forced to comment as follows:

'. . . Following upon what one heard in the lobbies of the Palace of Justice the decision could cause no one any surprise. To outsiders, however, the trial has not demonstrated such certainty of the complicity of General Capello as would justify a sentence of such severity. But as the trial was to pass judgment on Freemasonry, and as Capello stood at the Bar as its exponent, the judgment given in the case of Zaniboni, who had confessed, had to apply to him also.'

In other words, Freemasonry had to be condemned.

'The case against Capello is, with the exception of the disputable statements of the informer Quaglia, nothing but political circumstantial evidence. But as such, and precisely as such, it had to suffice for the Fascists, who were already convinced that Freemasonry was inimical to the State, to enable them to obtain a conviction, since there had to be either one thing or the other, no middle course being possible.

The chain of evidence against Capello might have been even weaker than his advocate demonstrated during his grim struggle; it would have made no difference to the verdict of that tribunal; in fact, the Court could not even be lenient to an old man who will certainly never survive the first third of his sentence. "A State must never be lenient," says the *Impero* to-day.'

So wrote the correspondent of the *Vossische Zeitung*.

It would be impossible to speak more clearly. A retrospective justification was required for the shockingly unjust treatment of Freemasonry and they wished to destroy it once and for all on this occasion. For that reason they passed a sentence upon the sixty-eight-year-old General Capello, now 'No. 3264', that amounted to a death sentence.

For that same reason they then went still further and devoted their attention to the Grand Master, Torrigiani. They had indeed had designs upon him from the very beginning! When the Grand Master was first summoned in connexion with the investigation, he was abroad. Many people would not have complied with the summons, no matter how innocent they might have considered themselves. But Torrigiani travelled to Italy and placed himself at the disposal of the examining judge. He told his friends that he had to leave. If he were to remain, it would be regarded as a proof of guilt and would probably serve as an excuse for the persecution of others.

As the investigation had an entirely negative result, Torrigiani was able to leave Italy again with a proper passport. Then he received a second summons! Once more he was warned, but Torrigiani took no notice. In the consciousness of his innocence he journeyed to Rome once more. There were further investigations, but not the slightest scrap of evidence was found against him.

Month after month the authorities searched the drawers in his private house, turned out every cupboard in his office, and examined every scrap of paper they could lay hands on in the hope of finding evidence against him, but, as already stated, they had not the slightest success. Quaglia, of course, related all the things which he afterwards 'divulged' in the course of the trial. But these statements did not give the authorities the slightest justification for proceeding against the Grand Master, and they were consequently obliged to close the investigation, though they did not yet acknowledge themselves beaten.

At the very beginning of his rule, Mussolini had made the wild assertion that Freemasonry was nothing but a bubble which only needed to be pricked with a needle to make it disappear into thin air. That had proved itself to be a fallacy. The self-sacrificing idealism which inspired Italian Freemasonry had for a long time been the bulwark against terrorism, fire, and murder. Only after the Fascist Act of Suppression had come into force did the Grand Orient stop its activity.

The fact that Torrigiani and his followers had not eaten humble pie when they received the first significant hint had increased still more the hatred against them. Torrigiani would have to fall!

He was now unable to obtain a visa and so had to remain in the country! In the meantime the 'administrative procedure' had been introduced, which permitted judgment without trial, and every one knew that, whatever the circumstances of the case, some way of disposing of Torrigiani would be found. But for this they required the grand *mise en scène* of Capello's trial.

This was carried on with such cunning that, whenever Capello was referred to, the shadow of Torrigiani loomed ominously in the background.

Day after day the newspapers filled their sheets morning, noon, and night with huge capitals:

'NOT ONLY CAPELLO—THE WHOLE OF FREEMASONRY IN THE DOCK!'
'THE MASONIC CRIME!'
'WHY IS NOT TORRIGIANI UNDER LOCK AND KEY?'
'WHEN WILL TORRIGIANI'S TURN COME?'

Naturally, every one imagined that the trial had disclosed much positive evidence against him and the Grand Orient, and the whole Italian Press, acting as one, made the country resound with cries of infuriated indignation. No one suspected for a moment that this furious rage was born of a brain working coolly and calmly in the background, or that the innumerable inflammatory articles were nothing more than variations of a single *communiqué* that had been given to the newspapers.

But they had their effect. The very department that had caused the whole agitation now suddenly took advantage of the storm they had themselves raised. And as Torrigiani could not be touched even by a special court they had prepared another way of 'keeping him from the light of day'.

Hardly had sentence been passed on Capello than the Secret Police drove up, in the early hours of the morning, before the house where Torrigiani had been living for some time past. The Grand Master was arrested and placed in the Regina Cœli Jail. Two hours later the Confinement Commission had banished him, without trial, to one of the miserable Lipari Islands for five years, 'because of his agitation against the State and Government'.

'In spite of the fact that the preliminary investigation had already established that he was not implicated in the conspiracy!' was the horrified remark of the anti-Freemasonic *Germania*.

The League for Human Rights, however, made a public protest in the following words:

'In view of the fact that General Capello and the Member of Parliament, Zaniboni, have been condemned with the utmost contempt for all principles of justice, to thirty years imprisonment by a Court of Fascist officers,

'In view, especially, of the fact that not the slightest proof of any description or even circumstantial evidence of the participation of General Capello in the alleged projected assassination has been produced,

'In view of the fact that it was Mussolini himself who staged this ridiculous mock assassination through the agency of the *agent-provocateur* Quaglia, in order to compromise the Socialist Party and the Freemasons,

'The League for Human Rights vigorously protests against this further travesty of justice and insult to the world's intelligence.'

In Italy, however, Mussolini abruptly closed the book of Fascist disgrace that bears the title 'Freemasonry'.

PART III

OLD AND NEW OPPONENTS

CHAPTER I

THE PAPAL BULLS

THE desire of the Fascists to please the Church of Rome, the oldest enemy of the Royal Art, also played an important part in the destruction of Italian Freemasonry. In that way Mussolini was able to efface many a bitter memory that the Catholic Church had of him. The suppression of the activities of the Grand Orient of Italy must have caused great pleasure at the Vatican, a fact that was frequently referred to at the meetings of the Supreme Fascist Council. Not only did they render the Pope a great service when they laid Freemasonry low: they also demonstrated anew the power of the Fascio. What the Church had been trying to do for two centuries, Mussolini had, by his ruthlessness, accomplished in a very short space of time.

The fight of the Church against Freemasonry began as early as fifteen years after the appearance of the Anderson Constitutions. At that time the Fraternity had already taken root in Italy, the Light having been brought into Lodges in Rome and Florence in 1733. Catholic priests of all hierarchical degrees associated with statesmen, diplomats, and artists in the work in the Lodge. This did not remain unnoticed and created great annoyance in Vatican circles, especially as religious zealots in other lands had already adopted a very unfavourable attitude towards the Masonic thought that was spreading with such amazing rapidity. On the 25th July 1737, a Sacra Congregatio Inquisitionis assembled in Florence, probably under the presidency of Pope Clement XII. This was an extraordinary conference, at which leaders of the three papal chancelleries, Cardinals Ottoboni, Spinola, and Zondadari, as well as the Inquisitor of the Holy Officium, participated. The subject for this grave discussion was the question of Freemasonry. The decisions arrived at at this conference were not at first disclosed. But, shortly after, the Berlin *Vossische Zeitung*, in its No. 85 of the year 1737, published a report from Lombardy in which the following information was given:

'The Holy Office of the Inquisition to which the established society of Free Masons has been denounced, is

that a secret Molinism or Quietism must underlie it. Legal action is already being taken against this Fraternity and various persons have been arrested, although there is strong reason to doubt that their principles can be compared with the enlightenment and deep meditation to be found in Molinism and Quietism.'

In the days that followed, anti-masonic riots broke out in several places. There was a definite feeling that steps of some kind were to be taken against the Freemasons. And on the 28th April, 1738, Pope Clement XII published the first anti-masonic Bull that has since become so celebrated. This began with the words 'In eminenti apostolatus specula', and, wherever it went, it caused a tremendous sensation. Such a step had not been expected of the old and feeble Pope, especially as it was not known with what vigour one of his intimates, Cardinal Joseph Firrao, Secretary of State, had agitated for the fulmination of an anathema. As this first Bull was referred to in many later Encyclicals, we quote it here in English:

'Condemnation of the Society, Lodges and Conventicles of Liberi Muratori, or Free Masons, under pain of excommunication to be incurred *ipso facto*, and absolution from it being reserved for the Supreme Pontiff, except at point of death.

'Clement, Bishop, Servant of the Servants of God, to all the Faithful in Christ Greeting and Apostolic Benediction.

'Placed by the disposition of the divine clemency on the eminent watchtower of the Apostolate, though with merits undeserving of it, according to the duty of pastoral oversight committed to us, we have with constant and zealous anxiety so far as it is conceded to us from above, given our attention to those measures by means of which entrance may be closed against errors and vices, and the integrity of orthodox religion may be best preserved, and dangers of disturbances may be repelled, in the present very difficult times:

'I. It has become known to us, even in truth by public rumour that great and extensive progress is being made by, and the strength daily increasing of some Societies, Meetings, Gatherings, Conventicles or Lodges, commonly named as of Liberi Muratori or Free Masons or some other nomenclature according to difference of language, in which men of any whatsoever religion or sect, content with a certain

NIGHT
Painted and Engraved by William Hogarth, 1738

The Weſtminſter Journal ; *or,* New Weekly Miſcellany.

By THOMAS TOUCHIT, *of* Spring-Gardens, *Eſq;*

SATURDAY, MAY 8, 1742.

From my own Apartment in Spring-Gardens.

THO' I belong to neither of the Fraternities mention'd in the following Pieces, and therefore am little concern'd in their annual Diſputes, I think it my Duty, as a Watchman of the City of *Weſtminſter*, to preſerve the Memory of the laſt extraordinary Cavalcade, the like to which hath never β.ppos'd ſince I have been .... As more ſolemn Proceſsions have of late Years been very rare, it cannot ſurely be taken amiſs, either by the *Free-Maſons* or the *Scald Miſerables*, that I give a Deſcriber in this ......

The FREE-MASONS Downfall ; *or,* The Reſtoration *of the* SCALD-MISERABLES.

The Re-aſſurance of the Right Worſhipful the Grand-Maſter, Deputy Grand-Maſter, Grand-Wardens, and Brethren of the moſt Ancient and Honourable SOCIETY of SCALD-MISERABLE-MASONS.

WHEREAS by our Manifeſto of laſt Year, dated from our Lodge in *Brick-ſtreet*, We did, in the moſt explicit Manner, vindicate the antient Rights and Privileges of this Society, and by incontestable Arguments evince our ſuperior Dignity and Seniority to all other Inſtitutions, whether Grand Volgi, Gregorians, *Bucks-makers, Oſtparians, Hurlothrumbos, Lumber-Troopers,* or Free-Maſons ; yet, ſpeerfulneſs, a few Perſons under the laſt Denomination, ſtill arrogate to themſelves the uſurped Titles of *Moſt Ancient and Honourable,* in open Violation of Truth and Juſtice,—ſtill endeavour to impoſe their falſe Myſteries (for a Premium) on the Credulous and Unwary, under Pretence of being Part of our Brotherhood, and ſtill run accuſtom'd with Drums, Trumpets, gilt Chariots, and other unconſtitutional Finery, to call a Reflection on the primitive Simplicity and decent Oeconomy of our Ancient and Annual Peregrinations : We think therefore proper, in Juriſdiction of Ourſelves, publicly to Diſclaim all Relation or Alliance whatſoever, with the ſaid Society of *Free-Ma-*

...... him, as the ſame muſt manifeſtly tend to the Sacrifice of our Dignity, the Impeachment of our Underſtanding, and the Diſgrace of our ſolemn Myſteries : And further, to convince the Public of the Candor and Openneſs of our Proceedings, We have preſent them with a Key to our Proceſsion ; and that laſt rather, as it conſiſts of many Things Emblematical, Myſtical, Hieroglyphical, Comical, Satirical, Political, &c.

And whereas many, perſuaded by the Purity of our Conſtitution, the nice Morality of our Brethren, and the peculiar Decency of our Rites and Ceremonies, have lately forſook the groſs Error and Follies of *Free-Maſonry,* are now become true *Scald-Miſerables* : It cannot but afford a moſt pleaſing Satisfaction to all who have any Regard to Truth and Decency, to ſee our Proceſsion increaſed with ſuch a Number of Proſelytes ; and behold thoſe whole Vanity, but the laſt Year, carried them into a borrowed Equipage, now condeſcend to become the humble Cargo of a Hand-Cart. *Dat—Magna of Veritas, & prevalent.*

A KEY ; or, Explanation of the Solemn and Stately PROCESSION of the SCALD-MISERABLE-MASONS, as it was martiall'd on Tueſday the 27th paſt, by their Scald Purſuivant, Black Mantle.

Set forth by Order of the Grand-Maſter of the SOCIETY.

Price TWO-PENCE.

affectation of natural virtue, are associated mutually in a close and exclusive bond in accordance with laws and statutes framed for themselves; and are bound as well by a stringent oath sworn upon the Sacred Volume, as by the imposition of heavy penalties to conceal under inviolable silence, what they secretly do in their meetings.

'But since it is the nature of wickedness to betray itself, and to cry aloud so as to reveal itself, hence the aforesaid Societies or Conventicles have excited so strong suspicion in the minds of the faithful that to enrol oneself in these Lodges is quite the same, in the judgment of prudent and virtuous men as to incur the brand of depravity and perverseness, for if they were not acting ill, they would not by any means have such a hatred of the light. And this repute has spread to such a degree that in very many countries the societies just mentioned have been proscribed, and with foresight banished long since as though hostile to the safety of kingdoms.

.   .   .   .   .

'2. We accordingly, turning over in our mind the very serious injuries which are in the highest degree inflicted by such societies or conventicles not merely on the tranquility of the temporal state, but also on the spiritual welfare of souls, and perceiving that they are inconsistent alike with civil and canonical sanctions, being taught by the divine word that it is our duty, by day and night, like a faithful servant, and a prudent ruler of his master's household, to watch that no persons of this kind like thieves break into the house, and like foxes strive to ravage the vineyard, that is to say, thereby pervert the hearts of the simple and privily shoot at the innocent; in order to close the wide road which might be opened thereby for perpetrating iniquity with impunity and for other just and reasonable causes known to ourselves, have determined and decreed that these same Societies, Meetings, Gatherings, Lodges or Conventicles of Liberi Muratori or Free Masons, or by whatever other name called, herein acting on the advice of some Venerable Brethren of ours, Cardinals of the Holy Roman Church, and also of our own motion, and from our certain knowledge, and mature deliberation, and on the plenitude of Apostolic Power, should be condemned and prohibited as by this present Constitution we do condemn and prohibit them.

'3. Wherefore we direct the faithful in Christ, all and singly, of whatever status, grade, dignity and pre-eminence, whether laics or clerics as well secular as regular, even those worthy of specific and individual mention and expression, strictly and in virtue of holy obedience, that no one, under any pretext or far-fetched colour dare or presume to enter the above-mentioned Societies of Liberi Muratori, Free Masons, or otherwise named, or to propagate, foster and receive them whether in their houses or elsewhere, and to conceal them, or be present at them, or to afford them the opportunity or facilities for being convened anywhere, or otherwise to render them advice, help or favour, openly or in secret, directly or indirectly, of themselves or through the agency of others in whatever way; and likewise to exhort, induce, incite or persuade others to be enrolled in, reckoned amongst, or take part in Societies of this kind, or to aid and foster them in any way whatsoever, but in every particular to abstain utterly as they are in duty bound from the same Societies, Meetings, Assemblies, Gatherings, Lodges or Conventicles, on pain of excommunication to be incurred by all who in the above ways offend—to be incurred *ipso facto* without any declaration, and that from this excommunication no one, except on the point of death, can obtain benefit of absolution except through Us, or the Roman Pontiff for the time being.

'4. Further it is our will and charge that as well Bishops or higher Prelates, and other local Ordinaries as the deputed Inquisitors of Heretical Depravity everywhere take action and make inquisition against transgressors, of whatever status, grade, condition, order, dignity or eminence they be, and inflict upon them condign punishment, as though strongly suspected of heresy, and exercise constraint upon them. To the above mentioned and any individual of them, we grant and impart free power of proceeding against the said transgressors, of making inquisition, of constraining by condign punishment, and of invoking thereupon, if need be, even the aid of the secular arm for that purpose.

'5. It is our will also that exactly the same credit be given to copies of these presents, subscribed by the hand of some public notary, and fortified with the seal of some person placed in ecclesiastical dignity, as would be given to the original documents if exhibited or displayed.

'6. Let it be lawful therefore for no man to infringe this

proclamation notifying our declaration, condemnation, charge, prohibition and interdiction, or to act counter to it with reckless daring. But if anyone presume to attempt this, let him know that he will incur the wrath of Almighty God, and of the blessed Apostles Peter and Paul.

'Given at Rome in the Basilica of St. Mary the Greater, in the year of Our Lord 1738 on the 28th April in the 8th year of our Pontificate.

'Registered in the Secretariat of Briefs, etc., on the above date and published on the doors of St. Peter's and other usual places.'

Despite its severity the Bull did not have the same effect in all places. Many Princes hastened to act upon it to the letter. King Augustus of Poland forbade Freemasonry in his State, whilst King Frederick I of Sweden put the death penalty on participation in masonic assemblies. For the temporal dominion of the Pope, Cardinal Firrao issued another special Edict in which Freemasons were threatened with excommunication, confiscation of goods, and even death. Such was the bitterness harboured by Firrao against the Fraternity that he even declared in his Edict that the houses in which assemblies of Freemasons took place would be razed to the ground. And, in many cases, these threats were actually carried out. At this time, countless Freemasons met the fate of martyrs under the barbarous tortures and persecution of the Inquisition. The Grand Master of the Knights of Malta also acted with great severity by banishing six of his Knights from Malta for life because they had not complied with the prohibition of masonic activity.

The fate of a work written in defence of Freemasonry is illustrative of the feeling that prevailed at that time. An anonymous pamphlet entitled *Relation apologique et historique de la Société des F.M. par J.G.D.M.F.M.*, written in the French language, but printed in Dublin, was published in 1738. Not only was this pamphlet placed on the Index by the Vatican, but it was condemned to be burned in public by the executioner. This ceremony was solemnly performed on the 25th February 1739, in the Piazza S. Maria Minerva in Rome, after a specially arranged religious service. But this did not prevent the *Apologia* from becoming the most popular book on Freemasonry of the eighteenth century. It was regarded as a 'semi-official' commentary on the Constitution and was translated into every European language. Within a short time it had run into six editions in Germany alone.

In 1751 the second ban was promulgated. Like his predecessor Clement XII, Pope Benedict XIV also published an anti-masonic Bull, 'Providas', the consequences of which were even more severe than those of the first one, for the persecutions were now carried on almost everywhere. As we have already seen, Freemasons were thrown into prison in Spain by the Inquisition and many were sent to the galleys; Ferdinand VI issued a Decree declaring that all Freemasons were traitors and therefore banished from the country. Fra Joseph Torrubia, a Franciscan, the Censor and Revisor of the Inquisition in Madrid, was particularly fanatical[1] against the Brotherhood. In order to combat Freemasonry with greater effect he had been initiated into a Lodge in Madrid, after having received a solemn dispensation from the papal penitentiar in respect of the vows of silence which he was about to take. In the accusation which he delivered to the competent authorities some months afterwards, he described the Freemasons as sodomites and magicians, heretics and atheists and, of course, as insurgents highly dangerous to the State, who 'should be burned at a devotional *auto-de-fé* for the glorification of the faith and the fortification of the faithful'. Such an extreme step was, of course, not taken, but a new Royal Decree against Freemasonry was issued.

But 'the most bloody letters in the history of Freemasonry' were written by the Inquisition in Portugal. Torture, labour in the galleys, and deportation were the order of the day.

It would be impossible to record all the persecutions in detail, but the Freemasons withstood them valiantly. Many of them became martyrs for the Royal Art. Now and again, of course, the severe measures were able to bring about a temporary stoppage of Lodge activities and occasionally to force Freemasons to take to flight, as, for instance, those in Lisbon; but they were unable to do any harm to the cause of Freemasonry as such. At the same time, it should also be remembered that leading members of the Catholic Church were then frequently members of Lodges and that there were even Lodges almost entirely composed of clerics.

The German scientist Reinhold Taute took the trouble to draw up a list of Catholic priests who became Freemasons in spite of all the Bulls. This list, when completed, was of

---

[1] Singer: *Der Kampf Roms gegen die Freimaurerei.*

considerable length. Especially in the time of Pope Clement
XIV, (1769–1774), that is to say, during the reign of Frederick
the Great in Prussia and Joseph II in Vienna, when the Order
of Jesuits was dissolved, it was by no means unusual for lay
brothers and monks, parsons and chaplains, abbots and
provosts to wear the masonic apron and take a lively interest
in Freemasonry. 'The Three Thistles' Lodge in Mayence was
composed mainly of members of the clergy, and amongst the
founders of the Lodge 'Frederick of the Three Beams' in
Münster, there were officials of the episcopal household, canons,
episcopal counsellors, and officers. Members of the clergy in
Hildesheim, Cassel, Breslau, Giessen, Fulda, and Cologne were
also enthusiastic Freemasons. The Erfurt Lodge 'Charles of the
Three Wheels' was founded in 1783 with the collaboration of
the subsequent Primate, Dalberg, and later—after a temporary
closing—reopened in the Cloister of St. Peter in the residence
of the Prelate and Abbot, Placidus Muth. Almost all Lodges
in the Rhineland had clerical members, as well as Hanover,
Munich, Paderborn, and Posen. The same applied to the
Lodges in Austria-Hungary. The Lodge 'Constancy' in
Vienna included on its roll two Royal and Imperial Chaplains-
in-Ordinary, the Rector of the Theological College, and two
canons. Thirteen priests belonged to the 'Crowned Hope'
Lodge, and a bishop, four monks, a lay brother and many
parsons were members of the Budapest Lodges 'Magnanimity'
and 'The Seven Stars'. The position in Prague, Brünn, Graz,
Innsbruck, Linz, Agram, etc., was more or less similar.
In Switzerland, Belgium, France also, and even in Italy,
Spain, and Portugal, Freemasonry always counted many
higher and lower members of the clergy amongst its
members.

Taute's[1] list contained the names of more than 500 Catholic
priests, of which only the following need be mentioned here:
Johan Baptist Albertini, Rector of the General Seminary for
the Training and Education of Tyrolese Clergy; Johann
Baptist Count Auersperg, Prince-Archbishop of Passau;
Prince-Archbishop Bevière of Liège; Dominikus von Bretano,
Chaplain-in-Ordinary and Spiritual Adviser to the Abbot
Honorius of Kempten; Johann Michael Brigido von Breswitz,

[1] The Catholic Reichsrat and Provincial Member of Parliament Dr. Victor
v. Fuchs, during the course of a lecture on 'Freemasonry under Joseph II',
given in Vienna in 1897, enumerated no less than 185 members of the clergy
who were Freemasons in Austria alone. Lecture printed in *Die Freimaurerei
Österreich-Ungarn*. Vienna: Herder. 1897.

Prince-Archbishop of Laibach; Abbé Cordier de St. Firmin, Paris, who introduced Voltaire to his Lodge; Gottlob Amandus, Baron von Dalberg, Councillor to the Archbishop of Speyer; Johan Freidrich Hugo, Baron von Dalberg, Capitular at Trèves, Worms and Speyer; Karl Theodor Anton Maria Reichsfreiherr von Dalberg, last Elector of Mayence, later Prince-Primate of the Rhine Confederation and Grand-Duke of Frankfort; Abbé Josef Dobrowski, the first revivalist of Czech literature; the Jesuit Lorenz Leopold, Haschka, Professor of Æsthetics at the Theresianum at Vienna, who wrote the words of the Austrian national anthem composed by Haydn; Urban Hauer, Abbot of the celebrated Benedictine Monastery of Melk in Lower Austria, who introduced almost all the monks of his abbey to the Brotherhood, and who, on his death-bed, directed that they should lay him in his coffin with his apron and trowel, and covered by his priestly robes, and then drive in the coffin nails with the Master's gavel; Johann Josef Klampt, Canon and Cathedral official in Glogau; Abbé Franz Liszt,[1] the great composer; Nordez, Bishop of Dijon; Archbishop Podowski of Gnesen; Franz Poschinger, Royal and Imperial Chaplain-in-Ordinary in Vienna; Nikodem Pucyna, Prince-Archbishop of Vilna; Louis René Edouard, Prince of Rohan, Cardinal-Prince-Archbishop of Strasburg; Maximilian Verhovac, Archbishop of Agram, whose portrait still hangs to-day in the Lodge bearing his name; Franz Karl Count von Wellbrück, Prince-Archbishop of Liège. It was not as though these men were priests who had become somewhat indifferent to the performance of their spiritual office. On the contrary, they were Church dignitaries, the majority of whom had attained the highest rank in their calling. Indeed, all of them must have recognized that Freemasonry was something quite different to what it was described as in the papal proscriptions. But they were not able to stem the tide of hatred that was pouring in upon Freemasonry.

In the 'sixties and 'seventies of the eighteenth century the anti-masonic campaign began in Germany also. The nature of this was illustrated by a sermon preached by the Capuchin, P. Schuff, in the Cathedral Church at Aix-la-Chapelle in Lent 1778, in which, supported by the Dominican, P. Greinemann, he made the following statement:

---

[1] Liszt, whose magnificent Oratorios *Christus, Legende der heiligen Elisabeth,* etc., which bear witness to such profound religious sentiment, was initiated in the 'Unity' Lodge in Frankfort-on-Main in 1841.

'The Jews who crucified the Saviour were Freemasons, and Pilate and Herod were the wardens of a Lodge. Judas had been admitted a Mason in a Synagogue before he betrayed Christ, and when he gave back the thirty pieces of silver before setting out to hang himself, he did nothing more than pay the fee for initiation into the Order.'

But the Freemasons could not allow such statements to pass without protest, and there is in existence a great number of open letters dating from those times in which they vigorously protested against such blind fanaticism. Hardly had this wicked calumny been published by a Rhenish newspaper than a German Prince[1] wrote as follows to the two reverend fathers:

'MY VERY REVEREND AND VENERABLE FATHERS,

'Various reports, confirmed by the public newspapers, have brought to my knowledge the zeal you are expending upon sharpening the sword of fanaticism against those peaceful, virtuous, and estimable people known as Freemasons. As an old officer of this most respectable Order, I must, as far as it lies within my power, refute these calumnies that insult the Brotherhood, and attempt to remove the heavy veil from your eyes that makes you regard the Temple which we erect to all the virtues as the meeting-place of all the vices. Why, my very reverend and venerable Fathers, do you wish to take us back to those centuries of ignorance and barbarity which were for so long the disgrace of human intelligence, those times of fanaticism which the eye of reason can only look back upon with horror; those times when hypocrisy, seated upon the throne of despotism, laid fetters about the world, and, without the slightest discrimination, had all those who could read burned as sorcerers?

'Not only do you call the Masons sorcerers, you also accuse them of being rogues, sodomites, wicked men and forerunners of the anti-Christ, and you exhort a whole nation to exterminate such an accursed body.

'Rogues, my very venerable Fathers, do not regard it as their duty, as we do, to help the poor and orphaned; rogues, on the other hand, plunder them and often rob them of their inheritance and live well on their booty in idleness and

[1] This letter was for a long time attributed to Frederick the Great, but it is now disputed that he was the author of it.

hypocrisy. Rogues finally deceive mankind—Freemasons enlighten it.

'Sodomites are not likely to populate the State with good family men ; a Mason, however, returning from his Lodge, where he has been taught only lessons beneficial to mankind, becomes a better father, and a better husband in his family circle.

'Forerunners of anti-Christ would probably direct their attentions towards the destruction of God's Law; Masons, however, cannot contravene the Holy Law without breaking down their own Temple.

'And how could the people who take pride in the untiring propagation of all those virtues that make an honest and good man be an accursed body?

'Potsdam, 7th February 1778.'

In 1784, when a prohibition of Freemasonry was issued in Bavaria, one of the most celebrated Freemasons of the time, the eminent naturalist Ignaz Edler von Born of Vienna, Worshipful Master of the 'True Harmony' Lodge in Vienna, returned his diploma as member of the Academy of Sciences at Munich and of the Bavarian Society of Learned Scholars, accompanied by a letter in which he enthusiastically professed his membership of Freemasonry, which he described as an association 'whose greatest characteristic is uprightness, and whose pre-eminent charges are fear of God, loyalty to the rulers of the land and charity and love towards their neighbours.'

Even in the nineteenth century the campaign of the Church against Freemasonry did not abate. Pius VII, who revived the Order of Jesuits, caused a new Bull against Freemasonry to be posted on the church doors, a Bull which was later followed by another 'against the canker and deadly pest of society', as he described Freemasonry:

'Brethren in Christ, say it after me: Death and destruction to Freemasonry! A thing that should be extirpated to the last root,' preached the Franciscan Espadeiro in Lamengo.

Even Pius VIII, who only occupied the Pontificate for one year, condemned Freemasonry; as also did his successor Gregory.

Pius IX, who wore the triple crown for thirty-two years, and under whose pontificate the infallibility of the Pope was raised to dogma, condemned Freemasonry no less than eight times in Encyclicals and allocutions. To him Freemasonry was 'the synagogue of Satan', a 'detestable and damnable sect of depravity'. One of the best known of German Freemasons, Professor Bluntschli, the celebrated expert in Constitutional Law, of Heidelberg, protested against this opinion in an open circular letter of 1865, which, even to-day, might serve as an answer to attacks from Catholic quarters. Bluntschli, who at that time was Worshipful Master of the Lodge 'Rupert of the Five Roses', wrote as follows:

'It is not the first time a Pope of Rome has anathematized our venerable Order. Clement XII did it as early as the 28th April 1738, and Benedict XIV confirmed and further explained the condemnation of his predecessor of the 18th May 1751. Since that date the same thing has also been done by Pius VII and Leo XII, although, of course on each occasion, as the present Pope laments, without success.

'These condemnations from the Holy See bear not the slightest resemblance to the judgments of our Courts of Law, the underlying consideration being secret calumniations not divulged to the accused. There is no public indictment and absolutely no defence either public or private. All guarantees of impartial administration of justice and a reliable judgment are conspicuous by their absence. Suspicion replaces proof, guilt is assumed, and people are condemned without having been heard.

'The Fraternity of Freemasons is a society of free men obeying the laws of the land, but as it is not an ecclesiastical institution, and as such does not belong to any Church, it is not subject to ecclesiastical authority. The papal condemnation, therefore, has absolutely no power over the Brotherhood. As, however, the sovereign of the Catholic Church constantly condemns us, it is of interest to know his reasons and to see how he arrives at his conclusions.

'The first and most important reason which all Popes have stressed in their condemnations is the reproach that our Brotherhood joins together men of various religions and sects as brethren. "The purity of the Catholic religion is thereby sullied," as Benedict XIV put it.

'The first and gravest reproach, my brethren, is founded on truth, as we freely admit. If it is a crime for men of various faiths to stretch out the hand of friendship irrespective of their several religious creeds, then we are guilty of this

crime and openly confess it. Moreover, our Brotherhood
has acknowledged from the very beginning and, as time
goes on, places greater emphasis on the sublime truth that
there are honest and good men in all religions who are worthy
to esteem and love one another as brothers. At all times
the Brotherhood of Masons has regarded it as a crime against
humanity to persecute people on account of their differing
religion. The moral fulfilment of duty is more highly
esteemed by Masons than orthodoxy. But these principles,
which for a long time had to be confined to the Lodge, have
long since become the principles of the civilized world,
despite all the efforts of ecclesiastical zealots to the contrary.
If Masonry is condemned on that account, then the enlightened world and all civilized states are subject to the
same condemnation.

'Thanks be to God that the anathema fulminated on this
ground is not capable, in this age, of inflaming fanatical
passions, but only serves to show, by contrast, the nocturnal
gloom of the intolerance that fathered it. It shows the world
how far Rome is still behind the moral progress of mankind.

'As a second ground for condemnation, Benedict XIV
cites the mystery in which our Brotherhood is cloaked.
It is true that the secrecy to which we bind ourselves by vow
has from all time aroused mistrust and provided an excuse
for many a misinterpretation. You are also aware of the
amazing misunderstanding, unfortunately not confined to
non-Masons, connected with it. Neither its principles, nor
its aims, nor its existence, nor its members remain secret.
Whosoever so desires can easily obtain the fullest information on all these points. Only the signs of recognition, which
are so designed that brethren may recognize one another
more easily in foreign parts, have to remain secret, as well
as the inner working of the Lodge, so that personal confidence
may there find most complete expression and so that
opinions may be more freely expressed. The secret and
personal influence that the Brotherhood has upon the
character and moral life of its members requires this protection. Is the Catholic Church any different? Is the confession public or secret? Are the discussions of the Catholic
Orders and authorities carried on in public? Has not every
family, every intimate circle of friends, every private company, secrets of its own? In an age that seeks publicity we
are perhaps a little too shy in this respect. But all the same,

this dislike of publicity cannot be termed a crime that justifies an anathema. . . .

'Furthermore, when Benedict XIV refers to the law of the Roman Church that does not tolerate any kind of association or corporation, the right of the Church is not in any way affected by it. The majority of civilized States who are alone qualified to decide in such a matter, have, for a long time past, allowed the Order to exist unmolested by virtue of their having recognized (in contradistinction to the Roman Empire) the general right of freedom in respect of associations. And even this reason collapses completely since individual governments have prohibited the Brotherhood, and where that has happened—as it has, by way of exception—the Lodges of the country concerned have obeyed without hesitation and dissolved at once, thus demonstrating their respect for the law of the land.

'Finally, as the last reason for his condemnation, Benedict XIV mentions the fact that many clever and honourable men have an unfavourable opinion of the Brotherhood. But the weakness of that assertion as a ground for such a condemnation should, we consider, be quite obvious to Rome, for the very reason that there are undoubtedly also very many clever and honest men who have an unfavourable opinion of all religious orders and monasteries; indeed, even of the whole Roman hierarchy.

'Therefore, of all these reasons, only the first has truth and weight. But the very ground upon which the Pope condemns us is, in the eyes of the civilized world, the greatest glory of our Brotherhood.

'Pope Pius IX expresses himself much more violently against Freemasonry than did his predecessors in the Holy See, although, to be sure, the style of Rome has never been spoilt for lack of terrible words. The fact that the present publication of Pius IX surpasses the previous condemnations in passionate outbursts of anger may be regarded as a sure sign of the pernicious influence which our worst and most implacable enemies, the Jesuits, have exercised over the sentiments and judgment of a Pope who is, by nature, mild.

'He calls our Brotherhood a criminal sect, although no other crime than that of humane tolerance can be proved against us, and he calls us an immoral sect, although the law of ethics is the very guiding principle of Freemasonry. He accuses us of having instigated the revolutions and wars that have set Europe ablaze, although all the world knows that the disturbances and wars in Europe have been caused by other and much more powerful forces than are at our disposal, and it is clear for any enquirer to see that our Brotherhood demands the conscientious observance of the law of the land, that the Lodges, in accordance with their Constitutions, refrain from any active participation in current political struggles and solely pursue humane and ethical objects, and that our Lodges are neutral ground and sanctuaries, the thresholds of which may not be crossed by partisan passions. He accuses us of harbouring violent hatred against the Christian religion, in spite of the fact that it is a principle with us to respect every sincere belief, in spite of the fact that the majority of the brethren profess the Christian faith, and in spite of the fact that the ethical ideal, which Christ demonstrated by his life and in his teachings, cannot be regarded by an ethical society otherwise than with admiration and respect. He even describes us as being antagonistic to God, although we address our prayers to Him and derive ethical refreshment from the divine source of all ethical life.

'Without avail he calls upon the State for measures against us; the State authorities have no fear of our activities, they know full well that we are peaceful and loyal citizens.

'Brethren, let us not follow the example of the Princes of the Church of Rome. Let us not retaliate with unjust accusations. Let us not answer the anathema of the Church with curses. Let us deplore the unfortunate delusions of a venerable old man whose heart has been deceived and misguided. Let us pray to the Almighty and All-seeing God that he may destroy the delusion that has stimulated the anger of the Pope and let his mind grasp the simple truth in order that he may change his curse to a blessing.'

This courageous letter had, of course, very little effect. On two further occasions did Pius IX attack the 'wicked society'; likewise Leo XIII, who stigmatized Freemasonry as 'wicked work' and 'this contagious disease' in his Encyclical 'Humanum genus' of 1884, to which, later on, Pius X gave his support. He took as his authority the works of the Jesuit, S. H. Pachtler, whose books *Der stille Krieg gegen Thron und Altar*[1] ('The Secret War against the Throne and Altar') and

[1] Amberg: Habbel, 1873.

Der Goetze der Humanität[1] ('The Idol of Humanity') had been published a few years previously, in which Freemasonry was described as a 'terrible system of sheer misguidance of minds and hearts', and as the supporter of an 'anti-theistical humanity', although not the slightest proof of these assertions has been put forward, despite all the subtlety of deduction and all the 'documentary evidence'.

The Encyclical issued by Leo XIII, which totally eclipsed the Bull of Pius IX, is perhaps the severest attack the Papal See has ever made upon Freemasonry, and is of such immense significance in respect of what happened to Freemasonry round about the turn of the century, and actually right up to the earliest days of the World War, that we cannot do otherwise than quote extracts from it here.

On all church doors the following was to be read:[2]

'THE MASONIC SECT

.   .   .   .   .

'The human race is divided into two different and opposing parties. . . . The one is the Kingdom of God on earth— that is, the Church of Jesus Christ; the other is the kingdom of Satan. . . . The one fights the other with different kinds of weapons, and battles at all times, though not always with the same ardour and fury. In our days, however, those who follow the evil one seem to conspire and strive all together under the guidance and with the help of that society of men spread all over, and solidly established, which they call Free-Masons. Not dissimulating their intentions, they vie in attacking the power of God; they openly and ostensibly strive to damage the Church, with the purpose to deprive thoroughly if possible Christian people of the benefits brought by the Saviour Jesus Christ. . . .

'The sect of Masons grew beyond expectation; and, creeping audaciously and deceitfully among the various classes of the people, it grew to be so powerful that now it seems to be the only dominating power in the States. From this rapid and dangerous growth have come into the Church and into the State those evils which our predecessors had already foreseen. It has indeed come to this, that we have

[1] Freiburg: Herder, 1875.   [2] Singer: *loco citato*.

serious fear, not for the Church, which has a foundation too firm for men to upset it, but for those States in which this Society is so powerful—or other societies of a like kind, and which show themselves to be servants and companions of Masonry. . . .

'The initiated must promise, nay, take an oath, that they will never, in any way or at any time, disclose their fellow-members and the emblems by which they are known, or expose their doctrines. So, by false appearance, but with the same kind of simulation, the Masons chiefly strive, as once did the Manichæans, to hide and to admit no witnesses but their own. They seek skilfully hiding places, assuming the appearance of literary men or philosophers, associated for the purpose of erudition; they have always ready on their tongues the speech of cultivated urbanity, and proclaim their charity toward the poor; they look for the improvement of the masses, to extend the benefits of social comfort to as many of mankind as possible. Those purposes, though they may be true, yet are not the only ones. Besides, those who are chosen to join the society must promise and swear to obey the leaders and teachers with great respect and trust; to be ready to do whatever is told them, and accept death and the most horrible punishment if they disobey. In fact, some who have betrayed the secrets or disobeyed an order are punished with death so skilfully and so audaciously that the murder escaped the investigations of the police. Therefore, reason and truth show that the society of which we speak is contrary to honesty and natural justice.

'There are other and clear arguments to show that this society is not in agreement with honesty. No matter how great the skill with which men conceal, it is impossible that the cause should not appear in its effects. "A good tree cannot yield bad fruits, nor a bad tree good ones." (Matt. vii, 18). Masonry generates bad fruits mixed with great bitterness. From the evidence above mentioned we find its aim, which is the desire of overthrowing all the religious and social orders introduced by Christianity, and building a new one according to its taste, based on the foundation and laws of naturalism. . . .

'But the war wages more ardently against the Apostolic See and the Roman Pontiff. He was, under a false pretext, deprived of the temporal power, the stronghold of his rights and of his freedom; he was next reduced to an iniquitous condition, unbearable for its numberless burdens until it has come to this, that the sectarians say openly what they had already in secret devised for a long time, viz. that the very spiritual power of the Pope ought to be taken away, and the divine institution of the Roman Pontificate ought to disappear from the world. . . .

'It is true, Free-Masons generally admit the existence of God; but they admit themselves that this persuasion for them is not firm, sure. They do not dissimulate that in the masonic family the question of God is a principle of great discord; it is even known how they lately had on this point serious disputes. It is a fact that the sect leaves to the members full liberty of thinking about God whatever they like, affirming or denying His existence. Those who boldly deny his existence are admitted as well as those who, like the pantheists, admit God but ruin the idea of Him, retaining an absurd caricature of the divine nature, destroying its reality. . . .

'The sect of the Masons aims unanimously and steadily also at the possession of the education of children. They understand that a tender age is easily bent, and that there is no more useful way of preparing for the State such citizens as they wish. Hence, in the instruction and education of children, they do not leave to the ministers of the Church any part either in directing or watching them. In many places they have gone so far that children's education is all in the hands of laymen; and from moral teaching every idea is banished of those holy and great duties which bind together man and God. . . .'

Leo XIII then proceeds to deal with the 'principles concerning the State' and asserts with obvious bias that it is the principle of the naturalists

'that the people are sovereign, that those who rule have no authority but by commission and concession of the people; so that they can be deposed, willing or unwilling, according to the wishes of the people. That the origin of all rights and civil duties is in the people or in the State, which is ruled according to the new principles of liberty. That the State must be godless; no reason why one religion ought to be preferred to another.'

It then goes on literally:

'The turbulent errors which we have mentioned must inspire governments with fear; in fact, suppose the fear of God in life and respect for divine laws to be despised, the authority of the rulers allowed and authorized would be destroyed, rebellion would be left free to popular passions, and universal revolution and subversion must necessarily come. This subversive revolution is the deliberate aim and open purpose of the numerous communistic and socialistic associations. The masonic sect has no reason to call itself foreign to their purpose, because Masons promote their designs and have with them common capital principles.'

Once more the Pope returns to the relations between Freemasonry and the authority of the State, and writes:

'Free-Masons, insinuating themselves under pretence of friendship into the hearts of Princes, aim to have them as powerful aids and accomplices to overcome Christianity, and in order to excite them more actively they calumniate the Church as the enemy of royal privileges and power. Having thus become confident and sure, they get great influence in the government of States, resolve yet to shake the foundations of the thrones, and persecute, calumniate, or banish those sovereigns who refuse to rule as they desire. . . .

'It would, therefore, be more according to civil wisdom and more necessary to universal welfare that Princes and Peoples, instead of joining the Free-Masons against the Church, should unite with the Church to resist the Free-Masons' attacks. . . .'

Leo XIII thereupon confirms all the proscriptions of his predecessors and implores the patriarchs, primates, archbishops and bishops of the Catholic girdle of the world to co-operate to root out this poison—*impuram hanc luem*.

The Encyclical closes with the exhortation to entreat the aid and intercession of the Mother of God, the Blessed Virgin Mary,

'that against the impious sects in which one sees clearly revived the contumacious pride, the untamed perfidy, the simulating shrewdness of Satan, she may show her power, she who triumphed over him since the first conception.'

FRONTISPIECE TO THE 'POCKET COMPANION', 1ST EDITION, 1735
Engraving by J. Clark, after T. Worlidge

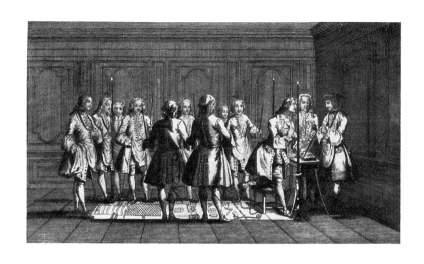

LODGES AT WORK
From a series of French prints, circa 1744

And to

'pray also St. Michael, St. Joseph, and the Apostles Peter and Paul . . . that God will condescend to piously help human society threatened by so many dangers. . . .'

This Encyclical was followed by innumerable pastoral letters, sermons, and pamphlets. The proclamation of the Pope was triumphantly circulated and, if at all possible, coarsened by newspapers, periodicals, and books. It need hardly be said that these publications were followed by counter-publications; and the struggle raged violently for years afterwards.

In this struggle the attackers suffered a defeat so severe that it shook the belief of thousands who had, up to that moment, regarded every false statement made as the absolute truth. This was brought about by the grotesque Taxil deception, which was one of the greatest and most notorious practical jokes ever played on the world, and which, when it first appeared, seemed to be a decisive blow against Freemasonry, but, when it ended, called forth an irrepressible laugh against the enemies of the Fraternity.

Leo Taxil, or to give him his proper name, Gabriel Jogand Pagés, a Frenchman, who had been brought up at a Reformatory by Jesuits and had then gone over to Radicalism and Latitudinarianism, had also been a Freemason for a short time, but did not get farther than the degree of Entered Apprentice, and had been excluded from the Lodge after he had only visited it on three occasions. Known as a passionate antagonist of clericalism, it caused great amazement when Taxil publicly renounced his past and went over to the Catholic Church. This victory over an erstwhile deadly enemy was counted a great triumph, for not a soul had any idea of the colossal deception which he was planning—a deception which was not perpetrated in order to do a service to the Freemasonry that he also hated, but in order to make a highly profitable business of the struggle against it. With this object in view, he first of all published a number of anti-masonic books, the first of which, *Les Frères Trois-Points* ('The Three Degree Brethren'), was put on the market in 1885, the way having been admirably paved by the Papal Encyclical. In this and his subsequent books, Taxil served up the most absurd, bloodthirsty fabrications. In order to make these more palatable, he sprinkled here and there a grain of truth about the masonic Ritual, although he disclosed nothing new. On the contrary the things he told had already become known from other books. But that consolidated the impression that the remainder was correct. Even in the *Three Degree Brethren* the swindler asserted that the Freemasons communed with the Devil, and that the whole cult was nothing more than the glorification of Lucifer. Especially

> 'the Areopagi and Chapters,' he asserts, 'are under the influence of the spirit of the Evil One, Lucifer, and Eblis, the supposed Angel of Light, with whom the Knights Kadosh (Masons of the thirtieth degree) commune by means of necromancy and the raising of evil spirits. I know full well that many of my readers will shrug their shoulders sceptically at such assertions. I must honestly admit that I myself at first, hesitated and laughed at such an assumption. After a thorough study of the documents I changed my opinion; I came to the firm conclusion that the fiendish spirit really does play a part in the secret direction of Freemasonry through the unapproachable Aeropagi. The organization and direction of the secret sect is too satanic to be humanly explicable.'

Giving full play to his imagination, Taxil went on to describe licentious happenings in women's Lodges and the 'Assassinations in Freemasonry', to which a separate book was devoted. The large majority of the Catholic newspapers at the time of Taxil filled whole columns each day with this fiction. Belief in the truth of Taxil's fabrications became a pious conviction when the 'convert' was received, on the recommendation of certain highly placed clerics, in solemn audience by Leo XIII. That encouraged him to act with even greater boldness; to think out even greater absurdities. In 1891 his book entitled *Les Sœurs maçonnes* ('Women in Freemasonry') was published. In this, and other writings, 'devil worship' in the higher degrees of Freemasonry, the so-called 'Palladism', was minutely described. In the palladistic Lodges of Satan very orgies of immorality were said to be celebrated. Lucifer was revered as the Prince of Goodness and the God of the Christians vilified as the Spirit of Evil.

> 'Here begins the cult and the direct worship of the Devil, the progressive brutalization through the black art, finally the adoration of Satan in the form of a snake. The adept

repeats the oaths of complete obedience to the orders of the Lodge, no matter what they may be or when they may be given. He thereby invokes Satan as his God; he invokes him according to the ritual of the black art; he worships him in the form of Baphomet, a disgraceful idol with goat's feet, the breasts of a woman, and the wings of a bat.'

According to Taxil, the climax of these orgies was always the profanation of the Host. In *Les Sœurs maçonnes*, Taxil had already invented Sophia Walder, the 'great-grandmother of anti-Christ', who, he alleged, had been elected palladistic Grand Mistress on the 21st January 1889.

In order to prevent any possible doubts from arising, 'disclosures' of a similar nature, but from other sources, suddenly made their appearance. A 'Dr. Bataille', in reality a German named Hacks, published a bulky work, *Le Diable au XIXe siècle* ('Satan in the nineteenth century'). The Italian, Domenico Margiotta, likewise devoted brochure after brochure to the subject of devil worship. Highly placed clerics, especially Mgr. Fava, the Bishop of Grenoble, whose sympathies Taxil had cunningly enlisted for his sinister purposes, became his enthusiastic apostles, and countless numbers believed that the American Freemason, Albert Pike, the leader of the Scottish Rite, was in reality the Pope of the Devil; that 60 per cent of all Lodges in France had, under the title 'Women's Lodge', a harem as an annexe, as it were; that the Devil himself very often occupied the chair at the sacrilegious orgies, and that he found pleasure on such occasions in dragging a living image of God around in filth.

Business was booming. The writings of Taxil, Hacks, and Margiotta met with a ready sale. Within a short time, according to Father Hermann Gruber, 100,000 copies of the *Frères Trois-Points* had been sold. Thus publication followed publication, and further assistance was forthcoming. Paul Rosen, ostensibly also a 'converted Freemason', added the books *Satan and Cie* and *L'Ennemie Sociale*, the last of which was particularly recommended by papal briefs. But even people who were not in the conspiracy did their share. The French Archbishop, Leon Meurin, wrote a particularly hair-raising book, taking Taxil as his sole authority, viz. *La Franc Maçonnerie-Synagogue de Satan*, in which he stated amongst other things:

'In the Lodge symbol Baphomet Lucifer has mimicked the Ark of the Covenant. The two cherubim on it are replaced by two horns. . . . We have not the slightest doubt that the Devil appears in person and makes announcements to his apostles and tools.'

In this work we cannot, of course, deal minutely with all the amazing statements that, by such an extraordinary means, created so vast an interest throughout the Catholic world, and also amongst many non-Catholics, in the 'nineties of the last century. The lies were supported in practically every publication by 'original illustrations', and it was a common thing for persons who actually existed to be shamelessly depicted as participators in the revolting atrocities that had been fabricated.

One of the swindlers attempted to outdo the others in powers of invention. 'Dr. Bataille' was especially gifted in the fabrication of ghastly ritual. According to his account, the brethren ranged themselves around the death's heads of Jesuits, execrated everything connected with God, and crushed the skulls and burned the fragments of bone before the idol Baphomet. Then began the raising of evil spirits amidst the roar of thunder and violent wind. Lucifer suddenly appeared as a gleaming apparition of supernatural brilliance. Then came the darkness once again. A fearful cry. Indescribable confusion. A brother falls down dead. 'The Devil in person has fetched him.' Satanic laughter of the hardened Freemasons. . . .

The Pope of the Devil, Pike, was naturally provided with the most modern technical devices and was connected with all the Grand Masters of Palladism by means of a Satanic wireless 'telephone organization'. Also a Devil's crocodile that played the piano, together with a soothsaying snake, belonged to the Freemasonic Ritual. And when any one suspected that, in spite of the favour displayed by the Pope, it might be a hoax, this was at once countered by numerous testimonies from the most eminent Church dignitaries.

The hoax reached its zenith when Taxil and his friends invented a second female figure, Miss Diana Vaughan, a Palladist, who was alleged to have been born in 1874 as the daughter of the 'Devil Bitru'. This absolutely non-existent woman seemed to be an extraordinarily prolific writer. Under the title *Mémoires d'une Expalladiste*, she first of all recounted her *mémoires* for the benefit of the public. At the age of ten she had been dedicated to Satan, initiated in an American Palladist Lodge and wedded to the Devil Asmodeus, who gave her as a wedding present the stolen tail of the Lion of St. Mark, which was endowed with extraordinary powers, and which, laid about her neck, came to life and kissed her.

Of course, Diana Vaughan was only known to the world through Taxil. Every month she published a long article in which she reproduced supposedly authentic documents of the Devil, and even produced the signature of the Devil Bitru. And all this was believed. The *Civiltà Cattolica*, the leading Jesuit organ of Rome, praised the 'noble Miss' and the 'other valiant fighters' who had 'often entered the lists at the risk of their lives'.

Enthusiastic letters were addressed from all quarters to Miss Vaughan, and when she sent a contribution to Cardinal Parocci for an Anti-Masonic Congress which was to be held in Trient, he sent her a blessing on the instruction of the Pope.

Such was the excitement aroused by this that in Switzerland it resulted in a trial for witchcraft. An exceedingly devout Swiss woman, Luzie Claraz, was accused of having participated in Freiburg in the Lucifrian orgies of the Freemasons and she was harassed by Catholic newspapers in an almost unbelievable manner. She was described as the mistress and ambassadress of the Devil and was accused of stealing the Host. This poor woman and her family were so severely persecuted that her mother died of sorrow at her daughter's shame.

The Anti-Masonic Congress that had been awaited with such keen interest was held in Trient in 1896. No less than 36 bishops, 50 episcopal delegates, and more than 700 other plenipotentiaries, of which the majority were clergymen, attended. The question of Miss Diana Vaughan seemed to form the chief topic of the Congress. There were two camps violently opposed to one another: The German clergy, who, after ten years, had gradually seen through the swindle, and the great body of the conference who still believed implicitly in Taxil and Miss Vaughan. When the German, Mgr. Gratzfeld, declared that the mysterious Miss Vaughan did not exist at all, the majority of the members of the Congress regarded him as the victim of a deceiver. Another German cleric, Dr. Baumgartner from Rome, had little more success. The very definite questions he put concerning the identity of Miss Vaughan were evaded by a French Abbé, and as this did not satisfy Baumgartner, Taxil himself intervened in the debate to the accompaniment of thunderous applause. He had been biding his time with a strong trump card up his sleeve, and this, which took the form of a 'photograph' of Miss Vaughan, he suddenly produced. He then proceeded to make violent attacks upon the Jesuit Father Hermann Gruber, who, at first, had himself been under the spell of the swindle, but, in the end, contributed more than any one else to exposing it. The majority of the audience broke out into enthusiastic applause as Taxil left the platform. Nevertheless, it was decided to set up a committee in order to settle the question of Miss Vaughan's existence once and for all.

But the popularity of Taxil, 'once a devil and now a saint', was by no means diminished. Even after the Congress, he was still tremendously acclaimed, and, although the campaign of the German Catholics against the swindle became more vigorous than ever, the committee appointed in Trient was not yet prepared to issue a report to the effect that Miss Vaughan was nothing less than a gigantic hoax; on the other hand, they arrived at what almost amounted to a judgment of Solomon by declaring that 'up to the moment they had not been able to trace any definite proof either for or against the existence' of Miss Vaughan. And this in spite of the fact that Dr. Hacks had publicly declared three months previously that he had been hoaxing the world. 'Miss Diana Vaughan' was very indignant about it and the leading German anti-Freemasons, Mgr. Gratzfeld and Father Gruber, found themselves being denounced as Freemasons.

However, the bombshell burst on Easter Monday 1897. Leo Taxil had convened for this day a grand assembly in the hall of the Geographical Society in Paris at which, 'after the raffling of a typewriter', a lantern-slide lecture was to be delivered on the Palladist cult. Taxil did not deliver the lecture, but informed the immense audience instead that he had succeeded in perpetrating the greatest hoax of recent times, that Miss Vaughan had never existed and that for twelve years he had duped the leaders of the Roman Catholic Church in a most flagrant manner. The sensation caused by this disclosure was almost greater than that caused by the hoax itself, not only at the assembly but also amongst the general public. For a certain length of time the question of Lucifer and the Devils Bitru and Asmodeus was a very delicate subject rarely touched upon. But only for a time, for it must not be assumed that the belief in the 'Devil worship of Freemasonry' has yet been finally disposed of. Even to this day the legend ekes out an obstinate existence and not merely amongst simple people who are easy to convince. Scarcely a year ago the statement of a French priest was published in the *Semaine réligieuse* of Grenoble, in which he declared that he had personally encountered Satan in a masonic Temple.

But those people who were conscious of the tremendous ridicule to which they had exposed themselves, sought to detract from the strong impression the Taxil swindle had caused in enlightened circles by pouncing all the more eagerly on the 'infamous crimes' of Freemasonry, as quoted in the Encyclical of 1884. It might well be said that the vast majority of the more important fabrications against and defamations of Freemasonry current to-day, politically, culturally, and socially, originate in the Catholic camp. Now, as before, there are a great many anti-masonic organizations at work, and especially in France does one find strong forces of such storm troops. The relentless campaign carried on from day to day against Freemasonry is described in a book by R. Mennevée, entitled *L'organisation antimaçonnique en France*, which is based on voluminous documentary evidence. The battle that was lost when Leo Taxil and his fellow-swindlers were sent into the front line had certainly not had an encouraging effect, but within a short time new anti-masonic societies were springing up like mushrooms. And in our times things have scarcely changed. A goodly number of daily newspapers has entered the lists against Freemasonry and, at the same time, there are also many periodicals whose sole object is to combat the Brotherhood. There is the *Revue Internationale des Sociétés Secrètes* (R.I.S.S.), which couples anti-semitism with anti-masonic activity and resolutely supports the legendary plan for setting up Jewish world-domination; also the *Cahiers de l'Ordre*, which, likewise anti-semitic, especially pursues the aim of proving the connexion between Freemasonry and the Soviets. The *Comité pour le bon goût français et chrétien*, which conducts a campaign against bobbed hair and short frocks, alleging them to be 'the diabolic work of the Freemasons', must on no account be forgotten.

However, the *Reveil français*, a newspaper under the management of Emile Bergeron, is the most clamorous of all. This paper feels not the slightest compunction in stuffing its readers with the old lie about masonic devil-worship, more in the way one would expect from a fanatical tract. Bergeron couples a wild hatred of Germany with his campaign against the Craft. So far as he understands politics, France is ruled by the Lodges, which have only one aim: 'To destroy the moral forces of the land, in order to be able to indulge in Bolshevism to their hearts' content.' As proof he cites:

> 'French Freemasonry favoured the entry of Germany into the League of Nations, it strove for the termination of the occupation of the Rhineland and desires the revision of the Treaty of Versailles.'

It is therefore a 'great national danger'. Is it to be wondered, in view of this state of affairs, that French Freemasonry, which, originally, was by no means anti-clerically inclined, has, in the course of time, taken up the quarrel forced upon it, and has, since that time, held anti-clerical views, although it certainly does not debar orthodox Catholics from joining the Brotherhood. We will deal more closely with this subject in a later chapter.

In quite recent times the Roman Catholic Church, the whole world over, has raised the cry that it was Freemasonry that had set in motion the cultural struggle raging in Mexico. 'The masonic war against the Church' is their term for the bloody conflict between the Mexican Government and the Catholics of that country. And, just as ten years ago it was preached from the pulpits that the Freemasons had instigated the Sarajevo assassination, and thus caused the world catastrophe, it is now being alleged in the pulpits that the Freemasons of Mexico regard it as their main object to torture and kill priests and nuns, which allegations continued to be made although it is an established fact that Mexican Freemasonry, as such, has taken absolutely no part in the religious conflict. It remained completely neutral, despite the fact that for a long time past unscrupulous propaganda had been made against it. Only on one single occasion did Mexican Freemasonry make a public declaration in favour of the Calles Government, and that was after that ghastly attack on a passenger train outside the town of Guadalajara in the Mexican State of Jalisco, when a horde of fanatical Indians derailed the train and murdered women, children, and old men, as well as the military escort of fifty, including their commanding officer (a Freemason), to the last man, and finally set fire to what remained of the train; all to the cry of 'Viva Cristo Rey'. The

Freemasons then made a public protest against such ghastly barbarity, but it was the only occasion on which they took part in the conflict.

It is, no doubt, quite unnecessary here to go deeply into the arguments upon which the 'holy war' of the Church against Freemasonry is based. The situation is clearly demonstrated in the Encyclicals and the clever analysis of Professor Bluntschli. Revealed dogma stands, as has already been said, in opposition to adogma. Even in the first Bull of 1738, expression was given to the conviction that Freemasonry constituted a danger to the Church, by reason of the fact that it formed a 'centre of union between good men and true and the happy means of conciliating friendship amongst those who must otherwise have remained at a perpetual distance', no matter what faith they may profess, so long as they are only unanimous in the 'religion in which all men agree. . . .' This conviction, which sees in that collaboration a serious danger to the purity of the Catholic religion, is also expressed in the latest Encyclical of Pius XI regarding the 'Unity of the Church'—issued in connexion with the religious conferences of recent years—an Encyclical which in itself was not directed against Freemasons. It condemned the endeavours 'that are being made to connect the true religion with the false ones and to awaken the belief that all religions are good'.

To this very day, therefore, the entirely untrue theory is propounded, viz.:

'That the aim of Freemasonry is to destroy the Christian civilization of the moment and to put the world under the domination of the Fraternity of Freemasons who would then replace Christianity by naturalistic and atheistic civilization with science and reason as religion. . . . The character of the struggle is therefore intellectual. It is the discord between materialism and the Christian idea, between the laws of God and the laws of man.'

To this only one answer can be given: that which the French merchant, Tournon, gave under examination before the Spanish Inquisition as early as the year 1757, when he was charged with indulging in masonic activities. To the question whether he was a Catholic he replied:[1] 'Yes. But in Freemasonry, indifferentism in matters of religion is not espoused. It is true, however, that in order to become a Freemason it is immaterial whether

[1] Arthur Singer: *Der Kampf Roms gegen die Freimaurerei*.

one is a Catholic or not. And the object of our Brotherhood is not to contest or deny the necessity and use of a religion. The masonic Lodges occupy themselves neither with maintaining nor with denying the mystery of the Holy Trinity, nor with the approval, nor the rejection of the religious system of the rationalistic philosophers.'

In Catholic quarters Freemasonry has frequently been confused with Protestantism, and this error has occasionally been fostered by the Protestants. For instance, a very eminent Freemason, the Rev. Dr. Gotthilf Schenkel, suggests in his excellent book entitled *Die Freimaurer im Lichte der Religions- und Kirchengeschichte* ('The Freemasons Considered in the Light of the History of Religion and the Church')

'that those men in particular, who, in the eyes of the enlightened people of German Evangelical circles, represent the German classical line of development, nationally and culturally, were Freemasons. The following are representative of such men: Frederick the Great, Klopstock, Lessing, Wieland, Herder, Goethe, Fichte, Freiherr von Stein, Blücher, Scharnhorst, Gneisenau, Rückert, and Frederick William III of Prussia, who caused a declaration to be made at the second Congress at Vienna in 1833, to the effect that he would always protect the Brotherhood, since he knew that those of his servants who were Freemasons were excellent servants of the State. The Emperor William I and Emperor Frederick III are also worthy of special mention in this list. And although,' Schenkel goes on to say, 'Kant himself did not belong to the Brotherhood, nevertheless, nowhere in enlightened society did Kant's range of ideas live on as they did in the German Lodges, which never open or close a meeting without thinking of the eternal Trinity of Truth, Goodness, and Beauty, as well as of God.'

Brauweiler, who belongs to the Catholic camp, also expressed this point of view very forcibly when he declared:

'It can be said that Freemasonry, as it has developed on Protestant soil, and in the form it has found in Germany, is wholly inspired with the spirit of Protestantism.'

And further:

'Protestantism does not demand unconditional belief. It concedes to its adherents the right to make the question of faith a personal matter—exactly the same right which Freemasonry emphasizes.'

Although the Protestant clergyman-Freemason and his Catholic counterpart may agree on this point, their statements are only correct to a limited degree. It is quite clear that the strict prohibition which the Catholic Church enforces in respect of Freemasonry has, in the Christian countries, brought about a predominance of Protestants in the Lodges. And it is quite a common thing for Evangelical clergymen to do great work there. But ignoring the fact that countless followers of all the other creeds are also enthusiastic adherents of the Royal Art, even Protestantism, and especially that of an orthodox and pietistic tendency, has by no means always and everywhere regarded Freemasonry with friendly eyes. Let us cite just one example. Towards the middle of the last century the well-known orthodox theologian, Ernst William Hengstenberg, Professor of Theology at Berlin University and founder of the *Evangelische Kirchenzeitung*, carried on so bitter a fight against Freemasonry that the King of Prussia personally intervened. And the violent attacks which, since the World War, have been made from national quarters arose almost entirely from Protestant circles, and were still further emphasized by the action of Behm, the Provincial Bishop of Mecklenburg, who, a few years ago, declared that his sympathies were entirely with the anti-masonic German National Officers' Association.

In recent times a kind of self-consciousness of an almost sensational nature has become manifest in prominent catholic circles. It is worthy of notice that it is again Father Gruber, S.J., who as already recorded, played such an important part in the Taxil affair, who is endeavouring to introduce fairness into the fight of Catholicism against Freemasonry. This may have great significance, for Father Gruber is not merely just one fighter amongst many antagonists of Freemasonry, he is the anti-masonic authority of clericalism. For more than a generation he has devoted all his strength, his mature and profound knowledge, and his brilliant pen to combating the whole range of masonic ideas; many opponents of the Brotherhood have been led astray by Gruber and many writers of anti-masonic literature have drawn the whole of their material from the writings of this militant Jesuit.

His entirely new attitude finds expression in an exceedingly important and extensive correspondence which he, now very aged and living in Holland, exchanged with Dr. Kurt Reichel, a Viennese Freemason. This correspondence, which has hitherto not been published, started with the series of articles which Father Gruber wrote for the leading Austrian Catholic weekly, *Das neue Reich*. These articles entitled 'Der Kampf gegen die Freimaurerei im Lichte jüngster Kundgebungen Pius XI' ('The Fight against Freemasonry in the Light of Recent Proclamations of Pius XI') displayed in a certain respect a remarkable and quite surprising consistency, inasmuch as Gruber there described the outlook of Freemasonry as the very antithesis of that of Catholicism, but confined himself to making this simple comparison. He who had so often accused Freemasonry of the most impossible things, now restricted the attack to a purely objective basis.

Father Gruber cites the following as being in his view, the most important features of modern speculative Freemasonry:

1. The ostensibly religiously or confessionally neutral, but really anti-supranaturalistic, in practice adogmatic and anti-dogmatic character, common to all fundamental liberalism.

2. The naturalistic and humanitarian fundamental principle.

3. The deistical basic idea.[1]

---

[1] Deism, according to Pachtler, the christening gift of the Fraternity of Freemasons of 1817, according to others the religion of the Lodges, comes from England. Whereas Theism embodies that religious conviction that explains God as a personal spiritual being, according to Whose Will the world was created and Who maintains and rules it, for which purpose He requires miracles, Deism, although it also acknowledges the personality of God, denies His miraculous intervention in the course of world events. For when God created the world, He also created the laws governing its gradual development from its imperfect state to perfection. A God who would have to work a miracle to keep the world in motion would destroy the perfection without which He is inconceivable. God's Will shows itself, therefore, in the ordered course of events of the world, more especially in Nature. That is what Deism says, but it is not inimical to Christianity on that account, for it merely rejects the dogma of supernatural miraculous phenomena. The father of this religio-philosophical movement was Lord Herbert of Cherbury (1583–1648), one of the younger contemporaries of the philosopher Francis Bacon, Baron Verulam. Amongst its forerunners was the latitudinarianism of the seventeenth century, the exponents of which declared that all the confessional differences of the Christian groups were immaterial and who considered only the 'basic truths', as laid down in the Holy Book, to be binding. The most important Deists, also called Freethinkers, were John Toland, who attempted by his work *Christianity not mysterious*, published in 1696, to prove that the gospel contained not only nothing unnatural, but also nothing irrational; Antony Collins (*Discourses on Freethinking*, 1713); Thomas Woolston (1669–1731), who re-interpreted the miracles of the Gospel as prophetic and symbolic narratives in his *Discourses on the Miracles of our Saviour*; and Matthew Tindal, who declared in his book *Christianity as old as the Creation*, that there is only one true religion, the natural one, which is really the fundament of moral conduct. According to him, this religion has existed from the very beginning, and what has since been incorporated in it

MASTERS' JEWELS: VARIOUS DEGREES

JUG WITH MASONIC SYMBOLS AND ARMS OF THE
GRAND LODGE OF THE 'MODERNS'

Gruber regarded Freemasonry as the chief exponent of 'Mundanity' and the supporter of a 'purely worldly culture'.
Dr. Kurt Reichel, who subjected these articles to a critical analysis,[1] described Gruber's statements as 'generally desirable in principle', and welcomed the opportunity to elaborate the masonic outlook thoroughly. The young Viennese philosopher drew attention to the fact that Gruber, in the attitude he had adopted, no longer accused Freemasonry of Atheism, but only of conscious Deism. This also is a reproach that has no substantial basis, but which seems much less serious since all that is adogmatic, in fact, all that is anti-dogmatic, applies to Deism. 'The freemasonic outlook,' writes Dr. Reichel, 'has, in its creed, the principle of a Supreme Being, a final spiritual *raison d'être*, known as God, but with the salutary "anti-dogmatic" difference to the dogma of the "one and only true Church holding the monopoly of all means of grace," that it leaves the inward conception of this idea of God to the subjectivism of each individual, in that it pursues the consideration that a religious faith may be there, but that it may not be dogmatized to an impossible monopoly of knowledge.'

As far as the ethics of Freemasonry are concerned, they are, according to Reichel, really 'mundane'; really materialistic. They constitute the ethics of designation, dedication to the Finite; not ethics of resignation, dedication to the Infinite. They are the ethics of worldliness rather than the ethics of unworldliness. In these ethics, Freemasonry is not the 'chief exponent' of 'secularization', but the 'chief exponent' of the human symbiosis for an ethically and æsthetically more valuable worldliness. Freemasonry regards the 'secularization' of human society as an actual and progressive fact following the commercial and social line of development of the history of mankind. In the face of this fact, its ethics are the ethics of acclimatization; ethics that are based on mundane society, in order, by all the means of 'materialism', to improve the state of civilization and minimize the suffering of humanity due to civilization. At the same time, they maintain the belief

is merely superstition. Viscount Bolingbroke also thought similarly. Amongst the Deists must also be reckoned Lord Anthony Shaftesbury, who made the æsthetic ideal the crux of his theory of ethics. He was a thinker who was, as it were, the spokesman of all those who sought to establish a moral and political ideal that would lead to universal peace and happiness.

In many views as to piety, morality, and, especially, tolerance, the contemporary attitude of Freemasons agreed with the theories of the Deists, not that Freemasonry has ever become a kind of Deist Church because of that.

[1] *Wiener Freimaurerzeitung*, No. 6, June 1928.

in a 'hereafter' for humanity, which, however, can only be gained by way of 'the life here below'. Humanity in its terrestrial social pain, not in its metaphysical original sin; the terrestrial inferiority of civilization, not the metaphysical inferiority of existence, seems to be the task to which their care and activity must first be directed. To this extent are masonic ethics humanitarian and naturalistic. In their metaphysics they see symbolized not the way from God, but the upward path to God.

Dr. Reichel closes with the statement:

'The masonic outlook as to metaphysics and ethics is opposed to that of the Catholics. But Freemasonry, which is not irreligious, but solely undogmatically religious, has never allowed the manifestation of its outlook on life to degenerate to an intentional struggle against the Catholic Church; this would be in direct contradiction to that which is "adogmatic" in the masonic view. When, however, the Church always finds occasion to construe a conscious anti-Church activity into the efforts of Freemasonry, which from its outlook on life can never coincide with those of Catholicism, it is because of the desire to bring into public disfavour that outlook which, by virtue of its "mundanity", its "materialism", and its "positive" religion, it knows only too well is a rival not to be despised.'

This polemic, which is so significant in principle, gave rise to the correspondence referred to above. This correspondence is still being carried on to-day, and may even cause the fight of Rome against Freemasonry to assume an entirely different aspect after more than 200 years of consistent bitterness.

Even the very first of Gruber's letters proved how right was the view of those few people who had perceived the new tendency of the articles in the *Neue Reich*; that is to say, the tendency to stress the antithesis of the outlooks of Freemasonry and Catholicism, and to abandon the weapons of clumsy invention and false legend in the feud against the Fraternity.

'I agree with you entirely,' wrote Father Gruber to Dr. Reichel, 'in the fundamental view that disputes between Catholicism and Freemasonry, which concern not only the highest interests of every individual person, but also of every nation and people, in fact, of the whole of humanity, should be carried on with suitable gravity and earnestness with the sole and only guiding principle of arriving at the objective truth and in the spirit of true Christian or Humanitarian love, as the case may be, seeing that, in so far as nationality, common descent, similar destiny, general human ideals and final basic principles are concerned, all men are, and will, in truth, always remain brothers, and belong to the same great human family, the children of God. Since only the objective truth can stand the test of life, and since unintentional errors and, similarly, intentional confusions may also hurl people and nations to destruction, it is indeed in the interests of all that the objective truth should prevail in all such important discussions. And here again, the criterion, which in respect of all people without exception leads most easily and most convincingly to its goal, is the criterion so often expressed by Christ himself: *Ex fructibus eorum cognoscetis eos* ("By their fruits ye shall know them"), that is to say: the true and the false prophets. . . .

'Neither the American nor the European Freemasons possess a materially more important secret. All that is of any importance, even of a ritualistic nature, has long been known the world over.

'Even from the true Catholic standpoint I consider it the most important task to combat, in the first place, the childish and erroneous conceptions of Freemasonry which still exist in wide circles. . . .'

Father Gruber became even clearer in his subsequent letters. Ludendorff's great anti-masonic campaign, with which we will deal later, and which, instead of making capital of alleged Devil worship, attempted to achieve the same object by warnings against the 'racial nationalism' of the Jews, was described by Gruber as the *'non plus ultra* of idiotic swindles on the part of one of the most celebrated of German military leaders of all time'. Gruber, of course, attributes a certain amount of the blame for this swindle to the Freemasons' 'mysteriousness', but he has repeatedly confirmed that it is an absurd lie to assert that Freemasonry really has any secrets to preserve.

It is also a remarkable fact that Father Gruber is not alone in his present attitude. A number of Jesuits from various countries have followed his new outlook and give support to his present principle that the struggle between Catholicism and Freemasonry must be confined to the differences in world outlook, and that an end must be put to calumny and false accusations. The endeavours 'to raise the methods of attack, at least, out of the moral slough' and to carry on the campaign, to make use of Father Hermann Gruber's words, 'in the spirit of Christian or Humanitarian Love, as the case may be', are, consequently, already bearing fruit. In Germany, it was Father Michael Gierens who gave up combating the Fraternity as the essence of all evil, but was antagonistic to it because the Church must insist 'that it, the Church, possesses its dogma revealed and, consequently, entirely, absolutely, and irrevocably binding truth in respect of all mankind'; in France, the publishers of the *Études Réligieuses* adopted a similar attitude, and in New York the *Catholic News* went so far as to call the Freemasons 'brethren in another camp', and there are signs of the beginning of an improvement in their tactics, even in the case of the leading organ of the Vatican, the *Civiltà Cattolica*.

All this has naturally resulted in trouble in Gruber's own camp. There are people who do not seem to wish to understand that a sense of justice and truthfulness that no longer permits them to calumniate their opponents has at last awakened in the breasts of the Jesuit Father and his friends, who are, nevertheless, amongst the strictest of orthodox Catholics. In consequence of this, extremely vehement attacks have been made against them in the Parisian *Revue internationale des Sociétés Secrètes*, which has already been described by us. The publisher of this paper, the late Mgr. Edouard Jouin, Protonotary Apostolic and pastor of one of the most aristocratic parishes of Paris, was, in spite of his eighty-five years, still a remarkably active enemy of Freemasonry. The views he expressed in this paper were, however, not solely of a purely Catholic note, the *Revue* being, as we have already said, extremely anti-semitic and national in character. Mgr. Jouin left the direction of operations in the feud against Father Gruber in the hands of the chief editor of his periodical, Pierre Colmet,[1] who performed this function with ruthless severity. Colmet complained bitterly that Gruber had written a letter to Dr. Reichel that 'had been all sugar and honey over Freemasonry'. It was inconceivable, he stated, that Gruber would not acknowledge the authenticity of the 'Protocol of the Wise Men of Zion'. Still more unbelievable was it, he said, that Father Gruber should implore Mgr. Jouin, for the sake of the honour of his whole work, to refrain from maintaining the correctness of the

---

[1] Pseudonym of the Abbé Boulin.

statements about a plan for the Jewish rule of the world. Even in France, he said, a regrettable 'change in the views of the publications of the Society of Jesus' was becoming noticeable. It was a question there, he said, of a universal campaign, and that could be seen from the attitude of the *Études* and its collaborators, Fathers Macé and Bonsirven. Colmet reproached these latter with wilfully underestimating the part played by Freemasonry, whose influence, he said, they were minimizing by representing that the Craft possesses no common leadership, and by denying the Jewish predominance in the Lodges.

This change of attitude is regarded by Colmet as 'a very sad picture' that is becoming increasingly glaring in colour.

'Father Gruber,' he wrote with indignation, 'has found a wonderful pretext for no longer finding it necessary to expose the secret societies or to wage any particularly severe campaign against them. So far as Father Gruber is concerned there no longer exists any secret in Freemasonry, or at least none of any importance, neither Phallus cult nor Satanism. This Jesuit rejects . . . the protocols of the Wise Men of Zion and our specialist's works on Occultism. He is kind enough to ascribe the responsibility for all the misunderstandings that have existed up to the present day, between the Church and the Lodges, to the annoying taste Freemasonry has for "mystification", which "mystification" lies in the legends concerning the origin of the sect, in its bizarre ritual and eccentric symbols! According to Gruber this mania, in itself innocent, has gradually upset relations and led to calumniations from opponents which are no less extravagant than this untimely masquerade.'

Father Gruber, he said, must therefore undoubtedly be in the pay of the Freemasons. This view seemed also to be borne out by the fact that he even went so far as to meet the Freemasons Dr. Kurt Reichel, Ossian Lang (New York), and the author of this book in the Jesuit Residence at Aix-la-Chapelle in June 1928, for the purpose of engaging in a conversation having the same aim as the correspondence that preceded it namely, 'to eliminate dishonourable, slanderous, personally offensive, or even silly tactics in the occasional and unavoidable intellectual battles between opponents whose fundamental principles are diametrically opposed', —to make use of Gruber's own words.

But these attacks did not succeed in making Gruber change his new attitude, even when Colmet, who harbours a bitter hatred of Germany, received help from such an extraordinary source as the German National Socialists, who declared that the alliance between Freemasonry and the Jesuits, so long suspected by them, was now an established fact. Father Gruber went out of his way to define his attitude even more clearly and unmistakably. A sentence from a letter addressed to Reichel on the 5th June 1928, illustrates this very clearly:

'In order to bring understanding to the Catholics, everything must be done first of all to break down gradually the deep-rooted mistrust of the "Brotherhood of Freemasons" in the narrowest sense of the word, whilst the Papal condemnations of Freemasonry should at the same time, be directed against the atheistical fundamental naturalism, which, since 1848, has made its appearance in other secret societies similar to Freemasonry and in profane schools of thought in a much more radically and aggressively pernicious manner than in Freemasonry itself, in the narrowest sense of the word, and which is, in general, combated with the greatest resolution by the Brotherhood itself.'

It is quite obvious that this new tone would not suit all those who, for decades, have been encouraging the most incredibly distorted views on Freemasonry;[1] for what Father

[1] These opponents should also read an 'open letter' that appeared in the *Irish Times* on the 15th March 1929. It was written by the then Deputy Grand Master of the Grand Lodge of Ireland, Col. Claude Cane, and was as follows:

'I have been reading with interest a good many articles and speeches dealing with the approaching centenary of Catholic Emancipation, but so far I have failed to find a single reference, either in a Roman Catholic paper, or by a Roman Catholic speaker, to the man whose influence and untiring work did more to secure the passing of that act of justice than anything else. That man was Richard, second Baron and first Earl of Donoughmore, Grand Master of Irish Freemasons.

'It was from a meeting of the Whig Club, held in 1792, at the house of John Forbes, in Kildare Street, and attended by Grattan, Lord Donoughmore and others, that the Catholic Convention of 1793 originated, and from that time onwards Lord Donoughmore devoted the whole of his energies and his very considerable political influence to the cause of his oppressed Roman Catholic fellow-countrymen. In doing so he was only carrying out one of the first principles of the Order of which he was the head—namely, that no man should be penalized or made to suffer on account of his religious beliefs. After the Union he continued his labours in the British House of Lords, and, in 1810, speaking on the "Catholic Petition," he made a most eloquent appeal on behalf of the Roman Catholic population. He also strenuously opposed all attempts to rule Ireland by coercion. On May 17th 1829, he rose from a sick bed to go to the House of Lords and move the second reading of the Catholic Relief

Gruber did, meant nothing less than the resolute rejection of a two-hundred year old system of persecution based on prevarication.

Bill. He never recovered from the effects of this exertion, but died on the 25th August following, a martyr to the cause of his Catholic fellow-countrymen, though himself a Protestant and a Freemason.'

'At a meeting of the Catholic Association held on the 10th November 1829, a warm tribute was paid to his memory as "the hereditary patron of the Catholics". Daniel O'Connell. the Liberator, expressed great gratitude to Lord Donoughmore for his public services rendered to the Irish people (FitzPatrick's *Correspondence of Daniel O'Connell*, vol i, pp. 76 and 88).

'In his efforts to secure justice for the Roman Catholics he was always supported, as far as could legitimately be done by a body which does not allow political activity—by the Freemasons of his Jurisdiction—but the result was rather paradoxical. Before and up to the time of the passing of the Catholic Relief Bill sixty per cent. of the Freemasons of Ireland were Roman Catholics, but as soon as their disabilities were removed the Church turned upon its former friends and attempted to rend them—Roman Catholics were forbidden to join the Order, and those who were already members were ordered to resign. They did so almost to a man, and I, for one, give them every credit for obeying the orders of their Church. Since that time the Order in Ireland has been almost exclusively Protestant, not more than about one per cent being Roman Catholic. That does not imply that any enmity is felt by the Order towards the Roman Church—the enmity is a one-sided one—but it does not encourage anyone to disobey the authority of the Church to which he belongs.

'The Roman Catholic papers have been very active lately in their denunciations of Freemasonry, but in common fairness they ought to give Lord Donoughmore, and the Order of which he was the head, the credit due to them for the great act of justice of 1829.'

CHAPTER II

'POLITICAL WORLD DOMINATION'

FATHER GRUBER was not the first Catholic anti-Freemason to think of disposing of the mythical plan to procure 'World Domination'. Just after the anti-Freemasonic Congress of Trient, Dr. Raich, the Capitular of Mainz Cathedral, who has already been mentioned by us, made the following statement at a mass meeting in Vienna:

'The idea of a central organization of all Lodges of the world is false, the idea of unknown rulers is false, and the idea of still unexplained secrets is also false. . . .'

And these words were not spoken at a time when polite words were called for, it was on the occasion of a violent demonstration against Freemasonry.

To-day, however, more than thirty years later, this absurd story is again being circulated. The men who blazon abroad these assertions, which have long since been discarded by the most competent of Catholic leaders as being exploded theories, come from nationalist camps and seem to have at their disposal unlimited vocal powers and inexhaustible pecuniary resources. In Germany, France, Italy, Hungary; in fact, everywhere, the same methods are adopted. Since the Revolution, there has, in Germany especially, been constant agitation against the Lodges. Shortly after the end of the War, when reaction against the new internal condition of the Reich began to set in, the word was passed about that the Freemasons, by virtue of their cosmopolitanism, were men who had not the slightest national feeling, that they worked with the direct object of eradicating the national sentiment from the population and that they were, therefore, entirely to blame for the circumstances and happenings complained of by the conservatives. A strange reproach when one considers that it was the Freemasons themselves who awakened the national feeling in Germany's most critical periods; not, it is true, a national feeling in any way related to the fanatical chauvinism which seeks nowadays to pass in many places as patriotism and true love of country.

The Freemasons who did such splendid work in the Prussia

of Frederick the Great, and those who came after them have already been mentioned many times. They were certainly cosmopolites, but, nevertheless, it was precisely amongst these men that the beginnings of the national consciousness, as now understood by the best of us, were to be found. They felt German and acted accordingly at a time when German nationals were being bartered by their princes like cattle; at a time when Prince (afterwards King) Maximilian of Bavaria and the Palatinate could still declare[1] that at every new success of the French arms he felt anew how much he was a Frenchman.[2]

One must really presuppose that those people who, because of their nationalistic views, have thrown down the gauntlet to Freemasonry, are fully conversant with this part of German history, but that they find it convenient to turn a blind eye to it. They are, however, more inclined to regard the patriotism of Fichte, Stein, Blücher and Scharnhorst as doubtful, merely because they were Freemasons.

This kind of campaign against Freemasonry was introduced in the early post-War days by a Viennese, Dr. Friedrich Wichtl, who had belonged to the Reichsrath in the days of the Monarchy and was, in consequence, also a member of the first provisional National Assembly of the new republic. His book *Weltfrei-maurerei, Weltkrieg, Weltrevolution*, which appeared shortly after the revolution, had, thanks to clever advertising propaganda, almost as telling an effect in certain circles as did the fabrications of Taxil in their day. In those days, of course, a 'scapegoat' was necessary, and the 'Freemason' was just the right one. Written without the slightest scruple, this book gave a provocative tone to the war-cries which have since been taken up in the most varied quarters. Not yet did Wichtl direct his attack—as his imitators afterwards did—chiefly against German Masonry.

His object was to 'prove' that Freemasonry—that is to say, also that of Germany—plays a very intimate part in all activities to a revolutionary end and in all political murders, and, in addition to this, he invented another lie that has subsequently appeared in print in so many other writings directed against Freemasonry, namely, that Freemasonry panders to the political ambitions of Jewry.

[1] In a conversation with the French Ambassador in 1799.
[2] Georg Kaufmann. *Geschichte Deutschlands im 19. Jahrhundert*. Berlin. 1912.

In fairness to Wichtl it must be stated that for years he had conscientiously collected reports that referred, or might possibly have referred, to Freemasonry and had filed them in a splendid filing cabinet. This cabinet also contained much that was not masonic, chiefly the names of politicians who had been deeply hated by what were formerly the Central Powers. In this way persons such as Wilson, Poincaré, Lenin, Trotsky, and Clémenceau, who were in no way connected with the Craft, became 'confirmed Freemasons'. Wichtl then gave the filing cabinet a good shake so that everything was jumbled up together, and lo and behold! there was the material for the most grotesque accusations, which, nevertheless, were believed and passed on by countless people. The main point of these accusations was to the effect that Freemasonry has only one ultimate object, namely, the creation of a world republic. Anything that ever happens anywhere to goad on the masses or to incite them to revolt is, he alleges, the work of Freemasons. The conclusion that this world republic is identical with Jewish world domination was not suggested by Wichtl, but it was this thesis of his, to the effect that the Jews play the predominating part in Freemasonry, that supplied the foundation for those who shortly afterwards made the 'discovery'. Let it be here stated that this assertion is ridiculous, and that amongst the four and a half million Freemasons in the world, the Jewish element is very small indeed, for instance, the number in German Freemasonry does not amount to 4 per cent. But the story gained credence, and more and more converts have been gained, until to many people the words Jew, Freemason, and revolutionary are synonymous.

In Wichtl's estimation the Freemasonry of every country, without one exception, is revolutionary. In his view, the French Revolution of 1789, the Republic of 1848, and the third Republic of 1870, were the work of Freemasons. All French radical politicians were Freemasons.

Freemasonry in Italy was naturally revolutionary; from the championship of liberty of the Risorgimento to the leaders in the World War. The murderer of King Humbert II was no doubt a Mason, and in all probability also Luccheni, the murderer of the Empress Elisabeth of Austria. 'For what other reason', asks Wichtl, 'should an anarchist have committed the murder?'

Serbian Freemasonry was, he alleged, revolutionary to the core. Among the assassins of Francis Ferdinand, Grand Duke

EIGHTEENTH-CENTURY MASONIC SONG

MASONIC SONG FROM BICKHAM'S MUSICAL ENTERTAINER

and heir to the throne, Čabrinović was a Freemason. The money for the execution of the assassination was provided by the Freemason Dr. Kazimirović. The plan for the murder had, he alleged, been conceived as early as 1912 by the Grand Orient of France.

In order to convince all those people who did not accept this without question, Wichtl produced his trump card; he cited an authentic source—a source from which, strange as it may seem, the imminent overthrow of the Hohenzollern dynasty had been announced as early as 1910. This was 'a well-known Parisian lady, Madame Savigny, or, as she was known to the public, Madame de Thèbes. . . . A highly fashionable soothsayer, in whose *salons* politicians and diplomats, highly placed personages, and audacious adventurers of all kinds were wont to forgather, and from whose statements and hints she drew the greater part of her prophecies.'

But how were the Freemasons brought into the plot? In the year 1910, (i.e. the year of this great prophecy), Italian, French, and English Freemasons met as the guests of the Grand Orient of France, amongst whom were 'Bro.' Clémenceau and 'Bro.' Poincaré. A war with Germany was discussed in all seriousness. William II, Francis Ferdinand of Austria, and others were to be rendered harmless. The secret plans were not only whispered in the *salon* of Madame de Thèbes, the Freemasons themselves spoke openly about them. 'The heir to the throne is uncommonly eminent; it is unfortunate that he is condemned; he will die on the way to the throne!' exclaimed a 'prominent Freemason from Switzerland'. But who this 'prominent' authority was, and where and to whom he is supposed to have made these nonsensical remarks is naturally not divulged by the wily Wichtl.

Wichtl's political ingenuity even enabled him to characterize English Freemasonry as revolutionary, although he was unable to deny its Conservative tendencies. The explanation is extremely simple. It stirs up revolution in other countries, or 'externally', as he puts it.

'Whenever unrest becomes noticeable in any country, England immediately does her best to encourage it and generously supplies the revolutionaries with money. . . . A revolution without money is even harder to promote to-day than in the past. The first thing revolutionaries require is money, more money, and then still more money. If they are Freemasons, and that is the general rule, for Free-masonry to-day is a kind of mutual indemnity and protection society against arrest and execution, then they have only to put their feet at the right angle and call for the help of their Brethren; the consequences follow with the same regularity and punctuality as a letter entrusted to the post in peace time. . . . There is, in the English Budget, always an item of expenditure of colossal dimensions regarding which no Chancellor of the Exchequer has ever been questioned by a Member of Parliament. This is the celebrated secret account for which five million pounds sterling are voted annually. This vast sum is at the disposal of the "Agitation Department for attaining political aims", under whose care falls the support of revolutionary movements in foreign countries, as well as the arrangements for, and the execution of, political assassinations. The money that was necessary for the assassination of Jaurès, the French Socialist leader, as well as in the case of the Russian Prince Witte, was supplied by this department. From the same source also came the sums that were needed for the murder plots against the King of Bulgaria and Sir Roger Casement and, perhaps, also for the Sarajevo assassination.'

And behind all this are the Freemasons, for

'uprisings and revolts are not counted as crimes in Masonry, and any one who wishes to strike a blow against "tyranny" (Monarchy) may, in certain circumstances, employ repre-hensible means. . . .'

Finally, the 'world-spanning and all-embracing' Freemasonry is also responsible for the fact that Germany and the Danubian Monarchy were opposed in the war, by a world of enemies. The timid question: Does not the 'world-spanning and all-embracing Freemasonry' also include Germany? is ignored by Wichtl. This question was too much even for the crafty pamph-leteer's imagination. However, one of his partisans, Karl Heise, who was no less clever at jumping to conclusions than his master, came to his rescue. Within Freemasonry itself there is, he declared, an international ring, 'which, at the out-break of war, shook itself free from all the purely German Lodges in the whole wide world'.

Why that happened is not explained, especially as Wichtl goes out of his way to state that the German Brethren have always pulled their weight in international political machinations. Relations with French Freemasonry, which had been broken off since the Franco-Prussian War, were resumed by them in 1909. Wichtl describes that as 'undignified', and quite overlooks the fact that by citing this incident he has made a great gap in his whole case. For since 1877 relations between French and English Freemasonry have been broken off, whereas, on the other hand, French and German Freemasons had, since 1909, become fraternally reunited. By what magical means, then, did an Anglo-French ring against Germany spring into being? Such tremendous mistakes in logic were of no importance at all to Wichtl's supporters: they continued to assert that 'Freemasonry seeks to establish a World Republic by means of a World Revolution'. It was of this that they wanted to convince the people; nothing would convince them that they themselves were wrong, and they went on repeating:

'All Freemasonic Congresses have always been dedicated to revolutionary aims. And thus those in the know could fix by the clock the exact moment of the downfall of the two Teutonic dynasties upon whom the Grand Orients the world over had passed sentence of death.'

Although all these assertions must be recognizable as the wildest hallucinations, even to those whose only knowledge of political events is gleaned from the newspapers, Wichtl attained his object. He was not at fault in his estimate of the mentality of his partisans. Just as even educated people believed in the devil worship of the Taxil hoax, many Conservatives accepted the 'Masonic World Revolution' as gospel, which led to a campaign of violence against Freemasonry being started by all sorts of nationalist associations, which was strongly reminiscent of the similar psychosis created by the papal Bulls. From that moment onwards the question of Freemasonry was permanently on the agenda of almost all the officers' associations, students' associations, and defence leagues. And when, finally, there dawned a day which saw grave doubts beginning to be entertained in the ranks of the nationalists also, this was due to the fact that a new warrior had arisen to challenge Freemasonry, one who so exaggerated the swindle that the anti-masonic movement became once again the object of universal ridicule; here again is a parallel with the case of Taxil.

This new warrior was General Ludendorff.

CHAPTER III

THE AARON APRON OF THE JAHVEH [1] BRETHREN

I T has been said of Leo Taxil that he made a crook comedy out of the feud against Freemasonry, but the war which Ludendorff declared on the Royal Art has become a tragic farce—tragic because a great part of the German nation venerated him for a long time as a very important, if not exactly successful, War Lord, who, however, has degraded himself more and more into a figure of ridicule.

He entered the new struggle with the same ruthless energy that we had learned to expect from him during the war. Great was the sensation he caused. It was on one of the most important days in German war history that he sent forth his message:

'To-day, Liège Day, General Ludendorff strikes a devastating blow against Freemasonry, that organization which puts power into the hands of, and upholds, Judah. Whosoever knows the secret forces of this powerful body, which has never drawn the line at murder, also knows that for centuries only fear of their diabolic power has sealed the lips of those who know.

'With one fell swoop General Ludendorff to-day tears the mask from the carefully veiled face of Freemasonry, and ruthlessly exposes the aims and objects, and the undignified usages, of this universal Brotherhood which makes artificial Jews of those of other blood, and which is inimical both to the State and to the person. There can be no shrinking away from the importance of this deed, as would so willingly be done, and the significance of this blow to the history of the world cannot be denied.'

The 'deed' was a brochure entitled *Vernichtung der*

---

[1] JAHVEH (Jehovah) is the most sacred of the names given in the Old Testament to the Supreme Being, regarded also as the God specially of the Jewish people. So holy was the name deemed that the Jews were afraid to allow it to escape their lips and therefore took means intentionally to mispronounce it by altering its vowel points when written. What the real vowel points and consequently the proper pronunciation should be is now doubtful. Many critics contend for YAHVEH, some for YAHVAH and some for YAHAVOH.—(*The Encyclopædic Dictionary*.)

Freimaurerei durch Enthüllung ihrer Geheimnisse [1] ('Destruction of Freemasonry by the Disclosure of its Secrets').   This pamphlet is inspired with a fanatical hatred of the Jews, and seeks to create the impression that the efforts of the last two centuries to combat the Brotherhood have been nothing but piteous sabre rattling, and that the world has been awaiting the advent of a great Liberator like Ludendorff to reveal the true nature of Freemasonry and to strike the death-blow.   'I have discovered the great secret, for which all who came before me have searched without avail,' seems to appear on almost every page of the book, but one encounters only the crassest ignorance and one seeks in vain for any original thought. The brochure is nothing but a hopeless jumble of phrases borrowed from hackneyed 'exposures', served up with the greatest impudence.   One seeks and seeks and seeks, and, finally, one discovers an amazing—bluff:

'The secret of Freemasonry is always the Jew!'   That is what it signified to Ludendorff.   He was well aware that only a small proportion of German Freemasons were Jews, that the Ancient Prussian Lodges, to which three-fourths of all German Masons belonged, were entirely Christian in their constitution, and that, in the long run, it would not be possible to maintain the fiction that such a Freemasonry 'puts power into the hands of Judah', and, for this reason, he elaborated a new theory, which, since that time has become the Alpha and Omega of his campaign, i.e. the theory of the 'artificial Jew'.   The Christian Freemasons may profess their belief in the Gospels a thousand times but, according to Ludendorff, that is only a blind;   they are really Jews, 'artificial Jews'.

For, in his view, every person who joins the Fraternity becomes one.   'All Germans who are initiated into Freemasonry are fettered with Jewish bonds and are lost to Germany for ever';   even the most Christian of them, those of the Grand National Lodge, 'in whose Chapter degrees the "cabalistic rabines", "known as rabbis", or "intermediaries", give instruction.'

Consequently, in Ludendorff's estimation, Freemasonry is

---

[1] During the printing of this book a second part of Ludendorff's brochure *Krieghetze und Völkermorden in den letzten 150 Jahren im Dienste des allmächtigen Baumeisters aller Welten* ('War Propaganda and Mass Murders of the last 150 years in the Service of the Great Architect of the Universe'), has appeared.   Its level may best be judged from the following sentence: 'The Brethren of the Ancient and Accepted Scottish Rite introduced the Charleston dance in order to show that the world dances to their tune.'

nothing but 'a Jewish institution, whose history, degrees, offices, passwords, and instruction are Jewish from beginning to end'.

References to the Bible ('a Jewish Book') which occur in the masonic Ritual, and instances where speculative Masonry has adopted those medieval customs of the operatives that are closely connected with the Old Testament, are cited by Ludendorff to substantiate his thesis. Does not Freemasonry speak of the Temple of Solomon? That signifies nothing less than the setting up of the Kingdom of Judah, that is to say, the betrayal of the German nation and its subjection to the rule of foreigners: 'the Jewish Capitalist Priestly World Monarchy' with headquarters in New York.

'The New Testament was only brought into Freemasonry as a bait, and only in so far as it is consistent with Mosaic-Jewish and Cabalistic views. In this way the Epoch of the "Great and Supreme Architect", the Architect of the Universe or the Cabalistic "Thrice Great Architect of the whole Universe" is prepared, of which even Dr. Stresemann spoke so proudly and happily at the League of Nations Conference in Geneva, which was held under the auspices of Freemasonry. It is the time of Cabalistic Jehova worship in the sense of Noah's laws in respect of the wider Judaization of nations and individual persons.'

Ludendorff is able to tell from afar whether anybody is a Freemason, that is to say, 'a morally and intellectually inferior person', for his activity as a Freemason 'invests him with the dissolute character of an untruthful hypocrite. His face quickly assumes that expression by which non-Masons may recognize a Freemason.'

As soon as this great calumniation of German Freemasonry became known it was at once greeted with strong disapproval in the German Press of all schools of thought. The Freemasons themselves were also up in arms. The Grand Masters of all the nine German Grand Lodges met in a demonstration of protest, and made the following unanimous declaration:

'The undersigned, legal representatives of approximately 80,000 true-German Freemasons, who are loyal to their Fatherland, wish to express on their behalf, their indignation at Herr Erich Ludendorff's insulting them in such a libellous manner in his pamphlet *Vernichtung der Freimaurerei* ('Destruction of Freemasonry') and at his attempts to lower their prestige in the eyes of the German people. At the same time they express their regret that they have lived to see a man of such former greatness and importance as General Ludendorff, stooping to such depths as to inflame the German people and to lead the masses astray. Although the pamphlet is unworthy of reply, since it attributes nothing less than maniacal aims to German Freemasonry and also relies upon the most obscure sources, except where it purposely makes use of unconscionable perversions and unbelievable mis-statements, we reserve to ourselves the right to make an exhaustive and impartial reply for the enlightenment of public opinion.'

Hundreds of leading persons from Lower Saxony, mostly ex-officers addressed the following open letter to Ludendorff:

'Your Excellency in your pamphlet *Vernichtung der Freimaurerei* has declared tens of thousands of German men who belong to the Brotherhood to be morally and intellectually worthless. In so doing you are attempting to dishonour true lovers of their Fatherland who, for the most part, have bled for Germany at your side and under your leadership. We indignantly protest against your entirely unjustified attacks, which, for the most part, are based on the crudest of mis-statements, for we are conscious of having at all times, and without any compulsion and from inner devotion, done our duty both to Freemasonry and to our Fatherland. To refuse to such men esteem and trust, which are the foundations of every civilized community, is an offence against the Fatherland "in the hour of Germany's direst need".

'A great Prussian War Lord, Field-Marshal Blücher, on being faced with similar calumniations, after more than thirty years of leading activity in our Brotherhood, once declared: "I am well acquainted with these persecutors, and know full well that many would like to exterminate us, but we have nothing to fear and the piteous attempts to calumniate us will not achieve their evil purpose. Truth and Virtue are the fundamental pillars of our Brotherhood, and our Temple stands firm in the opinion of all good men, through the patience, courage, and stoical indifference of the Brethren." We agree with him from the bottom of our hearts.'

Ludendorff replied with a scurrilious attack on Blücher, in which he alleged that the latter had not kept his oath of allegiance to the King. At the same time the General announced the imminent publication of further disclosures, not having dared previously to make known the whole terrible truth.

First of all, however, he travelled to East Prussia in order to take part in the unveiling of the Tannenberg Monument by Hindenburg. At this ceremony he made an amazing discovery:

'The astonished eye beheld on the battle-field a structure erected strictly in accordance with the rules of Jehovah, the sacred masonic symbol. In the interior, in the 'Court of Honour', was a great cube, before which, during the ceremony, the President removed his helmet in an act of homage. For four long hours I witnessed a scene of amazing mockery in which our race was derided by the Chosen People and its horde of Levite priests, the Freemasons. I also gazed with astonishment at the ten swords affixed to the front of the entrance-arch of the Court of Honour, the ten swords representing the Jewish Cabalistic Tree, the most sacred symbol of the Jewish masonic domination of the world, with its three pillars strictly in accordance with the rules of the Cabala.'

That was the end of all restraint. The last shred of the veil must now, 'of necessity and with inner repugnance', be removed, and 'the secret of the Ritual mercilessly described by its proper name'. The secret of the Ritual, which would even convince the sceptical of the out-and-out Judaization of Freemasonry!

'The apron of the Freemasons is not the apron of the Masons of the medieval Lodges, but the apron of the vestments of the Jewish High Priests. . . .

'The Mason is clothed as a Jahveh priest, with the Apron of Aaron and the Levite's Hat. The apron represents "the essence of Freemasonry". The masonic people is to consist of Jahveh priests, who, themselves nationless, are spreading over the earth as an appendage to the Jewish race, carrying out everywhere their secret "missions".

'Such an appendage is also formed by the expatriated Freemasons of German blood, being sons of Noah or sons of the widow of the tribe of Naphtali, the Jewish tribe which, according to biblical tradition, made camp to the extreme north of the Tabernacle . . . and was thus called upon to enslave the northern peoples, that is to say, to alienate them from their own nations and to rob them of their pride and trust in God.

' "Whosoever is born of a Jewess is a Jew," said the Rabbi Unna, and that requires of the Freemason not only superficial Levitical Priestdom, it calls also for the symbolical act of circumcision. The imperfect northern man is the rough ashlar of the masonic Ritual. . . . The Royal Art of Freemasonry makes him into a perfect cube, known to orthodox Jews as the "perfect" ashlar.

'In order to be able clearly to understand the Freemasonic Ritual in this connexion, I must describe the Jewish Ritual of the Miloh (circumcision), which is so repulsive to German ideas.

'After entering the Synagogue, the Mohel (the circumciser) takes the child, greeting it with the words: "Baruch habbo", which means, "Blessed is he who comes". He carries it to the stool of Elijah and lays it in the lap of the Godfather, grasps the foreskin of the male member, and cuts a small piece from it with a pair of scissors, which particle is afterwards burned, and tears the rest of the foreskin with the nails—which is the most important part of the Jewish circumcision, known as Prio—and he then fills his mouth with wine, sucks the blood from the wounded member and spits the mixture of wine and blood from his mouth into a chalice. . . .

'The Prio ceremony is of particular importance to the Jews. Other races and secret societies having circumcision as ritual, as, for instance, the secret societies of the Papuans, know nothing of the Prio, the tearing with the nails, and are only acquainted with the cutting. Father Abraham, who, according to the Talmud, sits at the Gates of Hell and closely inspects every new-comer, recognizes from the Prio the properly circumcised, that is to say, a Jewish co-racial and rescues him, but never an impostor, from the fiery torments of Hell.

'That is the Jewish Ritual of the circumcision.

'And the following is the symbolic Ritual of the Freemasons:

'In order that the important ceremony of the Prio may also be applied to the artificial Jews, i.e. the Freemasons, the unlined leathern apron of the first two degrees has another important symbolic meaning . . . "the symbol of the flesh".

'At the raising of the fellowcraft to the Master Mason's degree, "the apron is swiftly and abruptly torn" from the candidate. This tearing off of the apron in the third degree corresponds to the circumcision, the tearing, the Prio.

'The Freemason, thus circumcised, then receives as Master Mason, an apron lined with silk and decorated with gold, in place of the purely leathern apron of the apprentice.

'Blue and gold are the colours of Heaven, the robe of Jehovah. . . . The Freemason is now a perfect Jehovah Priest, having acquired citizenship of the Heaven of Jehovah.'

That was Ludendorff's 'secret'. Needless to say, no sane person took him seriously. But when, in spite of this, Ludendorff's friends sought to win President Hindenburg over to the view of his old Chief of the General Staff, Hindenburg replied:

'I know quite well what I am to think of Freemasonry. My grandfathers were Freemasons, and they would certainly never have belonged to an association whose aim was to place the world under the domination of the Jews!'

But universal disapproval made not the slightest difference to Ludendorff. He cheerfully continued his fight against 'the Freemasons, Jesuits, and Jews', in his periodical *Die Deutsche Wochenschau*, on lecturing tours throughout Germany and in innumerable assemblies. No impartial refutation was able to divert him from his course; not even the established fact that nowhere in the Old Testament is mention made of an 'Aaron apron', nor of an apron of the Jewish priests, nor even the evidence of certain learned students of Hamburg to the effect that the 'Protocols of the Wise Men of Zion', which were so often quoted by Ludendorff's supporters, and are supposed to contain the exact plans for the constitution of the Freemasonic-Jewish control of the world, are nothing less than uncommonly impudent forgeries, collected together from an old French satire against Napoleon III and a blood-curdling sensational novel.

'Having occupied the position of leader during the World War, I am now acting in a similar capacity against the masonic pest, and I do not rate this fight any less important than the struggles of the World War.' [1]

That is Ludendorff's watchword.

[1] From a letter to the Association of German Students.

However, as the many prominent Freemasons who made both private and public protest against him included also a goodly number of Protestant ministers, he withdrew from the Evangelical Church.

'A Church which harbours, generally, the Freemasonic immorality, has just as much ceased to be a Church as that which surrenders itself to Jesuitism. . . . Is there a more deplorable picture than that of innumerable Protestant ministers of German blood wearing the Aaron apron and practising the ritual of the symbolical circumcision, or that of many Protestant clergy of Jewish blood, who did indeed, as children, undergo the Jewish rite of circumcision? . . .'

But neither this withdrawal, nor his 'complete truth', roused to any great extent the masses which the General sought to nauseate. He therefore entered upon new investigation, faithfully assisted, both verbally and in writing, by his wife, whose untiring studies produced a fresh harvest of fruits every week. Here are some of the most important:

The 'Lodge Brother' Melanchthon stole Luther's seal, 'Petschaft und Gemerk', in order to prove that the great Reformer had presided over the Jewish-Cabalistic and secret Order of the Rosicrucians.

The Freemason Lessing, who 'overstepped the circle', died an unnatural 'Lodge death'.

Mozart, whose 'Magic Flute' is generally accepted as the most brilliant glorification of Freemasonry, also wove into his work an anti-masonic fundamental theme and, in consequence, was poisoned.

'But in order that suspicion might not fall on the Lodge, they let him compose one more Lodge cantata. What was ostensibly a new act of masonic love then followed—"his hands and feet became swollen, coupled with sudden vomiting". Death ensued a few days later, on Jahveh Day 1791. Mozart himself often said that he had been poisoned, and knew that the fact that he had been commissioned to compose the Requiem was a sign of the imminent execution of the judgment passed by the Lodge. . . .'

Schiller, who, since he did not belong to the Fraternity, 'stood in the way of the invisible Fathers', and upon whom Goethe unavailingly attempted the 'polishing of the Ashlar', fell to the vengeance of the Order. His death took place 'at the right time'. 'The Cheka of the international secret Order took Schiller in the bloom of life. . . . He was murdered.'

And Goethe made himself a party to the crime by his 'mysterious lack of sympathy' at the 'criminal's funeral' that fell to Schiller's lot, and 'by his cowardice in bowing to the secret orders'. 'Bro. Goethe, whose shameful betrayal of Schiller makes him no longer fit to rank with inspired men!' [1] Ludendorff's wife explains all these horrible deeds as being possible by the discovery she herself has made, namely:

'Jews, Jesuits, and Freemasons, are children of the moon. They show only one side and turn the other, which is very different, away from the public gaze.'

From which it becomes clear

'that all campaigns carried on against these moon natures not supported by a sufficient knowledge of the reverse side, can be nothing more than futile baying at the moon'.

Now, however, the moon natures have been revolved on a potter's wheel by the historic endeavours of the Ludendorffs, so that their reverse side has gradually become visible. This gives new courage—courage which manifests itself strikingly in the following call of the Field-Marshal's wife:

'Come to the wheel whose name is Enlightenment! Turn untiringly, but not too hastily, nor too abruptly, so that it does not shimmer before the eyes of the German people; turn it slowly and steadily so that the people may see it clearly; as clearly as the face of the moon. This reverse side must be shown to all before the fight, for through it Jew, Jesuit, and Freemason will become, in the future, fantastic things of the past, for moon natures can only deceive and rule so long as they succeed in avoiding the potter's wheel.'

However, in the face of all this nonsense, it did shimmer before the eyes of the German people, but the moon natures were not to blame; the Ludendorffs turned the wheel a little too violently.

---

[1] In the latest publications of the Ludendorff circle, Goethe is even called the 'mute dog' and the 'living corpse of Weimar'.

CHAPTER IV

WOMEN AND FREEMASONRY

WHEN in the past the enemies of Freemasonry were discussed, women, strange as it may seem, were often included amongst them. In many places, and especially in France during the eighteenth century, the dislike in which women held the Brotherhood made itself very clearly felt at times. The reasons for this antagonistic attitude are not difficult to find: In the first place, women were only too readily inclined to see in Freemasonry all the evil attributed to it by the Church, and in the second place, Freemasonry has from the very beginning always been a society for men, and women have, on principle, been barred from admission. This is not intended to express any lack of respect; indeed, as has already been mentioned, it is the custom in some Continental Lodges to think affectionately of the women, who are termed Sisters, at the most solemn moment of the ceremony, that is to say, at the time of incorporating a new link in the chain, and to hand the Neophyte white gloves 'for the woman nearest his heart'.

This is not the place to discuss the question as to why Anderson, in his *Antient Charges*, expressly barred women from admission into the Society and why there has been no subsequent change. In any case, Anderson only followed the principles of the ancient operatives, to whose gilds members of the female sex were in no circumstances admitted. Only one member of the fair sex has ever been accorded a share of homage from the gild, namely, the Queen of Sheba. The inclusion of her effigy in the rows of statues on German cathedrals, especially since it generally occurs in conjunction with that of King Solomon, can be no accident. The gild honoured her as a person belonging to the legendary figures connected with the building of the Temple. But it adhered rigidly to its principle as regards all other women, even in the case of Queen Elizabeth of England. Anderson could not resist incorporating the following sentence in the historical preamble to the *Antient Charges:* 'Queen Elizabeth, who was so well-educated and magnanimous, and who favoured all the other arts, was not graciously disposed towards Freemasonry; merely because she, as a woman, could not become a Mason.' And another contemporary, Charles Johnson, wrote the following in 1723:

'Unfortunately an eminent princess could not be admitted because of her sex. Her curiosity was thus aroused and this was perhaps the only occasion during her long reign on which the woman gained ascendancy over the queen.'[1]

It may also be that similar motives gave rise to Maria Theresa's celebrated order for the suppression of the 'Three Canons' Lodge. There was, in fact, a widely-circulated story in Vienna in the eighteenth century that she had on one occasion attended a meeting of a Viennese Lodge clothed as a man.

In any case, complaints regarding the exclusion of women from the activities of the Lodges very soon made themselves heard. The newspapers of the eighteenth century give us a good idea of these. In January 1733, the *Vossische Zeitung* reported from Great Britain:[2]

'. . . The secret [of the Freemasons] is revealed to the members of the society on admission; but they must, at the same time, bind themselves by a strong oath to disclose it to no one, so that when a certain princess, wishing very much to learn this secret, persuaded a certain well-born gentleman to betake himself amongst the Freemasons and subsequently desired him to reveal the secret, he was constrained to refuse her request.'

In 1737, a Paris correspondent of the same newspaper believed that it would soon be 'all up' with the Freemasons in France.

'The women are giving vent to their jealous envy because the male sex has excluded them from the secrets of their Brotherhood. . . .'

The women of Berne were even able to stir up the Government against the Order.

'In spite of their caresses, wiles, and artifices,' says a contemporary book, 'the wives of Freemasons were, to their great annoyance, never able to fathom the pretentious secret of the Freemasons.'

---

[1] Dr. Oskar Posner: *Wiener Freimaurer-Zeitung*, No. 9/10. 1923.
[2] Eberhard Buchner: *Das Neueste von Gestern*. Munich.

THE HON. MRS. ELIZABETH ALDWORTH
THE LADY FREEMASON

ADMITTANCE TO THE ORDER OF THE MOPSES

There was vexation also in Germany. In 1785, in his *Teutschen Merkur*, Wieland gave an essay on this theme, in which he said, 'The hearts of Freemasons are certainly open to women, but the Lodges are closed to them.' And Goethe also contributed his quota. On the occasion of a Ladies' Night of the 'Amalia' Lodge, when his son August was called upon to reply on behalf of the ladies, he directed him to poke sly fun by putting the following question:

> 'Sollen aber wir, die Frauen,
> Dankbar solche Brüder preisen,
> Die ins Innere zu schauen
> Immer uns zur Seite weisen?'

The gist of which was: Are we women expected to express our grateful appreciation of Brethren who cast us aside for the sake of Freemasonry? Masonic widows, as it were!

Herder, in his masonic discourse, attempted to give an answer to this question, which, to this very day, crops up again and again. He makes Linda (his wife Karoline), say to Faust (Herder himself):

'A man requires a tonic, and we willingly grant it him. Now and again he must expand, he must stretch his wings, so that he may live as a man amongst men, otherwise, even with the greatest care and love, he will become common-place even to us.—Do not take it amiss my friends: as a sex you are too narrow-minded, your outlook is too limited and you tire too quickly of your bonds. You often sink beneath their gentle but constant weight and grow old, prematurely old, through habits you do not wish to alter. Prejudice surrounds us perhaps more easily than you; but to you it is more fixed and oppressive. With our greater elasticity and freedom of spirit we are born Freemasons for the building up and continuation of humanity.—What great and beautiful thought did Socrates have that was not inspired by Aspasia?'

Herder answers:

'And yet, in spite of your great ideas, you do not belong in that closed rectangle of council and work. Does not your imagination too often run away with you? Are you not always carried away by your kind impulses? You are too energetic, too merciful; the moment overwhelms you. With one tremendous effort you would try and help the whole of humanity and thus spoil everything. For this very reason your place is not in that chamber of calm and dispassionate deliberation and work.'

Even at a time when their emancipation had made very little progress this answer did not satisfy many women. Many of them only too willingly lent a hand when it was a question of fighting Freemasonry or of profaning its secret. Many of them endeavoured, in spite of all restrictions, to get into Lodges. In some cases they were even successful. The first female Freemason is said to have been Mrs. Elizabeth Aldworth, daughter of Viscount Doneraile, who held Lodge meetings at his seat in Ireland. She is supposed to have been a witness at a meeting and to have been initiated in order to ensure her silence. The same story is related also of other women. It is an established fact that, under the French Consulate, the wife of General Xaintrailles, who was made a captain of cavalry by Napoleon, and acted as adjutant to her husband, appeared at a meeting of the 'Les Artistes' Lodge in Paris, and that Countess Helene Hadik-Barkoczy was admitted into a Hungarian Lodge in 1877. On the death of her father (the last male heir of the Barkoczy family) the Countess was substituted as a son and thereby regarded as a man under the civil law. The study of masonic literature had inspired this gifted woman[1] with a desire to become a member of the Order, and the Lodge in Ungvar acceded to her request in spite of the objection of the Grand Orient of Hungary, who declared the admission to be invalid.

Such initiations were very rare, however. But in order to cater for the wishes of the women, societies similar to Freemasonry were specially created in the eighteenth century. There arose, in France, the Order of the Knights and Nymphs of the Rose, the Society of the Companions of Penelope, the Order of Felicity, the Order of Woodcutters, and the Order of the Anchor, etc. All these more or less secret societies were open to both men and women. The meeting-places were called 'groves', 'retreats', or 'temples of love', and the women members were known as 'lady friends' or 'cousins'. Many of these societies, which naturally had nothing to do with Freemasonry were founded to create a diversion for great men, such as the

---

[1] She was the wife of Count Bela Hadik, Adjutant-General to the Archduke Max, subsequently King of Mexico.

CHINA FIGURES
RELATING TO THE ORDER OF THE MOPSES

THE THREE PHILOSOPHERS
From the Painting by Giorgione in the Art-History Museum, Vienna

Duke of Chartres, to whom the earnestness and dignity of the masonic Lodges became a little wearisome after a while.

This degeneration also strayed over to Germany, and, under the patronage of the gallant ecclesiastical Elector, Klemens August of Cologne, the 'Mopsorden' ('Order of Pugdogs') was formed. The members, male and female, had to be Roman Catholics, and they carried as emblems tiny pugdogs of porcelain. The customs of this 'Order', which was chiefly to be found at the small German Courts, were extremely nonsensical; every vestige of profound ethical significance was lacking. The emblem of the society was the 'pugdog', the symbol of Fidelity in the Order, and the circle of each Lodge, according to the Ritual, taught the members: 'that just as every cross section of a circle must pass through one and the same centre, so must all the actions of a "Pug" spring from the same source, i.e. Love'.

The 'Mops' Order, which arose shortly after the appearance of the first Papal Bull, consisted chiefly of members of Court circles, who wished to have nothing to do with Freemasonry, such as members of the anti-masonic society of the pietistic Count Heinrich XII von Reuss-Schleiz. On the other hand, what was known as 'Adoption' Masonry, had some connexion with isolated Lodges and was intended for both men and women. This emanated from France. It had its own ritual, which, however, was in no way connected with that of Freemasonry. This ritual was based on the story of the Creation, and the activities of 'mixed Freemasonry' were staged with the Garden of Eden as a background. It was a matter, as a well-known contemporary masonic author, Baron de Tschoudy, expressed it, of a 'pleasant bagatelle', which pandered to the wishes of the great ladies of the Court and satisfied the curiosity of all the various duchesses, princesses, countesses, and other ladies of rank. The first Grand Mistress was the Duchess de Bourbon, who was succeeded in the chair by Princess Lamballe. The Duchesse de Chartres and Mme Helvetius the gifted wife of the philosopher, were also prominent in 'Adoption' Masonry. 'Everybody participates,' wrote Queen Marie Antoinette on the 26th January 1781. They were happy in the thought that they were thus doing the same things as the men. How great was this desire is best illustrated by the fact that quite a number of the theatrical pieces of that period dealt with the question of why women were not admitted into Freemasonry. In most of these plays, as, for instance, 'Franc-Maçons' by

Pointinet, and 'Les femmes curieuses ou les francs-maçons' by Castaing, the women were finally able to open the magic doors.[1] That their curiosity seemed insatiable is illustrated by Meusnier de Querlon's charming novel entitled *Les soupers de Daphne*, which described the idea of a strike of young married ladies who wished at any cost to see their husbands' 'secret' betrayed. The 'Garden of Eden' produced for them, consoled them to some extent, especially as the women's Lodges were invested with much pomp and great splendour. The most celebrated artists attended. Learned and artistic lectures were held, concerts were arranged, prizes were offered, medals for meritorious acts of philanthropy were created, and charity meetings were convened. Charming songs were sung, as for instance:

> Amour! ne cherche plus ta mère
> Aux champs de Gnide ou de Paphos.
> Vénus abandonne Cythère
> Pour prendre part à nos travaux.

A brilliant ball always concluded the evening.

However the 'Adoption' Lodges were not very long-lived, although they were revived after the Revolution, and it is said on good authority that the Empress Josephine, Napoleon's wife, visited the 'Adoption' Lodge 'Les Francs Chevaliers' in Strasburg. But the frivolity gradually died out. In recent times the Grand Lodge of France has again created two 'Adoption' Lodges, which are, however, very different indeed to those of the eighteenth century. These two Lodges are associations in which women are trained for collaboration in the ethical tasks confronting mankind. With Freemasonry, as such, there is no connexion whatsoever.

The so-called 'Co-Masonry' of the Grand Lodge 'Droit humain', which arose through Maria Deraismes, the advocate of women's rights, becoming a member of a clandestine Lodge in Pequ in France in 1881, has also absolutely no connexion with Freemasonry, as such. After her admission Senator Georges Martin advocated the idea of admitting women generally, and as he did not succeed, he formed a 'mixed Order' which took the name of 'Droit humain'. This was recruited in a number of countries, principally amongst the Theosophists. Its spiritual head was the leader of the Theosophists, the late Mrs. Annie Besant.

[1] Albert Lantoine: *Hiram couronné d'épines*. Paris. 1926.

PART IV

MASONIC INTERNATIONALISM

CHAPTER I

THE BEGINNINGS OF AN INTERNATIONAL ORGANIZATION

ALTHOUGH the incorrigible opponents of Freemasonry are united in their assertions that Masonry is a secret society, with ramifications all over the world, whose members obey the orders of the headquarters with amazing alacrity, opinions as to the composition of this 'government' are very divided. The most popular theory is that of the 'unknown rulers', and this 'secret governing body' has been described by the 'initiated' in a thousand different ways. Only possessors of the highest masonic degree, the mysterious members of the 'thirty-third degree', are supposed to have seat and vote in this governing body, and the brethren of the lower degrees have naturally no idea of who really issues the orders they execute so blindly.

How fertile is the imagination in this respect is illustrated by a work entitled *Freemasons' Pyramid*, published by Professor Gregor Schwartz-Bostunitsch,[1] a Russian. Above the thirty-third degree there were supposed to be further invisible degrees, all of which were subservient to the 'Alliance Israélite Universelle', at the head of which was the 'Council of Seven' guarding the throne of the 'Patriarch', the 'Uncrowned King of the World'.

So long as General Albert Pike was at the head of the Scottish Rite in Washington he was regarded as Taxil's 'Pope of the Devil', the supreme ruler of Freemasonry. Subsequently, the Palazzo Giustiniani in Rome was said to be the headquarters of the invisible rulers. Recently, however, many people have gained the impression that the masonic headquarters are to be found at the Grand Orient in the rue Cadet in Paris; many suggest even London or New York, and state that American Freemasons send immense sums annually to their European brethren in order to give their political machinations the necessary financial backing.

This suggestion is made principally by those people who do

---

[1] *Die Freimaurerei, ihr Ursprung, ihre Geheimnisse, ihr Wirken.* Weimar: Duncker. 1928.

not believe altogether in the 'unknown rulers', and who know that nowadays great organizations can no longer carry on a secret existence, and, therefore, declare oracularly that one of the masonic Grand Lodges issues the decisive orders. Sometimes it is the Grand Orient of France, sometimes the Grand Lodge of New York, sometimes the Scottish Rite in Washington, and sometimes even the Grand Lodge of England, that holds the reins of world politics.

When a Masonic Congress was held in Vienna a short while ago, a nationalist newspaper reported it to its readers under the caption: 'Whilst in Paris the Apprentices and Fellow-Crafts are signing the Kellogg Pact, the Masters, the controllers of world events, are assembling in Vienna'. It went on to state that Freemasons are not necessarily serving the idea of the World Republic or the Jewish domination of the world, or even the anti-Church. There are other and nearer aims to be achieved, such as the furtherance of English Imperialism. For instance, the French author Leonce Juge, is taking great pains to prove that the formula of the symbolic Temple, the erection of which results from the perfection of humanity, is always understood by Freemasons to be merely a parable to be interpreted in the sense 'that it signifies the setting up of Anglo-Saxon sovereignty over the widest possible surface of the world', which leads him to the conclusion that 'Catholicism has its Pope in Rome; Freemasonry its Pope in London. . . .'

Such a view is naturally strengthened by the overwhelming predominance of the Anglo-Saxon element in Freemasonry:

'The Anglo Saxons are the masters of the world organization. If there is a masonic policy, this can, in the circumstances, only be Anglo-Saxon.'

But what is the real state of affairs? There exists, as we have repeatedly said, neither a supreme board of control of Freemasonry, nor even a strong international organization. The idea of Brotherhood is, to be sure, common to all Grand Lodges, but up to the moment, it has, for a variety of reasons, not been possible to exploit it in such a way as to organize a universal league of Grand Lodges, or even an international masonic union embracing the majority of them, although there has certainly been no dearth of attempts to realize the idea of a world-spanning fraternal chain: not, however, a fraternal

FRONTISPIECE TO THE 'CONSTITUTION OF 1784'
Engraving by Bartolozzi after Cipriani

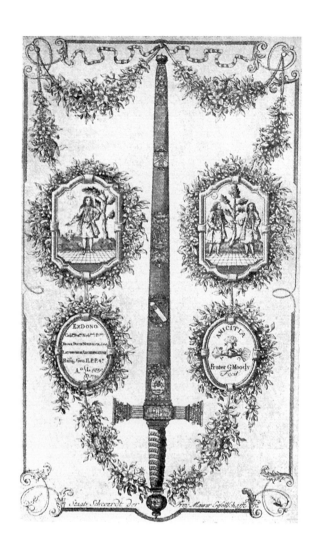

THE SWORD OF STATE OF THE GRAND LODGE OF ENGLAND
From an eighteenth-century German Engraving

chain aiming at securing political power, but a magnificent organization for the preservation of peace.

It is a peculiar fact that a goodly number of organizations which have been founded on the lines of Freemasonry have the very form that is generally attributed to Freemasonry itself. The mother society directs the groups springing from it in accordance with the most exact basic principles. But this is not so in the case of Freemasonry. Since its foundation, the Grand Lodge of England has never taken the initiative in advocating common action by all masonic Lodges, nor has it even issued any form of instructions. In no way does it regard itself as a central organization, and it is only authoritative in so far as Grand Lodges recognized by it are absolutely 'just, perfect, and regular'. But this does not mean that only Grand Lodges recognized by the Grand Lodge of England are to be considered regular.

The 'question of recognition' is one of the most delicate problems in masonic life. That no comprehensive Masonic International exists is mainly due to the fact that many of the masonic Obediences do not recognize one another; that is to say, they are not in touch with one another. The Grand Lodge of England is particularly strict. At the end of the 'seventies of the last century it broke off relations with the Grand Orient of France, as every reader knows. The alteration made at that time in the Constitutions of the Grand Orient of France created an effective bar to 'universal Freemasonry', for the Grand Lodge of England, and with it the greater number of the Anglo-Saxon Grand Lodges, has not only carried the breach to the logical conclusion of stopping all intercourse with the Grand Orient of France, but it will in no circumstances enter into anything that has the slightest savour of an association with the 'atheistic' Grand Orient of France.

But besides this there are other considerations. After the Franco-German War of 1870–1871, relations between French and German Freemasonry were also at an end, and, as is well known, decades passed before friendly relations were resumed. The efforts of all those people who, before the World War, were working for the creation of a Masonic International, were chiefly directed towards bringing French and German Freemasonry into closer touch with one another, and it was no easy matter. There were, it is true, a number of assemblies at which the masonic desire for the common weal was demonstrated, but, for the most part, these were demonstrations by individuals.[1] The Grand Lodges held themselves aloof.

After the war, when the conviction grew in masonic circles that the Spirit of Peace should be made to spread over devastated Europe, and that it was the avowed duty of Freemasonry to work for an understanding between the peoples of the various nations, there was undoubtedly no lack of people who took up the work seriously, and did great things. But the endeavours to create an organization under the auspices of Freemasonry itself had but scanty results, and the same remark applies at this very moment.

In recent years much has been written about the 'Association Maçonnique Internationale', which is, at least, an honest attempt to unite Freemasonry internationally in an organized form. This association, known briefly as the A.M.I., was founded in 1921 and, at first, was in the nature of an extension of the 'International Masonic Bureau' which was founded before the World War by Quartier-la-Tente, who devoted his whole life to the idea of Freemasonry Universal. But in spite of the fact that Quartier-la-Tente did all in his power to give to his 'International Masonic Bureau' that significance which its name implied, for the reasons cited above, he made very little progress, and was happy to make his institution the centre of the manifestations to which we have just referred. He also supplied much of the initiative that led to the creation of the A.M.I., but it had hardly come into being before it was beset with tremendous difficulties. It was not easy to find common ground, as the Grand Lodge of New York participated in its formation solely on the understanding that it would only contribute to the new work if the Anglo-Saxon, and not the French, conception of the principles of Freemasonry was adopted.

Optimists had naturally seen the dawn of a new epoch in the incipient collaboration of Latin and American Freemasons. They hoped that it would very soon be possible to bring German Freemasonry into the new Association, which elected as its first Chairman M. Reverchon, and then M. Magnette, Vice-President (now President) of the Belgian Senate. But even before any work in this direction could be performed, the

---

[1] On the German side, Dr. Kraft, at that time Professor at Strasburg University, and Ludwig Bangel in Frankfort-on-Main, devoted themselves in particular to this work of reconciliation; on the French side, Charles Bernardin performed untiring work to the same end in Nancy.

Grand Lodge of New York withdrew from the Association, only to be followed in 1925 by the Grand Orient of Holland.

Quartier-la-Tente died that year and the Chancellor's office passed to his countryman, Professor Reverchon of Geneva, formerly Grand Master of the Swiss Grand Lodge 'Alpina', and the Belgian, M. Gottschalk. They directed their attentions to persuading the Grand Orient of Holland, which might be regarded as a bridge to Anglo-Saxon Freemasonry, to rejoin the A.M.I. This actually took place in 1927, when a promise was given that the Association would adopt principles which would also make it possible for those Freemasons whose whole conception of Freemasonry was bound up in spiritual ideas to render faithful services under the auspices of the A.M.I.

A new declaration of principles, as a possible compromise between the diverging points of view, was proposed. The most important points of this were the following:

1. Freemasonry is a spiritual movement in which there is room for the various schools of thought and conviction and the object of which is to uplift mankind both in a material and in an ethical sense.
2. Freemasonry, as well as the Obediences constituting it, is not the organ of any political or social party; Freemasonry can, however, study in an impartial manner all problems concerning mankind with a view to inculcating a more fraternal spirit.
3. Freemasonry recognizes the existence of a higher and ideal principle that is generally known under the designation, 'The Great Architect of the Universe'; it combats no particular religious creed, nor does it advocate any particular creed.

Of these points the third, of course, caused the most trouble, and it became the subject of heated debates at the Paris Convention of the A.M.I. in December 1927. The Grand Orient of France declared again on this occasion that it could not deviate from its point of view. But when it came to the vote, the Dutch principles were adopted by seventeen votes to two (the Grand Orient of Luxemburg voting with the Grand Orient of France). However, as these principles had not been adopted unanimously, the Grand Orient of Holland declared that it was not satisfied, and a few days after the Convention—to be exact, on the 31st December 1927—it again withdrew from the

A.M.I., which was reduced once more to a mere skeleton from which great things are not to be expected.

And yet it is said that the A.M.I. is highly political in its activities. Various 'outward signs' have contributed to this theory, chief amongst which must be counted the magnificent peace demonstration in Belgrade in 1926, which brought together delegates from all the Grand Lodges affiliated to the A.M.I., the enthusiastic young Grand Lodge of Yugoslavia having expressed the wish that the very spot where hostilities first started, and where the first shot signalled the opening of the ghastly World War, should be the scene of an impressive peace demonstration. Peace was to be the sole topic of discussion throughout the meeting, and actually, nothing else was discussed. A strong desire for peace was expressed at all the sessions and a resolution advocating pacific ideals was passed, whilst the Great Hall of the University was the scene of an impressive gathering where masonic ideas and ideals were elaborated and where expression was given to the ardent desire for peace which springs from them.

The resolution, which was published for all the world to see, was worded as follows:

'The Freemasons of 18 nations, of which 16 are European, who have assembled in Belgrade under the auspices of the A.M.I., congratulate the Yugoslavian Grand Lodge on the creation of the necessary atmosphere of affection and sincerity amongst the brethren whose only wish is to work for the future. The Assembly expresses the heartfelt desire that democratic and liberal ideas, which alone ensure justice and mutual respect, will become the predominating elements in the international intercourse of the emancipated nations who are united in the endeavour to render impossible a recurrence of the catastrophes of war which are such a disgrace to the civilized world. The Assembly hopes that to achieve this object, for which the whole of mankind yearns, Freemasonry, imbued with a passionate desire for peace, will leave no stone unturned to attain the adjustment of quarrels solely by means of arbitration. The Assembly expresses its best wishes for the endeavours being made by the League of Nations in this direction, as well as for the pacts which aim at the restriction of armaments until they may one day be entirely dispensed with.

'It seems, however, that the chief conflicts develop in the

sphere of commerce. The solution should only be sought by peaceful means. They can, to a very large extent, be avoided by thorough investigation and sagacious foresight. The Assembly is of the opinion that, on the initiative of each national Freemasonry and in complete agreement with the A.M.I., committees should be created whose task would be to seek likely ways and means of peaceably disposing of economic strife.'

This was the result of the Belgrade Assembly, but the echoes which reverberated suggested that the manifestation had been nothing less than a large-scale meeting of conspirators against Italy. For week upon week 'details' were given in Italian newspapers of the 'resolutions passed in secret conclave,' and much was said of the very close relations of Yugoslavian Freemasons, the 'murderers of Francis Ferdinand', and the chauvinistic 'White Hand', and even to-day one can read in a certain section of the Press that Belgrade had but one object: the preparation of the coming war against Italy.

Furthermore, it is said that even if Belgrade cannot be regarded as proof of the political aspirations of the A.M.I., then surely they are made plain by the fact that its headquarters are to be found at Geneva, the home of its third Grand Chancellor, John Mossaz, the successor of Reverchon, who died in 1927, and who was also a native of Geneva. That shows quite unmistakably that the leader of the A.M.I., is the man who receives all the secret instructions for the League of Nations.

'In order,' wrote Mgr. Jouin in the *R.J.S.S.*, 'to open the eyes of those people who are still in doubt as to the connexion between Freemasonry, Zionism, the Spartacus movement, Communism, and Bolshevism, we remind them that the League of Nations will hoist the blue and white flag of Judaism. Horizontal stripes, the lower one white, the middle one blue; that will be the proud banner of all nations groaning under the Jewish yoke.'

CHAPTER II

FREEMASONRY AND THE LEAGUE OF NATIONS

ON the very day when the League of Nations met for the first time in the Reformation Chamber, it was reported 'from reliable sources' that all that was going on in Geneva could be blamed on the Freemasons. Hitherto people had only been able to make very hazy suggestions as to how the national leaders were influenced by the 'central board of control'; now, however, they had merely to point, with a triumphant gesture, to Geneva. 'The Central Bureau of Freemasonry commands and Briand, Chamberlain, and Benesch obey.' This refrain recurred with a thousand variations. The fact that on one occasion Albert Thomas, the Director of the International Labour Office attached to the League of Nations, like so many other members of the Congress, informed the participators in one of the A.M.I., Conventions of the setting up of his institution, and also the declaration which Valot, the French publicist, made in a Viennese Lodge to the effect that it was proposed to form a circle in Geneva for those Freemasons regularly attending the sessions there, in order to facilitate friendly discussion, were sufficient proof for the opponents of Freemasonry of the masonic dominance of the League of Nations, of the incessant machinations of the Chancellor of the A.M.I., and of the influencing of ministers, delegates, chairmen of committees, and members of the League secretariat by emissaries of the 'unknown rulers' specially sent for this purpose to reside in Calvin's own city. But when Germany entered the League of Nations and Stresemann made reference to the Great Architect of the Universe in one of his great speeches, there was then no end to the volley of abuse. The lie was circulated—and believed—that 'the Reichminister for Foreign Affairs had given the secret sign of the Freemasons', and the public were firmly convinced that the *salons* of all the leading delegates were connected by a private telephone line with the rue Bovy-Lysberg, where the Lodges of Geneva have their home.

An important point was overlooked, however—and that

the most important of all—namely, the circumstance that although the League of Nations may perhaps have sprung from the idea of a Freemason, it was without a doubt strongly advocated by members of the Fraternity whilst the World War was still raging. From the 28th to the 30th June 1917 a masonic congress was held in Paris at which representatives of allied or neutral Grand Lodges discussed thoroughly the idea of a League of Nations and expressed their determination that organized mass murder should be rendered impossible in the future by means of meetings of a League of Nations Parliament. The Deputy André Lebey, member of the Council of the Grand Orient, was Secretary to the Congress. He was a man of powerful intellect, who believed implicitly in the eventual victory of the Allies, but under no circumstances did he allow himself to be led astray by the prevailing thirst for vengeance against the German nation. Even whilst the great battle was still raging on French soil and unbridled propaganda was stirring up violent hatred against the 'Bosches', he could still speak of the necessity of one day making a treaty with Germany, as only an alliance between England, France, and Germany, together with complete disarmament, could guarantee the peace of the world, which might be described as the quintessence of Freemasonic desire. A horror and hatred of war is beneficial, but if we are to do away with the horrors of war, we must first of all create a League of Nations, which, of course, would be unthinkable without the collaboration of the Central Powers.

'La guerre elle-même a été si bien deshonorée par l'excès de ceux qui l'ont élevée à la hauteur d'une institution normale qu'il n'est pas interdit d'espérer qu'elle ait reçu une atteinte mortelle.' ('War itself has been so deeply dishonoured by the excesses of those who have raised it to the level of a normal institution that one may be permitted to hope that it has received a mortal blow.')

These words were spoken in June 1917, that is to say, at the very moment when the War had assumed a very different aspect because of the intervention of the United States of America and, according to official phraseology, was anything but 'dishonoured'.

The Congress unanimously approved the rough outline which Lebey submitted for the creation of a League of Nations, and also the principles which were later to materialize in the League of Nations Pact,[1] viz:

'Solidarity is the basis of civilized society. Each nation takes part, within its own boundaries, in the common work of Humanity, in which rights and obligations play equally important parts.

'Mankind is an immense family which only excludes those who violate national and international laws.

'The unity, autonomy and independence of each nation is inviolable.

'The Code of Human Rights was set up in 1789. The first task of the League of Nations is to set up a Code of National Rights.

'No nation has the right to declare war upon another; for war is a crime against the human race. (Eleven years before the Kellogg Pact!) Every quarrel between States must be brought before the international Parliament. Nations which do not conform thereto shall be automatically excluded from the League of Nations.'

This meeting in Paris is something of which all Freemasons who took part in it may be justly proud. They let themselves be guided by the spirit of the glorious verses of Lamartine:

> Et pourquoi nous haïr et mettre entre les races
> Ces bornes ou ces eaux qu'abhorre l'œil de Dieu?
> De frontières au Ciel, voyons nous quelques traces?
> Sa voûte a-t-elle un mur, une borne, un milieu?
> Nations, mot pompeux pour dire: Barbarie,
> L'amour s'arrête-t-il ou s'arrêtent vos pas?
> Déchirez vos drapeaux, une autre voix vous crie:
> L'égoïsme et la haine ont seuls une patrie,
> La Fraternité n'en a pas!
>
> .   .   .   .   .
>
> Ce ne sont plus des mers, des degrés, des rivières
> Qui bornent l'héritage entre l'humanité;
> Les bornes des esprits sont leurs seules frontières,
> Le monde en s'éclairant s'élève à l'unité

L'Acacia, June 1928

The author who made this avowal was not a Freemason himself. But the masonic ideals were his also. 'You are,' he wrote to the Mâcon Lodge in the year 1858, 'the great eclectics

---

[1] We have omitted all those proposals which applied to the organization of the League of Nations; the Assembly, Council, Arbitration Court, etc., were all planned as they were subsequently created.

of the modern world. From all times, from all countries, from all systems, and all philosophies you draw the leading and eternal principles of universal morality, and acquire therefrom the great infallible dogma of fraternity. You combat what divides spirits; you advocate what joins hearts. Your trowels spread the mortar of virtue that binds the foundations of society. . . .'

But the Paris meeting in 1917 naturally does not mean that Freemasonry interferes in any way in the destinies of the League of Nations, or that it has crept into its organization either as a visible or as an invisible element. The advocation of an idea of peace that seems likely to prove a blessing to all humanity and implication in diplomatic intrigues which could only result in the destruction of this fine ideal, are as far apart as the poles, and the very suggestion is ridiculous. How could it possibly be anything but ridiculous? Quite apart from the fact that at every meeting of the Council great differences of opinion illustrate the lack of any unanimous desire, and that in Geneva representatives of States openly antagonistic to Freemasonry are also powerful, any kind of intervention on the part of the Freemasons is rendered quite unthinkable by the lack of unity in Freemasonry itself.

Even if it so happened that the English, French, and German Foreign Ministers for the time being were all Freemasons, they would never arrive at an agreement just because of that.

CHAPTER III

OUTLOOK

I N this book we have been able to record only the beginnings of world-wide masonic activity. When we say this we do not wish, in any circumstances, to be misunderstood. It is not our desire to deny things that perhaps really exist, in order to confute those people who assert in their campaign against us that Freemasonry is a world political power; we are, on the contrary, deeply grieved that the language of Humanity should still have so many dialects and that Grand Lodges which, in their own particular circles, have the same ideals, should find it so difficult to work together in harmony. This failing in the past has not been due to any lack of true desire; the cause is to be found in all the tumults and ferments which the men constituting the Brotherhood during the last 200 years have been unable to avoid, and also in all the campaigns and persecutions to which they have been subjected, and in the amazing changes which have come to pass in the era of the most revolutionary technical innovations. The increasing mechanization and the disappearance of the personal element in present-day life is—in principle—contrary to the idea of Freemasonry. For Freemasonry aims at making men who are no machines; at forming a humanity consisting of persons who —to use the exquisite words of Emil Svoboda, the philosopher— possess, besides the miracle of a brain, also the wonder of a heart; a task whose very immensity makes it easy to understand why the foundations of the masonic edifice are not yet more uniformly laid.

However, we believe that we have demonstrated that since the time of Montesquieu, the first great representative on the Continent of the English philosophy and one of the first founders of Lodges there, many a good stone has been well and truly laid. That the idea of tolerance could spread with such amazing rapidity over so large a surface of the globe during the era of enlightenment may be regarded as the achievement of Freemasonry; an achievement that is still less open to dispute as the very powers that had from time immemorial been opposed to the idea of tolerance, entered the lists against Freemasonry

MASON'S CERTIFICATE, 1805

CERTIFICATE OF SCOTTISH ROYAL ARCH
MID NINETEENTH CENTURY

for that very reason. In his sociological essay *Zur russischen Geschichte und Religionsphilosophie* ('Russian History and Religious Philosophy'), Thomas G. Masaryk[1] writes:

'Culturally, it was the great movement of the eighteenth century, which, under the name of Enlightenment and Humanity, characterized the efforts made for the regeneration of all the peoples of Europe; these efforts . . . also spread to Russia. The Freemasons were . . . particularly prominent as organizers of European culture and ardent propagators of the Ideals of Humanity. . . .'

The statements made in respect of Russia by a philosopher of such undeniable authority as the President of the Czechoslovakian Republic, who, as we have already stated in another chapter, is himself not a Freemason, apply also to a large part of the rest of the world. Credit must also be given to Freemasonry for the fact that many a great and successful battle for freedom of thought and for the removal of encumbering and chafing fetters of intellectual repression could thus be fought, and that out of soul-destroying medieval restriction, a new and beautiful path to freedom was cleared and inviolable human rights incorporated in the Constitutions of many States.

Such work will, and must, be continued further, be the goal ever so distant and the step possible to the individual ever so small. Good men will always strive for more than they can attain. 'Go thy imperceptible step, O Eternal Providence. Only let me not despair of thee by reason of this imperceptibility, when e'en thy step retreat may seem,' said Lessing humbly in his wisdom. Freemasonry does not therefore mean crying for the moon. Only when one does not live for the moment, but from the very beginning strives for the furthest and highest aim is there a possibility of attaining, in the end, the highest possible ideal. The Freemason of to-day knows that he himself will not approach this ideal. But he is filled with the blissful consciousness of at least actively striving to attain it and he is inspired with the desire to conform to the exhortation of Herbert Spencer, that is, to couple with the desire to discover the Truth the eagerness to employ it for the benefit of mankind. Ludwig Keller, the distinguished Freemason, once declared that what Freemasonry lacked was unanimity in its great self-imposed tasks and unity of action for their execution according to plan. The task is there: the

[1] Quoted in *Die Drei Ringe*, 1st year, No. 11. Reichenberg. 1925.

work of Freemasonry can to-day only be that which has already been initiated by so many brethren, namely, the work for Peace; a work which, paradoxical as it may sound fifteen years after the end of the World War, was never so urgent as it is to-day. Many lips extol the great mission of certain institutions as a means of creating friendly relations between the various nations, without, however, having anything positive in mind. The phrase is used because it sounds well and ennobles aims which, only too often, stand in need of justification. But, in reality, the consciousness of what Peace really means has dawned upon but few minds. For four long years (and even after) men tore each other to pieces. One would have thought that this fearful self-destruction would have opened their eyes and made their hearts fertile soil for the idea of Humanity. But the reverse is the case! Hatred and bellicose instincts are welling up more and more to the gloomy surface. When, before 1914, we spoke of peace, we meant peace between nations, but to-day we have come to such a pass that large sections of one and the same nation are opposed to each other as the bitterest enemies, so that sensible people are forced timidly to ask how we can at least arrive at peace among ourselves.

The endeavours of Freemasons must be directed towards both external and internal peace. If Freemasonry will only foster the desire for unity, it can become a mighty power. Not a world power of a political or religious stamp, but an ethical power whose unity rests upon the common possession of the same profound symbolism; an ethical power against boundless egoism—a power centre that radiates Humanity and the desire for social morality into the political, religious and social struggles.

Fourier, the great precursor of Socialism, who once asserted that the law of Love applied to all peoples, a saying forgotten by many who now call themselves Socialists, on one occasion said of Freemasonry:

'A new question confronts the century. Up to now the century has not appreciated the valuable power which Freemasonry constitutes. It is like an unpolished diamond which we, being ignorant of its great value, fail to appreciate. The natives of Guahana trod nuggets of gold under foot with the utmost contempt before the covetousness of the Europeans opened their eyes to their value.'

Fourier was only too right. Freemasonry has shown its strength without having become a world-wide power. This manifests itself above all in the indestructibility of the masonic idea. Lack of organization, the petty jealousies between the systems and all the acts of suppression have not succeeded, during the course of 200 years, in rendering it ineffective. The hopes for the future also depend upon it.

The task of the Brotherhood to-day is none other than that which Lessing and Fichte and the other prophets of Freemasonry set it in the past, the only difference being that mankind, with so much agony behind it, must approach the solution more resolutely. In times when the world, so far as it takes thought at all, regards the outlook for the future with pessimism, the Freemason must be an optimist, like Prometheus, who, fettered to the rock and dying, still called out to Zeus:

> Think'st thou that I despair that ev'ry
> Dream hath not itself fulfill'd ?
> That ev'ry bloom did not itself unfold ?

SUPPLEMENT

to the 3rd English edition of

THE FREEMASONS

B. P. Hutton

CHANGES AND DEVELOPMENTS

Wars and political upheavals have been the cause of both the abolition and revival of Freemasonry, but the Order itself has continued its adaptation to social changes as it has continued to do, successfully, since its distant origins.

One important change which was confidently foreseen by the author was the attempt to create some kind of International Freemasonry, or a Freemasons' League of Nations. He did not know that the League of Nations was to be a failure, and that an international organization of Freemasons would not receive support from most of the world's Grand Lodges.

There has been much more progress with agreement on the basic principles of Recognition and it has been shown that adherence to these is effective and they can be maintained. Several countries have succeeded in forming Regular Grand Lodges after their original sovereign Grand Lodge had begun to deviate from the principles. This is very convenient for freemasons who travel abroad because they are able to find out in advance, from their Grand Secretary, where visiting can be made without embarrassment.

The most profound changes have been brought about by World War 2 and the Cold War which followed, when Freemasonry was banned by dictators, masonic leaders were imprisoned or executed, and in some cases the brethren were ill-treated. After a long period of darkness, many countries have been liberated and there has been an astonishing revival of Freemasonry where the memory of it was kept alive, often in secret and in great danger. There have been many instances where nations which had been enemies have given assistance and brotherly love in the difficult process of rebuilding their lodges, based on the masonic ideals which had never been extinguished.

Perhaps the most important change in Freemasonry has been in the matter of secrecy which had developed into an unnecessary concealment of trivial matters which are not secret, and not even of interest to the popular world. Moves were made, particularly in England and the United States of America, to consider public relations, leading to press conferences, open days and videos to show the good intentions of Freemasonry, and its complete lack of improper interference or influence on others.

In England, the Duke of Kent introduced a completely new outlook, eliminating the unnecessary secrecy and allowing the Order to show itself more openly to the public. A permanent exhibition was installed in Freemasons' Hall which is open to the public, and there are guided tours of the library, museum and the Grand Temple. There have been public performances in the Grand Temple of Mozart's *Magic Flute* and *Don Giovanni* as well as Haydn's *Creation* and Britten's *Midsummernight's Dream* by arrangement with the Covent Garden Festival.

In America there have been films, radio and television appearances to bring Freemasonry to the attention of the public, and there have been many instances of open meetings and shows where non-masons have been given the opportunity to ask questions and receive answers. The uniquely American *Ancient Arabic Order, Nobles of the Mystic Shrine* (Shriners) is not a masonic organization but all its members are freemasons, and their charitable activities such as hospitals for burns victims and for crippled children of all creeds and races are widely known and respected. The Grand Charity in England distributes huge sums to non-masonic charities but it is not so well known to the public as the Shriners in America.

AN OPEN MEETING

The new policy of masonic relations with the public was demonstrated at a special quarterly meeting of the United Grand Lodge of England on 10 June 1992 in London to celebrate the 275th anniversary of the formation of the premier Grand Lodge in 1717. Because the attendance was over 12,000, the meeting was held at Earl's Court and on this special occasion Ladies and the Press were admitted.

The arena had been specially prepared and decorated to recall as far as possible the Grand Temple in Freemasons' Hall. Before the meeting, those present were entertained by three Choirs, including one from the Masonic Girls' School and an orchestra of 46 ladies and brethren from London orchestras.

Grand Lodge had first been opened in Earl's Court's Westminster Room, and Called Off. A procession then accompanied the M.W. Grand Master, H.R.H. The Duke of Kent, into the arena to be greeted by a fanfare by eight masonic trumpeters. The Three Great Lights were presented by representatives of the Time Immemorial Lodges and an Opening Ode was sung. Eighty four Grand Masters, or their personal representatives, and Visiting Deputations from all over the world entered and were welcomed and applauded. Replies were given by the Grand Master of the Grand Lodge of the Commonwealth of Massachusetts, and the

Grand Master of the Symbolic Grand Lodge of Hungary. Grand Lodge was Called On and the business transacted.

The meeting also celebrated the 40th anniversary of the accession of H.M. Queen Elizabeth II, the 20th anniversary of the Installation of the Grand Master, and the birthday of H.R.H. The Duke of Edinburgh.

Grand Lodge was Called Off after the business transactions, and the Grand Charity held a meeting at which grants of £300,000 were approved to non-masonic charities, and £500,000 to the Cancer Relief Macmillan Fund. To mark the 275th anniversary there were grants of £2 million for mental handicaps, and the new community at Rowde in Wiltshire. The Grand President of the Grand Charity then dedicated the Foundation Stone of the community on the black and white carpet of the Lodge floor.

Grand Lodge was addressed by the Grand Masters of Ireland, Scotland and Canada in the Province of Ontario. In his address, the Duke of Kent referred to the Dark Age when our habit of responding to criticism with a wall of silence seemed to confirm people's worst fears about Freemasonry. He said that we are now firmly committed to an era where we can and do respond sensibly, remembering that only very few matters are private. In preparing our explanations, we have taken a close look at ourselves, and improvements have been made. Occasionally going back to first principles helps us to navigate by the right stars. Grand Lodge has no corporate policy towards the community and masons are expressly forbidden, as masons, to attempt to influence any of the country's institutions. Freemasonry will survive in the future if we all maintain our adherence to the basic principles by which we recognize our Freemasonry as Regular.

After a prayer of thanksgiving and the National Anthem, a Closing Ode was sung while the Grand Master and his Officers retired in procession from the arena. Grand Lodge was Called On in the Westminster Room, and Closed. Afterwards 4,000 brethren, ladies and gentleman dined in Earl's Court 2 when the Grand Master received a memento of the anniversaries, and the Grand President of the Grand Charity presented a cheque for £250,000 to H.R.H. The Duchess of Kent as Patron of the Camphill Village Trust.

Two weeks later, brethren were invited to St Paul's Cathedral where Evensong was celebrated by the V. Rev. the Dean of St Paul's, and the preacher was the M. Rev the Archibishop of the West Indies. Similar services were held in Cathedrals and Churches all over England.

THE WORLD'S LEADING FREEMASONS AT AN OPEN MEETING IN LONDON IN 1992 TO
CELEBRATE THE 275TH ANNIVERSARY OF THE FIRST GRAND LODGE, WITH A
GATHERING OF 12,000 INCLUDING LADIES AND THE PRESS. TERRY MOORE.

THE VILLA MEDICI IN ROME, HEADQUARTERS OF THE GRAND ORIENT
OF ITALY.

DOMIZIO TORRIGIANI, THE GRAND
MASTER WHO WAS MARTYRED BY
THE FASCISTI WHEN ITALIAN
FREEMASONRY WAS SUPPRESSED
IN 1937.

W BRO MAJ-GEN DR JOSEPH SAIDU
MOMAH, WHEN HE WAS PAST
MASTER AND PRESIDENT OF
SIERRA LEONE.

THE VAST MASONIC AUDITORIUM IN SAN FRANCISCO USA WITH 3,000 PLACES
FOR CEREMONIALS, AND AS A CONCERT HALL AND THEATRE.

THE FOYER OF THE MASONIC MUSEUM OF OUR HERITAGE IN LEXINGTON, MASSACHUSETTS USA.

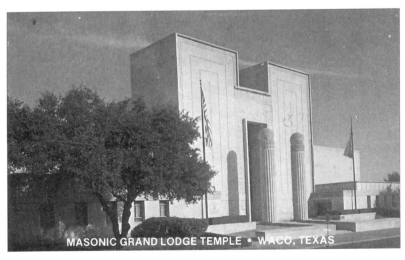

THE GRAND LODGE TEMPLE IN WACO, TEXAS USA ERECTED IN MEMORY OF FREEMASONS WHO SERVED TO PRESERVE FREEDOM AND DEMOCRACY IN THE LAND OF LIBERTY, EQUALITY AND FRATERNITY.

FREEMASONS IN HAMILTON, BERMUDA FOLLOWING THE MILITARY BAND
DURING THE 'PEPPERCORN' CEREMONY WHEN THE STATE ALLOWS THE
FREEMASONS TO USE THE GOVERNMENT BUILDING.

THE MASONIC HALL IN FORT
BEAUFORT, SOUTH AFRICA.

THE MASONIC HALL IN LINKÖPING,
SWEDEN.

A TYLER IN THE UNIFORM WORN IN
THE 18TH CENTURY.

THE MASONIC HALL IN ISTANBUL,
TURKEY WHERE FRANZ LISZT, THE
COMPOSER AND FREEMASON,
ONCE LIVED.

THE AMERICAN UNION COLONIAL DEGREE TEAM OF THE COLONIAL
CRAFTSMEN'S CLUB, MASSACHUSETTS AFTER A RE-ENACTMENT OF AN
ANCIENT CEREMONY.

SCHLOSS ROSENAUER, ZWETTL WHERE THE AUSTRIAN STATE MASONIC
MUSEUM ARRANGED BY THE GRAND LODGE OF AUSTRIA, IS OPEN TO
THE PUBLIC.

A STREET IN AITRÉ, FRANCE IS NAMED
AFTER GRAND MASTER
DR DESAGULIERS WHO WAS BORN
THERE IN THE HUGUENOT DISTRICT OF
LA ROCHELLE IN AQUITAINE.

Above: BRO EDWIN D. ALDRIN JR, FIRST MAN ON THE MOON 1969.
Above right: LUXEMBOURG, 175TH ANNIVERSARY OF THE SMALLEST GRAND
      LODGE.

Above: STATE HOUSE BERMUDA, LEASED AS A MASONIC HALL FOR SCOTTISH,
      ENGLISH, IRISH AND AMERICAN LODGES.
Above right: PRINCE HALL, FOUNDER OF AFRICAN GRAND LODGE, BOSTON 1791.

Above: BRO SIR WINSTON CHURCHILL ON A FIRST DAY COVER.
Above centre: BRO SIR CHARLES WARREN, A FOUNDER OF QUATUOR CORONATI
      LODGE.
Above right: BRO FRANKLIN D. ROOSEVELT, PRESIDENT OF USA.

FREEMASONRY ON STAMPS

THE MASONIC HALL AT FAVERSHAM, KENT WAS BUILT IN 1587 AS A SCHOOL.
THE LODGE OF HARMONY NO 133EC WHICH MEETS THERE WAS FOUNDED
IN 1764.

THE ROYAL SHAKESPEARE THEATRE, STRATFORD-ON-AVON.
THE FOUNDATION STONE WAS LAID IN 1929 BY LORD AMPTHILL,
PRO GRAND MASTER OF ENGLAND.

WORLD FREEMASONRY

To give an explanation of all the Grand Lodges in the world would require a separate book for each country, and the author of *The Freemasons* did not attempt a comprehensive survey. Those countries which were included were relevant to the main subject, but many changes have taken place in the last sixty years.

A brief outline to show the present position is included in the Supplement but there could be further developments by the time of publication.

EUROPEAN FREEMASONRY

An Association with the object of promoting masonic friendship and brotherhood in Europe was formed in Frankfurt on 2 December 1989 at a meeting of 12 freemasons from nine countries. The seat of the European Masonic Association is to be located in London with English as its official language. Membership is restricted to Master Masons of good standing in regular recognized lodges. No ritual or ceremony will be used and meetings take place twice a year in Spring and Autumn at locations in different countries. At the Autumn meetings, families of members will be welcome to attend.

THE COMMONWEALTH

The British Empire was still in existence when *The Freemasons* first appeared but it has now been replaced by the Commonwealth in which the members are independent States. Freemasonry was introduced into the old colonies by settlers and travelling military lodges who naturally used their own rituals and practices. However, these were diverse and interesting because of the variety in the sovereign Grand Lodges in the British Isles of England, Ireland and Scotland.

After the Union with Scotland the inhabitants of the United Kingdom became Britons but the distinctive differences among the three races of English, Irish and Scots are unchanged. This is particularly noticeable in Freemasonry where the three Grand Lodges continue their independence. At the same time, it is of interest that while nationalists continue to quarrel, the lodges in Northern Ireland and the Republic all work in close harmony together under the sovereign Grand Lodge of Ireland in Dublin.

There is complete amity among the three Constitutions, with intervisitation, and they frequently meet overseas in the same premises. Visiting among these three jurisdictions at home can sometimes produce a very wide range of different masonic practices whereas a visit to a lodge on the other side of the world could be found to be more familiar.

NORTH AMERICA

A glowing description in Part II, Chapter II of *Freemasonry in the United States of America* refers to the immense size and the volume of support which it receives from the male population. In addition, there are other groups supported by masons and involving the whole family. At the time of publication, President Harding had attempted to translate the masonic ideal into practice, and the failure of his Disarmament Conference did not shake his belief. Today it is less likely for masonic ideals to be mentioned at international meetings, but the more members who have these standards the greater will be the opportunity for success.

American bodies such as the Scottish Rite take an interest in current affairs and education while their large membership, not all active freemasons, is kept well informed.

In addition to the recognized Grand Lodges in all the States, there is a separate obedience for black masons in Prince Hall Lodges, a very large organization dating back to 1775 with some 5,000 lodges, but not generally recognized. However, this situation is already changing, and recognition has been given by Connecticut and some other Grand Lodges. There is every possibility that this process will continue.

The situation in Canada is similar, with the first Grand Lodge in Ontario being followed by eight more as the country developed, and also with Prince Hall lodges.

FRANCE AND BELGIUM

These two countries are included in Part II, Chapter III, probably because they both ceased to be recognized at the same time, in 1877, when they abandoned the necessity of belief in the Great Architect of the Universe.

The author shows considerable respect for these views and only makes brief reference to the regular *Grande Loge Nationale Française* which had originally been formed with a longer title in 1913. The freemasons in France and Belgium were also exponents of International Freemasonry, and they were interested in peace, especially for an understanding with Germany, which was so harshly treated by the Allies after 1918.

The present situation is that the GLNF in France has grown considerably and the Regular Grand Lodge of Belgium, although of more recent origin, can look forward to expansion in the future. Both are recognized by most of the Grand Lodges in the world, and visiting is permitted.

RUSSIA

The last of the freemasons in the Kerensky (a freemason) provisional government were crushed by Trotsky and Lenin and it is possible that there can be no living memory of Freemasonry to kindle after so many years. However, a Charter has been received by a group of 14 masons in Moscow for the revival of Harmony Lodge No 1 which once met there. They are to meet in premises which are available, but they have the intention one day to occupy their own original building which is still standing.

GERMANY

In Part II, Chapter IV ends with the complete abolition of Freemasonry by the Nazis. After the end of World War 2 it was revived in Western Germany, although headquarters was in Berlin, but the ban continued in the East, the so-called DDR (German Democratic Republic) under the control of the Soviets. Before the war the complicated system in the whole of Germany consisted of 11 Grand Lodges with differing practices, and when the revival took place in the West there was a *Magna Charta* which brought everyone under the United Grand Lodges of Germany, consisting of five mainly independent Grand Lodges.

Most of the surviving masons in Western Germany came under the Grand Lodges AF & AM of Germany in Bonn, using the Schröder ritual. The Grand Land Lodge of Freemasons in Germany in Berlin works the Swedish rite, and also in Berlin is the

National Grand Mother Lodge of the Three Globes using the Fessler ritual which is similar to Schröder. The American-Canadian Grand Lodge AF & AM in Frankfurt was formed for the convenience of service men, and their workings are of various American rituals. The Grand Lodge of British Freemasons in Düsseldorf caters for British troops, working in English predominantly with the Emulation ritual.

The revival of Freemasonry in East Germany (the DDR) following Unification has already begun but there is considerable prejudice against freemasons because of the misinformation which was widely spread by Nazi and Soviet propaganda. The Grand Lodges of Germany are committed to awaken Freemasonry in the East, and in Ludenscheid the Deputy Grand Master has already conducted a ceremony of 'Bringing in the Light' in Jena Lodge and there are now two lodges at work there.

AUSTRIA

The Grand Lodge of Austria existed between the wars but after the *Anschluss* it was abolished by the invading German Nazis. Austrian freemasons had been in the forefront of the international movement in the cause of world peace, but this was brought abruptly to an end.

After the end of World War 2 the Grand Lodge was revived and Freemasonry prospered in liberated Austria. Most lodges work the Schröder rite but there is one English speaking Sarastro Lodge in Vienna which uses Emulation. The members of this multinational lodge come from many countries, and represent the major religions of the world. There are now some 2,000 members of Austrian lodges which are located in Vienna, Burgenland, Graz, Klagenfurt, Linz, Salzburg and Villach.

The Grand Lodge of Austria undertakes, on behalf of the State of Lower Austria, the arrangement of the Austrian Masonic Museum which is housed in a large 18th century baroque mansion, the Schloss Rausenau, near Zwettl. In 1982 an exhibition of 'Freemasonry in England—the Senior Grand Lodge of the World' was held in this historic masonic meeting place. The exhibits included Austrian items from the 18th century and others on loan from the United Grand Lodge of England.

HUNGARY

Freemasonry was revived in Hungary on St John's Day 27 December 1989 when some 450 brethren met in a hotel in Budapest to restore the light in the Symbolic Grand Lodge of Hungary. The Grand Master of Austria opened the Grand Lodge and handed the gavel to the elected Grand Master, M.W. Bro Istvan Galambos. There were delegates from 14 countries as well as brethren of Hungarian descent from 50 countries. The United Grand Lodges of Germany were represented and they are already engaged in the revival in Romania, Yugoslavia and Czechoslovakia, although the breaking up of the two latter countries is likely to delay the process.

SCANDINAVIA
Sweden, Norway, Denmark, Iceland and Finland

In Part II, Chapter VII under the heading of Neutral Countries, the Swedish system in Scandinavia is described but Finland is omitted, probably because changes were taking place at the time. This chapter also includes Holland and Switzerland because they were considered neutral, but these countries differ masonically from Scandinavia and they will be considered separately.

King Edward VII of England was initiated in Stockholm when he was Prince of Wales in 1868, by Prince Oscar, later King of Sweden, and he was advanced through the ten Christian degrees of the Scandinavian Rite. He was Grand Master of England from 1874 until he ascended the throne in 1901. At the time when Sweden ruled Norway, Iceland and Finland, they all used the same masonic system and this was also adopted by Denmark in 1858.

When Finland was ceded to Russia in 1809 all the lodges were closed but on gaining independence in 1918 the Swedish lodges were revived but another masonic system was introduced from America. Some Finns who had been made masons abroad received a Charter from New York, and Suomi Lodge No 1 was consecrated. One of its earliest members was the composer Jean Sibelius, and in 1924 the Grand Lodge of Finland was constituted by the Grand Lodge of New York. Freemasonry was suspended during the war but from 1945 there has been considerable growth. The Swedish lodges cater for the Swedish-speaking minority in Finland, under the authority of Stockholm, while the Finnish lodges use a working similar to that of New York. The relations between Stockholm and Helsinki are most friendly, and Freemasonry is firmly established.

Norway was a possession of Denmark until it was ceded to Sweden in 1814, and was granted independence in 1905. The earliest lodges were English from 1749, and German lodges followed with a Provincial Grand Lodge. In 1891 the Grand Lodge of Norway was formed and the Swedish Rite is used.

The earliest lodges in Denmark were English and German but in 1792 recognition was given by the Danish Crown and the National Grand Lodge of Denmark was formed. The Swedish Rite was introduced and this became mandatory for all lodges in 1855.

Freemasonry did not come to Iceland until 1919 under warrant from Denmark. The National Grand Lodge of Iceland was constituted in 1951 and the small number of lodges there work the Swedish Rite.

SPAIN

The first lodge in Spain was formed in Madrid in 1728 by the renegade Duke of Wharton but it did not survive. The Grand Lodge of Spain was founded in 1767 and it had very close links with the Grand Orient of France, so that when the break came in 1877 recognition was withdrawn. Freemasonry was brought to an end by General Franco but in 1975 the few masons who remained set about reconstruction. This time they approached the regular *Grande Loge Nationale Française* who helped them to open lodges, first under the French Province of Occitaine where Spanish is widely spoken, then in 1982 the G.L.N.F. constituted the Grand Lodge A.F. & A.M. of Spain and Madrid. Recognition soon followed and by 1990 there were some 50 lodges in Spain. Since then lodges have been formed in the Balearic Islands, some English speaking, where visitors are warmly welcome.

GREECE

The first lodge was founded in Corfu in 1809, and the English Star of the East Lodge still works there under the number 880EC. It was not until 1866 that lodges were formed on the mainland. The Grand Lodge of Greece was reconstructed after World War 2 with one of its lodges working in English. The present position is that recognition has been withdrawn from this Grand Lodge, and a new National Grand Lodge of Greece was recognized by England in 1994.

ITALY

Freemasonry came to the separate sovereign states in 1733 before the unification of Italy, and Garibaldi was the Grand Master of several organizations in the 1860s. The Grand Orient took over in 1873 and this was recognized by England in 1993. Some lodges broke away from the Grand Orient to form the new Regular Grand Lodge of Italy, which was recognized by England in 1994.

THE NETHERLANDS

The well known initiation of the Duke of Lorraine by Dr Desaguliers in a lodge specially convened in 1731 was the first appearance of Freemasonry at the Hague. The Grand East of the Netherlands had its origin in 1756 and there has been a long period of stability and recognition. All the lodges were closed during World War 2 but a rapid recovery was made after the war.

SWITZERLAND

A country with three languages and many Cantons had difficulties in 1736 when some Englishmen formed a lodge in Geneva. The Grand Lodge of Geneva was formed, but there were also French and German speaking lodges which set up obediences in 1777. The Grand Lodge Alpina of Switzerland became the central authority in 1844 and is recognized by England today, although other irregular bodies exist.

TURKEY

After years of suppression, Freemasonry was revived in 1948. The Grand Lodge of Turkey is now widely recognized and the many lodges include some which work in English, French, Greek and German.

LUXEMBOURG

The smallest Grand Lodge in Europe, the Grand Lodge of Luxembourg, was founded in 1868 and its earliest lodges were of Belgian and French origin. It has only four lodges now and recognition was given from England in 1969, although this Grand Lodge is not widely recognized. A modified form of Grand Orient working is used by the lodges, which all meet at the Masonic Temple in rue de la Loge.

WOMEN AND FREEMASONRY

This was the subject of Chapter IV in Part III and it ends with a mention of Co-Masonry of the *Droit Humain*, led in Britain by Mrs Annie Besant of the Theosophical Society. This was for men and women but, from a breakaway group, a society for women only was formed, the *Order of Women Freemasons*, which has grown, with over 350 lodges in Britain and overseas, working the degrees of Freemasonry. An official magazine is issued and there is a very good record of charity, but the Order is not recognized by the United Grand Lodge of England. There are similar women's masonic Orders in Europe and there is some visiting, but there are others which have a connection with the irregular *Grand Orient*. The *Order of the Eastern Star* for women is a large and widespread organization to be found in America, Canada, Australia and some other countries. In a modified form it is tolerated in Scotland but not in England. There are masonic connections but the ceremonial is based upon the stories of women in the Bible. There are thought to be some three million members worldwide.

The *Order of Amarinth* is for Master Masons and their ladies in America, and the Order of the *White Shrine of Jerusalem* is restricted to Christian members. There are some other Orders of different kinds, light and serious, open to men and women but the *Order of Rainbow* and the *Order of Job's Daughters* are for girls, similar to the boy's *Order of Molay*.

OUTLOOK

The sub-title to *The Freemasons* was 'The History, Nature, Development and Secret of the Royal Art' and we should remember that the book was written soon after the end of World War 1.

At that time many people thought that it had been the war to end wars but we know, from hindsight, that much worse was to come. However, the idea of peace was of tremendous importance and Eugen Lennhoff clearly thought that it should be given priority. To this end he was willing to work openly with all freemasons, regardless of their regularity, in an attempt to influence others by the demonstration of masonic principles.

Alas, we now know that revenge, bitterness, hatred and inhumanity did not disappear with the end of the 'Great War'. The League of Nations, with such bright prospects, was a failure and the genuine peacemakers were disappointingly outnumbered. Freemasons, with their principles unaltered, are still in the minority but they retain the power to influence others by their own behaviour. The Royal Art is strong and world wide, while the political changes which have liberated more countries provide conditions for the further spread of the Craft.

The system of Recognition has been applied successfully and it is necessary for the understanding of lodges world wide, but we should not forget that it is more important to demonstrate our way of life to the uninitiated who may then want to join with us. As one of our great leaders once said, it is more important to get Freemasonry into men than more men into Freemasonry.

In his Outlook in Part IV, Chapter III, Lenhoff looked forward to making Freemasonry into a mighty power, not political or religious, but ethical. The idea is still valid and its achievement depends upon the ability of freemasons to demonstrate, by their own lives, the benefits available to everyone.

LITERATURE

I. IN THE ENGLISH LANGUAGE

Ahiman Rezon, Or a Help to a Brother, etc. A new edition.

ANDERSON, JAMES: *Constitution of the Freemasons*, etc. London.
1723.

—— *New Book of Constitutions*, etc. London. 1738.

BAIRD, GEORGE W.: *Great American Masons*. Washington.

CALVERT, ALBERT F.: *Grand Lodge of England 1717–1917*. London.
1917.

—— *Grand Stewards' and Red Apron Lodges*. London.

CARLILE, RICHARD: *Manual of Freemasonry*. London. 1845.

CHURCHWARD, ALBERT: *Origin and Evolution of Freemasonry*.
London. 1920.

CONDER, EDWARD: *Records of the Hole Crafte and Felawship of
Masons*. London. 1894.

CUNNINGHAM, W.: *Notes on the Organization of the Mason's Craft in
England*. London.

DAYNES, GILBERT W.: *The Birth and Growth of the Grand Lodge of
England 1717–1926*. London. 1926.

GOULD, ROBERT F.: *History of Freemasonry*, etc. London. 1885.

HALLIWELL, JAMES O.: *Early History of Freemasonry in England*.
London. 1892.

HAWKINS, E. L.: *Concise Cyclopædia of Freemasonry*, etc. London.
1908.

HAYDEN, SIDNEY: *Washington and his Masonic Compeers*. New
York. 1869.

HUGHAN, WILLIAM J.: *Constitutions of the Freemasons*. London.
1869.

—— *Memorials of the Masonic Union of 1813*, etc. London.
1874.

—— *Origin of the English Rite of Freemasonry*, etc. Third edition.
Leicester. 1909.

JOHNSON, MELVIN M.: *Freemasonry in America Prior to 1750*.
Anamosa. 1925.

LANG, OSSIAN: *Freemasonry in France*. New York. 1928.

—— *Freemasonry under Fire in Continental Europe*. New York.
1927.

—— *Freemasonry and Medieval Craft Gilds*. New York. 1916.

—— *History of Freemasonry in the State of New York*. New York.
1922.

MACKEY, ALBERT G.: *History of Freemasonry*. 1898.

MACOY, ROBERT: *General History, Cyclopædia and Dictionary for Freemasonry*, etc. New York. 1870.

MORSE, SIDNEY: *Freemasonry in the American Revolution*. Washington. 1924.

NEWTON, JOSEPH F.: *The Builders. A Story and Study of Masonry*. Iowa. 1915.

Pocket Companion, A, and History of Free-Masonry. London. 1754.

PALMER, DR. JOHN C.: *The Morgan Affair*. Washington. 1924.

PIKE, ALBERT: *Morals and Dogma of the Ancient and Accepted Scottish Rite of Freemasonry*. Charleston. 1881.

—— *The Meaning of Masonry*. Washington.

POUND, ROSCOE: *Masonic Jurisprudence*. Washington.

PRESTON : *Illustrations of Masonry*. London. 1772.

QUATUOR CORONATI LODGE: *Ars Quatuor Coronatorum*, etc. Sundry volumes.

SADLER, HENRY: *Masonic Facts and Fiction*. London. 1887.

—— *Masonic Reprints and Historical Revelations*. London. 1898.

SPETH, GEORGE W.: *Builders Rites and Ceremonies*. Margate. 1894.

STREET, OLIVER DAY: *Symbolism of the Three Degrees*. Washington.

TATSCH, HUGO, J.: *Short Readings in Masonic History*. Iowa. 1926.

TELEPNEF, BORIS: *An Outline of the History of Russian Freemasonry*. London. 1928.

VIBERT, LIONEL: *Freemasonry before the Existence of Grand Lodges*. London.

—— *Story of the Craft*. London. 1921.

WAITE, ARTHUR EDWARD: *Real History of the Rosicrucians*. London. 1887.

—— *The Secret Tradition in Masonry*. London. 1911.

WARD, I. S. M.: *An Outline History of Freemasonry*. London. 1924.

WILSON, WOODROW: *History of the American People*.

WRIGHT, DUDLEY: *Robert Burns and Freemasonry*.

—— *The Ethics of Masonry*. Washington.

YARKER, JOHN: *Arcane Schools*. Belfast. 1909.

II. IN THE GERMAN LANGUAGE

ABAFI: *Geschichte der Freimaurerei in Österreich-Ungarn*. Budapest. 1893.

Adhuc stat! Die Freimaurerei in zehn Fragen und Antworten. St. Gallen. 1870.

ALBRECHT, JOHANNES: *Versuch einer Lehre nach dem Gebrauchtum der Grossen Nationalmutterloge z. d. 3. W.* Mecklenburg. 1925.

Allgemeines Handbuch der Freimaurerei. 3rd edition. Leipzig. 1900/01.

Alten Pflichten der Freimaurer, Die. Pressburg. 1914.

ANDREAE, JOH. VALENTIN: *Fama Fraternitatis oder Entdeckung der Brüderschaft des Hochlöblichen Ordens des R.C.*
―― *Confessio Fraternitatis,* etc.
BAKUNIN, MICHAEL: *Gesammelte Werke,* Vol. II. Berlin. 1923.
BEEK, GOTTFRIED ZUR: *Die Geheimnisse der Weisen von Zion.* Charlottenburg. 1927.
BEGEMANN, DR. WILHELM: *Die Tempelherren und die Freimaurer.* Berlin. 1906.
―― *Vorgeschichte und Anfänge der Freimaurerei in England.*
―― *Vorgeschichte und Anfänge der Freimaurerei in Irland.* Berlin. 1911.
―― *Vorgeschichte und Anfänge der Freimaurerei in Schottland.* Berlin. 1914.
BEYER–BAYREUTH, DR. BERNHARD: *Das Freimaurermuseum;* Vol. 1: *Das Lehr-system des Ordens der Gold und Rosenkreuzer.* Leipzig. 1925.
BIBL, VICTOR: *Der Zerfall Österreichs.* Vienna. 1922.
BISCHOFF, DIEDRICH: *Die Religion der Freimaurer.* Gotha. 1922.
―― *Maurertum und Menschheitstum.* Leipzig. 1900.
―― *Wesen und Ziele der Freimaurerei.* Berlin. 1910.
BOEHN, OTTO: *Wege zur Freimaurerei.* Berlin. 1922.
BOOS, HEINRICH: *Geschichte der Freimaurerei.* Aarau. 1906.
BRICHT, BALDUIN: *Was ist, was will die Freimaurerei? Was sind die Ziele der Grossloge von Wien?* Vienna. 1919.
BRUNNER, ARMIN: *Der 18. Grad des A. und A. Schottischen Ritus.* Vienna. 1929.
BUCK, J. D.: *Mystische Maurerei.* Gross-Lichterfelde. 1908.
BUDDECKE, ALBERT: *Das Freimaurerideal.* Berlin. 1924.
CASPARI, OTTO: *Die Bedeutung des Freimaurertums.* Berlin. 1910.
DEILE, GOTTHOLD: *Goethe als Freimaurer.* Berlin. 1908.
ECKERT, E. E.: *Magazin der Beweisführung zur Verurteilung des Freimaurerordens.* Schaffhausen. 1855/56.
ENGEL, LEOPOLD: *Geschichte des Illuminatenordens.* Berlin. 1906.
FALLOU: *Die Mysterien der Freimaurerei usw.* Leipzig. 1848.
Fascistisches Gesetz, Das Gesetz gegen die Freimaurerei. Rome. 1926.
FENSCH, DR. LUDWIG: *Fessler (Maurerische Klassiker).* Berlin.
FINDEL, J. C.: *Geist und Form der Freimaurerei.* Leipzig. 1883.
―― *Geschichte der Freimaurerei.* 7th edition. Leipzig. 1900.
FLUHRER, WILH.: *Die Freimaurerei, wie sie ist usw.* Frankfort-on-Main. 1926.
FRANK, B.: *Arbeit.* Lennep. 1928.
Freimaurerei, Die, Österreich-Ungarns. 12 lectures. Vienna. 1897.
FRIEDELL, EGON: *Allgemeine Kulturgeschichte.* Munich. 1928.
FRIEDRICHS, ERNST: *Geschichte der einstigen Maurerei in Russland.* Berlin. 1904.
GRUBER, HERMANN: *Freimaurerei, Weltkrieg und Weltfriede.* Vienna. 1917.

GRUBER, HERMANN: *Betrug als Ende eines Betruges.* Berlin. 1897.

—— *Der 'giftige Kern' oder Die wahren Bestrebungen der Frei-maurerei usw.* Berlin. 1899.

—— (*Gerber Hildebrand*) *Leo Taxils Palladismusroman.*

—— *Mazzini, Freimaurerei und Weltrevolution.* Regensburg. 1901.

HAARHAUS, JULIUS: *Deutsche Freimaurer zur Zeit der Befreiungs-kriege.* Jena. 1913.

HALLIWELL, JAMES RICHARD: *Alteste Urkunde der Freimaurer in England.* (Translation.) Hamburg. 1892.

HARTLAUB, G. F.: *Giorgiones Geheimnis.* Munich.

HECKETHORN: *Geheime Gesellschaften usw.* Leipzig. 1900.

HEINICHEN, OTTO: *Die Grundgedanken der Freimaurerei im Lichte der Philosophie.* Berlin. 1927.

HEISE, KARL: *Okkultes Logentum.* Leipzig. 1921.

—— *Entente-Freimaurerei und der Weltkrieg.* Basle. 1920.

HELDMANN, FRIEDRICH: *Die drei ältesten geschichtlichen Denkmale der teutschen Freimaurerbrüderschaft.* Aarau. 1819.

HENKE, PROF. DR. OSKAR: *Die Freimaurerei in Deutschland.* Berlin.

HENNE AM RHYN, DR. OTTO: *Kurzgefasste Symbolik der Freimaurerei.* Berlin. 1906.

HERGETH, DR. FRIEDRICH: *Aus der Werkstätte der Freimaurer und Juden im Österreich der Nachkriegszeit.* Graz. 1927.

HORNEFFER, AUGUST: *Der Bund der Freimaurer.* Jena.

—— *Die Freimaurerei.* Leipzig.

—— *Symbolik der Mysterienbünde.* Vienna. 1924.

—— *Die Lehrart der Grossen Loge von Preussen.* Berlin. 1924.

HORNEFFER, ERNST UND AUGUST: *Freimaurerisches Lesebuch.* Berlin.

HOTTINGER, J. J.: *Rückblicke auf die Vergangenheit usw.* Zürich. 1848.

JENNINGS, H.: *Die Rosenkreuzer.* Berlin. 1912.

Illuminaten, Drey merkwürdige Aussagen, die innere Einrichtung des Illuminatenordens in Bayern betreffend. Munich. 1786.

Journal für Freimaurerei. Vienna. 1784, 1785.

KATSCH, FERDINAND: *Die Entstehung und der wahre Endzweck der Freimaurerei.* Berlin. 1897.

KELLER, LUDWIG: *Die geistigen Grundlagen der Freimaurerei und das öffentliche Leben.* Jena. 1911.

—— *Die Tempelherren und die Freimaurer.* 1906.

—— *Die Freimaurerei.* 1918.

KLOSS, GEORG: *Geschichte der Freimaurerei in England, Irland, Schottland.* Leipzig. 1847.

—— *Die Freimaurerei in ihrer wahren Bedeutung.* Berlin. 1855.

KNEISNER, FRIEDRICH: *Geschichte der deutschen Freimaurerei in ihren Grundzügen.* Berlin. 1912.

KRAUSE, KARL CHRISTIAN FRIEDRICH: *Die drei ältesten Kunstur-kunden,* etc. Dresden. 1819.

KREHAN, ARNO: *Zu neuen Ufern lockt ein neuer Tag.* Weimar.
1926.

LANZ-LIEBENFELS. J.: *Der Taxil-Schwindel.* Frankfort-on-Main.

LESSING, GOTTHOLD EPHRAIM, ERNST UND FALK: *Die Erziehung des Menschengeschlechts.*

LEWIS, DR. L.: *Geschichte der Freimaurerei in Österreich.* Vienna.
1861.

LUDENDORFF: *Vernichtung der Freimaurerei durch Enthüllung ihrer Geheimnisse.* Munich.

—— *Krieghetze und Völkermorden in den letzten 150 Jahren,* etc.
Munich.

MERZDORF, J. F.: *Ernst und Falk.*

MICHALER: *Beruhigung eines Katholiken über die päpstlichen Bullen wider die Freymaurerey.* Cosmopolis. 1782.

NEUMANN, DR. OTTO: *Das Freimaurertum.* Berlin. 1909.

—— *Die Gegner der Freimaurerei.* Berlin.

NORMANN, H.: *Die Freimaurerei in England und Amerika.* Berlin.

OHR, WILHELM: *Der französische Geist und die Freimaurerei.*
Leipzig. 1916.

PACHTLER, S. U.: *Der stille Krieg gegen Thron und Altar.* Amberg.
1873.

—— *Der Götze der Humanität.* Freiburg. 1875.

PAUMGARTNER, BERNHARD: *Mozart.* Berlin.

PEUCKERT, WILL-ERICH: *Die Rosenkreutzer.* Jena. 1927.

PHAROS: *Der Prozess gegen die Attentäter von Serajewo usw.* Berlin.
1918.

PINKOW, HANS WILHELM: *Macht und Einfluss der Freimaurerei.*
Hamburg. 1912.

PLANTAGENET, ED. E.: *Die französische Freimaurerei.* Basle. 1928.

POSNER, OSKAR: *Am rauhen Stein.* Reichenberg. 1925.

—— *Bilder zur Geschichte der Freimaurerei.* Reichenberg. 1927.

REBOLD, EMANUEL: *Allgemeine Geschichte der Freimaurerei.* Basle.
1884.

REITZENSTEIN, ALBIN FREIH. V.: *Wieland.* (Maurer. Klassiker.)
Berlin. 1907.

—— *Fichte.* (Maurer. Klassiker.) Berlin.

—— *Herder.* (Maurer. Klassiker.) Berlin.

—— *Lessing.* (Maurer. Klassiker.) Berlin.

SCHENKEL, GOTTHILF: *Die Freimaurer im Lichte der Religions- und Kirchengeschichte.* Gotha. 1926.

SCHIFFMANN, G. A.: *Andreas Michael Ramsay.* Leipzig. 1878.

—— *Die Freimaurerei in Frankreich.* Leipzig. 1881.

—— *Die Entstehung der Rittergrade.* Leipzig.

SCHULTZE, DR. ERNST: *Die Kulturaufgaben der Freimaurerei.*
Stuttgart und Berlin. 1912.

SCHWARTZ-BOSTUNITSCH, GREGOR: *Die Freimaurerei usw.* Weimar.
1928.

SINGER, ARTHUR: *Der Kampf Roms gegen die Freimaurerei.* Leipzig. 1925.

SMI͡T, WILLEM: *Katechismus der Freimaurerei.* Leipzig. 1891.

STARCKE, DR. C. N.: *Freimaurei als Lebenskunst.* Berlin. 1911.

—— *Die Freimaurerei, ihre geschichtliche Entwicklung usw.* Hamburg. 1913.

TAUTE, REINHOLD: *Katholische Geistlichkeit und Freimaurerei.* Berlin.

TIEDJEN, JOHANNES: *Die deutsche Freimaurerei.* Marburg. 1913.

Vernichtung, Die, der Unwahrheiten über die Freimaurerei. Leipzig. 1928.

WALTHER, HUGO: *Die Freimaurerei.* Vienna. 1910.

WEISS, EUGEN: *Steinmetzart und Steinmetzgeist.* Jena. 1927.

WERNEKKE, HUGO: *Goethe und die Königliche Kunst.* Berlin. 1923.

WICHTL, FRIEDRICH: *Weltfreimaurerei, Weltkrieg, Weltrevolution.*

WOLFSTIEG, AUGUST: *Ursprung und Entwicklung der Freimaurerei.* Berlin. 1921.

III. IN THE FRENCH LANGUAGE

AMIABLE, LOUIS: *Une Loge Maçonnique d'avant 1789. La R. Loge 'Les Neufs Sœurs'.* 1897.

—— et COFLAVRU, J. C.: *La Franc-Maçonnerie en France depuis 1725.* Paris. 1927.

Association Maç. Int. Compte-rendu du Congrès Maç. Intern. 1921.

—— *Compte-rendu du Congrès Maç. Intern. 1923.*

—— *Compte-rendu du Congrès Maç. Intern. 1927.*

BARRUEL: *Mémoires pour servir à l'histoire du Jacobinisme.* Paris. 1797.

BATAILLE: *Le diable au XIXᵉ siècle.* Paris and Lyons.

BÉDARRIDE, ARMAND: *La Doctrine maçonnique.* Paris. 1928.

BÈGUE-CLAVEL: *Histoire pittoresque de la franc-maçonnerie.* Paris. 1843.

BOIS, GEORGES: *Maçonnerie nouvelle du Grand Orient.* Paris. 1892.

BORD, GUSTAVE: *La Franc-Maçonnerie en France,* etc. Paris. 1908.

Bureau International de relations maçonniques, Deux Siècles de Franc-Maçonnerie 1917.

Congrès des Maçonneries des nations alliées et neutres. Paris. 1917.

COROYER, GASTON: *Étude historique sur la Maçonnerie.* Paris. 1923.

CORO. S. C.: *'Fama Fraternitatis' Rosae Crucis.* Paris. 1921.

FEUILLETTE, R. C.: *Précis de l'histoire du Grand Orient de France.* Paris. 1928.

Grand Orient de France, La Franc-Maçonnerie.

KAUFFMANN ET CHERPIN: *Histoire philosophique de la Franc-Maçonnerie.* Lyons. 1856.

LANTOINE, ALBERT: *Histoire de la Franc-Maçonnerie Française.* Paris. 1925.

—— *Hiram couronné d'épines.* Paris. 1926.

—— *Hiram au jardin des oliviers.* Paris. 1928.

LARUDAN, ABBÉ: *Les Franc-Maçons écrasés.* Paris. 1747.

LEBEY, ANDRÉ: *Dans l'atélier maçonnique.* Paris.

LE FORESTIER: *Les Illuminés de Bavière et la Franc-Maçonnerie allemande.* Paris. 1919.

LEROUX, ADRIEN: *La Franc-Maçonnerie sous la 3me république.* Paris. 1886.

MARGIOTTA, DOMENICO: *Le Palladisme.* Grenoble. 1895.

MARTIN, GASTON: *La Franc-Maçonnerie française et la préparation de la Révolution.* Paris. 1926.

MAISTRE, JOSEPH DE: *La Franc-Maçonnerie.*

MENNEVÉE: *L'Organisation anti-maçonnique en France.*

MOUNIER: *De l'influence attribuée aux philosophes, aux francs-maçons et aux illuminés sur la Révolution française.* 1801.

PAPUS: *L'Illuminisme en France (1767–1774.)* Paris. 1895.

PIGNATEL, FERNAND: *Batailles maçonniques.* Paris.

RAGON, J. M.: *Cours philosophique et interprétatif des Initiations,* etc. 1842.

SAVOIRE, CAMILLE: *L'esprit maçonnique.* Paris. 1925.

TAXIL, LÉO: *Les Frères Trois-Points.* Paris.

—— *Y a-t-il des femmes dans la Franc-Maçonnerie.* Paris.

TEMPELS, PIERRE: *Les Francs-Maçons.* Brussels. 1888.

WIRTH, OSWALD: *L'idéal initiatique.* Paris. 1922.

—— *Livres de l'apprenti, du compagnon et du maître.* Paris. 1923-4-6.

WITTEMANS, FR.: *Histoire des Rose-Croix.* 1923.

IV. IN THE ITALIAN AND SPANISH LANGUAGES

BACCI, ULISSE: *Il libro del massone italiano.* Rome. 1922.

BELLETTI, G. B.: *La Massoneria e l'Italia alla fine del secolo XVIII.* Rome. 1913.

BODRERO, EMILIO: *Inchiesta sulla massoneria.* Milan. 1925.

Discorsi del Adriano Lemmi, etc. Rome. 1893.

IMBRIACO, ACHILLE: *I misteri massonici rivelati al popolo.* Naples. 1922.

LETI, GIUSEPPE: *Carbonari e Massoneria nel Risorgimento.* Genoa. 1925.

LUZIO, ALESSANDRO: *La Massoneria e il Risorgimento.* Bologna. 1922.

MONTI DI MARCO, CARMELO: *La Massoneria.* Palermo. 1869.

MORAYTA, MIGUEL: *Masoneria española.* Madrid. 1915.

SBIGOLI, F.: *Tommaso Crudeli e i primi Framassoni di Firenze.* Milan. 1884.

SORIGA, RENATO: *Settecento massonizante e Massonismo napoleonico nel primo Risorgimento Italiano.* Pavia. 1920.

TIRADO Y ROJAS: *La Masoneria en España.* Madrid. 1892.

TORRIGIANI, DOMIZIO: *Massoneria e Fascismo.* Rome. 1923.

—— *Principi e propositi. Discorso.* Rome. 1919.

INDEX OF NAMES